Navigating Research in an Applied Graduate Program

Navigating Research in an Applied Graduate Program

A Guide for Students in Psychology, Mental Health, and Education

Hilary B. Vidair
Pam L. Gustafson
and
Eva L. Feindler

OXFORD
UNIVERSITY PRESS

OXFORD
UNIVERSITY PRESS

Oxford University Press is a department of the University of Oxford.
It furthers the University's objective of excellence in research, scholarship,
and education by publishing worldwide. Oxford is a registered trade mark of
Oxford University Press in the UK and in certain other countries.

Published in the United States of America by Oxford University Press
198 Madison Avenue, New York, NY 10016, United States of America.

CIP data is on file at the Library of Congress.

ISBN 9780199352272

DOI: 10.1093/oso/9780199352272.001.0001

Printed by Marquis, Canada

MIX
Paper | Supporting
responsible forestry
FSC® C103567
FSC
www.fsc.org

Contents

Worksheets and fillable forms can also be accessed and downloaded by searching for this book's title on the Oxford Academic platform, at academic.oup.com.

List of Tables, Figures, and Worksheets

Tables

Figures

Worksheets

Preface

Who Is This Guide For?

Congratulations! If you are holding this guide, you likely already made it into a graduate program in an applied field of psychology, mental health, or education. By applied, we mean you are learning to apply theories and methods in your field in practice (e.g., with clients, students, or organizations in clinical, educational, or community settings). We are certain this is after a lot of hard work and persistence, because being accepted to graduate school and then making your way through the coursework and practicums are major accomplishments. As you begin your program, you will likely be exposed to various opportunities to get involved in research. Along the way, you will be expected to develop your research competence, which will often include embarking on your own research or scholarly project(s). Typically, students in a doctoral program are expected to complete a dissertation; in a master's program the final project is often referred to as a thesis, which usually takes less time and is shorter in length. Some doctoral programs also require a thesis project prior to the dissertation. Other doctoral programs do not require a dissertation, but require a final doctoral paper or project. Generally, throughout this book, we will use the following terms interchangeably: final project, dissertation, thesis, and research or scholarly project. We know these projects can lead to a range of feelings, from exciting to downright daunting. These feelings can occur at any stage of the process, such as selecting a topic, choosing a project advisor, writing a proposal, deciding on a study site, managing obstacles to the project's completion, and fostering a meaningful mentor–mentee relationship.

Our experiences with students indicated the need for a guide that addressed everything from getting involved in research early in your graduate school experience to developing and completing your own project, beyond basic information provided by graduate programs such as program timelines, general project content, and formal advising procedures. That is why we wrote this guide: to help you navigate the nuts and bolts of these experiences. Wherever you are in this process, we have included information meant to help graduate students at all levels take their next steps.

This guide will be helpful to students in applied graduate programs within the professional human services fields. This encompasses students in psychology doctoral programs (e.g., clinical, counseling, and school PhD and PsyD programs) that range from a scientist-practitioner model to a practitioner-scholar model. In addition, this guide is relevant for students in other applied doctoral and master-level programs, such as social work, mental health counseling, vocational counseling, marital family therapy, art therapy, and education. We have included information related to each stage of your training, from entering your program to completing your final research project and beyond.

This guide will also be helpful to faculty members serving a variety of roles, including teaching courses in applied research, leading professional development seminars, advising students during the development of their research or scholarly projects, and mentoring students in applied labs. It is important for faculty to consider how they can help students achieve research competence while under their advisement and/or mentorship. We have included strategies to help mentors and mentees navigate their relationships throughout this process.

How This Guide Is Structured

Your knowledge, skills, and attitudes (KSA) about research will likely be the foundation for competently conducting and completing a successful final project. The importance of KSA is based on a well-recognized national competency model developed by the National Council of Schools of Professional Psychology (NCSPP, 2007). NCSPP established seven competencies in their model, including the "Research and Evaluation" competency, which includes three domains: critical evaluation of research, conducting research in applied settings, and ethics and professional competence (NCSPP, 2007, p. 31). Each of these domains includes a set of KSA that students should obtain at three developmental achievement levels of training: the beginning of their programs, as they begin their internship, and as they complete their degrees. There are similar competency-based models across various types of mental health and education programs. Our goal is to help you learn how to develop the KSA necessary in each stage of your graduate training to successfully embark on research and scholarly work from the beginning through the end of your program.

This guide is divided into three sections based on each stage of your research and scholarly trajectory: Section 1, "Becoming Familiar with Research and Scholarly Work;" Section 2, "Developing Your Proposal and Managing Your Final Project;" and Section 3, "Finishing Your Final Project and Beyond." The three sections are each divided into three chapters, addressing, respectively, (a) knowledge, (b) skills, and (c) attitudes that will help you achieve success at each stage. Generally, the knowledge chapters focus on what you need to know to succeed during each stage of research in graduate school and as you develop a project. The skills chapters include strategies for navigating each component of research competence and through all the steps of your project. The attitudes chapters focus on how you are thinking about each stage of the process. Worksheets, visual aids, and checklists are included throughout the book to help you assess and develop your KSA throughout your graduate program.

The first section of this guide includes information about types of project designs, narrowing down your areas of interest, strategies for choosing a mentor, examining your resources and supervisory needs, assessing your applied research competencies, developing strategies for critically evaluating relevant literature and starting to write, and assessing your attitudes toward research and readiness to work on a project. The second section focuses on strategies for selecting a project topic; understanding the pieces of a proposal; how to organize and write your proposal (e.g., introduction and methods section); assessing, building, and maintaining your mentor and collaborator relationships; proposing, starting, and managing your project; working with research assistants; and troubleshooting concrete obstacles and procrastination. It is designed to help you to keep up with all the requirements and deadlines while balancing other responsibilities (including those in your life outside your program). Finally, the third section includes understanding the components of a full dissertation or thesis and guidance on completing your project, including collaborating with your mentor, writing up your results and discussion sections, and finalizing and defending your project. We discuss practical strategies for presenting and publishing, as well as ways to think about moving forward after your final project into your career.

Types of Applied Dissertation and Thesis Projects

Your program likely has a range of types of dissertation or thesis projects that meet their requirements. These projects might include quantitative research, including true experiments, quasi-experiments, and correlational research (e.g., cross-sectional surveys, observational research designs). Behavioral programs often also include single-case designs such as ABAB and multiple baseline designs. Many professional programs have expanded the range of acceptable projects to include qualitative research (e.g., grounded theory studies including interviews and focus groups). Still others allow nonempirical dissertations such as theoretical or scholarly papers, extended case studies, program evaluations, and the development of treatment or educational protocols. We wrote this guide to reflect the general requirements for all these types of projects. The best way to determine what type of projects your program approves (other than asking!) is to review your program's specific handbooks or materials, as well as recently completed projects by graduating students and new alumni. We note throughout the guide when there are points that may vary based on different program requirements.

Mentors and Mentor Models

Project experiences can be greatly enhanced through a productive and supportive relationship between mentor and mentee. Ideally, faculty will go beyond their official role as chair of a final project and mentor their student through the graduate school process, into the beginning of their career, and beyond. Applied graduate programs include different types of mentorship models, ranging from those in which students conduct their final project with the same mentor they were assigned to in their first year to those where students choose a mentor at the dissertation or thesis stage. Students may also find that they need more than one mentor to serve in different types of mentor roles. Our guide includes strategies for fostering mentor–mentee relationships based on recent NCSPP and American Psychological Association conferences and guidelines. We review the KSA related to selecting a mentor, finding a balance between student and mentor interests, building a mentor–mentee relationship, and knowing when to seek additional assistance. Finally, we discuss ways to transition from the mentor–mentee relationship to professional colleagues.

We also discuss the KSA necessary for selecting and managing project chairs and committee members. Specifically, we provide factors to consider for selecting a project chair and committee members and strategies for working through generation of the proposal idea, writing the proposal, proposing, conducting the project, writing up the results and discussion, and defending. We also review how to manage disagreements among committee members and what to do when one of these professional relationships becomes challenging.

How This Guide Can Be Used

There are several ways you can make use of this guide. We understand that you will be trying to fit the use of this book into your already busy schedule! Table P.1 provides specific recommendations about which chapter students should read at each stage of graduate school, as well as related recommendations for workshops, assignments, and activities that faculty members can orchestrate when they are teaching research courses, running labs, and/or serving as advisors or chairs.

As a student, you can use this book independently to assess, build, and maintain helpful KSA for each step in the process. We guide students with varying levels of program support through how to use these materials on their own and en route to working with a chair. We recommend you show this guide to your chair to help you align what you learn with your program's requirements.

Throughout the book, you will find worksheets, visual aids, and checklists that can help you develop your KSA. Worksheets and fillable forms can also be accessed and downloaded by searching for this book's title on the Oxford Academic platform, at academic.oup.com. They are designed to help you generate your ideas for your final project, develop each component of your written draft, critically evaluate your work, prepare for project milestones (e.g., proposal and defense meetings), and keep track of your progress. We also provide steps you can take to implement a remediation plan, if needed. You can complete these items on your own or with chairs, advisors, or peers to supplement the project-related activities your program has in place. In addition, sections focused on mentorship can serve as a springboard for class and/or lab discussions or conversations about navigating these relationships.

Table P.1 How Students and Faculty Can Use This Guide

If you are	We recommend you read:	We recommend faculty/advisors/chairs:
Starting graduate school	Chapter 1: "Knowledge Needed for Beginning to Build Your Research Competence"	• Provide a program orientation, including how science is incorporated into their program's model of training, types of research and scholarly designs possible for final projects in the program, the program's advising structure, and ways to form advising and mentoring relationships. • Assign Chapter 1 as part of an introductory research course. • Assign or advise students to complete Worksheets 1.1 and 1.2 to help determine their interests and narrow them down to a potential project area (e.g., in an introductory research course or professional development seminar, with an initial advisor, or as an activity in a faculty lab).
In your first semester or year of graduate school	Chapter 2: "Skills to Develop for Beginning-Level Research Competence"	• Assign Chapter 2 as part of an introductory research course. • Provide a class or workshop(s) for students focused on how to collaborate with faculty; succeed as a mentee; find, read, and critically evaluate research; and navigate conducting research in applied settings, university resources, and the IRB. • Advise students to complete Table 2.2 to identify relevant university and program resources (e.g., in an introductory research course or professional development seminar, with an initial advisor, or as an activity in a faculty lab). • Ask students to select a research article and assign the questions in Table 2.4 for reading and critically evaluating research articles. • Ask students to become familiar with IRB procedures and assign them to assist a faculty member or upper-level student with an IRB application. • Select a research evaluation tool from Table 2.5 and assign it to students. • Review Table 2.6 with students who need to improve their research skills and help them identify potential solutions. • Assign or advise students to complete Worksheet 2.1 to evaluate their current writing skills and develop a plan for any needed improvement.

| In your first semester or year of graduate school | Chapter 3: "Attitudes toward Research" | • Assign Chapter 3 as part of an introductory research course.
• Provide a class or workshop and discussion about attitudes toward research in an applied field, their graduate program, and applied settings.
• Assign or advise students to complete Worksheet 3.1 to help determine which stage of change they are in and strategies for progressing through the stage (e.g., in an introductory research course or professional development seminar, with an initial advisor, or as an activity in a faculty lab).
• Assign or advise students to complete Worksheet 3.2 to evaluate their attitude toward self-evaluation and feedback and see if they might benefit from making some adjustments. Review the accompanying Table 3.1 with students who could benefit from seeing examples about how to generate a more positive attitude (e.g., in an introductory research course or professional development seminar, with an initial advisor, or as an activity in a faculty lab). |
| Preparing to write a research or scholarly proposal and/or select a project chair | Chapter 4: "Knowledge Needed for Selecting Your Final Project Topic and Developing Your Proposal" | • Assign Chapter 4 as part of a course or seminar where students write a research or scholarly proposal or as a chair working with a student at the beginning phases of developing a proposal.
• Provide a class or workshop(s) to review how to select a chair and/or committee, final project–related program timeline and deadlines, acceptable proposal formats, and/or purpose and structure of the proposal meeting.
• Assign or advise students to complete Worksheet 4.1 to help them move forward with a final project topic (e.g., in an introductory research course or professional development seminar, with a chair, or as an activity in a faculty lab). |

continued

Table P.1 *continued*

If you are	We recommend you read:	We recommend faculty/advisors/chairs:
Working on writing a research or scholarly proposal or preparing to conduct a research or scholarly project	Chapter 5: "Skills for Writing Your Proposal and Managing Your Final Project"	• Assign Chapter 5 as part of a course or seminar for students writing a research or scholarly proposal, preparing for their proposal meeting, and/or conducting a research or scholarly project or as a chair working with a student on a project. • Provide a class or workshop(s) for students focused on how to write each section of their proposal, work with their chair and/or IRB, and/or manage their final project (e.g., preparing and assembling materials, obtaining and managing research assistants, keeping track of progress, managing changes over the course of the project). • Assign or advise students to complete Worksheet 5.1 to help plan and evaluate progress on their written proposal (e.g., in an introductory research course or professional development seminar, with a chair, or as an activity in a faculty lab). • Assign or advise students to develop a tentative timeline, ideally with their chair, for selecting committee members and drafting their proposal through conducting and completing their procedure using Table 5.3 as a template. • Assign or advise students to complete Table 5.4 to evaluate their readiness for their proposal meeting and identify skills still needed. • Ask students to create a project to-do list using Table 5.5 as a guide. • Help students keep their project timeline on track by asking them to review Tables 5.7 and 5.8 to evaluate whether they are managing their time effectively and are aware of important program requirements, deadlines, and resources. • Use Worksheet 5.2 to help students in need of remediation at the proposal stage.
Working your way through a research or scholarly project	Chapter 6: "Attitudes toward Your Research and Your Collaborators"	• Assign Chapter 6 as part of a course or seminar for students conducting a research or scholarly project or as a chair working with a student on a project. • Provide a class or workshop and discussion about maintaining a positive attitude toward your research and your collaborators. • Assign or advise students to revisit Worksheet 3.1 from Chapter 3 to help determine which stage of change they are in and strategies for progressing through this stage. Review Table 6.1 with students who are procrastinating and could benefit from considering potential solutions (e.g., in an introductory research course or professional development seminar or with a chair).

		• Advise or assign students to review Table 6.2 if they could benefit from generating more positive attitudes about receiving feedback. Then ask them to complete Worksheet 3.2 in Chapter 3 to restructure these thoughts.
Preparing to analyze your data and/or write up a research or scholarly project	Chapter 7: "Knowledge Needed for Finalizing Your Final Project"	• Assign Chapter 7 as part of a course or seminar where students will be completing their final research or scholarly project or as a chair working with a student finalizing their project. • Provide a class or workshop(s) about factors to consider when completing a final project (i.e., revisions to make, roles of chair and committee members, determining project findings and implications, project limitations and directions for future research, timeline), key components of results and discussion sections, ethical principles related to completing a project (e.g., authorship), and/or purpose and structure of the defense meeting. • Assign or advise students to complete Worksheet 7.1 to help them plan the final stages of their project (e.g., in a professional development seminar or with a chair).
Working on analyzing and/or writing up the results of a research or scholarly project	Chapter 8: "Skills for Finalizing Your Final Project"	• Assign Chapter 8 as part of a course or seminar for students analyzing and writing up the results of a research or scholarly project, for students preparing for their defense, or as a chair working with a student on finalizing a project. • Provide a class or workshop(s) for students focused on how to analyze and write up results of a final research or scholarly project, successfully work with their chair, finalize their project (e.g., keep their project timeline on track, finalize their written draft, prepare for their defense, tasks to complete postdefense), present, and publish. • Assign or advise students to complete Worksheet 8.1 to prepare to conduct their data analyses and write their results and discussions sections, as well as track progress as they complete each task (e.g., in a professional development seminar or with a chair). • Help students continue to keep their project timeline on track by asking them to revisit Table 5.7 to evaluate if they are managing their time effectively and complete Table 8.1 to ensure they are aware of important program requirements and deadlines. Table 8.2 can then be used to develop a tentative timeline, ideally with their chair.

continued

Table P.1 *continued*

If you are	We recommend you read:	We recommend faculty/advisors/chairs:
		• Assign or advise students to complete Table 8.3 to evaluate their readiness for their defense meeting and identify skills still needed. • Refer students back to Worksheet 5.2 to help students in need of remediation during the final stages of their project.
Thinking about next steps beyond your final project and graduate school	Chapter 9: "Attitudes about Research after Your Final Project and Beyond"	• Assign Chapter 9 as part of a final professional development seminar for students conducting a research or scholarly project or as a chair working with a student on finishing a project. • Provide a class or workshop and discussion about transitioning into an early career professional, attitudes toward lifelong learning, and decisions about commitment and focus for the future.

Note: IRB, institutional review board.

Faculty can also assign this guide as part of required reading for students at all levels of building research competence, from an introductory applied research course or professional development seminar to independent study. Faculty can assign these worksheets as in-class or lab activities, peer mentoring activities, or homework. Finally, this guide will be useful for applied graduate programs to adopt. The step-by-step process laid out in this book can serve as a supplement to program dissertation and thesis project guidelines.

Acknowledgments

We are incredibly grateful to Sarah Harrington, senior editor at Oxford University Press (OUP), for your belief in this book, ideas for broadening its scope, and patience with us over the past several years. We also greatly appreciate Hayley Singer, our editor, for all the helpful suggestions and tips that allowed our book to move into the preproduction phase. Thanks also to Kayley Gilbert, our project editor, for addressing numerous questions and providing support throughout the end stages of this project. Thank you to the entire editorial staff at OUP who made this publication possible.

This book would not be complete without the research and editing efforts of the following current and former research assistants: Carly Apar, Emma Bernstein, Katie Darvin, Alexander Dorfman, Olivia Gesimondo, Lauren Goldsamt, Danny Gur, Chaya Lieba Kobernick, Katerina Levy, Mehrnaz Mirhosseini, Rose Alicea Oliveras, Nicole Rosenfield Davis, Alexandra Mercurio Schira, Miriam Smith, Shira Wein, Morgan Weinstein, Tali Wigod, Ami Zala, and Sara Zelmanovitz-Bistritzky. Thank you all for your work on this project.

Special thanks to Shira Wein for being our chief book assistant. Your ability to coordinate, offer insight, and hold us accountable for meeting deadlines fostered our progress on this project. In addition, special thanks to Emma Bernstein and Katerina Levy for working on chapter-by-chapter edits and suggestions, as well as helping to develop worksheets and tables from a student perspective. The three of you truly facilitated our ability to finish this project!

We also thank the following LIU Post program alumni for granting us permission to share their experiences conducting research and scholarly work: Carly Apar, Emma Bernstein, Jacquelyn Bogdanov, Cassady Casey, Adam Clark, Elise Cohen, Alexis Conason, Gustavo Cutz, Sonja DeCou, Mary Elsharouny, Danielle Francois, Meghann Gerber, Chani Goldfeder, Benjamín Gottesman, Stefanie Iwanciw, Rebecca Kason, Chaya Lieba Kobernick, Kristin Kunkle, Sharon Levi, Katerina Levy, Rebecca Lieberman, Matthew Liebman, Amanda Lytle, Melyssa Mandelbaum, Melissa Melkumov, Alexandra Mercurio Schira, Megan Moxey, Bethany Pecora-Sanfeski, Christina Petitti, Esther Raminfar, Kimmy Ramotar, Jessica Renz, Erika Rooney, Marina Ross, Allison Rumelt, William Rung, Gina Sita, Alexander Stratis, Sophie Strauss, Lauren Taveras, Daniel Tieman, Kristen Ullrich, Shira Wein, Tali Wigod, and Eric Yellin. We believe your experiences will shed light on the research process for other graduate students in the years to come.

In addition, we wish to thank LIU Post faculty who chaired dissertation projects mentioned in the book: Orly Calderon, Marc Diener, Geoff Goodman, Danielle Knafo, Camilo Ortiz, Jill Rathus, and David Roll. Special thanks to Robert Keisner for encouraging our emphasis on qualitative research, both in our program and in the book. You all have shaped our ideas about how to conduct and mentor student research in applied programs, and your collective wisdom is portrayed throughout this book.

Overall, our inspiration for this book came from the students we worked with over the years in our clinical psychology doctoral program at LIU Post. Thanks to all of you who shared your courage, creativity, and passion for your research and scholarly work with us, as well as the challenges you encountered along the way. Though we served as the mentors and/or administrators, we learned a great deal from you.

HBV

I want to extend my deepest gratitude to my coauthor Eva Feindler for your initial idea to turn the development of a program dissertation handbook into a book for students in applied graduate fields, as well as your creative ideas, innovative contributions, and never-ending faith in our ability to finish this project. I learned many of my best mentoring skills from being your faculty mentee, colleague, and friend.

I also wish to extend my sincere thanks to my coauthor Pam Gustafson for sitting side by side with me to build the foundation and structure for this book. Your administrative experience and knowledge as a librarian brought unique perspectives that have had a significant impact not only on the book, but also on our program today.

I am forever grateful to Jill Rathus for believing in this project and my ability to do it, and for cheering me across the finish line. Several parts of the book were inspired by your wisdom and experience as a professor, researcher, mentor, and clinician. Thank you for sharing your clinical research methods course materials with me early on, for collaborating on so many dissertations with me, and for being the best all-around colleague and friend I could ask for! Special thanks for modeling how to write beautiful acknowledgment sections.

At Hofstra, where I earned my PhD, I give heartfelt thanks to my own graduate school mentor, Phyllis Ohr, for providing me with so many valuable opportunities throughout graduate school and beyond. I am still so thankful for your support of my dissertation research, particularly given the vigor and speed with which I worked on it, and feel lucky to call you my colleague, coauthor, and friend. I also extend my thanks to the late Richard O'Brien, who had confidence I would be a professor before I did and, in many ways, set me on my academic career path. Thanks also to my committee members, Joseph Scardapane, Kimberly Gilbert, and the late Marla Ince, for cultivating such a delightful committee and defense experience that shaped the kind of defense I aspire to give each of my doctoral students today. And thank you to Mitchell Schare, whose charisma and career as a director and professor I have aimed to emulate.

I am also grateful for my colleague Ruth DeRosa's continuous encouragement and willingness to listen to my progress on this project and about everything else. Thank you for being my confidante, time and time again. Special thanks to Moira Rynn for teaching me so much about what a combination of solid career and psychosocial mentorship looks like. It meant more than you could know.

Thank you to my entire family for your unwavering love and support. To my mother, Fredrica, I am thrilled you knew about this book and honored by how excited you were about it. Thank you for having been such a huge inspiration for my education and for having been so involved, all the way through my dissertation research and beyond. To my father, Steven, thank you for all your support and advice throughout my schooling. I have always remembered the three rules and have strived to implement them.

To John, my husband, thank you for giving me the time and space to work on this project, even when it was wildly inconvenient, from my time spent in Queen's Room, to a window seat in the mountains during the pandemic when you wanted to ski, to our Astoria basement while you took care of our son. Thank you for always believing I could write this book, even when I had my doubts. Now it is your turn!

Finally, my heartfelt thanks to my children. Elliot, having you made me more efficient in my work and, in many ways, more productive. It was always most rewarding to come upstairs, back to your smiling face and curious questions. Leia, your pending arrival provided the impetus needed to finish the revisions for this book, just in time to complete our family. It is a beautiful end to an exciting beginning.

PLG

I would like to thank my coauthors, Hilary Vidair and Eva Feindler. Eva, you have always found innovative ways to support junior faculty and staff. This project was no different. You are a mentor to us all on how to support students, colleagues, family, and friends. Hilary, the marathon writing sessions and constant refining of our frame and our focus very much dictated how I now approach big projects, making sure to weave in some fun (and good food) throughout.

To my LIU family—both students and former colleagues: getting to be a part of the clinical psychology doctoral program in such a significant way for so long shaped the trajectory of the rest of my professional and personal life. I have taken the frame of our program and applied it to so much of my work elsewhere. That I worked among the "How are you feeling?" people who always dug into the answers to that question has been the biggest influence of them all. The list of alumni whose work is included in this book brings back great memories—and I thank you for sharing that experience with me and with this book. Special thanks to Jill Rathus who, like Eva, has always encouraged me to keep writing, with humor, even in the darkest of times.

To my own mentors and writing soundboards: Your influence and support shaped me into the writer and librarian-teacher I am today. Jeanie Attie and Sara Gronim, my former history professors and now friends, set me on my academic path many years ago and were so crucial to that journey. Jeanie, you have made me a better writer with every correspondence, every paper, every conversation. Sara—the reason I found myself back at LIU for graduate school—knowing you has made me a better thinker and a better person. To one of my oldest friends, Emily Intravia, who has read almost everything I have ever written—the dry and the creative—your careful eye and thoughtful feedback are much appreciated.

To my colleagues and students at SUNY Empire State University: Thank you for your unwavering support of me over the past 7 years, especially Mildred van Bergen. Working with Empire students has allowed my mind to stay fresh in a myriad of disciplines and enabled me to keep working with college-level students on research projects as diverse as it can get. You help keep my love for it alive.

A big thanks to my new professional home, Brentwood Schools, for supporting research in our curriculum. With that support, we ready students to approach the world with a critical eye and the knowledge, skills, and attitudes necessary to approach a topic fully. I cannot wait to share this publication with our young scholars and hopefully watch many of them go into research fields like applied psychology themselves. The field needs you.

To my two boys, Beyrim and Quinn, who put up with years of late-Thursday-night writing sessions and me away at writers' weekends—thank you. Bey, I can still remember you putting your foot in a book to make a joke about footnotes when you were little and we had just started this project. And Q, your interjecting of much-needed silliness into Thursday-night sessions kept us sane. The humor and poise you both carry with you as young men has been my grounding force. You were both so young when this project started. I love that you have grown up surrounded by writers and academics and have seen firsthand the work that goes into creating and maintaining that world.

An enormous thanks to Jill Silverstein—who spent all of those years hearing about this book and being a support in every aspect of my life, even when I talked endlessly about the structure of the book and the process. I am heartbroken that we cannot toast to its publication together. I can hear you saying, "Dude that's awesome." But I am thoroughly happy that a copy of this will live on my shelf next to the title you helped craft into the world, *The Autism Experience*.

ELF

I would like to start with thanking my coauthors for all of their efforts and creativity. We worked on this through some really difficult times and here it is, a finished product that we can all be proud of. I wish to further thank all of the many doctoral students who were first the inspiration for the project and then participants in oh so many ways. I also thank my family for their constant support for all of my projects, academic or not. And finally, this is in remembrance of my mother, who was an amazing teacher and writer and who helped me really know that I could accomplish anything I set my mind to.

SECTION 1
BECOMING FAMILIAR WITH RESEARCH AND SCHOLARLY WORK

Chapter 1
Knowledge Needed for Beginning to Build Your Research Competence

Introduction

At the beginning of your graduate program, you should aim to develop your *knowledge* about critical evaluation of research, the conduct of research in applied settings, and ethical and professional competence by reviewing the following areas of this chapter:

- Why include research in an applied graduate program?
- Science versus practice training models: a continuum
- Why be scientifically minded?
- Types of research designs and scholarly projects
- Foundational concepts in research: statistics, psychometrics, and ethics
- Navigating your way toward a final project topic: a developmental process
- Advisors and mentors: purposes and roles

Why Include Research in an Applied Graduate Program?

Why do you need a strong foundation in research? You likely enrolled in an applied graduate program because you have an interest in professional practice. Your program will be training you to work with clients, students, or organizations in clinical, educational, and/or community settings. However, as a student in an applied program, you are also expected to demonstrate research competence. You may be interested in conducting research or other academic work; however, students from applied programs often desire to enter the practical side of their fields. If this is the case for you, research may seem like a program requirement rather than a set of skills you can acquire and use in your career.

We encourage you to begin to view research as an important, even exciting, part of your training. Although what *research* means varies across disciplines as well as programs, becoming competent in research in your field will at the very least enable you to become an educated consumer of scientific findings that can improve your practice and at most help you become an active contributor to the knowledge base in your field. Practically speaking, students who demonstrate competence in the understanding and conduct of research can be more marketable when entering

Navigating Research in an Applied Graduate Program. Hilary B. Vidair, Pam L. Gustafson, and Eva L. Feindler, Oxford University Press. © Oxford University Press (2024). DOI: 10.1093/oso/9780199352272.003.0001

their field as beginning professionals. As you read on, you will learn the benefits of applying scientific information to your practice.

Science versus Practice Training Models: A Continuum

Students in graduate programs are often expected to conduct *basic research*, or research that aims to increase the field's understanding of a particular theory or build on our knowledge about a specific phenomenon. The results of such studies are usually important for scientific advancement, but typically do not have direct or immediate implications for real-world, practical application.

In contrast, most applied graduate programs adhere to a balance in training between scientific research and practice, making this type of education unique in comparison to nonapplied fields. Students who conduct research in these applied programs are typically encouraged to conduct *applied research*, which refers to research designed to address problems found in actual practice. The development of an applied research project can build on what has been found in basic research, but the goal is to produce findings that elicit direct and immediate real-world implications.

Applied graduate programs vary in the degree to which they emphasize science versus practice. For example, among clinical psychology doctoral programs, there are three models of training: the scientist-practitioner model, the practitioner-scholar model, and the clinical scientist model (which focuses predominantly on training students to produce research) (see Ready & Santorelli, 2014). Originally, the scientist-practitioner model was developed by the American Psychological Association during a famous meeting referred to as the Boulder Conference (Raimy, 1950). The goal of this model was to place equal emphasis on research and clinical work in the clinical psychology PhD, because the expectation was that students would integrate the two areas and undertake careers in both.

Over time, critics of the scientist-practitioner model asserted that training in such programs was still relatively scientific and did not prepare students for the responsibilities and challenges of actual clinical practice, which many ultimately pursued. This dissatisfaction inspired the Vail Conference, where the need for programs focused primarily on training students to become practitioners was discussed (Hoch et al., 1966). This led to the development of doctor of psychology (PsyD) programs. The goal of these programs was to train students in the practitioner-scholar model, meaning they would be educated to critically evaluate science, but primarily trained to practice professionally.

Currently, there is often more overlap between these two training models than originally expected, so much so that a program's mission and curriculum necessitate review to determine its placement within the science-versus-practice continuum. Most graduate programs in related applied fields (e.g., education, social work, counseling) vary in their place on the science–practice spectrum, with a range of research requirements. Overall, scientific research and practice can be thought of as intertwined, with research informing practice, practice informing further research, and practitioners providing the most evidence-based services possible (Jones & Mehr, 2007). In fact, Gelso (2006) stated that clinical practice may be the most potent source of ideas for research, while research in turn relates directly to practice and can enhance it. Regardless of the applied field you are studying or where your graduate program falls on the science-versus-practice continuum, we recommend thinking of science and practice as interdependent.

Why Be Scientifically Minded?

Traditionally, research is conducted via the scientific method. The philosophy behind this method is that one can determine the objective reality of a phenomenon by developing a hypothesis (i.e., prediction) and seeing if it is supported. The hypothesis is tested in an experiment that isolates the variable of interest and controls the researcher's potential biases. Practically, the researcher performs the following steps: (1) forms a question area of interest based on an observation or experience, (2) conducts a review of the empirical literature in this area, (3) develops a hypothesis (i.e., what you expect to happen) supported by prior theory and empirical research that predicts the answer to the question, (4) tests the hypothesis in an experiment using appropriate research methods, (5) analyzes the results of the study, (6) interprets conclusions, and (7) presents the findings. In the future, other researchers replicate the study to determine whether they obtain further support for the findings. Quantitative research follows this method.

Rather than test a theory-driven hypothesis, qualitative research involves exploring an experience from the perspectives of the participants and developing common themes and/or generating a theory based on data collected in a narrative, or nonnumerical, manner. This type of research includes strategies for systematic collection, organization, and interpretation of phenomena; however, qualitative research allows researchers to explore research questions that are difficult to measure quantitatively. Sometimes this is difficult because little to no research has been conducted on a topic, and it is premature to generate hypotheses. Other times, the research question may best be addressed by developing a narrative of participants' experiences, rather than a statistical analysis of the findings. We will explain more about the differences between quantitative and qualitative research designs shortly.

Regardless of where your graduate program falls on the science–practice continuum, part of becoming a competent professional in your field includes becoming scientifically minded. This means that what you practice in your field should be guided by empirical evidence. Here, we review a five-component competency model that was developed for scientifically minded psychologists (Bieschke et al., 2004; see also Bieschke, 2006); however, we view these components as important for practice in any applied field:

1. Learn how to routinely consume current research and appropriately apply it in practice.

This involves becoming familiar with the latest empirical literature in one's field, taking into account the fact that an ever-changing scientific knowledge base requires continued training and education beyond graduate school. Practice is then conducted in an evidenced-based manner that integrates findings in the empirical literature and clinical expertise with client characteristics, culture, and preferences (e.g., Spring, 2007). The goal is to identify a practical problem, turn to the literature to determine what evidence-based strategies are available for managing the issue, and combine this knowledge with your experience, the unique aspects of the client, and the client's individual values.

2. Actively contribute to the advancement of scientific knowledge.

This can be accomplished in several ways, with a broad definition including the traditional production of research presented at conferences and published in journals, as well as communication of practice-related information to academic researchers, engagement in peer supervision, and providing education within a community. Students in applied programs will vary in their desire to produce their own research as part of their careers. However, even those in practice can enjoy benefits from engaging in research. For example, conducting applied research can make you more marketable for jobs, and conducting systematic evaluations of your services can enhance your credibility.

3. Critically evaluate your practices and their outcomes.

The main idea here is to actively implement critical thinking into your practice, remaining skeptical about ideas until they earn credibility and being open to alternative ideas. This is often referred to as becoming a *local clinical scientist*, a term developed by Trierweiler and Stricker (1992; see also Stricker & Trierweiler, 1995). A local clinical scientist applies a rigorous scientific approach to their practice by collecting information from a client, formulating hypotheses about their problems and what interventions might be helpful, and deciding how to test these hypotheses, with the understanding that they may be either confirmed or disconfirmed. Client progress should be evaluated over time, with intervention decisions based on the data, including continual revisions to the case formulation. The National Council of Schools of Professional Psychology based their research and evaluation competency on the premise that students will be trained to function like a local clinical scientist (Trierweiler et al., 2010).

4. Be aware of how sociocultural variables impact your practice.

This means being aware of how various research and sampling methods, as well as interpretations of research findings, influence what we know about working with people from individually and culturally diverse backgrounds. For example, a research study's internal validity is the degree to which we can conclude that one variable had effects on another, controlling for extraneous variables. External validity is the degree to which we can generalize findings from a study to actual people in a real-world setting. Usually, one of these types of validities is strengthened at the expense of the other; for example, on the one hand, the more confident we are that a study is well controlled and will provide accurate findings (i.e., internal validity), the less we can be certain that the results will apply to people outside the study (i.e., external validity). On the other hand, the more we focus a study on a particular group of people in a real setting, the less likely we can be confident in the rigor of a study's findings. Kazdin (2016) emphasized that we need to go beyond knowing *who* research findings fail to generalize for and ask *why*. Doing so can help us determine whether extraneous variables are at play or if there is a true difference in how we can understand and/or assist a specific population.

Unfortunately, research has been conducted with predominantly White/ Caucasian samples (e.g., Sue, 1999). Several groups have been grossly underrepresented, including, but not limited to, racial and ethnic minorities, children, geriatric populations, women, sexual and gender minorities, people with disabilities, those from rural areas, and those with a lower socioeconomic status (Mapes et al., 2020). The sociocultural component of the competency model calls for a broadening of the types of research methods (e.g., qualitative methods) used in order to expand our understanding of diverse groups. We need to interpret research findings within their social context, because what has been true for one group (e.g., culture, generation, socioeconomic status) is not necessarily true for another, and subgroups of people from a larger group may demonstrate within-group differences based on factors such as language,pt cultural customs, and level of acculturation.

5. Allow your work to be examined by others.

This involves holding yourself accountable to people both in and outside your field (e.g., a mental health organization, the public, interdisciplinary scholars) to ensure that your practices are scientifically based. It means that you should demonstrate how your practice decisions were guided by the scientific process, including which intervention strategies you chose, how you decided to measure change over time, and revisions you made to the course of an intervention based on your findings.

Knowing what it means to be a scientifically minded professional will likely help you integrate current knowledge in your field with your applied activities, starting now as a student. It will also help you begin to view your interests through a scientific lens, something you will need to do as you explore areas of interest.

Types of Research Designs and Scholarly Projects

In the beginning of your program, you will want to focus on generating potential research areas of interest. We will discuss ideas for generating these areas later in this chapter. For now, it is important to understand that you will eventually narrow down from a research area of interest to a project topic. The topic you select will then be further narrowed down to your overall research question(s). These questions will be based on what is already known in your field, gaps in the literature, and what your study could potentially contribute to existing knowledge in this area. The appropriate research design or scholarly project will follow from the question(s) you are interested in answering. Knowing about different types of research designs and scholarly projects can help shape a topic area into a project with an accepted methodology.

Across applied fields and programs, various schools of thought exist about which research designs are most appropriate for final projects. An applied graduate program usually accepts several types of research designs and projects for a dissertation or thesis. The types allowed will depend largely on the structure of your program, as well as other factors, including theoretical orientation and faculty expertise. Check your program's requirements regarding the types of research designs or scholarly projects you can pursue. At the beginning of your training, you will want to familiarize yourself with the types of designs acceptable within your program. That said, having knowledge of additional types of research designs is an important part of learning how to critically evaluate and build on existing literature.

Many applied programs offer a research methods course designed to teach students about a variety of research designs, including which ones would be appropriate to pursue for their final projects. Programs typically support students pursuing quantitative and/or qualitative research designs. Some programs also support theoretical or scholarly projects, some of which may be nonempirical (i.e., projects that do not involve data). There are several kinds of research designs and scholarly projects with slightly different terminology used across applied fields and textbooks. Although it is beyond the scope of this guide to provide an exhaustive review of project designs, we provide an overview of the kinds of research designs and scholarly projects typically used for student dissertations and theses. Table 1.1 compares some of the key differences between quantitative and qualitative research designs. See Kazdin (2016) and/or McMillan (2021) for more comprehensive information about specific quantitative and qualitative research designs.

Quantitative Research

The goals of quantitative research are usually to describe, predict, or ultimately explain a phenomenon. Traditionally, research in the social sciences used quantitative research designs similar to those found in the natural sciences. In accordance with the scientific method, quantitative researchers typically use deductive reasoning to develop hypotheses based on theory and prior research about a particular phenomenon (see Figure 1.1). They remain skeptical about their

Table 1.1 Key Components of Quantitative versus Qualitative Research Designs

	Quantitative	Qualitative
Purpose	Test a theory, demonstrate relationships among variables, describe characteristics of a sample or a phenomenon, assess the effects of one variable on another variable	Cultivate understanding of a particular group's experiences, explore participants' perspectives and experiences, ground a theory, observe behavior over time
Sample	Larger, ideally representative of the population of interest	Smaller, nonrepresentative, selected for uniqueness
Research design	Premeditated, typically remains the same as data are collected	Flexible and evolving, emerges as data are collected
Data collection and analysis	Surveys, structured interviews, physiological measures, observations, self-report measures, data analyzed numerically, using statistics	Open-ended interviews and/or focus groups, participants' own words, narratives, participant observation, review of text documents, pictures and/or artifacts, field notes, data often coded to identify themes or patterns
Researcher	Typically removed from participants, less involved	Typically immersed with participants, more involved

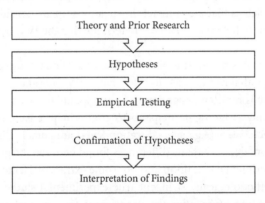

Figure 1.1 Deductive reasoning in a quantitative study

hypotheses until they have tested them empirically and gathered enough evidence to confirm them and interpret the meaning of the findings. Note that exploratory questions can also be examined quantitatively when there is not yet enough theoretical or empirical support to form specific hypotheses. Even when hypotheses are confirmed, quantitative researchers remain open-minded to alternative explanations and question all claims until they are well replicated. Though there are numerous quantitative research designs that are often described slightly differently across fields, we review those we find most suitable for student final projects in the following categories: experimental, correlational, observational, and descriptive designs. In addition, meta-analyses, scale development, and program evaluations are reviewed.

Experimental Designs

Experimental designs are used to compare differences between two or more groups when the researcher is able to manipulate the effects of an independent variable (IV) on one or more dependent variables (DV). The IV is divided into two or more levels (e.g., receiving an intervention versus not receiving one). Experimental studies can be used to make three types of comparisons. First, they can be used to compare an experimental group (e.g., treatment, program) to a control group. There are several types of control groups. One kind of control group is a no-treatment control group, in which participants do not receive or do anything, but complete the same pre- and/or posttest measures as the experimental group. An alternative is a wait-list control group, where participants wait until the experimental group is finished before receiving the same program as the experimental group. Another option is an attention placebo control group, in which participants engage in activities that are similar to those of the experimental group but lack the proposed "active" ingredients of the experimental program.

Second, experimental studies can compare two active interventions or programs to each other (e.g., cognitive-behavioral versus psychodynamic therapy for panic disorder). Third, they can compare two sets of instructions or experimental conditions (e.g., being told to attend to negative words versus being told to attend to positive words). Each group is treated in exactly the same manner except for the difference in levels of the IV. The DV (e.g., level of anxiety) is expected to change as a result of the IV. Other variables that may impact this relationship are considered extraneous and controlled for to help the researcher determine that the IV caused the change in the DV.

A *true experiment* is the most well-controlled type of quantitative design. It is the only group design that can be used to infer that an IV caused a change in a DV. Its key characteristic is random assignment of participants to two or more conditions of an IV. Randomly assigning participants to groups helps ensure that participants' individual characteristics (e.g., age, education level) are equally distributed, giving the researcher confidence that any differences found between the groups are likely a result of the experimental condition and not some extraneous factor.

The most methodologically stringent true experimental studies include assessment at baseline and again after the experiment (i.e., pretest and posttest). An example of the structure of this design is shown in Figure 1.2A. Assessing data at both points has several benefits, such as the removal of many threats to internal validity, as well as the ability to assess change over time, check whether randomized groups are indeed equal on baseline characteristics, statistically control for differences in the groups at baseline that randomization did not address, and assess whether there are differences between participants who drop out of the study at baseline versus participants who complete the study.

A second true experimental design only assesses the DV at posttest. An example of the structure of this design is shown in Figure 1.2B. Although this is a slightly weaker design, sometimes it is more feasible (e.g., when pretesting would be unethical, impossible, or expensive). In addition, skipping a pretest can eliminate something called a pretest sensitization threat, which can occur when participants are primed to focus on a certain aspect of a study via the pretest assessments conducted.

Student Example: True Experimental Design

JB trained student clinicians to conduct an evidence-based treatment via a peer training model. She randomly assigned students to either a peer group condition or a self-reflection condition. She conducted pre- and posttest assessments focused on areas such as knowledge of this treatment, treatment adherence on case vignettes, and attitudes toward evidence-based practice.

Students often shy away from true experimental designs because of difficulties with randomly assigning participants to groups. For example, in a randomized, controlled intervention study for children with learning disorders, you must find participants who are willing to enter the study with the possibility that they will not receive the intervention, at least not right away. It can be challenging enough to find children who meet your eligibility criteria! Even if a fully randomized controlled intervention trial is not feasible, we recommend you strongly consider whether you can find a creative way to randomize participants on an independent variable(e.g., randomly assigning the order in which participants read two vignettes).

Student Example: Randomly Assigning Order of Vignettes

ER was interested in parents' preferences for treatment of anxiety in preschool children; however, she did not have access to this type of sample. She decided to ask parents of any preschool-aged children to imagine their child was experiencing anxiety (as described) and read vignettes about two types of treatment for child anxiety to determine if they preferred one over the other. She randomly assigned which vignette parents would read first to assess whether there were differences in preference based on the order in which vignettes were read. This is a version of what is called a counterbalanced design. It allowed ER to benefit from the methodological rigor of random assignment without needing participants to agree to random assignment to conditions over time.

The *quasi-experimental design* occurs when randomization is not possible, but the researcher still wants to manipulate an IV. For example, you might want to compare an innovative classroom behavior management program to the usual classroom management in a school, but students have already been placed in their respective classrooms. This design affords the researcher less experimental control than the true experiment, making it less likely that change in the DV can be interpreted as being "caused" by the IV. Other variables might account for a between-group difference. For example, perhaps one class has already been exposed to a teacher with effective behavior management skills. This makes having a well-developed theory about the reasons that the IV is thought to be the variable impacting the DV even more important to specify in advance. There are ways to try to increase equivalence across groups (e.g., match the groups on relevant variables such as age or gender; statistically control for potentially confounding variables). Both pretest and posttest designs (see Figure 1.2C) or posttest-only designs (see Figure 1.2D) can be conducted. Like true experiments, the former include more control over threats to internal validity.

Single-case designs, also referred to as single-subject designs, are studies that can be considered as methodologically rigorous as true experimental group designs. They

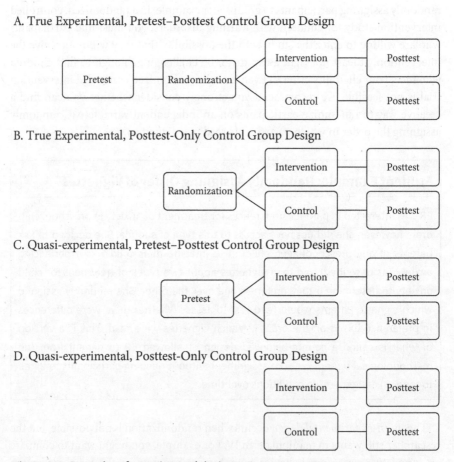

A. True Experimental, Pretest–Posttest Control Group Design

B. True Experimental, Posttest-Only Control Group Design

C. Quasi-experimental, Pretest–Posttest Control Group Design

D. Quasi-experimental, Posttest-Only Control Group Design

Figure 1.2 Examples of experimental designs

originated in animal studies and were later used in applied behavior analysis with humans. These designs typically involve a small number of participants (even an *n* of 1 at times), where each participant serves as their own control. Data are collected about each participant at multiple points in each phase of the study (e.g., in the baseline phase, during the intervention phase, and potentially after implementation of an intervention). Ideally, baseline assessments demonstrate stability before moving to the intervention phase, because the baseline is supposed to predict how the participant would function if no intervention was implemented, and variability makes it more difficult to interpret changes across study phases (Kazdin, 2016). The goal is to determine whether there are effects of the intervention on the outcome of interest by comparing the intervention phase to the baseline phase. Data are most commonly examined via visual analysis. More recent research has used statistical analyses to calculate effect sizes. Outcomes are often changes in specific behaviors. These designs are particularly useful when one wants to closely and systematically assess change in individual participants. They are also often used to pilot test new interventions.

One type of single-case design is referred to as the *ABAB or ABA design* (also referred to as a reversal design). In this case, the first "A" is the baseline phase condition and the first "B" is when the intervention phase is implemented. For example, let's say the goal was to increase a boy's appropriate participation in class. The intervention is the provision of stickers each time he raises his hand (see Figure 1.3). Several baseline observations would be conducted to determine how often he typically raises his hand before the intervention is implemented (first "A"). Several observations would also be conducted once the intervention is taking place (first "B"). The *reversal* occurs with the second "A." This is when the intervention would stop to determine whether his lack of appropriate participation would resurface. Finding a return to baseline would help confirm that the intervention was responsible for the

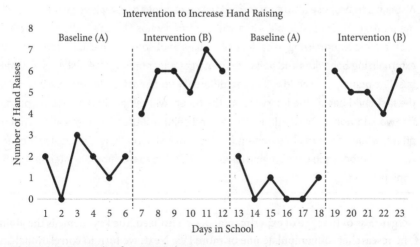

Figure 1.3 Example of an ABAB design

increase in his hand raising. The second "B" would be reinstating the intervention, which is sometimes added to an ABA design. If his hand raising once again increased at this point, we could be confident that the intervention was responsible for the changes. In some cases, however, the first intervention would be enough for the child to learn new behavior, and we might not see a return to baseline in the reversal phase. In some cases it may be unethical to remove an intervention that appears to be working (e.g., to reduce head banging).

For interventions in which we expect a more lasting change over time, a *multiple baseline design* can be used. Instead of using a reversal phase, there are a number of baseline participants, settings, or behaviors, and the intervention for each one begins at a different point. This allows the researcher to determine whether change occurs at the time the intervention is implemented, regardless of the time that this occurs. For example, consider a study designed to reduce nail-biting behavior for three participants (see Figure 1.4). Each participant is observed every minute for thirty minutes to see if they spend any of each minute biting their nails. One participant is observed for five baseline days and then begins the intervention, while the other two remain in the baseline phase. After five additional baseline days, the second participant begins the intervention, while the third remains in the baseline phase for another five baseline assessment days. Finding a reduction in each participant's nail biting after the intervention is implemented, regardless of the number of baseline days, reduces the possibility that extraneous factors, rather than the intervention, are responsible for the change observed. The closer the observed change happens to the intervention, the more confident the researcher can be that the intervention caused the change in behavior.

Student Example: Multiple Baseline Design

AMS aims to propose a study assessing the efficacy of an innovative anger management program for preschoolers in a school setting whose teachers identify specific, problematic externalizing behaviors. She plans to observe each child's frequency of externalizing behaviors and ability to use target anger management skills at several baseline points. Each child will have a different number of baseline observations. As the first child begins the intervention, the others will remain in the baseline phase for two additional observations. The second child will then begin the intervention phase, while the third child undergoes two more observations. The goal will be to assess whether each child's behavior improves close to the time the intervention is implemented.

Regardless of the type of experimental design utilized, the key theme is the ability of the researcher to manipulate one or more IVs. Next, we turn to correlational and observational group designs, where variables are examined as they occur naturally, without any experimental manipulation.

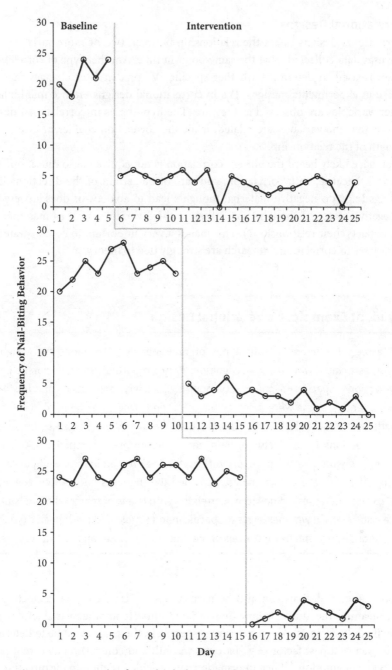

Figure 1.4 Example of a multiple-baseline design

Correlational Designs

Correlational designs assess the relationship between two or more variables. One type uses data collected all at the same point in time. Another type of correlational design is used to determine whether specific IVs predict later changes in a DV. Unlike in experimental designs, IVs in correlational designs are not manipulated; rather, variables are observed as they are. The hypotheses in correlational designs test whether the variables are related, while the correlation coefficient assesses the strength of the relationship.

You have likely heard the phrase "correlation is not equivalent to causation." One reason is because, with correlation, you cannot be certain of the directionality of findings (e.g., do negative maternal thoughts lead to anxiety, or does anxiety lead to negative maternal thoughts, or is there a third variable, such as maternal age, that impacts their relationship?). This makes it very important to demonstrate how hypotheses in correlational research are strongly tied to theory.

Student Example: Correlational Design

CC assessed whether specific types of maternal negative mood were significantly associated with maternal cognitions during reportedly stressful parent–child interactions. Specifically, maternal mood (e.g., anxiety, depression, and hostility) and parenting stress were assessed via self-report. One week later, mother–child dyads were videotaped in their homes during what they reported to be stressful interactions (e.g., mealtime, bath time). The mothers watched these videos immediately afterward and reported thoughts they remembered having during a series of thirty-second increments. CC coded the thoughts into various cognitive categories and assessed how they correlated with levels of maternal mood states. She also assessed whether levels of specific mood states predicted specific types of cognitions above and beyond levels of the other mood states and parenting stress.

Correlational designs can also be used to assess risk factors or protective factors, meaning the study of how one variable impacts another variable at a later time. If adults were asked questions retrospectively, the goal would be to determine the impact of a past factor (e.g., parental warmth and control) on a current factor (e.g., current emotions). Such information can provide insight into the directionality of a relationship between variables. However, this is still not providing causal information. As with a correlation, B could still precede A (e.g., a child's emotions could have impacted how a parent reacted to them). There could also be a third variable related to the outcome (e.g., a child's school experiences could affect their emotionality).

Observational Group Designs

Observational group designs, also sometimes called nonexperimental group designs, typically compare two groups that differ on an existing variable (e.g., level of education, gender), meaning there is no manipulation of an IV or random assignment of participants to groups. For example, two groups could be adults with and adults without children. The researcher did not create these differences; they already existed. Similar to correlational studies, finding significant differences between groups in an observational study does not indicate that the IV was the cause of these differences. The order of the IV and DV often cannot be determined, and even if this can occur, other variables may be impacting the findings. Strong theory is needed regarding why group differences on a clearly defined outcome are expected.

Some observational group designs are commonly used in educational research. One type is sometimes referred to as a *comparative design* (McMillan, 2021). This kind of design assesses two or more preexisting groups to compare them on an outcome of interest. A popular example of this design is differences between two genders (e.g., female vs. male) on a particular outcome (e.g., ability to be empathetic). The researcher does not assign gender, but compares the two preexisting groups to assess differences in amount of empathy. Findings are interpreted as relational rather than as a causal relationship, because we cannot infer that gender type causes an ability.

Another type of observational group design is called a *causal-comparative design* (called an ex post facto design when conducted retrospectively), where preexisting groups need to have occurred before an outcome of interest, allowing causality to be inferred with caution (McMillan, 2021). In this design, preexisting groups are chosen for their similarities (e.g., same socioeconomic status or educational level), except for the IV of interest. This way, differences in the DV can be attributed to the IV. Because there is no random assignment, a strong theoretical reason for inferring a causal relationship is necessary.

Student Example: Causal-Comparative Design

DT is interested in conducting research comparing levels of stress and perceived social support between couples who manage residential houses together and more traditional residential care workers. These potential participants are already working in their respective applied settings, so they cannot be randomized to groups. However, DT plans to control for potentially extraneous variables, such as being in a relationship and the socioeconomic status of the neighborhood in which they live.

Traditionally used in epidemiology, *case–control design* is a type of observational group design, where *case* means the participant has a particular condition or characteristic (e.g., adults with children), whereas the *controls* do not (e.g., adults without children). The two groups are then compared on other variables of interest (e.g., level of education). For example, it could be hypothesized that adults without children are likely to have a higher level of education as compared to adults who have children. However, a third variable may also be at play in this relationship (e.g., if they are married).

Cross-sectional case–control designs involve collecting data from cases and controls about their current characteristics at one point in time. These designs are commonly used for applied dissertations and theses because they can assess several variables at once and can even be conducted online (e.g., asking adults to complete a set of questionnaires via a survey-making website).

In a *retrospective case–control design*, the researcher starts with two groups that differ on an outcome variable (the DV) and retrospectively assesses variables that are possible antecedent causes (the IV). For example, could certain parenting styles (permissive vs. authoritarian) increase the likelihood of having a diagnosis of borderline personality disorder later in life? To answer this question, the researcher would ask participants with and without this disorder about their parents' style of parenting. This design can be useful for obtaining information about two or more variables that occurred at different times relatively quickly, because the prior variable has already occurred. A key limitation to this design is that participants may remember past information inaccurately (e.g., what their parents' parenting style was actually like).

Descriptive Design

A descriptive design focuses on the exploration of characteristics of a sample or a phenomenon. This design is useful as a first step toward quantitative understanding in an original line of study. Research questions are often used as opposed to hypotheses because these designs tend to be used when little is known about a topic of interest. Hypotheses may be generated from the findings, however. Typically, the researcher assesses frequencies (e.g., number of students who request an event), averages (e.g., test scores), and/or percentages (e.g., program completion rates).

Student Example: Descriptive Design

Although several studies have demonstrated the efficacy of dialectical behavior therapy for adolescents (DBT-A) as it was created, clinicians often find it challenging to engage adolescents and their parents in this treatment. ER and CG thought it would be innovative to assess parent and adolescent expectations of DBT-A and preferences for various treatment format options (e.g., attending multifamily groups vs. adolescent-only groups). Families were asked to participate after they were informed about the treatment procedure at intake. The goal of these two dissertations was to explore whether parent and adolescents entering this treatment understood what they would receive and whether they had other preferences, which could indicate the need to further orient families to the rationale for the existing treatment procedures.

Now that we have reviewed experimental, correlational, observational, and descriptive designs, you may want to think through how to choose which type makes sense for a particular quantitative project idea. Figure 1.5 may help you determine which design would be most appropriate.

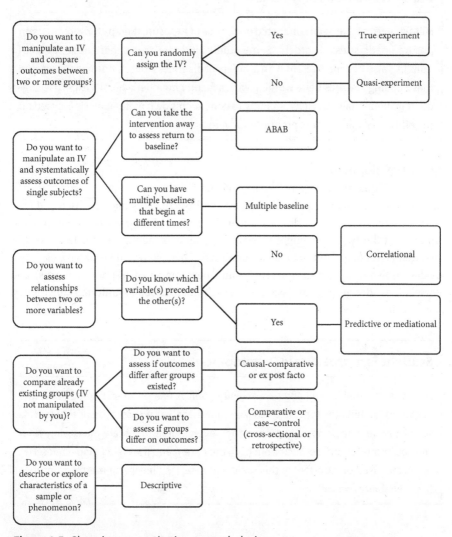

Figure 1.5 Choosing a quantitative research design

Meta-analysis

A meta-analysis is designed to aggregate and compare the findings of a number of existing empirical studies focused on a particular type of intervention. Typically, effect sizes, which measure the magnitude of an effect, can be used to standardize results across studies that used different assessments. Data are composed of results sections from methodologically rigorous published studies, dissertations, and even unpublished data sets if they can be made available. Researchers often contact the authors of studies to ask for access to relevant data that are not found in publications.

Student Example: Meta-analysis

Meta-analyses have been conducted on the use of exposure therapy for veterans with posttraumatic stress disorders. Some studies indicate that mindfulness interventions can also benefit veterans with a variety of diagnoses, but no one has aggregated these findings. AC has been working with a faculty member who has expertise conducting meta-analyses. He is planning to conduct his own meta-analysis focused on the efficacy of mindfulness programs for veterans.

Scale Development

This type of quantitative study focuses on assessing the psychometric properties of a scale of measurement (e.g., reliability and validity, concepts that are discussed later in this chapter). You might develop a new scale and test it for various types of reliability and validity, or you might be evaluating an existing scale to further assess its psychometrics (e.g., conduct a factor analysis). These studies tend to have elements of descriptive design (e.g., frequencies and percentages of responses, means) and correlational design (e.g., assessment of psychometrics such as internal consistency, convergent validity).

Student Example: Scale Development

DF was interested in studying parent–child conflict related to technology use. She began researching the topic and realized that there was no assessment tool for this specific issue. She decided to pursue the development of a scale measuring what she has termed technoconflict, from both the parent and the child perspectives. Her project focused on developing this scale and assessing its psychometric properties (e.g., reliability and validity).

Program Evaluation

Program evaluation is the systematic collection, analysis, and reporting of information about a particular program to assist in decision-making about that program. Often, it is linked to outcomes assessment in terms of an applied program's impact, efficacy, or efficiency in attaining specific goals. Many in applied fields already assess their services or efforts without necessarily calling it an evaluation. A more formal program evaluation starts with a description of the program being evaluated and an explanation of the program's goals and methods. Using a program evaluation as a research project requires that you fully understand the program's aims. Then, you will need to figure out: (a) what to measure, (b) how to measure it with either existing data collection methods or new sources, (c) who will conduct these assessments, (d) when to measure (will this be a single time or multiple times across the process of the program?), and (e) who will complete the assessments. This can be a complex process because many folks are interested in the outcomes of programs, including participants, therapists and providers, clients, students, educators, managers and administrators, sponsors, and researchers. Program evaluation can focus on short-term and/or long-term outcomes and will help an agency or funding source address the following questions:

- Is the program being implemented as intended?
- How is the program achieving its goals?
- What activities and/or interventions are being conducted toward the program's goals?
- What services did the clients and/or students receive?
- What were people's experiences during and as a result of this program?

The researcher helps to analyze and interpret the information and/or data obtained to understand the program's impact and to make recommendations for change. Further, the results of such a project can help agency personnel to design better or different services to further improve the desired outcomes.

Qualitative Research

The historic origin of qualitative research lies in the fields of anthropology, sociology, humanities, and philosophy. The nature and scope of a qualitative research study are distinct from those of a quantitative study, because the study is inductive rather than deductive. In other words, the researcher approaches the topic of interest with an open mind. They begin with an overarching research question in mind, though this question may change as the research evolves. This is different from the scientific method, because qualitative studies do not start with a theory and are not bound by specific hypotheses; instead, data are collected from participants to explore and understand their perspective on their experiences.

There are several qualitative methodologies, including narrative, phenomeno-logical, grounded theory, participatory action research, ethnography, and case study approaches. Although they differ from traditional research, students con-ducting qualitative projects still need to demonstrate satisfaction of the research and evaluation competency included in various training models. All of the types described next require a review and synthesis of the relevant scientific and concep-tual literature, as well as a demonstration of implications for practical significance and innovation.

Narrative Research

In narrative research, the researcher explores an individual or individuals' experi-ences over the course of their lives. Participants are often interviewed and asked to share their personal stories. Additional materials may also be reviewed, such as diaries, photographs, and letters. The researcher places this material into a narra-tive, taking verbal and nonverbal information into account to construct a meaningful narrative of their experiences. Usually, the write up includes both the participants' and the researcher's perspectives. Sometimes, this type of project is in the form of a biography that reflects a narrative about one individual.

Phenomenological

Phenomenological design stems from the fields of philosophy and psychology. It involves describing the experiences of individuals who all experienced a similar phenomenon. This description typically comes from open-ended interviews. The researcher can focus on describing participants' perspectives and experiences to shed light on their meaning or can go a step further and interpret them. The researcher "brackets" their preconceived biases to fully explore participants' experiences while attempting to keep their biases at bay.

Student Example: Phenomenological Research Design

MM lived in New York City during the 9/11 terrorist attacks and had strong ties to the first responder community. She wondered about the experiences of the spouses of first responders who spent an enormous amount of time at Ground Zero. In the hope of truly understanding their experiences, MM conducted individual interviews with spouses of firefighters and police responders and asked them to talk about their experiences at home.

Grounded Theory

Grounded theory is a sociological research approach designed to generate theory, grounded in the words of the participants. This type of qualitative study typically involves constant comparison of participant interview data as it is obtained over the course of the study to identify and categorize common concepts across participants. The researcher may also engage in theoretical sampling, a process by which participants with slightly varying experiences are interviewed over time to help understand myriad perspectives. The goal of this approach is not to identify hypotheses beforehand, but rather to allow the data to unfold into meaningful patterns, exposing themes surrounding the topic(s) of interest. This hypothesis-generating approach is "particularly well suited for the study of diversity because it does not assume that there is one universal truth to be discovered" (Auerbach & Silverstein, 2003, p. 26).

Typically, individual interviews or focus groups with small numbers of participants are asked a question about the topic of interest. This question and a few follow-up questions are designed to be general so as to invite the respondent to create their own narrative response. For example, one of our students asked his participants, "What was it like to grow up with an artist as your parent?" These interviews are audiotaped and then transcribed so that the researcher and/or coders can group the text into relevant ideas, repeating themes, and finally theoretical constructs that weave the idea and themes together cohesively.

One type of grounded theory only involves the researcher's coding of the data, because the goal is to capture the researcher's subjective experience of the information collected (Charmaz, 2006). Another method of grounded theory involves coders, who work with the researcher to help identify biases and come to a consensus about how to best categorize the data. Auerbach and Silverstein (2003) describe their method of working with coders in detail, including the various stages of coder training, transcript coding, and data analysis. The final step, grounding the data in the literature and with existing theories, allows one to develop a theoretical framework. The researcher can then generate a theoretical narrative and hypotheses directly from the participants who have a particular experience.

Student Example: Grounded Theory Design

SD was interested in engaging low-income, depressed mothers in mental health treatment. She found a good deal of research indicating the types of barriers to treatment these women endorsed; however, proposed solutions appeared to come from the researchers, not the mothers. She conducted a grounded theory study in which she interviewed low-income, depressed mothers to learn what they wanted from the mental health system. She and two coders generated themes and theoretical constructs from the data that were then placed in an innovative theoretical framework, including support from the unified theory of behavior change and concepts from dialectical behavior therapy. The new theory included ideas about what factors influence these mothers' intentions to enter treatment, entering treatment, and remaining in treatment.

Participatory Action Research (PAR)

PAR is an approach to inquiry that includes action as a major objective and outcome. PAR is an interactive process between researchers and participants that evolves from the unique needs of a specific group of individuals. According to Kidd and Kral (2005), a colloquial description is a process wherein "you get the people affected by a problem together, figure out what is going on as a group, and then do something about it" (p. 187). PAR is not necessarily a method, but a qualitative, collaborative approach that uses various research methods to inform actions that can be taken to address the problem of interest. Researchers and participants work together to identify goals and methodology, collect and analyze data, and use results of the project to advocate for desired changes in the participants' lives. The researcher involves participants in each step of the research. Historically, this approach has connections to community psychology and social justice initiatives. Rather than traditional research approaches in which research questions lead to the methods, in PAR, the problem is explored over time, with questions revised in the ways that are expected to best lead to action (Kidd & Kral, 2005). The methods used to generate knowledge around the problem can range from a traditional survey to interviews, focus groups, and narrative recordings that are more typical in qualitative research.

Example: Participatory Action Research (PAR)

Chen and colleagues (2010) included girls in five cities as evaluators of their after-school programs. The authors found that over the three-year period, PAR was a promising evaluation tool; the girls determined what offerings worked well and what could be improved to make after-school programming more engaging for them. Additionally, staff learned that the girls were capable of participating in research, which challenged their assumptions about the girls and had implications for future programming. The PAR approach was used in this program evaluation to improve data collection, showcase the skills and talents of the girls, and alter relationships between the girls and after-school program staff.

Ethnography

Ethnography is a research approach originating in anthropology and sociology. The researcher examines patterns of behavior in a particular cultural group's natural setting across a long period of time. The researcher is considered a participant observer, or someone who fully engages in the group's daily activities and culture while observing and/or interviewing participants across the duration of the study.

Case Study

Case study is an approach used to develop an in-depth analysis of a case, which can include one or more people, a group, event, or situation. The case study method has a long tradition in the social sciences. There is ample evidence of psychodynamic applications, but often these were *uncontrolled case studies* and relied heavily on subjective interpretation by the therapist. These differ from the quantitative single case designs discussed earlier, which are considered *controlled case studies* use hypotheses, a rigorous design, stringent methods of data collection, and results that remain separate from their discussion (Luyten et al., 2006). Researchers collect detailed information via multiple data sources, including observations, interviews, and additional relevant documents and/or materials. The case study involves a detailed description of a setting and its participants. Case studies are typically implemented when there is something exceptional or unique to examine about a particular case that could make a significant contribution to the field.

Mixed Methods Research

Mixed methods research includes a purposeful combination of both qualitative and quantitative approaches used in one research study (Shannon-Baker, 2016). This combination of these approaches can occur in a variety of places throughout a study, including the research aims, research design, methods for data collection and analyzing data, and interpretation of the findings. The goal of using a mixed methods approach is to develop a more comprehensive understanding of a situation than one research method can provide (e.g., Creswell & Plano Clark, 2011). For example, perhaps you have determined through a literature review that a certain anger management intervention developed by others might be promising for adolescents with mild brain injury with whom you have begun working. There is a good amount of research evidence supporting the cognitive-behavioral strategies incorporated into various anger management treatment manuals. To consider its generalizability to this type of adolescent population, the first step might be a case study of one such application and then a larger group design if the case study is successful. Another example might be assessing results from several assessment inventories you administered to your sample about how their anger changed from before to after the intervention. Are these tools giving you all the information that you want, or can you also conduct interviews with a smaller number of research participants on questions that should have been asked, to broaden your understanding of their experience? Combining results from your quantitative data as well as the qualitative interviews will likely best inform your next steps.

Theoretical or Scholarly Project

In some graduate programs, final projects can take the form of scholarly research. Sometimes these projects are considered theoretical or scholarly projects. Some of them can also be referred to as nonempirical, if data are not collected or analyzed. The following are some examples of theoretical and scholarly projects.

Theoretical Project

Theoretical projects are carefully reasoned efforts to synthesize existing theory and research in order to propose a new and original way of explaining or understanding aspects of human behavior. This could be a modification, a reformulation, or an advanced application of a relevant theory germane to the practice of your applied field. These projects include a comprehensive and critical review of the existing literature, a proposed model for understanding the literature in new ways, and a discussion of the practical implications of this new model.

Student Example: Theoretical Project

WR theorized that four clinical presentations—depression, obsessive–compulsive, dissociative, and psychotic—could be conceptualized as psychopathological disturbances maintained through dissociation, based on the dissonance between moral values and human nature. For his dissertation, he first reviewed how morality is conceptualized across the field of psychology. He then reviewed the literature on defense mechanisms, particularly as they pertain to dissociation and its impact on the self. Next, he presented the theoretical interaction of these concepts based on varied awareness of the dissonance between oneself and one's moral ideals. He then proposed four positions along a continuum, including a theoretical justification for each one, accompanied by a clinical example. His dissertation ended with a review of clinical and theoretical implications for his proposed theory.

Critical Analysis of the Literature

This includes the synthesis, analysis, and critique of the existing conceptual literature and research focused on an applied problem. This review can include a newly proposed model for understanding the literature and a discussion of implications and future directions in this area. A systematic review involves identifying a question of interest and developing a comprehensive method for searching databases, identifying search terms and eligible studies, and evaluating relevant information to address that question, synthesizing all evidence available.

Example: Critical Analysis of the Literature

The first author published a review of the literature examining whether treating parental anxiety or depression improves child anxiety outcome. Various studies in this area had been conducted, but this was the first literature review to compile all relevant information from the parent and child treatment literature. The authors critically evaluated this literature and suggested directions for future research.

Extended Case Study

According to Bloomberg and Volpe (2012), case study is both a methodology (a type of qualitative and quantitative design, as described under "Single Case Designs" and "Case Study") and an object of study. Data collection in case study research is typically extensive for either a single case or multiple case studies. For example, you might conduct an intervention with a client or student at a practicum or externship site for a full academic year. Your project would likely include sections such as a comprehensive client or student background and description of the presenting problem, your case formulation, intervention plan with a justification, description of your client's or student's progress, and a self-evaluation of your work with the case. Typically, this will include some kind of continuous data collection or monitoring of treatment outcomes and/or impact. In a single case of psychotherapy, you might analyze transcripts of all individual sessions across time to look at aspects of the psychotherapy process, development of therapeutic alliance, or the occurrences of rupture-and-repair cycles.

Systematic Development of an Innovative Program Manual, Curriculum, Book, or Guide

These types of projects include the development and comprehensive description of a new professional program manual, curriculum, book, or guide, based on the scientific and theoretical literature. For example, an anger management manual already accepted as an effective treatment approach could be adapted for use with a different population (e.g., developmentally delayed adolescents). In many graduate programs, developing or adapting a manual would be the first step. The next step would involve a pilot study of the intervention with several individual cases or a focus group asking clinicians about their perspectives on the intervention. This type of pilot study can set the stage for future researchers using the manual with a larger sample. Alternatively, you might develop a book to serve as bibliotherapy or an adjunct to an intervention or lesson plans. You would likely have to demonstrate how your approach fills a gap among existing manuals or books. Similarly, you could write a guide based on existing literature for a group of people, such as clinicians, teachers, or parents, designed to provide strategies for addressing a particular issue (e.g., social media use, obtaining various clinical or educational services).

Student Example: Development of a Children's Book as a Bibliotherapy Resource

As part of KL's clinical training, she treated a child suffering from emetophobia, or a fear of vomiting. KL noticed there were few resources available to help facilitate her treatment. She conducted a review of the treatment literature and found bibliotherapy had demonstrated efficacy for treating child anxiety, but she did not come across any therapeutic books about this phobia. After consultation with her dissertation chair, KL decided to propose the development of a children' storybook for her final project. Specifically, she proposed conducting a review of the available treatment literature as well as a review of published children's books for various types of child anxiety to help her develop her book. She then planned to submit a book proposal to the American Psychological Association's children's book publishing company, Magination Press. KL's dissertation committee found her proposal important and innovative.

Student Example: Development of a Manual for an Innovative Program

CK developed a stress management program for mothers of teens with attention deficit/hyperactivity disorder based on her clinical understanding of the various stressors facing mothers when managing the high school years with their teens. Her dissertation research focused on the implementation and evaluation of this new protocol with three mothers. Both continuous stress-log data and pre–post assessments were gathered for all three.

Foundational Concepts in Research

Now that you are familiar with a variety of types of project designs, we briefly review some foundational concepts in quantitative research about statistics and psychometric properties that you will likely be asked to familiarize yourself with at the beginning stages of your graduate training. We then review key criteria for judging qualitative research. Finally, we provide an overview of the types of ethical information you will need to learn about when conducting research.

Understanding the Statistics You Read and Need

We know that some of you are going to groan when you see the word statistics. And we get it. Many students who enter an applied graduate program shudder at the mere mention of numbers. In fact, statistics are one of the reasons students might lean toward conducting a more qualitative or nonempirical study. But you cannot escape statistics entirely. As someone pursuing a graduate degree in an applied field, you need to at least be an educated consumer of research, which includes the ability to generally understand and critically evaluate the statistical sections of quantitative articles. After all, it is important to be able to evaluate authors' discussions about their findings and come to your own conclusions. A review of specific statistical concepts and tests is beyond the scope of this guide; however, our goal is to make sure you know what you need to learn.

Needing to have a basic understanding of statistics does not mean you have to automatically be familiar with the specifics of every statistical test; however, you should have a general understanding of what descriptive statistics (e.g., means, standard deviations) look like in an article, as well as what they mean. You should also know how to recognize and when to use inferential statistics, which are tests of significance that either confirm or disconfirm a hypothesis via a predetermined p value (e.g., <.05). These statistics include t-tests, analysis of variance, chi square, correlations, and linear regression analyses. Several articles use more complex statistics, such as logistical regression, path analyses, or factor analyses. It is good to be familiar with when each of these types of tests makes sense to use. Beyond whether your findings are significant, it is good to know how to assess effect size or the magnitude of your findings. You will also want to be familiar with when to control for potentially extraneous variables.

For applied research projects, it is important to remember that statistical significance is not the same as clinical significance, which refers to the practical difference a change makes in a person's life. Kazdin (1982) discussed an example of a child who self-injures by banging their head approximately one hundred times per observation. If an intervention is conducted and subsequently the child reduces their head banging to fifty times per observation, this would likely be a statistically significant change. Practically, however, it would not be clinically significant, because the child would still be getting injured. Keep in mind that when you complete a research study in an applied setting, the staff there will likely be collaborating with you in the hopes of achieving clinically significant changes. You cannot control your results, but you can design your project with these concepts in consideration. In addition, when you eventually write up your final project, you can differentiate between research and clinical implications of your findings based on these concepts.

So how do you get comfortable with statistics? It really is like learning a language—the more you learn and apply your knowledge, the greater comprehension and fluency you will have. As part of your graduate program, you will likely have to take some statistics courses. Take good notes in those courses and save your textbooks, because you may want to reference the materials down the line. At this point, you also likely have opportunities to get involved in some research. We urge you to engross yourself in all aspects of faculty or upper-level student projects (or projects outside your school) that you work on, including understanding the rationale for and running of specific statistical analyses. One of the best ways to learn statistics is by having to run analyses. We suggest volunteering to run analyses for a poster presentation or ask a faculty member to walk you through analysis of their data. You may find you have more of an interest in statistics than you thought that you did—stranger things have happened! Some of our most clinically-focused students have become highly skilled and interested in statistical analyses, often based on their desire to adequately conduct applied research.

Foundational Knowledge of Psychometrics

Psychometrics in quantitative research generally refers to theories and methods for measuring participants' characteristics, such as clinical outcomes, educational achievement, personality traits, or attitudes. These characteristics may be assessed at one point or over time. Common types of psychometric measures in research include self-report questionnaires, diagnostic and cognitive tests, and systematic observations.

Two major concepts used to evaluate the value of specific measures are reliability and validity. Generally speaking, reliability assesses how consistently a measure provides the same results. Validity focuses on whether the measure is assessing the construct it is intended to measure (e.g., does a measure purporting to assess depression truly capture what depression looks like?). Table 1.2 presents a basic overview of common types of reliability and validity. We will discuss these terms again when reviewing the knowledge needed to select measures for your project in Chapter 4.

Table 1.2 Common Types of Reliability and Validity

Reliability	Basic definition
Internal consistency	Level of consistency across items on a measure; one type is called Cronbach's alpha
Test–retest reliability	How consistent scores on a measure are at different points
Interrater reliability	How consistent scores are between raters; one type is called kappa

Validity	Basic definition
Face validity	An informal way to review a measure and determine whether it appears to assess the target construct
Content validity	A more formal method for determining whether a measure is assessing the target construct (e.g., experts review the measure)
Convergent validity	How much a measure correlates with a measure assessing a similar construct (i.e., how similar the constructs are)
Predictive/concurrent validity	How much a measure is predictive of a future or concurrent construct (e.g., how much do SAT scores predict college grade point average?)
Divergent/discriminant validity	How much a measure does not correlate with a measure of another construct (i.e., how discriminant the constructs are)

Criteria for Evaluating Qualitative Research

Qualitative researchers tend to disagree with quantitative approaches to assessing reliability and validity. The goal is not to determine how much specific constructs reflect real world occurrences, but to capture participants' subjective experiences.

Lincoln and Guba (1985) outlined alternative criteria for evaluating reliability and validity in qualitative research. Specifically, they described four criteria related to the trustworthiness of the data: credibility as analogous to internal validity, transferability to external validity, dependability to reliability, and confirmability to objectivity. Credibility refers to the extent that qualitative research results are accurate and believable, according to the participants' viewpoints. One way to assess for credibility is to conduct a participant member check, which is described in Chapter 8. Transferability is how much qualitative research findings is applicable to other settings or contexts. Because qualitative research is conducted within a specific group of people or situation, it is challenging to relate the findings to other environments. Researchers can increase the possibility of transferability by thoroughly describing the context in which the study was conducted, unique factors about the sample, and any biases considered. Dependability refers to the consistency of the results within a context that can change over time. To assess dependability, researchers can maintain an audit trail, or a detailed record of their data collection and coding process so others can determine the stability of the results over time. Confirmability is defined as the extent to which other researchers could confirm the findings as objectively as possible, given each researcher brings their own perspective and biases to a study. This can involve keeping a comprehensive record of the way data is coded and interpreted over the course of a project and then having this process examined by an outside researcher to examine the data for any potential bias and/or contrasting perspectives.

Demonstrating Basic Knowledge of Ethical Principles in Research

Before you become involved in conducting any research, you will need to become cognizant of the guidelines for ethical conduct of research in your field. Ethical guidelines related to research include issues such as obtaining informed consent from participants, debriefing participants after a study, avoiding plagiarism, and taking appropriate publication credit. As part of your graduate training, you will likely take an ethics course that exposes you to this information and enables you to demonstrate competence in these areas. In Chapter 4, we provide a brief overview of ethical principles to consider and adhere to when you propose to conduct research with people, based on the American Psychological Association's (2017) "Research and Publication" section (standard 8) of the *Ethical Principles of Psychologists and Code of Conduct*. The goals of these guidelines are to protect research participants and inform people about the field's ethical standards for research activities. Several applied fields have similar ethical guidelines for the conduct of research, so you will want to compare this list to the guidelines in your field.

If you conduct an empirical project in graduate school, the project must be reviewed and approved by your school's institutional review board (IRB) before the research can be conducted. IRBs are federally mandated groups present in organizations such as universities and hospitals designed to protect the rights and well-being of human subjects and prevent them from harm when they participate in research. For IRB purposes, research is federally defined as a "systematic investigation" that aims to "develop or contribute to generalizable knowledge" (US Department of Health and Human Services, 2018). In accordance with federal policy, the IRB evaluates whether subjects will be exposed to greater than minimal risk or greater than the possible risk involved in a typical day or in a routine physical or psychological examination. If so, a cost–benefit analysis is conducted to determine whether the benefits of conducting the research outweigh the amount of potential risk. The IRB also assesses factors such as voluntary participation, ability to withdraw from the research at any time; informed consent and/or assent materials; research study procedures, including recruitment; and how confidentiality of the data will be ensured. Particular consideration is given to applications involving vulnerable populations, such as children, people who are ill, pregnant women, prisoners, and those who have a disability. College students are also often considered vulnerable because of the possibility of exploitation (e.g., feeling pressure to participate for course credit).

It is common for IRBs to require research training (e.g., how to ethically conduct research with human subjects) before you conduct your own research. Some universities offer this training in person, while others offer it online. We begin to explain how to navigate the IRB, including information about these courses, in Chapter 2. We will also help you determine what to include in your IRB application (see Chapter 5).

Navigating Your Way toward a Final Project Topic: A Developmental Process

Identifying Your Research Interests

Now that we have gone through foundational knowledge concepts (phew!), it is time to start thinking about ideas! Your final topic is selected through a developmental process that begins with identifying your research areas of interest. The beginning of graduate school can seem fragmented as you rush from course to course, and from school to your practicum site, and as you learn from a variety of faculty and clinical supervisors. Over the course of your program, you will likely develop many interests within the field. It can seem difficult to then have to come up with a single final project. Regardless of whether you think you have a solid research topic in the beginning, you will want to keep your mind open to several possibilities. Good brainstorming involves thinking about all possible options while withholding evaluation. Catalysts for topic selection include the following:

- Applied experiences with particular populations or intervention methods
- Your own life experiences
- Class projects, papers, and presentations
- Conversations with faculty and peers
- Issues encountered in your professional training
- Working in an active research lab
- Joining organizations and attending professional conferences and student poster sessions
- Reading, reading, reading!

We suggest you keep a running list of ideas as they come to mind. If you keep track of potential topic areas, the focus for your final project will likely evolve naturally.

Graduate students arrive at final project topics from a number of pathways. You can begin this process by simply noticing what caught your interest in your field from the beginning. After reading this section, we recommend you complete Worksheet 1.1 to determine areas you may be interested in pursuing.

You may have had potential project topics in mind before you entered your graduate program. This may be the case if you participated in research as an undergraduate, if you were employed or volunteered in an applied clinical and/or research setting, or if you have already completed an undergraduate honors or master's thesis. These early experiences may have engaged and excited you to the point where you would consider further exploration in an existing area of interest.

Students often apply to graduate school with a passion for a particular topic because of their own life experiences or interests. Personal experience can serve as a springboard for developing a professional area of interest. When this occurs, it is often referred to as *MEsearch*. Speculation exists that most professionals have some personal connection to their area of interest. Use caution, however, in conducting this kind of work. Dedicating significant time to something that has strong personal relevance for you in your life has advantages because of your experience in this area. However, there are risks associated with personal disclosures, such as difficulty being objective and receiving feedback. We recommended discussing the pros and cons of pursuing a MEsearch topic with a trusted advisor.

A great deal of information can be obtained about the research conducted by faculty, graduate students, and alumni. You can usually review the faculty interests, grants received, conference presentations, books and chapters, and published articles on the program site. If a particular faculty member has published in an area you have interest in, we recommend reading some of their work early on, because once your academic year begins, you will likely have less time to do it. You can also read dissertations or theses completed by former students in your program and review final projects supervised by a faculty member you might be considering for your project chair.

Once you begin graduate school, you may find areas of interest through class lectures, articles you read, conversations about your ideas with faculty and peers, and issues encountered in your professional training. Start with broad areas of interest. For example, do you find yourself engaged in discussions about treating child anxiety? Did you begin a practicum in a homeless shelter and realize the staff could benefit from trauma training? Did you encounter some students or clients who experienced barriers to improvement while others did not and wonder how they differed?

Early academic projects, such as term papers, group projects, or classroom presentations, can also provide the impetus for areas of interest. To formulate a well-designed research study, you must become knowledgeable about the topic. Some programs have a research course or seminar that focuses on topic area selection and often includes a draft proposal as a term paper. These assignments may eventually represent portions of the proposal for your final project.

Student Example: Personal, Clinical, and Research Experiences Lead to Final Project Topic

MM started her doctoral program with an interest in working with children and families. She had a particular interest in the diagnosis and treatment of attention deficit/hyperactivity disorder (ADHD) based on some familial experience with this issue. In her second year of graduate school, she wrote a paper for her child therapy class about treating a client with ADHD, which helped her start to cultivate treatment literature in this area. In her third year, she participated in an externship largely focused on assessing and treating this disorder in children. Throughout her first three years of graduate school, she served as a research assistant in a lab focused on parents and children. As part of this position, she conducted qualitative research focused on exploring parents' commentary about time-out and toilet-training videos found on YouTube. Collectively, these experiences taught her quite a bit about ADHD and qualitative coding; however, over time, her research interests shifted to wanting to understand the experience of parents who are members of underrepresented ethnic groups seeking ADHD diagnosis and treatment for their daughters. For her dissertation, she was able to build on her personal, clinical, and research experiences while pursuing in-depth qualitative interviews with parents about a topic she found meaningful.

Early in your graduate training, you may be assigned as a research assistant in a particular lab or to a faculty member who is conducting applied research. There are pros and cons to "growing" your final project out of a faculty member's research lab. If you spend a good deal of time working as a research assistant, perhaps even helping upper-level students with their dissertations, you can put that time to good use by continuing a line of research from that lab. Certainly, your research faculty advisor, who is well versed in that particular area, will be uniquely suited to guide your research. You may have access to data sets, assessment measures, data collection methods, and a clearly defined content area for your literature review. In addition, working in an active research lab allows collaboration with others, which guards against the isolation that many graduate students face once they begin to work on their own final project. Research has shown that both faculty and students from psychology doctoral programs report having positive experiences with the dissertation process when they cultivated a positive working relationship through conducting research together early on (Burkard et al., 2014; Knox et al., 2011).

Since research assistants are typically "assigned" as part of their financial aid, however, you may have little interest in the lab's focus area. Instead, your genuine interests may lie in other areas, with other populations or other methods. Pursuing a project as an outgrowth of the research of others may seem to be an easier route, and that may be true, but it is hard to devote extensive time and resources to a topic you find underwhelming.

As you work on identifying your research interests, we recommend you consider joining a couple of professional organizations. Organizations can be broad based, addressing national or international issues in an overall field, or they can be more locally based. They can focus on particular characteristics of their members (e.g., ethnicity, gender), be interdisciplinary, or be specific to interests in a particular sub-field. Ask your faculty and supervisors which organizations they are active members of; this can help you determine which organizations it might make sense for you to join. You will often hear professionals refer to an organization as their *professional home*. The goal of these organizations is typically to provide their members with the most cutting-edge, up-to-date developments in the field. They will also provide opportunities to interact with like-minded researchers and practitioners in your field. Many graduate programs advertise the conferences that are most relevant to their program's mission or orientation. Over time, you can likely obtain opportunities to present at these conferences with your advisor and other student researchers.

Factors to Consider When Narrowing Research Interests into a Potential Topic Area

How do I turn my research interests into a potential project area? Several factors go into answering this question (see Figure 1.6). Once you have a few key interests, think of each of the following issues as part of a whole that will need to be balanced as you narrow your interests into a potential project area. After you read this section, we recommend you complete Worksheet 1.2 to help you think through this process.

What Interest Areas Inspire Me and Capture My Attention?
Look at the list of interests you have accumulated. What parts of the field do you feel excited to become an expert in? You will be focusing on your topic for quite some time, likely at least for a year, and often longer. No matter how much passion you have for your topic, chances are you will want a break from it by the time you complete your project! Therefore, it is extremely important to choose a topic area that seriously motivates you and holds your interest.

What Has Not Been Studied among My Interests That Could Advance the Field?
As you think about what areas interest you, figure out what appears important, but has not been studied. Keep in mind that you will need to develop a project within

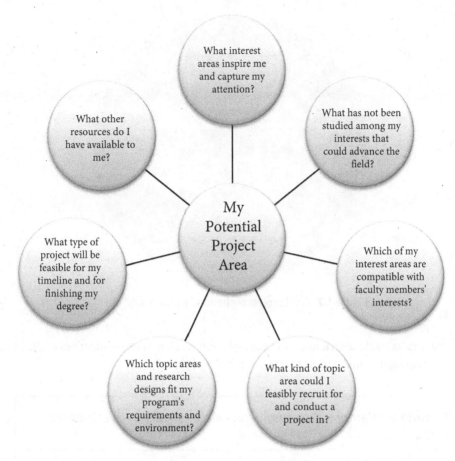

Figure 1.6 Factors to consider when narrowing interests into a potential project area

the context of existing knowledge in your field. As demonstrated in Figure 1.7, you will want to familiarize yourself with the state of the applied subfield that your area of interest fits into. Passion for an area of interest is a good start; however, in a scientifically minded program, you will be expected to understand how your idea fits into what is already known in the field. Start by reviewing recent and relevant articles to understand current problems in this area. What appear to be important next steps? What do the authors describe as future directions for research in the discussion sections? Independent of what the authors discuss, where do you see gaps in the existing literature where you could potentially make a contribution? What questions remain in your mind about the topic as a potential project area for further study? As a graduate student, your time and money is limited and you are not expected to discover something earth shattering. This is understood; however, a worthwhile final project should address a problem in the field and generate new information that

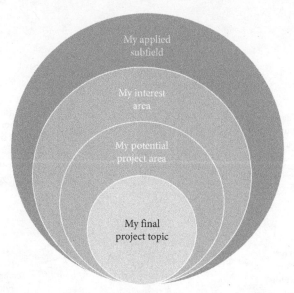

Figure 1.7   Final project embedded within a subfield

makes a valuable contribution to existing literature. Here is one student's example of developing her final project topic within her subfield.

Student Example: Developing an Interest within the Context of a Field

KK entered our program with a general interest in parent training for child behavior problems (applied subfield). She was encouraged to expand her knowledge of evidence-based parent training programs and the theories behind the efficacy of specific parent training techniques (interest area within applied subfield). As KK researched the topic, she determined that there were gaps in the literature about parental acceptability and preferences for various parent training techniques (potential project area). She eventually determined she could meaningfully contribute to the existing literature in this subfield by assessing parents' acceptability and preferences for two types of time-out procedures (final project topic).

Which of My Interest Areas Are Compatible with the Interests of Faculty Members?

Another key part of a successful project is finding a good faculty member match. As you get to know the faculty in your program, think about your options for a project chair. Several factors will go into selecting a chair, such as the type of mentor model used in your program and how students are assigned to advisors. We will discuss various types of mentor models and roles later in this chapter and review tips for selecting a project chair (i.e., project advisor, sponsor) as you get closer to developing your project proposal in Chapter 4. From the beginning of your program, however, you may be assigned to a particular research lab or faculty advisor. This will give you exposure to their existing lines of research and the types of projects they appear eager to collaborate on. Each semester, you will likely also take classes from several professors in their areas of competence. At the start of your program, think about the following questions.

Who Has Expertise in an Area That Interests You?

Your project will likely cover more than one literature base, and your project chair does not have to be familiar with all areas. However, having a chair who is knowledge-able about at least one of your topics will greatly facilitate their ability to guide you and make it more likely that you will receive meaningful feedback. Think about it: yes, advising you will be their job, but they will likely be more motivated and engaged if they are professionally invested in your topic area.

What Are Your Professors Interested In?

Begin reviewing your faculty's websites to learn about each of their areas of expertise and interest. If you belong to a professor's lab, think about the work you are involved in and whether you could see yourself pursuing that topic or a related one. If not, consider asking to work with a faculty member on one of their projects to gain some experience about what it is like to work with them. To the extent that your program allows, consider sitting in on an additional lab to learn about the work they are doing. We discuss skills for how to get involved in faculty's research in the beginning of Chapter 2. Many of the best projects come from a combination of two topic areas, and you may find that your work exists at the intersection between two faculty members' labs.

Which Faculty Member's Feedback on Class Assignments Do You Find Most Helpful?

The types of editing and suggestions you receive on class papers will likely be similar to what you would receive if they were the chair of your final project. Faculty can have very different styles of providing feedback. For example, some will provide suggestions for rewriting and specify ways to improve. Others will criticize something you have written and tell you to rework it, without suggesting how to do so. Some make grammatical and content edits, line by line. Others will tell you to seek writing assistance before they read further. If you are interested in working with a faculty member who is a stickler for writing and this is an area where you could improve, you should devote sufficient time to improving your writing as soon as possible.

Which Faculty Members Seem Most Interested in You?
An advising relationship is a two-way street. As you engage in your coursework and program activities, you may find that some professors seem intrigued by your ideas more than others. Is there someone who particularly complements your coursework or asks you to work with them on something? If so, they may have already thought about their interest in working with you!

Who Is Rumored to Be a "Good" Chair?
Who is reputed to be overly positive without providing substantial input? Who is known to provide direct feedback? Who is quick to return written drafts? Who sounds too rigid in their decision-making or slow in giving permission to move forward? Talk to upper-level students who have spent a few years working with the faculty. Ask them to describe what their experiences have been like and what factors they attribute to any issues they faced. It is important to remember that different students have different experiences, expectations, and working styles. We believe in finding a good fit between a chair and a student. One faculty member will not fit all students. For example, some students may avoid working with a faculty member who has developed a reputation for requiring substantial rewriting and execution of complex statistical analyses. Other students will want to work with that same professor because of their emphasis on methodological rigor and interest in student publication. In other words, take into account that what you hear will be filtered through factors related to the student who provided you with the information. Even so, a faculty member's reputation among upper-level students can give you a sense of their general strengths and weaknesses as a chair.

What Supervisory Style Is the Best Fit for You?
In their book on completing a professional practice dissertation, Willis et al. (2010) describe Gatfield and Alpert's (2002) conceptual supervisory style model, which focuses on interactions between a dissertation supervisor's amount of support (e.g., encouragement, raising of morale, assistance with problems) and amount of structure (e.g., selecting topic, setting timelines, skills training). These interactions lead to four types of supervisory styles, including: (1) laissez-faire style (low structure, low support), (2) pastoral style (low structure, high support), (3) directorial style (high structure, low support), and (4) contractual style (high structure, high support). The same faculty member can ideally fluctuate in style depending on the student they are working with and the point in the project process. For example, a student may benefit from a directorial style when they are learning how to implement a specific methodological design. In contrast, the same student may benefit from a pastoral style when they are in a time of personal crisis or need to change their project for some reason. However, broadly speaking, faculty may lean toward one of these styles. You likely also prefer one style or another. Some students will appreciate a laissez-faire chair who is hands-off and lets them proceed with their project independently. Others will want a contractual-style chair who walks them though each

part of the project process, setting deadlines and providing regular feedback and encouragement. In Chapter 4, we review more specific characteristics to consider when selecting potential project chairs.

What Kind of Topic Area Could I Feasibly Recruit for and Conduct a Project In?

It is important to have interests you are passionate about, a topic that could make a valuable contribution to your field, and faculty who are on board with your ideas. Next, you should ask yourself what kind of project is realistic to recruit for and feasible to conduct. For example, if you want to recruit adults with anxiety disorders, will you have access to such a sample? If so, how? Do you have evidence to suggest that enough people will be willing to participate? Have other students had success recruiting a similar sample within your geographic region?

Student Example: Making a Potential Project Idea Feasible to Conduct

EB was interested in issues parents face when their college-aged children participate in dialectical behavior therapy. However, access to this sample appeared difficult for her to obtain. After her own clinical experiences providing this therapy for emerging adult clients, she became interested in conducting a qualitative study exploring clinicians' experiences incorporating parents into their treatment.

There may be creative ways to study an area of interest that is difficult to recruit for. For example, if you are interested in studying children with cancer, but think it would be hard to obtain such a sample, you could develop a project idea focused on interviewing the health professionals who work with such children. Another idea is to broaden your inclusion criteria to include a more feasible sample (e.g., children with any chronic medical illness or adults who had cancer as children).

If you want to develop or conduct a project in an applied setting, do you have a setting in mind? How open do you think the staff and organization will be to you conducting a project in their facility? Whose permission would you need to recruit and/or conduct the project? They may allow you to collect data in their setting. How much would they assist you, expect to have control over your project, or allow and/or expect you to work independently? Will the setting's directors and staff be interested in helping facilitate your data collection or will you need to do it on your own? Would they want to claim primary ownership of your project? Would they allow you to publish your findings? Would you be the first author?

Another idea is to explore whether you have access to an existing data set with some of your variables of interest. Many organizations, agencies, and institutions collect data on a routine basis, at times for research, but also for other reasons (e.g., absentee records at a school, employee turnover at a foster care placement). This archival data might be stashed in a file drawer or be a part of the agency's database. The agency might agree to let you analyze their data, particularly if you can find ways that your project could help them understand or improve their services. However, whose permission would you likely need to access the records? Would they help you extract the data and/or analyze it?

If you are thinking of pursuing a topic that does not involve traditional data collection and analysis, such as the development of an innovative educational curriculum, do you have access to the needed materials or people? If you are completing a theoretical review, do you have a clear understanding of what is involved? Is there enough relevant literature to support the development of your theory? Overall, potential hurdles will exist in any topic area and every research project. We suggest brainstorming possible solutions early on, so you have time to evaluate the pros and cons of pursuing a particular topic.

What Topic Areas and Research Designs Fit My Program's Requirements and Environment?

Programs typically have a mission statement that relates to their overall curriculum. You may be strongly encouraged to carry out a project that fits with that mission, such as assessing the efficacy of an intervention in an underserved population, conducting interviews focused on a social justice issue, or contributing to the field's knowledge of a specific type of therapy or philosophy. Some programs have special tracks or concentrations for students to select that may be related to their project topic. You typically can pursue a topic outside these areas, but be sure to familiarize yourself with your program's specific project guidelines.

Graduate programs also typically have certain types of methodological designs they allow for the completion of dissertation or thesis requirements. For example, some scientist-practitioner programs will expect their students to conduct a quantitative, empirical research project, while some practitioner-scholar programs will encourage qualitative projects and theoretical narratives. Acceptable data collection practices can also vary. Some programs only allow their students to complete projects for which they have collected their own data, rather than using archival data or their advisor's data. A good way to determine what types of research designs are allowed is to survey the designs taught in your program's research course(s) and, again, review the guidelines for student final projects.

Effective graduate training environments must do far more than teach research skills and set guidelines within which students can conduct their projects. Students in applied fields often enter graduate programs with a certain ambivalence toward research involvement, and some programs work to create more of a research training environment than others. For example, faculty can model scientific behavior and attitudes, and students can be encouraged to get involved with research early (Gelso, 2006). Factors like these are hypothesized to influence students' attitudes toward research, such as their interest in doing research and the perceived value of research for their careers. You will soon be able to determine whether scientific activity is reinforced in your program and whether students are able to get involved with research early. Hopefully, your graduate community will showcase a variety of approaches to research and demonstrate how integrated science and practice really are. Gelso (2006) hopes that "students [will] be aided in seeing themselves as an integral part of the knowledge-generating process and in owning their research ideas rather than experiencing research as personally alien" (p. 11). Be sure to assess your program's research approaches and the integration of research and practice by talking with faculty, current students, and alumni from your program.

It is a good idea to get a sense of what projects in your program typically look like early on. From the first semester of your program, you will have opportunities to be exposed to upper-level students' research projects. Most programs can give you access to an electronic and/or hard copy library of successful projects. Pay attention to the types of topics and methodologies that have been approved and which faculty members were involved. A good way to decide if you would like to pursue a similar topic is to become familiar with what the work on an existing project entails. Find out if the researcher needs an assistant and volunteer! Many programs also allow students to attend project defenses. If so, we recommend attending at least one defense to hear about a recently completed project and observe what the final process looks like, particularly with specific faculty in the room.

What Type of Project Is Feasible for My Timeline and for Finishing My Degree?

A key part of getting your degree is choosing a final project that is doable within your graduate school timeline. We recommend that you quickly become acquainted with the final project timeline in your program. What are each of the steps (e.g., proposal meetings, forms to be completed), what research courses and/or competencies are required, and when are program deadlines for each part of the process? Although some students are able to pull off a well-written paper at the last minute, we cannot emphasize enough that you will not be able to do that with research projects, particularly the final project that will serve as the capstone to your graduate school training.

How many years are you willing to stay matriculated in school to complete your project? How much does it cost to stay matriculated for extra semesters? Some students are open to staying in school longer to complete a more methodologically rigorous research project or recruit a difficult-to-obtain sample. Think about this when you are considering project ideas. Ask faculty and upper-level students about the amount of time different types of projects have taken in your program. For example, many students are interested in conducting intervention studies, but these studies often take a long time to complete. You may need a specific number of participants to complete your intervention study, but some may drop out over the course of assessment, treatment, and potentially follow-up sessions, leading to further recruitment efforts.

Coming to the realization that a research idea would take too much time does not mean you have to give up on your topic area; you can often find a creative way to study a similar topic using a more timely method. For example, there may be ongoing research in your program; upper-class students or faculty often have projects going and could offer you an initial "applied lab" experience. You may be able to parse out a piece of their research or recruit participants from their research projects.

Student Example: Finding a Timely Way to Study an Area of Interest

SL asked for access to unused videotapes from a faculty member's group anger management project completed in a group home setting. She wanted to study group process in adolescent therapy groups and was able to test several coding methods using these videotapes rather than conducting a new intervention study. This balanced her interest with the concept that "a good dissertation is a done dissertation."

With any final project, you will have to juggle a number of timelines, academically, professionally, and personally. It is important to develop a plan to balance these components of life. For example, you can plan to take courses and workshops to help build your research competence and think through the feasibility of potential project ideas (e.g., in terms of time and resources availability). Your program may include a heavy amount of academic work in the first semester or the first year, but an expectation that you will move into the research project phase by your second semester or second year. By thinking this through, you can better plan for how you will juggle your responsibilities as you move through your program.

What Other Resources Do I Have Available to Me?
Be sure to consider the following additional resources when working on developing your potential project area.

Faculty Who May Not End Up Directly Involved in Your Project
Your idea may originate from something discussed in class. Faculty may also be useful to consult with on a number of issues, such as types of methodology and statistics. In the long run, you may develop a close mentor–mentee relationship with a faculty member who can provide career or psychosocial support, supplementing what you receive from your project chair. They may also become your project's committee members (we discuss selection of committee members and their typical responsibilities in Chapter 4).

Your Graduate School Peers

The best ideas may stem from conversations you have with your peers. This can occur in a formal setup, such as in a research class where you are paired with another student to work on a mock version of your project, or after class, while socializing. Some of your peers may know you well and be able to reflect what they hear you saying you are interested in, which may help you shape your idea. Peers can also set aside project-focused time with you. We recommend that students help each other set up contingencies for working on their projects (e.g., going for ice cream or watching a movie if a specific task is completed).

Your School's Library, Computer, and Information Technology (IT) Services

It is important to become familiar with your library's resources as soon as possible. Do you know what journals you will have access to? Do they have an interlibrary loan for articles or books they do not possess? How long will it generally take to fulfill such orders? What kinds of software do they have to help you develop surveys or organize references? Many libraries hold tutorials for how to use computer programs related to research and writing.

Does your program have computers and/or printers you can access? What statistical and computer programs will you have access to? Can IT help you build a website or a survey that changes the questions presented based on participants' prior answers? Can they fix your personal laptop? Finding out this information will help you understand your options at school and what you would need to obtain independently.

Staff and Supervisors at Local Applied Settings, Externships, and Internships

Individuals located in the various settings you will come across during your time in an applied graduate program will be tremendously valuable. Whether they provide anecdotal information and insight about the site, the field, or your project, they can serve as your professional network outside your program. Sometimes these staff members and/or supervisors can grant you access to data already collected or help you navigate the correct channels to discuss feasibility of research at a particular clinical site. Ultimately, they can also become your colleagues.

Support from Family and Friends

Life will continue throughout your time in your graduate program. Whether your program requires a lot of time away from the rest of your life and other responsibilities or is part-time, you will need to balance both the personal and the school aspects of your life. Try to be proactive about identifying where and when the stresses in your life and your schoolwork will build up. Work on ways to continue to balance both, even during more stressful times of the year. Just as you turn to different faculty for different reasons, the people in your life will serve different roles at different times. Are there people who can help support you emotionally? Practically? Financially? How? Build time into your schedule with people who will serve these roles.

For example, you can make it a point to seek out people who make you laugh, as well as those who can validate the stress you are experiencing as a student and problem-solve challenging situations as they arise. It is helpful if you can also identify people who can support you practically when you have a lot of work to get done (e.g., people who can run errands for you or babysit your children). It is an extra bonus if you have family who can help support you financially.

Building Your Own Professional Network

What happens when your resources do not suffice for your potential project idea? There are two answers to this question. First, students' ideas are often larger than necessary to get through the research component of their program. If your project is too far from what your program can offer in terms of resources, you may need to save that research project for after graduation. Second, as your knowledge about the process of conducting a project in your applied field grows, you may want to go outside the established resources of your program to build a network of support. This might include a study group, a peer group, individuals in a related field, or other professionals (including those who can provide writing and/or editing assistance, statistics, or some other area that you may need help in).

Research Funding

When investigating a potential project area, it is useful to learn about potential funding sources. Funding may be helpful for a number of project-related items (e.g., measure purchases, participant compensation, data analytic software), but can be hard to obtain. This is why it is important to become aware of any funding opportunities early on. Sometimes universities offer small internal research grant opportunities to students and/or faculty (who might apply as your advisor). Others offer dissertation research assistance. Externally, professional organizations often offer grant opportunities for students (e.g., the Association for Behavioral and Cognitive Therapies and the American Psychological Association). Reviewing possible eligible grant topics early on might also help fine-tune your ideas. Ask your faculty advisor and other faculty if they know upper-level or former students who have obtained funding and if they can put you in touch with them.

Advisors and Mentors: Purposes and Roles

As you start to narrow down your interests, think about the type of professional guidance you are interested in. Are you looking for a project advisor only, or are you looking for a mentor? Perhaps both? Keep in mind that there are different types of relationships you can have with your project chair, as well as with other faculty members and professionals in your field. Schlosser and Gelso (2001) defined an advisor as "the faculty member who has the greatest responsibility for helping guide the advisee through the graduate program" (p. 158). They found that doctoral programs use several terms to describe the person who serves as an advisor (e.g., mentor, major professor, supervisor, committee chair, dissertation chair). However, these terms often do not encapsulate all the ways in which graduate advisors and advisees interact, and certainly the task focus and time frame must be considered. Over time, the advisee may transition across a developmental arc from being a student to becoming a colleague. Your professional, collegial, and social relationship with your advisor and/or mentor may last well beyond your successful project completion and thus warrants important consideration.

Early academic advising might be seen as the gateway to final project supervision and eventual professional mentorship (Schlosser et al., 2011). Students are typically assigned an advisor when they enter a graduate program. Their initial responsibilities might include assistance with basic tasks such as course registration and practicum placements. Some programs have a rationale for this pairing (e.g., similar interests, requests from either students or faculty, funding sources). Some programs assign advisors per student cohort, whereas other assignments are more random or based on equity in faculty load. This advising relationship may or may not continue and it is a good idea to ask about this up front, before a more substantial interpersonal process begins. As soon as you know who you have been assigned to for advising, do some research and be prepared to know about your advisor before your first meeting.

The academic advisement process has been studied via measures such as the Advisory Working Alliance Inventory–Advisor Version (Rogers, 2009; Schlosser & Gelso, 2001). Research using this instrument indicated that students' perception of the working alliance positively correlated with advisee interest and self-efficacy in research, as well as perceived attractiveness, trustworthiness, and expertise of their academic advisors (Schlosser & Gelso, 2001). Another study on graduate advising relationships across Canadian psychology programs revealed different predictors of advisees' perceptions of positive advising relationships based on program type (Peluso et al., 2011). From 387 graduate students participating in an online survey, these authors determined that for clinical students, advising in self-care and life balance best predicted satisfaction and quality of their advising relationship. In contrast, experimental students reported that advising in research design and publications were predictors of their satisfaction. For counseling students, advising on clinical work was the best predictor.

There are some clear differences between academic advisors and mentors. Johnson (2003), who has examined the process of mentorship in doctoral programs, indicates that mentoring is differentiated from teaching, supervising, advising, and counseling, some of the many roles played by graduate school faculty members. Whereas an advisor might be an assigned role that could have both positive and negative aspects, a relationship with a mentor is more likely chosen and positive in valence.

Ideal mentoring relationships at the graduate school level, where the faculty mentor guides, instructs, sponsors, and serves as a role model to their mentee, are mutually rewarding to faculty and students (Schlosser et al., 2011). Mentors provide a range of career and relational functions to students, and mentoring signifies intentional and generative career development (Johnson, 2002). Ragins and McFarlin (1990) developed the Mentor Role Instrument based on two distinct career and psychosocial role domains. The career roles a mentor can serve included project sponsor, coach, protector, and provider of challenges and exposure to career activities. The psychosocial roles of a mentor included friendship, social relationship, parent role, role model, and provider of counsel and/or acceptance and support. The most common characteristics of mentorship are as follows: (a) mentorships are continuous personal relationships that are more reciprocal over time, (b) compared to the mentee, mentors have more experience and provide mentees with a role model and career guidance, (c) mentors provide social and emotional support, and (d) mentors offer a safe place for the mentee's self-exploration, which facilitates growth and identity development (Schlosser et al., 2011).

Unfortunately, clinical and counseling graduate students in psychology have reported receiving less mentoring than experimental and other psychology doctoral students (Johnson et al., 2000), and students in PsyD or professional psychology doctoral programs have reported less mentoring than those in PhD or traditional university-based programs, respectively (Clark et al., 2000). One possible explanation is the student-to-faculty ratio and the potential availability of mentors. Mentorship relationships can vary across the training model of a program and should be tailored to the appropriate developmental level of the mentee. If your program follows the traditional scientist-practitioner model, where there is often an equal emphasis on training in both research and practice, an effective mentor would embrace this integration and encourage you to conduct applied clinical research. If your program is more in line with the Vail model, your mentor will emphasize preparation for clinical practice while acknowledging the importance of understanding research and using it to inform your work.

Research mentoring involves a developmental process whereby a faculty member provides students with opportunities to join their research team, have access to data sets, and collaborate on specific projects. The mentor might help their students participate in conference or workshop presentations, meet other research colleagues, and be a part of publications or grants (Brown et al., 2009). Research mentors can help students to achieve competence in both foundational (understanding of research ethics, scientific foundations of psychology) and functional (specific methodologies, randomized control trials) competencies. Successful mentors embrace a "scaffolding" model of progression, from more basic tasks and objectives (i.e., directing a specific research project) to more advanced tasks (i.e., collaborating on articles for publication) (Brown et al., 2009). Some faculty members are more successful in this mentorship role than others and it will take some time to get to know which faculty member could serve as the best mentor for you.

Do not be reluctant to search for a mentor for your research ideas. For the most part, clinical researchers enjoy the induction of new students into clinical research. Drotar (2013) suggested that mentees become critical to the career of the research mentor because they play important roles in the mentor's ideas for new research, help to complete research studies, and provide personal satisfaction to the mentor. Additional rewards for mentors include a sense of generativity and career fulfillment (Brown et al., 2009). Research mentors take great pride in growing their network of applied clinical researchers and often form special interest groups or collaborate on multisite investigations long after the dissertations have been defended.

Brown et al. (2009) provide a comprehensive set of skills and behaviors of highly effective mentors that you might keep in mind when considering a faculty mentor. They include:

- Supporting the transition to independence using a developmental framework.
- Educating, encouraging, and inspiring work in clinical and research settings.
- Fostering professional development.
- Providing a hands-on modeling approach to learning research skills.
- Using relationship skills that communicate empathy, positive regard, and genuineness.
- Developing compatibility between mentor and mentee over time through mutual trust.
- Providing contingent positive reinforcement.
- Exposing mentees to a variety of clinical research methodologies.
- Guiding the development of clinical research.
- Evaluating and critiquing the mentee's ideas and work.
- Providing corrective and timely feedback.
- Being available for consultation.
- Opening doors for mentees in clinical research organizations and settings.
- Promoting scholarly values, scientific integrity, and ethical decision-making. (p. 311)

In 2012, the Association for Counselor Education and Supervision published guidelines for research mentorship that included characteristics of mentors and mentees in the hopes of enhancing the research productivity of counseling psychology students (Borders et al., 2012). In addition to their comprehensive listing of mentor skills, the following are highlighted for the mentee, and each includes a subset of clearly defined characteristics (p.174-175):

- The mentee "is an ethical researcher who applies this knowledge in practice."
- The mentee "is forthcoming about one's needs in the mentoring relationship."
- The mentee "is an effective learner who enters the relationship with a desire to learn and gain knowledge or skill in a particular area of research..."

It may be far more difficult for students from underrepresented groups and cultural backgrounds to find and develop good mentorship relationships. Alvarez and colleagues (2009) emphasized that there has been little growth in the number of students of color who have earned doctoral degrees since a peak in 2000. Recent data demonstrated underrepresentation of Black/African American and Hispanic/Latino groups in psychology doctoral programs compared to the population of these groups in the United States, even without significant differences in academic qualifications (Callahan et al., 2018). In addition, students of color had high attrition from these doctoral programs. Alvarez et al. (2009) indicated mentoring students of color warrants added expertise, including in topics such as ethnic and racial self-awareness, racial discrimination, and the role of culture in academic settings. Our third author spearheaded an alumni mentorship program aiming to match mentors with PsyD students who were similar in some capacity, including the opportunity to match based on ethnic minority status (Feindler et al., 2019). In the first year of the program, 40 percent of alumni mentors who volunteered identified as nonwhite, perhaps reflecting the type of support they wished they had in graduate school. If the opportunity to find a mentor extends to alumni of your graduate program, perhaps some of the unique issues related to being a student of color can be addressed by finding an alumni mentor who has a similar background.

Worksheet 1.1 What Areas of the Field Grab Your Interest?

Answering these questions can help you determine a number of areas you may be interested in pursuing as a potential project area. Use the information in the "Identifying Your Research Interests" section of Chapter 1 to help you complete this worksheet.

Which of my early experiences engaged and excited me (e.g., as an undergraduate, as an employee or volunteer in an applied clinical and/or research setting, during completion of an undergraduate or master's thesis)? Which of these ideas am I ready to leave behind?

Experience	What about it . . .

What personal experiences might I explore as areas of interest? Would I want to? What are some pros and cons of my exploring these topics as MEsearch?

Experience	What about it . . .

What faculty research have I learned about so far that interests me? What labs or projects might I join to develop an interest?

Faculty member	What about their research/labs/projects?	My related interest

What projects have been done by students in this program that pique my interest? Who was their chair?

Project title	Chair	What about it . . .

What are some class lectures, conversations with peers, articles I have read, conference presentations I have attended, or personal observations I have had that could be explored further as an area of interest?

Lecture/discussion	What about it . . .

What term papers, group projects, or classroom presentations have I done or will I be doing that I might pursue as an area of interest? What upcoming assignments can I selectively use to pursue a tentative idea?

Paper/project/ classroom presentation	What about it . . .

What are some pros and cons to pursuing an area within my current lab and/or with my current advisor?

Area:	
Pros	Cons

Which professional organizations should I consider joining? Which ones do my advisors, lab members, and/or upper-level students attend?

Professional organization	What about it . . .

Worksheet 1.2 Factors to Consider When Narrowing Interests down to a Potential Project Area

Once you have a few general areas of interest, use the information in the "Factors to Consider" section of Chapter 1 to help you complete this worksheet. Answering these questions can help you narrow your interests down to a potential project area.

What interest areas inspire me and capture my attention? What parts of the field do I feel excited to become an expert in?

What has not been studied among my interests that could advance the field? Based on what I've read so far, what appear to be important next steps in the area?

What do the authors describe as future directions for research?

Independent of what the authors discuss, what do I see as questions for further study? What problem do I see in this area of the field? How might I generate new information that would make a valuable contribution to existing literature?

Consider	Comments
Independent of what the authors discuss, what do I see as questions for further study?	
What problem do I see in this area of the field?	
How might I generate new information that would make a valuable contribution to existing literature?	

Which of my interest areas are compatible with faculty members' interests?

Consider	Comments
Who has expertise in an area that interests me?	
Which faculty member's feedback on class assignments do I find most helpful?	
Which faculty members seem most interested in me?	
Who is rumored to be a good chair?	
What supervisory style is the best fit for me (Laissez-faire? Pastoral? Directorial? Contractual?)? Under what circumstances?	

What kind of topic area could I feasibly recruit for and conduct a project in?

Consider	Comments
How might I have access to the sample of interest?	
What evidence do I have to suggest that enough people will be willing to participate?	
Have other students had success with recruiting a similar sample within my geographic region? Who? Where?	
Are there ways I could study the same topic with a different population or broader criteria?	
To develop and/or conduct a project in an applied setting: Do I have a setting in mind? How open do I think staff and the organization will be to my conducting a project in their facility? Whose permission would I need to recruit and/or conduct the project? How much do I think they will assist me? Expect to have control over my project? Allow and/or expect me to work independently? Will the setting's directors and staff be interested in helping facilitate my data collection? Would they want to claim primary ownership of the project? Would they allow me to publish my findings?	

To use existing data: Do I have access to an existing data set with some of my variables of interest? Who could I ask? How could my project idea benefit the owner of the data set or the organization? Whose permission would I likely need to access the records? Would they likely help me extract the data? Analyze it?	
To pursue a project that does not involve traditional data collection and analysis: Do I have access to the needed materials or people?	
To pursue a theoretical review: Do I have a clear understanding of what is involved? Is there enough relevant literature to support the development of my theory?	

What topic areas and research designs fit my program's requirements?

Consider	Comments
Would my topic fit into my program's mission, track, or concentration area?	
What methodological designs fit with my program's requirements?	
What data collection methods are allowed?	
Where and how can I access completed student projects in my program?	
Which current students may be looking for research assistants for their final projects?	
When are upcoming defenses in my program? Can I attend?	

What type of project is feasible for my timeline and for finishing my degree?

Consider	Comments
Approximately how long do I anticipate this project taking to complete (e.g., writing, time for data collection)?	
How many years am I willing to stay matriculated in school to complete my project?	
How much does it cost to stay matriculated for extra semesters?	
What are creative ways I might study a similar topic with a more feasible method?	

What other resources do I have available to me?

Consider	Comments
What faculty members might be useful to consult with on my potential project topic? Who might be able to provide me with career and/or psychosocial support?	
Which of my peers might be able to think through my potential project topic? When? How? What kinds of contingencies might we set up for completing tasks?	
Library resources: What journals do I have access to? Do they have an interlibrary loan for articles or books? How long will it generally take to fulfill such orders? What kinds of software do they have to help develop surveys or organize references? Are tutorials available?	
Computer and IT resources: Does my program have computers and/or printers I can access? Statistical or other computer programs? Can IT help me build a website? A survey? Can they fix my personal laptop? How can I find out? What will I have to take care of independently?	

Do I know any staff or supervisors at local applied settings, externships, or internships who might be able to help me develop an idea or collect and/or access data in their setting? Do I foresee any possibilities like this occurring in the near future?	
Who among my family and friends can help support me emotionally? Practically? Financially? How? Who do I want to regularly keep in touch with? How?	
What other kinds of resources might I need to build into my professional network for this project idea? Do I anticipate needing a study group? A peer group of some kind? A professional to assist me with writing and/or editing? Statistics? Other areas?	
What are possible funding sources? Internally? Externally? What might I need to purchase to conduct my potential project? Who can I ask about this, and who can I contact who has received funding?	

Chapter 2
Skills to Develop for Beginning-Level Research Competence

Introduction

At the beginning of your graduate program, you should aim to develop the *skills* to critically evaluate research, conduct research in applied settings, and practice ethical and professional competence by learning about the following:

- Collaborating with faculty: when and how to get involved
- Skills for becoming an excellent mentee
- How to navigate conducting research in applied settings
- Navigating your university's research resources
- Finding your literature
- Skills for reading and critically evaluating research
- Navigating your way through the institutional review board (IRB) process
- Self-evaluating and improving your research skills
- Self-evaluating and improving your writing

This section will teach you how to build these skills while you begin to think about possible projects and expand your research competency.

As you build your knowledge base about research in your field, ideas for potential project areas, and the related faculty you may connect with, you will also begin to develop a sense of your skills as a researcher. This chapter focuses on the skills you will need to be successful in your research, both interpersonally and academically. As you read through the skills expected of someone at the beginning of a graduate program, think about the areas that are strengths for you as well as those that may need some work. You will have the opportunity to conduct an evaluation of your research skills at the end of the chapter.

Collaborating with Faculty: When and How to Get Involved

In Chapter 1, we discussed a variety of ways to identify your interests, including spending time reviewing your faculty's research areas of interest. We also reviewed

Navigating Research in an Applied Graduate Program. Hilary B. Vidair, Pam L. Gustafson, and Eva L. Feindler, Oxford University Press. © Oxford University Press (2024). DOI: 10.1093/oso/9780199352272.003.0002

the pros and cons for developing an idea based on a specific faculty member's research. Before you can do that, however, you need to find a way to collaborate with the faculty member in the first place! We recommend you begin collaborating with faculty during your first semester. Even though you might feel overwhelmed and anxious about your performance as a beginning graduate student, see if you can find at least a few hours to get your "research feet" wet. As we mentioned, sometimes your program will assign you to be a particular faculty member's research assistant. This person may or may not also serve as your academic advisor. Here are some steps you can take to develop relationships and even venture beyond what you are assigned.

Some faculty collaborate often with graduate students, whereas others do not. Look at a listing of projects that have been successfully completed in your graduate program. Are there several students who seem to have had related projects? For example, we had a faculty member in our department who is an internationally known expert on dialectical behavior therapy for adolescents. If you were to look through our program database of completed doctoral dissertations, you would see many dissertations related to that therapy, sponsored by that faculty member. This underscores the support of student research in the faculty member's area of expertise. Similarly, review the faculty's conference presentations and publications to determine whether faculty collaborate with students at these levels. You can also ask more advanced students about their experiences with various faculty members.

Find out which faculty members have a research lab or group. The concept of a lab does not have to imply the type of traditional laboratory setting found in more basic psychology research; rather it can be a type of group collaboration on a particular area of inquiry. For example, there might be a lab sponsored by a faculty member focused on several types of projects, all broadly related to attachment disorders. Or there might be a group who provides trauma-focused services for children in school and community settings and then conducts research on their work. Participating in a lab or group like this might be your first opportunity to collaborate with faculty and other graduate students. Small research teams may also help reduce the gap between research and practice because they have been found to be more collaborative, less intimidating, and more pleasurable than working independently (Crane et al., 2002; Gelso, 2006; Owenz & Hall, 2011).

You can ask a faculty member if they need any help with their current research projects. In addition, you will hear about upper-class students needing help on their final projects. Usually these tasks are somewhat mundane, like transcribing interviews, coding data, entering data into the computer, or watching videotapes and measuring discrete behaviors. But go ahead and volunteer: not only will you learn about that particular project, but also you will learn skills more broadly related to conducting applied research and demonstrate your enthusiasm for an area of research supervised by a specific faculty member. Another way to demonstrate your interest in a faculty member's work is to sit in on their student's project defense. This will also help you learn about a project the faculty member was interested in and allow you to watch interactions between the faculty member, the committee members, and the student. Most programs require a public listing of the defense date, so keep your ears and eyes open and then ask about the possibility of your attendance.

Whether you volunteer for a faculty member or an upper-level student, you are helping them out, but you are also establishing a collaborative relationship. This context will allow you to learn the nuances of the research process and the ways the faculty member and the student negotiate the research process. This will help you assess your interest in this research area, as well as your comfort level working with the faculty member. This type of initial volunteering is not typically a commitment for who you will work with on your final project, but it affords you a first look. Research from a retrospective faculty perspective indicated that in positive dissertation experiences, chairs and students collaborated in some way before the dissertation project began (Knox et al., 2011).

Student Example: Shifting Areas of Interest and Faculty Members

---

SW began her doctoral program serving as a research assistant for a faculty advisor whose work focused on evidence-based treatment with families. She enjoyed her experiences in the faculty member's lab, found she learned a lot, and was able to present posters and submit an article for publication with upper-level students. However, over time, she realized her primary research interest focused on the relationship between attachment to God, hope, and mental health. SW had developed a great relationship with her advisor and was able to talk with her about the shift in the type of research she hoped to pursue for her dissertation. Fortunately, her advisor was supportive of the change and helped her brainstorm which faculty it made sense to approach about the new topic area, which she was then able to pursue.

Challenges with Collaboration

In your first year, you might feel intimidated by the research of faculty members who are well published and well-known in the field. You might even be a bit intimidated by an upper-level student, such as a fourth- or fifth-year dissertation student. But you will eventually be part of the upper-level student body, too! It might take a little courage, but rarely do researchers reject the idea of volunteers! Most everyone is very receptive and grateful for any help they can obtain. And everyone, including the (inter)nationally known faculty members at your school, started out in the same beginner spot you find yourself in, so they can relate.

Figuring out your role as an early research collaborator can also be challenging. Just what is it that is expected of you and for how long? And will there be any gains for you? Sometimes, you will be added onto a poster, conference presentation, or community presentation, which is a plus for you in terms of expanding your curriculum vitae, gaining presentation experience, and having an opportunity to network at a professional convention. Sometimes you will be given later access to a data set for your own project if you decide to do similar research. Sometimes it will simply result in a positive impression that a faculty member has of you (which might be helpful, because you will invariably need letters of recommendation for any applied practica or clinical positions you apply for). As you develop a relationship with a faculty member, there may be opportunities for coauthoring publications. The challenge is whether these things are articulated clearly at the start or whether the gains are offered over time as the research team gets to know you.

We recommend asking about the procedures for getting involved with these types of opportunities up front; however, it is important to convey interest in learning about what might work rather than sounding entitled, as if you expect to be included. Be patient, observe how other students approach this issue with specific faculty or in specific labs, and model effective behaviors. If you demonstrate that you can be relied on to conduct solid and timely work, over time you will likely be included and even welcome to take the lead on something!

Skills for Becoming an Excellent Mentee

In Chapter 1, we discussed factors to consider regarding compatibility between you and your faculty, as well as the roles an advisor and/or mentor can play in your graduate training. Here, we discuss skills to help you cultivate a positive working relationship with faculty with whom you are thinking of collaborating on your final project (and potentially beyond). In other words, as much as you should consider the characteristics of various faculty, you should also aim to develop the mentee characteristics that faculty members look for. For example, the American Psychological Association's (APA's) (2006) *Introduction to Mentoring* recommends that mentees be reliable, on time, and able to work independently to facilitate their mentor's ability to help them meet their goals. This mentoring guide also lists key "mentee dos and don'ts," which we address next.

Do Identify Specific Expectations and Goals

When you begin to conduct research with a faculty member (or upper-level student), make sure you regularly communicate with them about what they expect you to accomplish. Identify specific, concrete goals, and follow through on any commitments you make. Be clear on when the deadlines are and meet them. Let them know as soon as possible if you will be delayed in your work or absent from a meeting. Include a revised timeline or an idea of how you will make up or complete the work.

It is also important to be clear about what you are hoping to get out of the working relationship, even in the short term. For example, when you begin "shopping around" for a project idea and chair, be transparent about your intentions. You can ask to meet with a faculty member to obtain their opinion about an idea or explore whether your interests are compatible. Be careful not to commit to working with them on your final project prematurely (e.g., say that you have a few ideas and are starting to discuss them with various faculty members).

As we mentioned in Chapter 1, you may find yourself working with a faculty member early on in your program who you decide does not fit your work style or interest area. In this case, we recommend consulting with another trusted faculty member or mentor about how to approach the situation. Many programs will support a student shift in advisor, and some have a procedure for doing so. Generally, it helps to maintain a respectful, interested attitude in their work while you remain a part of it. At the same time, it is important to be clear about your development of another interest.

Student Example: Deciding to Switch Research Advisors

A student entered her doctoral program with an avid interest in bipolar disorder in adults. She opted to work with a faculty member who had written substantially in the area, but about children. Over the course of the student's first year, she served as a research assistant for the faculty member, but found their relationship was tense and not rewarding. During the same period, she volunteered on another faculty member's project focused on hospitalization experiences and began to think more about ways their interests could overlap. She decided she no longer was interested in a dissertation project focused on bipolar disorder specifically, but rather wanted to examine outcome data for adults who had spent time in inpatient units. In a sense, she had to "break up" with her research advisor, because she wanted to complete her research assistant responsibilities and change advisors. She hoped that her new advisor would eventually become her dissertation chair because they had an energetic relationship and both loved talking about how patients are treated in inpatient settings. Her initial advisor was quite angry, because he had hoped she would continue conducting research with him. It is always hard for a faculty member to lose a bright and articulate graduate student. Her program director maintained that it was a student's choice about whom to work with and that she could make the change in her second year.

Don't Expect Your Mentor to Decide Things for You

You are in the beginning stages of your profession, which means you are preparing to be a professional. When it comes to making choices about your advancement in the program, you need to balance seeking input from others with coming to your own conclusions about how you will proceed. It is fine to seek assistance with evaluating the pros and cons of a decision, such as the type of topic to pursue or an appropriate project timeline. It is also acceptable to describe problems you are having with your work, such as understanding a particular concept or knowing how to approach a particular person. Ideally, however, you will offer some potential solutions along with your description of the problem, and ultimately, you will need to take the lead on resolving the issues. Your ability to do so will be a testament to your competency as a researcher and a budding professional.

Do Be Proactive with Your Mentor

Faculty are busy! They are more likely to take particular interest in you if you make the effort to maintain contact with them and keep them up to date on what you are working on. Consider it your responsibility to schedule your future meetings together. It is important to present yourself as a self-starter, taking the initiative to accomplish tasks and troubleshoot problems as they arise before you are asked to do so. It is a bonus if you offer to take on responsibilities above and beyond what is required.

Faculty will also appreciate you showing interest in their research interests. As we mentioned earlier, feel free to approach faculty about opportunities to get involved with their research. Sometimes you might even be able to encourage a faculty member to pursue a lab project that incorporates both of your interests. We know of students who were hoping to work with specific faculty members on specific types of lab projects. Their enthusiasm and prep work inspired these faculty members to pursue the ideas with them! Such extra efforts can lead to presentations, publications, final projects, networking opportunities, and lifelong collaborations.

Don't Take Advantage of Your Mentor's Time and Support

Make sure to respect your faculty's time and assistance. For example, there is a difference between knocking on a professor's door and asking if they are available to talk for a few minutes and just walking in, expecting them to address your question or concern right there in the moment. Furthermore, understand that there will only be so much support they can offer you for one issue or at one time. Occasionally, you may need someone else's opinion, writing assistance, statistical consultation, or perhaps therapy.

Do Treat Your Mentor Ethically and Professionally

It is important to remember that the faculty you work with are human! Like you, they are juggling many professional and personal responsibilities. They will often be dealing with life hurdles that will not be within your awareness. Think about how you want to be treated and treat the faculty with whom you work with the same respect and care. Be sensitive to their feelings and their time.

Like other humans, faculty are likely to respond well to positive reinforcement. For example, express appreciation for any opportunities or constructive feedback they provide you. You might also try shaping a faculty member's behavior by selectively attending to the behaviors they exhibit that you would like to increase.

Don't Spread Gossip about Your Mentor

It may seem obvious, and yet this happens often. We understand that it is natural to discuss your academic experiences with others, particularly other students and faculty. At the same time, you want to be careful that your statements remain professional and avoid name-calling, complaining about them, or sharing their personal information (which anyone in a close working relationship may become privy to). First, think about how you would feel if you thought your faculty member was gossiping about you. It would probably feel hurtful and provoke some anger. This goes back to the concept of treating your advisor as you want to be treated. Second, the people who you call your peers and faculty will likely become your future colleagues. You do not want them to think that this is how you normally speak about those with whom you have working relationships. Third, sometimes focusing on negative aspects about a person or interaction just magnifies them in your mind. It will likely be more useful for you to focus on the positives and think about addressing any problems in your working relationship professionally. Fourth, imagine if they found out what you said—it would probably be an awkward situation to manage and might have serious consequences. In contrast, loyalty can go a long way.

Don't Take a Rejection from a Potential Mentor Personally

You may want to continue working with a faculty member who decides to no longer work with you. Or you may approach a faculty member you are interested in working with only to find they say no. It is important to be levelheaded about such a rejection. The faculty member may already be overloaded and cannot take on more students at the time. Alternatively, they may think you would be better off pursuing another interest or that your work style would be more compatible with someone else's. Reflect on your experiences with the faculty member or in their lab and do a comprehensive self-assessment across your professional and personal interactions.

There may have been unresolved conflicts or differences that influenced the decision. We recommend that you consult with another faculty member or supervisor about how to handle the situation, which might include asking the faculty member who let you go if they can give you an explanation. At the very least, you will hopefully determine if there is something you can do to remediate your professional work ethic or behavior now. At the very best, you will come to see it as an opportunity for professional growth in another (and potentially better) direction, as well as an opportunity to build new working relationships. Remember, your graduate training only encompasses a certain amount of time in your life. You will be involved with many people over the time of your career—and this is what a career in an applied field involves—navigating interactions with people.

How to Navigate Conducting Research in Applied Settings

As a student in an applied graduate program, one of your goals will be to learn to collect data to address a local practical issue. In other words, you will want to become able to make decisions in a particular applied setting that are informed by systematic assessment. Even if you are planning to have a more practice-based career, it is becoming common to expect practitioners in applied settings to collaborate with researchers and explain the research process to other professionals and consumers in a site. The best way to learn how to do this is to gain hands-on experience. If you are thinking about conducting research in an applied setting, you should seek out opportunities to volunteer in a practical or research setting early on. Doing so will help you begin to understand a particular setting's culture and available resources (e.g., computer access, time that staff can devote to research participation), as well as site limitations that may affect the feasibility of your research ideas (e.g., no ability to have an after-school program, lack of parental involvement, lack of physical space to conduct interviews).

Navigating working in applied settings may require you to adjust your work style to fit with that of the site and the professionals working there. To do so, you will need to reflect on your work style and its fit with the sites' abilities and limitations. Through this process, you will become more aware of your own biases (personal or field specific) that may impact the research design or procedures you thought you could implement in a project.

Conducting successful research in an applied setting takes time because there are many steps involved in the process. For example, to even begin to volunteer in a hospital setting, you typically must apply for an identification card; show proof of a recent physical exam, several immunizations, and a tuberculosis test; and attend more than one orientation (e.g., on hospital policies, fire safety, sexual harassment, infectious control training). School environments have their own set of policies and procedures for outside personnel. It is helpful if you know someone in the setting who can walk you through the steps of gaining entry. Volunteer work and/or working on others' projects can help you become familiar with the processes involved and build your interpersonal skills for interacting with professionals, administrators, and consumers (e.g., clients) in applied settings. Next, we give some suggestions for how to become actively involved in conducting research in applied settings.

How to Get Involved

Continue Your Prior Applied Experience

Upon entering graduate school, you likely have already had relationships with staff in applied settings. You might have been a teacher's assistant, an in-home applied behavior analysis trainer, a volunteer at a summer camp for children with diabetes, or a recreational therapist at an assisted-living facility. These relationships might become the key to having access to your population of interest for data collection. During your time working or volunteering at an agency, you and the staff likely had discussions about issues facing your target population. For example, you might have wondered with others about the best ways to get children to be compliant with their prescribed medical regimens. Or you might have worried about the supportive resources available to the family members of nursing home residents. Returning to these relationships and settings when you are considering your research ideas may make the most sense, given your interest in the population and the topic and your established history with the agency and/or setting. However, etiquette requires that you still have the collegial relationships to make this dialogue happen and that the individuals at the agency support your research efforts in a positive way. No setting or staff member would want to feel that you were merely using your connections without genuine interest in their mission.

Learn from Faculty's Current Research in Applied Settings

Faculty members working in applied fields will often already be engaged in research in applied settings. Even if you are engaged in other research assistant tasks, we recommend making your interest in that part of their research known, because they may appreciate extra assistance. They may also have upper-level students conducting research in these settings who would appreciate a research assistant for help with tasks such as recruitment, data collection, or the cofacilitation of a group. Even if you are asked to code already collected data, you can learn a lot by listening to transcripts or watching videotaped observations of people who are involved in or attend the setting.

Coursework

It is common for some classes in applied graduate programs to include assignments that require you to observe, interview, or implement a brief intervention in the community. For example, you may be required to find a child to observe in class, interview clinical staff about their daily experiences, or present a workshop to parents. One benefit to such assignments is the opportunity to experience what it is like to practice your applied skills in a real-world setting. They are also excellent opportunities to start thinking about ideas for research projects! Even if you only need to enter the setting one time, you can observe elements such as the people, the environment, and information on bulletin boards. If possible, you should introduce yourself to key staff in these settings: introduce yourself, the school, and the program you are from. Always keep good interpersonal skills in mind (e.g., smile, make eye contact, do not interrupt them). Find something complimentary to say about their site, thank them for allowing you to conduct your assignment there, and ask if you can contact them about opportunities to become involved in the future. If they would like to invite your program to participate in other ways, take down that information and offer to introduce them to your program director via phone or email. Networking in this way will enable you to leave a positive impression, which staff will hopefully remember if you contact them about the possibility of conducting a project in the future.

Lab or Research Group

As mentioned earlier, joining a lab provides you with an opportunity to work with faculty and students whose interests overlap with yours. This can create an opportunity to collaborate on group projects in applied settings that specialize in your area of interest (e.g., children with cancer, a charter school, an anxiety and phobia center). If the lab is not currently involved in the type of setting you are interested in, you can try to build a connection between your lab and a community you are interested in working with, creating possibilities for future applied experiences, networking, and research.

If your school does not already offer labs or research groups, you could consider creating a lab-like team for yourself. Often, students develop study groups or special interest groups that can function as a collaborative team with which to undertake a research project.

Student Example: Building Connections between Applied Settings and a Lab

LT joined a lab in her first year that focused on providing a three-session assessment and referral service for parents of young children. When she joined, the lab was focused on increasing recruitment. One strategy they were using was to offer free psychoeducational parent workshops in community settings where parents could gain parenting skills and learn about the three-session service. LT was interested in providing workshops within her church and to Spanish-speaking parents in local agencies. She offered to spearhead communication between these applied sites and her lab's advisor. She was able to arrange student-led workshops in several sites, including her church, which became interested in a series of workshops. This led to a new area of interest in the lab, focused on providing parent workshops within religious organizations. Students from the lab eventually presented pilot work on this topic at national conventions.

Your Program's Applied Practica, Externships, and Internships

Throughout your graduate training, you will have several practica, externships, and/or internships. These applied settings might seem ideal for conducting your research, and they may work out well. However, keep in mind that most placements are time limited, and some may operate on a different calendar than you may need (e.g., you might not be able to collect data at a school in the summer). We recommend only conducting research in a setting where you can sustain some kind of a multiyear relationship. This will enable you to form relationships over time with key staff who may be able to serve in a consultative or collaborative role with regard to research questions germane to the setting. Demonstrating your ability to successfully collaborate and conduct research will help you build professional relationships that could lead to future career opportunities.

Student Example: Maintaining a Collaboration in an Applied Site for a Final Project and Beyond

JR was an extern in a hospital unit for eating disorders in the third year of her doctoral program. Based on her clinical experiences there, she became interested in excessive exercise in adolescents in the target population. She learned that the unit had collected a large data set that included information from approximately 250 adolescents regarding their demographics, mood, dietary restraint, and excessive exercise at intake, as well as their treatment placement. She spoke with her clinical supervisor, who was eager to help her develop a feasible final project idea and gain access to the data. She found out the name of the principal investigator of the original research project and met with him to discuss her ideas. He granted her permission to access the data and helped her obtain IRB approval, both in the hospital and in her university. In JR's fourth year, she externed at another site, but obtained a volunteer ID card to maintain access to the hospital. She also kept in regular contact with the staff there, set up days to be on-site to extract data, and invited her supervisor to be on her dissertation committee. She later published her dissertation results in a peer-reviewed journal, with her chair and hospital staff serving as coauthors. JR's continued positive collaboration with the hospital staff may be one of the reasons she was later selected for a postdoctoral fellowship in another part of the hospital.

Overall, we recommend you really get to know a setting you are interested in to assess their interest and involvement in conducting applied research. Some sites are already involved in conducting research projects, and some have intervention components that are grant funded and research based. Larger agencies, such as medical centers or large state institutions, often have their own IRB, which you would likely have to go through to conduct research in their settings (see the IRB section later in this chapter for more information about this). Revisit the section in Chapter 1 where we discussed factors to consider regarding topic areas that you could feasibly recruit for and conduct a project in. Then assess these factors about any applied site of interest. For example, who on staff is open to collaborating on research? Does the site have data you can have access to, or will they allow you to collect data? If possible, find out what other students' experiences conducting research in the site have been like to give you an informed idea of what might be feasible.

What Can You Offer a Site in Return? Creating a Quid Pro Quo Relationship

Student Example: Conducting Presentations in Exchange for Permission to Recruit Research Participants

BP had worked in a nursing home before pursuing her doctoral degree in clinical psychology. For her research methods course, she wrote a proposal for an investigation of the relatively new concept of *ambiguous loss*, which captures the emotional experience of losing a loved one, but not through death. This loss might occur via military deployment or divorce. BP's previous work had sensitized her to the complicated grieving process of losing a loved one with Alzheimer's disease. She wanted to recruit family members with loved ones in nursing homes and have them complete several assessment measures. BP could easily recruit participants through the networks she had previously established, but she needed to offer them some kind of incentive or benefit. She offered to do a presentation of the concepts and issues relative to ambiguous loss for any caregiver support group that might have members interested in research participation. Not only was she able to recruit research participants, but also the nursing homes were able to offer a specialized presentation.

If you use an applied setting for your research, you will need to propose ways for your work to somehow also benefit the setting. One option is to offer a service or workshop to the facility that may or may not have to do with your research project.

Another option is to offer your data to the agency for their own purposes. Many clinical settings do not have the resources, either time or staff, to conduct any type of research, nor are they necessarily skilled or motivated for data collection and analyses. However, agency administrators and/or managers may welcome an objective look at various aspects of their services and outcomes. By conducting a pre–post evaluation of a particular treatment program (i.e., parent training for children with autism), you might help them expand the program, obtain more funding for the program, or convince administrators of the program's efficacy. A note of caution: agency personnel might express interest in your outcome data but be less prepared for negative results.

Student Example: Conducting an Applied Program Evaluation That Finds Negative Results

MG worked with an agency to examine the effectiveness of an anger management program they incorporated system-wide in multiple group homes for court-adjudicated youth. After MG obtained self-report data at admission and discharge for youth across several years, the data analyses revealed that the anger management program had virtually no impact. These outcome results were certainly disheartening to the agency staff and compromised their abilities to secure funding for future programming.

Be prepared to encounter challenges when trying to balance benefiting a site and conducting your own research project. In addition to the previous example where data outcomes were not what the agency expected, having to manage dual roles can interfere with successfully conducting your project. Unfortunately, at times you may have to make the tough decision to move on and conduct your research elsewhere.

Student Example: Dual Roles Lead to a Change in Project

A student was going on internship at a day treatment program and approached the internship director about conducting his dissertation research with the attending youth. The staff were generally supportive of psychoeducational skills training groups and encouraged him to implement this type of group for adolescents. However, when the staff wanted to sit in on the groups to learn the curriculum, the

Table 2.1 Opportunities to Get Involved with Research before Your Final Project

Your program	Faculty labs
	Research course
	Externship/internship connections
	Continue your prior applied experience
	Learn from faculty's current research in applied settings
	Coursework
	Your lab, your program's applied practica, externships, and internships
	Research assistantships
	Coding assistance
Peers	In your program
	In other programs
	Alumni
	Local clinicians
In the field	Student organizations
	Local, regional, national, and international conferences
	Professional membership organizations in your applied field

dynamics of the group changed significantly. The staff began to contradict the adolescents' reports about conflict and aggression occurring in the program. This put the student in a very awkward situation and he could not implement his skills protocol as it was written. Rather, he facilitated a staff–student conflict resolution process that, although it was helpful to the day treatment program, was not helpful in data collection for his dissertation. He then completed a separate pilot investigation of his protocol at a local private high school.

As described in this section, there are many ways to get involved with research before you begin your own. Next is a summary of ideas about how to first get involved in research to get you started (see Table 2.1).

Navigating Your University's Research Resources

As you get more involved with faculty, applied settings, and the process of reviewing academic literature, make sure to also become familiar with the research training resources available to you from your university. Your development of beginner-level research competence includes making competent use of the resources available, as well as seeking out other resources that are lacking but necessary for you to be successful. You want to become comfortable with the resources available to you early on. Doing so will reduce the amount of time you spend accessing these resources later. In addition, when you move into your career after graduation, you may not have access to such an immense number of resources. Because of this, we urge you to make use of all your resources now! This section will discuss common student resources you will want to become acquainted with to understand how to use them efficiently and help build your research competency.

Academic Libraries and Writing Centers

As a student, you will have access to your institution's library. This may include hard-copy stacks, access to electronic databases, and special collections. This means that you have access to librarians who have a wealth of experience in helping researchers find what they are looking for and who spend much of their professional time learning new tools for doing so. Your institution may have a library liaison who has been assigned to your academic program to assist students and faculty. This person will likely have worked within the field before and may have developed a libguide or other resource for your program community. A libguide is a webpage that is set up to guide the library search for individuals within that field. For example, a psychology libguide might include databases relevant for psychology research, links to webinars, or library holdings.

In addition, your academic library may have access to interlibrary loans from other institutions. In some institutions, you will use a system called ILLiad for requesting interlibrary loan copies of books or articles from another institution. In others, you may need to contact a reference librarian (at your institution or the other institution) to make the request. If you are unsure whether you will be granted access to another institution's holdings, you can always call ahead, email, and/or have a letter from your chair or program director confirming your student status in your program. Many institutions offer visitor passes for students at other institutions. If you know of another library that has holdings that would be useful for you, you may inquire about a visitor's pass as a student.

Many institutions also subscribe to various organizational tools. Systems like RefWorks and EndNote are downloadable tools to help researchers organize their materials. RefWorks and EndNote help you manage your bibliography and citations. The software may be downloaded on one or more computers, depending on your institution's license. Plug-ins also help store citations offline that plug right into Word (or other word-processing programs). These tools may include options as simple as creating a citation list or as complicated as organizing PDF copies of actual articles stored under your account. Some tools will allow you to maintain a "bookshelf" online, whereas others will not. Most institutions will have librarians or information technology staff to help you with these online tools. Check with your university's librarians to see what is available to you. Getting to know how to use these tools for shorter class papers or projects will allow you to be an expert in utilizing them by the time you need to use them for your final project.

In addition, a university-based writing center may provide you with a writing tutor for academic papers, reports, annotated bibliographies, or other work. In some cases, these centers may provide help that is very extensive, but in other cases they may not be designed to do so. In any case, you will want to explore these resources and become acquainted with the processes, limitations, and possibilities. If you are working on a dissertation for a doctoral program that is one of the only doctoral programs on campus, you may not have access to the level of writing help you need from the campus resource. In that case, you may want to review other options with your program director, faculty, or graduates of the program (e.g., an alumni or peer writing mentor, professional writing assistance).

Your Program's Resources

You will want to find out if your program has its own holdings or if a faculty member whose work you are interested in is willing to loan you titles from their own collection. Programs may have internal libraries of DVDs or audiotapes available for students concerning interventions or mock client cases. Reviewing these may spark an interest for you or supplement the interests you have already developed.

Many programs house their graduates' theses and dissertations within their program's offices. In addition, some programs require their students to publish their work online in ProQuest Dissertations & Theses Global (which we will discuss in Chapter 8). In any case, you will want to review previously approved work.

The above-mentioned resources will likely be established at your university and can be found by simply asking about them in your program or library office or by looking up the information on the university website.

As a beginning student, you will also have people available to you whom you should consider asking for tips on how to navigate the research resources in your program, as well as your university. Peers and alumni, as well as faculty, have all conducted research within the same academic setting—their experiences may be valuable to you. Additionally, as noted earlier, getting involved in research as a beginning student can help you build your skill set for completing a research project within your program's institutional resources (or beyond, if necessary).

Overcoming Hurdles to Using Research Resources

Use a template like the one in Table 2.2 to help you organize your resources. This will help you get a clear sense of what your resources are and the name and contact information of someone who can help you with them. It is also helpful to be (and stay) aware of any concerns you have about accessing or using these resources. Then you can identify proactive solutions for these concerns, such as engaging in a tutorial or requesting assistance from a specific contact. Learning how to overcome hurdles when using research resources on your own allows you to bring helpful information back to your prospective chair, your advisor, your peers, or staff in an applied setting.

Table 2.2 Your Resources Template

Resource	Contact	Concerns/hurdles	How concern may be overcome

Finding Your Literature

Working on a research project is not like following a course syllabus. You will not be handed a magical list of readings that will fit simply into your literature review. But do not worry—one of the best things about research is learning the conversation that has been going on about your topic. Think of all the conceptual papers and research studies that have been written up as a network of capillaries of thought. Some go off in this direction and that direction; some lines of thought diverge suddenly because of a framework of thinking or new data. Some exist in one discipline, but have not yet been explored in others. Others form new networks when combined with those from other disciplines. Your efforts to digest research from other fields with an open mind will allow you to expand your knowledge base and form a well-researched project.

First, get to know the foundations. Who are the major researchers in your field? Look at their work. It is important to read the early research on your topic, as well as the seminal research articles that have shaped your area of research. You should also check the reference sections of relevant articles and books to find other important articles and sources that were previously written and related to your topic.

Second, get comfortable with searching for sources (e.g., articles, books, prior dissertations and theses). You will often want to search for peer-reviewed sources within the past ten years, but this depends on your topic. If you are looking at a historical change in the field, using the publication date filter will require searching within a historical period (e.g., 1950–1970) rather than searching only current literature.

You can also search articles to see which other authors have cited them after they were published. Many databases have a search tool that will tell a researcher how often, and by whom, the article has been cited. For example, say you use Google Scholar to search a topic. Under each article listed, you will see a link listed as "Cited by . . ." with a number at the end to indicate how many times it has been cited. You can click on the link to see what publications have cited a particular article. This is a great way to search for literature relevant to your topic that was published after the initial source.

Be sure to search multiple databases (e.g., PsycINFO, ERIC, PubMed) to ensure that you have access to as wide a variety of articles as possible. You can use the keywords from abstracts of articles pertinent to your topic as search terms to find related articles. You can also use authors' last names as search terms. Databases tag articles with subject descriptions, which you may want to use to further search topics adjacent to your main topic that have been explored by others. These have been added by editors and librarians to help guide researchers.

As you read relevant sources, you will become more familiar with terminology you might use in your searches to find more sources. For example, perhaps you have been searching for "cognitions" and find several articles that use the term "thoughts." Revising your search terms could help you expand your search.

It is also useful to become familiar with database search techniques. Putting any phrase in quotation marks will tell the database to search those words as if they were one thing. For example:

- Cognitive behavioral therapy = will yield results with any of these three words in any order (or nowhere near one another)
- "Cognitive behavioral therapy" = will yield results with these three words, in this order, in the article.
- Albert Ellis = will yield results with Albert and Ellis (Ellis Island, Albert Einstein, Little Albert, etc.).
- "Albert Ellis" = will yield articles with Albert Ellis mentioned.

Another useful technique to help refine your search is called Boolean. Boolean will allow you to search for specific terms together with other terms, as well as limit certain terms from your results. There are three Boolean operators. They must be capitalized for the database to understand what you are asking it to do. The operators are "AND," "OR," and "NOT." Here are some examples of this search method.

Example 1: childhood AND trauma NOT adolescence
    This will find results that include childhood and trauma, but do not include adolescence.

Example 2: "anger management" NOT trauma
    This will find results that include anger management (as one term) but do not include trauma.

One note of caution with using Boolean is that authors may include something about other related topics in the introduction. For instance, if the author says, "In this study we purposely focus on childhood and not adolescence," then using the Boolean operator "childhood NOT adolescence" has limited your search too much. So start with a broad search, and then use the search-within features of the databases after you get a sense of how scholars talk about your topic.

Many students wonder how they will know when they are "done" with their literature search. It is normal to feel overwhelmed at times with the number of directions the search can take you. One general rule is to notice when your search efforts elicit the same sources, without relevant additions. As you read and write, you will get a better sense of what other information you might need. Also, keep in mind that unless you are conducting a comprehensive literature review as the focus of a project, you do not need to write an exhaustive review. The goals are to use enough sources to show you are knowledgeable about a topic area, build an argument for your project based on the existing literature, and demonstrate familiarity with what has and has not been done. We discuss skills for writing your literature review in Chapter 5.

Skills for Reading and Critically Evaluating Research

One of the key pieces of your final project will be a written review of the literature. This literature review will embed your project in the context of the larger subfield and support the rationale for what you plan to study. Reading, critically evaluating what you read, and synthesizing this information in writing can be a complex process. We review a general strategic set of steps, including organizing your articles (and other sources), reading and summarizing literature, critically evaluating research articles, outlining and beginning to write, and welcoming and incorporating feedback. Please see other authors for additional suggestions about organizing, analyzing, and synthesizing relevant literature (e.g., Bell et al., 2019; Efron & Ravid, 2018; Galvan & Galvan, 2017).

Please note that we write specifically about using journal articles in this section. This is because they are the most common source students use to support their project ideas; however, relevant sources for your ideas might also include articles, books, websites, newspaper clippings, videos and/or audios, listservs, personal communications, and perhaps even photography and/or art. In addition, although we discuss these steps as if they are sequential, note that this is a bit misleading, because you will likely find yourself going back and forth between steps as you refine your project ideas. For example, once you have read some articles and begin writing, you will likely realize you need to become familiar with another part of the literature. Once you read some more, you will be able to sharpen your written explanation regarding what your project adds to the literature, be more informed about possible methods, and so on. Because you have to start somewhere, we first suggest strategies for organizing what you read.

Organize Your Articles

In Chapter 1, we suggested you keep a running list of your ideas. Once you identify an area you would like to explore, your next step will be to search for scholarly readings in this area, using the just-noted skills for finding literature. As you conduct your literature search, skim the abstracts of articles to determine if they contain key concepts relevant to your idea. When you find potentially pertinent articles, download them and organize them into electronic folders by subtopic, which can later turn into categories for your outline, helping you form the order of your written proposal. You can also get a better sense of which authors and articles are continually cited and which are not.

As you go through the program, it is useful to have an organizational tool in place where you keep a running list of the articles you use on assignments that match the saved files you keep. Table 2.3 provides an example template for how to create a database of articles from courses and from your own independent research. In Excel, you may want to have multiple tabs in one spreadsheet—one for all articles and others for your particular interests. The last tab might include articles listed on faculty syllabi that you want to keep. We recommend using this method, or something like it, to organize the articles you accumulate over time in your program. Consistency is key here; for example, you can repeat the same names of categories to help you sort through various sources on the same topic later. You might also create a column indicating if you think an article could be relevant for a specific part of your written proposal. For example, some articles will provide background information, like the prevalence of a problem in a particular population, while others may be studies similar to what you hope to study, provide support for your project's rationale, or include potential ideas for your method. Saving the

Table 2.3 Example Database of Sources

Author(s)' last name, first initial	(Year)	Title	*Journal*	*Volume (issue)*	Pages	Category/ topic	Notes

articles by the authors' last names and year of publication is also helpful for locating them more easily later. Note that the order listed here will also allow you to easily copy and paste into a Word document with the citation pieces in the correct order for your eventual references section: Authors. (Year). Title. *Journal, Vol*(issue), pages.

Read and Summarize

Once you have organized the literature you found into categories, you will want to engage in two levels of reading. The first level involves skimming readings you collected in each category to gain a general understanding of what they cover. For example, when reviewing a research article, you will want to initially understand the purpose of the study, what the authors proposed the study would add to the literature, the hypotheses and/or research questions, who the participants were, the research design, the overall procedures of the study, the major findings of the study, the study's limitations, and the clinical and/or applied implications of the results. We suggest first reading the abstract, the end of the introduction, the participants and procedure section, and the discussion section to get a general gist of what the study contributed to the literature and where there may be room for improvement or ways to build on the study. At this level, you are reading to determine how the prior study could support the need for your idea and the general development of your project. Your goal is to review a breadth of readings rather than go into too much depth with any one article, because this can slow down your broad understanding of the subfield. At the same time, you can take notes or highlight any similarities or differences in the methods and results among articles as you read.

The second level of reading involves taking a more in-depth look at articles and generating a summary of key points that will directly help you build the rationale for your project. Unfortunately, it is easy to do a lot of reading only to find a few weeks later that you do not really remember key points or findings! Make efficient use of your reading time by finding a method for retaining essential information. Research articles typically include introduction, method, results, and discussion sections. The second column in Table 2.4 provides questions to answer about each section of a research article in order to summarize the main points. We recommend placing the answers for articles you read in depth into a table or spreadsheet in a program like Microsoft Word or Excel. This can help you absorb the article's information and keep it organized for future reference.

Critically Evaluate

Once you have summarized the content of a research article, the next step is to critically evaluate its components, including the authors' support for the purpose

Table 2.4 Questions to Help You Summarize and Critically Evaluate Research Articles

Section of article	Summary of reading	Critical evaluation
Introduction		
Background literature, operational definitions, and previous studies reviewed	What were the key concepts or areas covered? What were the operational definitions of these concepts? What major studies were reviewed?	How comprehensive was the literature review? Do all important prior studies appear to be included? Were details of studies most related to the article reviewed in detail? Were they critically reviewed? Were diverse perspectives and mixed findings presented and discussed? How well organized was the review?
Theory	What theory or theories, if any, supported the hypotheses and/or research questions?	If a quantitative study, was the study guided by theory? If a qualitative study, did the review take a neutral, open-ended stance?
Statement of the problem, study purpose, and rationale for the study	What is described as lacking in the literature? What was the purpose of the study? What were the independent and dependent variables? What was the rationale for conducting the study?	Were gaps in the literature connected to the main studies reviewed? Did the literature review support the need for the current study? Was the purpose of the study clear and specific? Were the variables and population clearly defined? Was the type of research design needed clear from the wording of the purpose of the study? Did the rationale for the study demonstrate its potential contribution to practice in the field? Theoretical knowledge? Methodology? Was the significance of the study made clear?
Hypotheses and/or research questions	What were the hypotheses and/or research questions? Were hypotheses directional and/or nondirectional?	Were the hypotheses/research questions clearly stated? Did they clearly follow from the stated purpose of the study? Based on the wording of the hypotheses/research questions, can you predict what research design was needed to test/explore the relationships between the included variables? How about the relevant sample? Were directional hypotheses clearly supported by the literature reviewed?

Section of article	Summary of reading	Critical evaluation
Researcher bias (for a qualitative study; might be found in the introduction or method section)	What, if any, personal or professional biases of the researchers were disclosed?	Did the authors acknowledge their biases? How about ways to monitor and attempt to minimize bias (e.g., making coders aware of the overarching research question and potential biases, selectively choosing coders with diverse experiences)?
Method		
Participants	Who was the sample of participants (e.g., demographics)? Sample size? What were the inclusion and exclusion criteria? What was the sampling strategy used?	Were the sample and sample size sufficient for the purpose of this study? How well did the sample represent the population studied? Was the sampling strategy suitable for this study? How do you think those who participated differed from those who did not? Was this addressed?
Design	What research design was used? In a quantitative study, if conditions/groups were created, what were they?	Was it clear what type of research design was used? If a quantitative study, did authors specify which variables were the independent and dependent variables? In a quantitative study, are potential threats to internal and/or external validity addressed?
Procedures	How were participants recruited? By whom? When and where did each part of the procedure take place? How was each part of the study conducted? If groups were created, what happened in each group? If an experiment, were there any manipulation or fidelity checks? If coders or research assistants were used, how were they trained?	Was the procedure clear enough that you could replicate it? Is there anything you think should have been done differently to improve the study's quality? **Ethical evaluation:** Do the authors note whether participants completed informed consent and/or assent before agreeing to participate? Was there any deception used in this study? Does it seem to have been important for the study's purpose? What was the degree of risk for the participants? Did the benefits appear to be worth any potential risks? Was there a procedure in place for participants who experienced discomfort or emotional or physical distress? Were participants debriefed at the end of the study? Did it seem necessary?

continued

Table 2.4 *continued*

Section of article	Summary of reading	Critical evaluation
Measures	What measures were used? What concepts were they measuring?	Did the measures used adequately assess the constructs the researchers aimed to measure? Was sufficient detail about each measure provided (e.g., number of items, range of scores, meaning of scores)? Did the measures used have adequate reliability and validity? If a qualitative interview study, did authors indicate whether they asked open-ended questions? Did they attempt to minimize bias?
Results		
Analyses conducted	What kinds of data or statistical analyses were conducted?	Were the analyses conducted appropriate for the research design used? Were appropriate analyses used for each hypothesis/research question?
Descriptive statistics	What are key means and standard deviations of continuous variables (e.g., age of sample, scores on measures)? What are key frequencies and percentages of categorical variables (e.g., ethnicity, gender, scores on measures)?	Were any descriptive statistics missing that would be useful to know?
Inferential statistics (quantitative study)	What inferential statistics were used? Were any variables statistically controlled for? Any corrections used?	Were the findings explained conceptually? Were any inferential statistics missing that would be useful to know?
Qualitative analyses	Was there a coding system? If so, what kind of data were generated (e.g. themes, theoretical constructs)?	If there is a coding system, does it appear there was a method for acknowledging potential biases? Did any analyses assess the trustworthiness of the data?
Tables and figures	What visual information is provided?	Do tables and figures used highlight key findings in the study? Do they accurately represent the study's results?

Section of article	Summary of reading	Critical evaluation
Discussion		
Summary of findings	What are the overall findings of this study?	Do the findings address the original purpose of the study?
	What are secondary findings that might be important to note?	Are the findings summarized accurately based on the study's results?
Comparison to current literature	What are similarities of this study's findings to other studies? Differences?	Do the authors adequately address how the current findings compare to prior findings?
Implications of findings	What are the practical implications of the study? Theoretical? Methodological?	Does the study meaningfully contribute to practice in the field? Theoretical knowledge?
	What are the strengths of this study?	Are there any methodological innovations?
		Are the implications addressed within the limits of the authors' findings (e.g., based specifically on who and what was studied)?
Study limitations	What are the limitations of this study?	Are all study limitations adequately addressed?
Directions for future research	What are suggested directions for future research? Could they provide support for my idea(s)?	Do future directions directly follow from the specific results found in this study?

and rationale of the study, hypotheses and/or research questions, methodology and data analytic techniques used, the findings, and the conclusions. This is where your knowledge of appropriate research methods comes into play. Cultivate your ability to critique published work early on in your graduate training, because you will be expected to synthesize information from articles you have read in the written introduction of your eventual project (rather than summarize several individual studies separately). For example, try critiquing a peer-reviewed article with a faculty member as part of a lab activity or with a group of peers. Use the questions on the right side of Table 2.4 to help you (based on McMillan, 2021). You can also refer to McMillan (2021) for more thorough criteria for evaluating specific types of research designs. Students are often surprised to realize that published work can include many limitations. You will likely find several unaddressed issues and have ideas for how things could have been done differently, which can aid in the development of your project idea. You will also be expected to critique prior work to support the rationale for why your project is a good next step in your field.

In addition, you will want to evaluate whether the research conforms to ethical standards. Some ethical issues may not be so easy to ascertain from an article, such as how participants were consented or if their data remained confidential. However, authors of a research article will ideally report on ethical issues in the procedure section, such as informed consent and/or assent procedures, any use of deception, potential risks to participants, methods for managing participants in distress, and a debriefing procedure (if applicable). The third column in Table 2.4 provides questions to ask to critically evaluate each section of a research article.

You can use time early on in graduate school to bolster your knowledge of research and scholarly literature written about topics that interest you. In addition, reviewing the existing literature can help you form an appreciation for others in applied fields, as well as strengthen your critical thinking by questioning assumptions your field may have about a topic and generating lines of thought that do not appear.

Outline and Begin to Write

Now that you have read several articles, it is time to start organizing your ideas in writing. There are a few ways this can be done. One approach for beginning to write involves writing down your thoughts freely, without thinking much about grammar, organization, or citations. This can be a good way to brainstorm what you are really interested in and hoping to say. You can do this on your computer or in a notepad. Sometimes it can help to sit and write freely in a visually pleasing place or with music on. The first author, HBV, wrote the first ideas for her method section of her dissertation while sitting in front of armor statues in the New York Metropolitan Museum of Art that her significant other was sketching for his own project. You can engage in writing freely while on the train, between classes, when you first wake up, or right before you go to sleep at night. If you drive long distances, you could even use voice recording to log your ideas and write or type them out later. Some of your best ideas will likely come at times when you are not officially working, and you want to be sure you remember them later!

A second way to begin writing is to draw flow charts, diagrams, or idea maps for what you want to say. You can start at the top of a page or in the middle, drawing branches between ideas. For example, HBV's dissertation focused on the effects of video self-modeling as an intervention for mothers of children with oppositional behavior. Figure 2.1 shows some of the plausible initial layouts for organizing her introduction.

Another example where a visual can be useful is when brainstorming how to balance methodological rigor with determining what is feasible in an applied setting. For example, you may want to conduct a single case design to address oppositional behavior of students in a school setting. This would involve determining how to balance

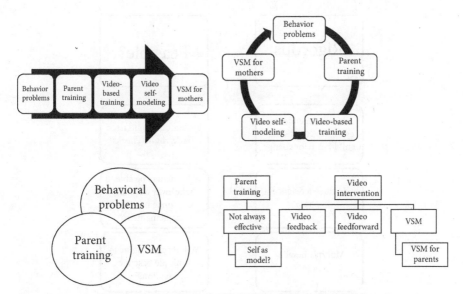

Figure 2.1 Examples of plausible initial layouts for organizing an introduction (VSM, video self-modeling)

threats to validity with ensuring the school and its teachers would be able and willing to participate. In this case, you could outline your thoughts as shown in Figure 2.2.

A third approach is a structured outline (e.g., a roman numeral outline). At some point, you will likely want to create one of these so that you can review it with your advisor or potential chair. Typically, a research project involves reviewing literature from a few major areas in the field and explaining how these areas can come together. You can begin organizing your outline via the categories you created when you were organizing the literature you acquired. For example, take HBV's dissertation involving using video self-modeling as an intervention for mothers of children with oppositional behavior. She needed to review literature focused on the following:

I. Development and Maintenance of Oppositional Behavior
II. Types of Parenting Interventions
III. Use of Video in Interventions
IV. Video Self-Modeling Interventions

Once this was clear, she was able to add subheadings under each part of the outline. For example, for the section on video self-modeling interventions, she added the following subheadings:

IV. Video Self-Modeling Interventions
    A. Definitions of Video Self-Modeling
    B. History of Video Self-Modeling
    C. Theory about Video Self-Modeling

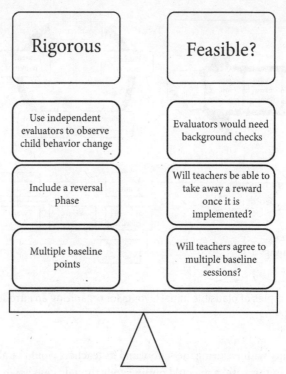

Figure 2.2 Example of visually balancing rigor and feasibility for potential methodology

D. Differences among Video Feedback, Video Feedforward, and Video Self-Modeling
E. Video Self-Modeling Interventions for Various Populations
F. Video Self-Modeling as a Parenting Intervention

Including subheadings like this can be a natural way to build in steps to follow as you work on writing up your idea. You can then break the work you do on each subsection down even further. For example, the section on video self-modeling interventions for different populations was broken down into interventions for children versus adults. An added benefit is that the headings in your outline can become the headings for your final project's table of contents.

Once you begin to write out each section of your outline, you will want to start synthesizing information from your various readings. For example, instead of reviewing one study at a time, you will want to group and review findings from multiple studies, highlighting key examples that help drive home your main points. The next step involves transforming your critical evaluations of the literature you read into what you write. Students often mistakenly limit their written review to descriptions of studies conducted and accept the authors' conclusions, rather than offering their own critique. If you are new to the field, or to writing, it can feel intimidating to assert your own perspective about the work of experts. However, that is the goal of any new piece of scholarly writing. The very goals of conducting research are to question theories and findings from prior studies, discover gaps in our knowledge base, and develop theories about alternative possibilities. Continuous questioning is the core of scholarly progression, and this will be your opportunity to contribute to this process. We will discuss more about writing the literature review for your research project proposal in Chapter 5. Before you get to that point, however, you will want to share your written ideas with faculty and/or peers for feedback.

Welcome and Incorporate Feedback

When should you share your ideas and submit your work to faculty or peers for feedback? We recommend doing this as soon as possible. Formal opportunities for doing so will likely depend on the structure of your program and the people with whom you work. One idea is to form a peer review group, perhaps as part of a faculty member's lab, where you can practice critiquing each other's ideas for projects. Another idea is to ask faculty you might like to work with if they would be open to meeting with you about an idea. Some faculty will appreciate being given an abstract or a short concept paper summarizing the purpose of and rationale for an idea before you meet. You will also have opportunities to receive more general writing feedback on papers you write for class.

It can be hard to receive feedback on your idea, however constructive it may be. It makes sense that after all the time and energy you spent developing it, the last thing you want to hear is why it does not make sense or might not work! Sometimes the tone in which others provide feedback, especially over email or by text, can be hard to accept, but the people providing it likely mean well and are trying to help you.

Even though it can be tough to receive feedback, we recommend being welcome to it for several reasons. First, it is good to hear feedback early on, when you still have plenty of time to make changes. Second, you can get others' perspective on whether your idea will make a valuable contribution to your applied field. Third, after getting some space from the feedback, you will likely begin to see ways to incorporate it that strengthen your idea. This is because you have been sitting close to your idea, whereas others have distance from it and may be able to come up with fresh perspectives and suggestions. Finally, hearing what others think about your idea can help you know what to expect when you have to explain your work in your proposal meeting or when you present your work to professionals in an applied setting or at a conference.

Students often wonder whether they have to incorporate every piece of feedback they receive into their idea. The answer is no: you do not have to take all feedback given to you, but be sure to remain nondefensive and appreciative when receiving it. On the one hand, for those who are not directly involved with your idea, you can thank them for their input, indicate what you find useful, and say you will think about it. On the other hand, you may need to incorporate more of the feedback from those who may be directly involved with your project, such as your prospective chair. This does not mean you always have to incorporate all of their feedback, however. When you do not agree with a key person's input, it is important to thank them for it and explain your rationale for doing it differently. Part of developing your final project is developing your own voice, something your eventual chair will hopefully appreciate. At the same time, hear them out about other ideas. They likely have experience with issues they are belaboring and may have good reason to suggest you do something otherwise. If you get to the point where you are in complete disagreement with a faculty member over the core points of your idea, this may be a sign to seek out another prospective chair and/or alter your idea.

Navigating Your Way through the Institutional Review Board (IRB) Process

As we mentioned in Chapter 1, you will need to apply for IRB approval to conduct any empirical research project that involves human subjects. Going through the IRB process will ensure that you are protecting participants in your study from harm and describing an ethical study procedure. It is helpful to familiarize yourself with this process early in your training. We recommend working with a faculty member or an upper-level student on an IRB application before you need to submit one for your final project. Another idea is to submit an IRB proposal in conjunction with a poster submission for a conference, alongside peer coauthors and a faculty advisor. In addition, you could ask a faculty member if they have any IRB applications on which they or their students could use assistance. You may find that they are relieved to get some extra help in return for guiding you through the application process. Learning how to navigate the IRB at your school well before you need permission to conduct your final project can help make part of the process easier for you. In this section, we review what you will need to do to become familiar with your school's IRB process.

Become Familiar with Your School's IRB Procedures and Timelines

Although the IRB follows federal and state laws, each institution will have its own policies. The board will also include institutional faculty from various academic departments (e.g., scientific and nonscientific) and members of the community, each with their own perspectives. Most IRBs will have a document of guidelines for investigators to follow, as well as application forms to complete. These documents can often be found on your university's website. There will likely be a schedule of times when the full IRB meets to review applications, as well as deadlines for when you must submit your application. For example, you may be required to submit your application to the IRB two weeks before the review meeting so that your application can be reviewed administratively and by reviewers prior to the meeting. The guidelines will also likely include the IRB's review criteria, as well as a general estimate of when you can expect to hear a response regarding the status of your application.

What Category of Research Am I Doing According to the IRB?

Once you know your IRB's general procedures and timelines, you will have to determine whether your project is considered research that the IRB will need to review. For example, some types of case studies may not be considered research because the data are not considered generalizable. Similarly, if your data collection involves systematic review of published texts or articles, the IRB will typically not need to review your procedure because you will not be using human subjects, but it never hurts to check with your IRB's administrator! Research that the IRB will need to review falls into one of the following categories: exempt, expedited, or full. Typically, you can find the definitions for these categories in your school's investigator guidelines. We provide a general overview of each category next.

Exempt Category
Research that falls into the exempt category is research that would not create more than minimal risk for the participants. Research deemed exempt by the IRB does not need to be reviewed by the full IRB committee; however, you typically still need to complete an exempt IRB application, which will be reviewed and approved by an individual member of the IRB or a subcommittee. An exempt IRB application typically includes a description of your project; a statement explaining why your project can be considered exempt according to federal guidelines; a description of who your subjects will be and your procedures for the research, including recruitment; a review of the benefits and risks of participating in your study; and copies of consent and/or assent forms, surveys and/or questionnaires, and letters of permission from individuals providing you with data or allowing you to conduct your research at their off-campus site.

According to current federal requirements (US Department of Health and Human Services, 2018), some types of research relevant to the applied fields that fall into the exempt category include:

- Research conducted in educational settings that will assess typically accepted scholastic practices. For example, this could be research examining typical teaching methods or comparing teaching techniques, classroom management strategies, or course content.
- Research that uses standard educational tests (e.g., cognitive, achievement), interviews, surveys, or observations of public behavior, if the data are collected

in a way so that participants cannot be identified and/or cannot potentially be subject to liability or damage to their finances, employment potential, or reputation.

- Brief and benign behavioral interventions (e.g., a game) when participants agree to the intervention and related data collection beforehand, if the data are collected in the ways listed in the previous point.
- Research involving the use of existing data or documents that are publicly available or if data are collected in a way in which participants cannot be identified.
- Research led or approved by a federal department or agency aiming to study one of the following: public benefit or service programs, procedures for obtaining benefits found in these programs, and various alternatives or changes to these programs or their practices.

Expedited Category

Research that falls under the expedited category means research that would not create more than minimal risk for the participants and includes certain types of procedures outlined by federal guidelines (US Department of Health and Services, 1998). For expedited research, you will have to complete a full IRB application (see overview of full IRB application below), but your application will be reviewed by an individual IRB member or an IRB subcommittee rather than the full board. In the applied fields, expedited research could include:

- Research involving data or documents that have been or will be collected for nonresearch purposes, such as diagnosis or treatment.
- Using data from voice, image, or digital recordings that were collected for research purposes.
- Research assessing individual or group characteristics or behaviors, such as research on language, cultural practices, or motivation, or research using data collection methods such as surveys, interviews, focus groups, program evaluation, or quality assurance.
- Research previously approved by the IRB that is near complete. For example, the research may be ongoing but does not include enrollment of new participants, only includes participants that have already completed research activities, has not been found to involved additional risks, only involves longitudinal follow-up of subjects, or only involves data analysis at this point.
- Research previously reviewed by the full IRB that requires modification before full approval can be granted. This is a common reason for an expedited review.

Full Category

Research that does not fall under the exempt or expedited categories means subjects may potentially be exposed to more risk. These applications will require full IRB board review of a full IRB application.

IRB Application Content and Turnaround Time

Generally, an IRB application will ask you to include the following: project description, description subjects, recruitment and enrollment, study procedure, any compensation you will provide, potential risks and benefits of research participation, confidentiality and storage of data, informed consent and assent forms, and copies of any unpublished measures you plan to administer. Some universities will ask for less information for an exempt or expedited application than for a full application. Be sure to review your IRB's specific guidelines about which application to use and what sections to include. We discuss general tips for writing each of these sections in Chapter 5.

Turnaround time can vary by IRB and category of application. The range is generally anywhere from a couple of days for an exempt or expedited application to a couple of months for a full IRB application.

Completion of Training Certificate

Most IRBs require investigators to complete training regarding ethics and legal issues in research before submitting an IRB application. Some universities offer this training in person, while others offer it online. One commonly required, free online course is called "Protecting Human Research Participants" and is offered by the National Institute of Health's Office of Extramural Research at http://phrp.nihtraining.com. Another online course is offered by the Collaboration Institutional Training Initiative at https://www.citiprogram.org. Your institution must have an affiliation for this course. Both courses require reading material and subsequent online tests about the information. The good news is that if you fail, the material can be reviewed and tests repeated until you pass. Then you can print out or save your certificate of completion, which some IRBs request you attach to your IRB application.

Tips for Successful IRB Submission

After reviewing your university's IRB guidelines, there are a few things you can do to prepare to submit your own application.

Review Your IRB Application with Your Faculty Sponsor
At a basic level, your faculty sponsor will serve as the gatekeeper for your submission to the IRB, since they will need to sign off on your application; however, your faculty sponsor can also help you navigate the IRB process. Faculty have experience with what your IRB is looking for and what they have approved in the past. As clear as you may think are in your writing, the IRB is looking for information

that is much more specific than what is typically expected in a research proposal or article. Meet with your faculty sponsor while you are preparing the application to discuss and agree on the specific steps your procedure will follow. Nailing these steps down now will aid you in conducting the study. Your faculty sponsor can then review a draft of your application and point out the issues they think need clarification or modification.

Sometimes faculty will talk about the IRB process as a major obstacle to conducting research. Understandably, the IRB's relationship with faculty as a checks-and-balance system can lead to tension, because projects can be delayed or even disapproved by the IRB. If you are having difficulty getting part of your research through the IRB, first meet with your faculty sponsor to receive their assistance in addressing the issue(s). In addition, find out if a member of your faculty serves on the IRB because this person will have firsthand experience with what your school's IRB tends to expect.

Review IRB Applications for Recently Approved Studies in Your Program That Are Similar to What You Want to Do

Reviewing recently approved applications similar to what you want to submit will give you an idea of your IRB's general expectations for a particular type of project and can serve as a template for your application. For example, if you are thinking of conducting a qualitative research project, it can help to ask faculty and/or upper-level students for copies of recently approved qualitative study applications and about issues they had to resolve to receive approval. It is important to remember, however, that because projects are assessed in isolation, the procedure you write may be almost identical to that of another student, but you may be asked to do something different!

Clarify Questions about Your School's IRB Procedures by Contacting an IRB Administrator

In our experience, administrators are usually eager to help students with their questions and prefer to address issues that arise before a student submits an application. It can even be helpful for your faculty to invite them to speak to you early on in your program. Keep in mind, however, that these administrators will typically only be able to provide general feedback, rather than "correct" answers for how to address issues specific to your research project.

Self-evaluating and Improving Your Research Skills

From the beginning of your applied graduate program, you will be expected to self-evaluate and expand on your research skills. It will be essential for you to determine which research skills you still need and what methods of skill building work best for you, in your program, in your field, and for your particular set of interests. For instance, a student in an applied setting with a lot of one-on-one faculty mentorship and peer support will need a different set of methods to begin applying research skills at the beginning of their program than a student in a program who must find their own connections to faculty, peers, or local professionals.

Importantly, the need to develop these methods is not solely contingent on how much support is already available in a program; rather, it is based on the particular needs of an individual student at the intersection of themselves, their program, and their field. These three pieces must meet in useful and productive manners that lead to research competence development. One might think of this process as being analogous to buying a car with a maintenance plan. While the support to maintain the car may always be there, it is the action the owner takes to initiate that maintenance that is necessary to keep the car running properly. Similarly, students in high-support programs must be able to self-evaluate their needs within their program and choose methods for seeking the right amount of maintenance assistance from that support network.

Get to know (and really grapple with) your preexisting conditions as a beginning student, and re-examine those issues (or new ones) as you develop your research skills. Advisors and mentors can be excellent resources for seeking honest feedback at this stage. In addition, there are a number of published evaluation tools that can help you, your advisor, and/or your mentor understand your current level of research competence in specific areas, as well as provide an evaluation of your research training environment, research motivation, and interest in research. Table 2.5 contains a list of several of these scales, including descriptions and sample items.

Each of these evaluation tools helps to gather information about yourself, your advisor or mentor, and your program in relation to the research process. This information can enable you and your advisor and/or mentor to begin talking about what skills you need to improve your research competence. For example, depending on the information elicited, you might need to find methods within your program and/or field to do the following:

- Create opportunities for building research competence
- Ask for assistance at appropriate times and/or developmental points
- Use assigned coursework or program experiences to enhance research competence (i.e., develop a poster or conference paper submission based on a class assignment)
- Develop communication methods particular to your advisor or mentor
- Make use of the technological tools (such as RefWorks) available or seek out additional needed organizational tools
- Find and utilize related resources, such as writing centers, consultants, or peer networks, for support with academic or related deficiencies (i.e., writing, time management, technology)

- Make use of or explore student professional organizations currently associated with either the program faculty or the subfield for workshops, networking, and resources
- Understand your resistances to conducting research
- Know which research competencies are already in your repertoire and which are your areas of weakness

Keep in mind that evaluation of your research skills is not enough. It is also important for you to identify proactive steps you and your advisor or mentor can take to improve these skills. Developing solutions for getting you to the appropriate level of research competence is an important step that students, and their advisors, often miss. Table 2.6 will help you, your advisor, and/or your mentors map out solutions (general and program specific) once you have determined your research competence levels, skills needs, and/or deficiencies (using the previously mentioned evaluation tools or more informal self-evaluation or evaluation of your academic competencies by your faculty).

Table 2.5 Evaluation Tools Related to Research Competency Development

Scale title	Scale description	Selected sample questions
Interest in Research Questionnaire (Bishop & Bieschke, 1994)	Assesses degree of interest in a variety of research activities. Sixteen items rated on a five-point Likert scale of degree of interest.	-Reading a research journal article. -Conducting a literature review. -Analyzing data.
Research Competence Rating Scale (Schlosser & Kahn, 2007)	Advisor-rated measure of research competence in doctoral students. Nine items rated on a five-point Likert scale of agreement.	My advisee has: - Knowledge of qualitative research designs, such as grounded theory and consensual qualitative research - The ability to perform a statistical analysis with computer assistance and interpret computer printouts. - The writing skills necessary to effectively write introduction, method, results, and discussion sections of a thesis, dissertation, or journal-length manuscript.
Research Motivation Scale (Deemer et al., 2010)	Used to measure research motivation, including three factors: intrinsic reward, failure avoidance, and extrinsic reward. Twenty items rated on a six-point Likert scale of agreement.	- I conduct research for the joy of it. - I sometimes want to avoid difficult research projects because I am concerned that I might fail. - I want to leave a mark on my field.

Scale title	Scale description	Selected sample questions
Research Outcomes Expectations Scale (Bieschke, 2000)	Used to assess level of agreement with statements about outcomes associated with research involvement. Twenty items on a five-point Likert scale of agreement.	- Involvement in research will enhance my job and/or career opportunities. - Doing research will increase my sense of self-worth. - Involvement in research will positively influence my applied skills.
Research Self-Efficacy Scale, Revised (Bieschke et al., 1996)	Reflects respondents' confidence in their ability to perform various research behaviors, including four subscales: early tasks, conceptualization, implementation, and presenting the results. Fifty-one-item scale with each behavior rated from zero to one hundred for the amount of confidence they have in their ability to successfully execute the behavior.	-Brainstorm areas in literature to read about. -Synthesize current literature. -Choose methods of data collection. -Write manuscript for publication.
Research Training Environment Scale (Gelso et al., 1996)	Assesses student perceptions of their research training environment, including nine subscales such as faculty modeling of appropriate scientific behavior and science as a partly social experience. Provides training programs with a checklist representing desirable components of research training. Fifty-four items rated on a five-point Likert scale of agreement. Eighteen-item short form also available (Kahn & Miller, 2000).	- My graduate program provides concrete support for graduate student research (e.g., access to computers, travel money for making presentations, research supplies, or free postage for mailing surveys). - Faculty members often invite graduate students to be responsible collaborators in the faculty members' own research projects. - Because of the diversity of research approaches among faculty members in my program, I would be able to find help learning about virtually any major research approach (e.g., field, laboratory, experimental, qualitative). - There is a sense around here that being on a research team can be fun, as well as intellectually stimulating.
Revised Attitudes Toward Research scale (Papanastasiou, 2014)	Assesses student attitudes toward research, including three subscales: research usefulness, research anxiety, positive research predisposition. Thirteen items rated on a seven-point Likert scale of agreement.	-Research is useful for my career. -Research courses make me anxious. -I find research courses interesting.

continued

Table 2.5 *continued*

Scale title	Scale description	Selected sample questions
Scientist Practitioner Inventory (Leong & Zachar, 1991)	Examines graduate students' interest in science and practice tasks psychologists often engage in, with seven subscales, including therapy activities, research activities, and teach–guide–edit. Forty-two items on a five-point Likert scale of degree of interest. Eighteen- and twenty-item short forms also available (Leong & Zachar, 1993).	- Writing an article commenting on research findings. - Conducting a diagnostic interview with a client. - Serving on a thesis or dissertation committee.

Table 2.6 Solutions for Expanding Your Research Skills

If you have ...	You may have trouble with ...	Possible solutions, in general	Program-specific solutions
Received feedback on academic papers concerning writing issues, such as grammar, paper organization, formulating of ideas	Writing in your program	Watch some videos on writing in your field; join a writing group; rework old papers for practice; take an additional graduate class that is writing intensive	Find a writing mentor (faculty member or upper-level student); meet weekly at your campus writing center; review completed theses or dissertations; ask a faculty member to review your drafts
Had little prior experience working with clinical populations	Using practical knowledge to inform your knowledge base	Find out what experiential activities others in your program are or have been involved in; look for opportunities to work on projects from student organization LISTSERVs, opportunities your faculty members may know about, or local clinical sites	See if your program has any clinical videos you can review; find out about opportunities to transcribe sessions or other preclinical work; volunteer for on-campus and faculty projects

If you have . . .	You may have trouble with . . .	Possible solutions, in general	Program-specific solutions
Trouble managing your time, often missing deadlines	Making your program's deadlines; balancing life and school	Set reminders (notes, alarms, calendar reminders) to keep yourself on track; set up a behavior management reward system for when you meet those deadlines on time	Work with a mentor to develop a timeline relevant to your program's deadlines; set an alarm to remind yourself of major and minor tasks and deadlines coming up
Found you work well alone	Class assignments that are group projects involving research	Working with others is essential to working in applied settings. Exposing yourself to these types of collaborative projects early on in meaningful ways will assist you later when you are working with professionals and/or populations in the field.	Get involved in a lab or project that requires you to collaborate with others in your program
Found you work well with constant feedback from peers	Working in a small program, an online program, or in a program that does not use a cohort model	Look for local or regional student professional chapters; develop study groups in your programs; look for students in similar local programs	Find a mentor or peer who will agree to act as a sounding board to provide feedback and support throughout your time in the program
Found you like to talk out ideas and issues	A chair, advisor, or mentor who gives very direct and short feedback, refusing (or not thinking) to elaborate on issues or ideas	Find or develop your own study group on a particular issue or a broader set of issues	Develop a peer-study workgroup that can meet formally or informally to discuss ideas or whatever is of interest in their studies/projects at that time.
Been given feedback about needing to explore or dig deeper into issues in papers or class discussions	Working on literature reviews, conceptualizing complex applied problems, being able to discuss and understand others' research outside the scope of your interests	Find a way to put yourself out there in a variety of settings with others who may or may not share your same interests or ideas. By hearing how others think, you can begin to develop a broader sense of your field and of the various ways of approaching issues within that field.	Meet with faculty, peers, and alumni across your interest and others. Ask if you can discuss a particular topic with them or just meet to hear about their research, interests, or the like.

Self-evaluating and Improving Your Writing

Developing your writing skills is key to embarking on a successful research project. Knowing how to attack writing remediation requires self-evaluation, reflection, and feedback. Use Worksheet 2.1 to assist you with self-evaluation of your writing. When completing the worksheet, reflect on your recent written work and the feedback you received to develop goals and strategies to improve your writing (either with or without a formal writing mentor).

Worksheet 2.1 Writing Evaluation Form

Part 1: Please complete the following self-review of your written work. It is important to look at your academic and clinical writing work over the past academic year (or more) to get a true sense of what kind of feedback faculty and supervisors have given you. This way, you (and your writing mentor) can work on specific writing goals over the course of the next academic year.

Your name:	Never	Seldom	Sometimes		Frequently	Always
	0	1	2	3	4	5
On writing assignments (e.g., coursework, clinical reports, research papers), I often get negative feedback from professors concerning:						
Grammar						
Punctuation						
Formatting						
Citation						
APA style						
Proofreading						
Wordiness						
Critical evaluation of literature						
Content/ organization						
Academic/ professional voice						
Other						
Other						

Part 2: Directions: State your writing goals in each box. If you have the opportunity to receive assistance (e.g., from a writing mentor, faculty member, or upper-level student), you can work with them on ways to achieve these goals by developing strategies to improve.

Writing Mentor Goal Setting and Strategy Form			
Your name: _____ Date developed: _____ Mentor's name: _____			
List the prior papers/reports/academic/clinical work you submitted to your mentor to begin to develop a writing mentorship plan:			
Writing areas to improve	Goal	Suggestions	Plan
Grammar		Review previous papers, articles, or other work similar to the assignment with your writing mentor.	
Punctuation		Conduct a spelling and grammar check (e.g., Word, Google Docs, Grammarly).	
Formatting		Use Purdue OWL (resource for citations, APA style, formatting).	
Citation		Maintain flow of writing within and between paragraphs by linking concepts together. Refer to the APA style manual (apastyle.apa.org) or other required style manual.	
APA style (or other required style manual)		Use RefWorks or EndNote software that can help you manage bibliography and citations.	
Proofreading		Have a peer or mentor review your work. Read it out loud. Use Grammarly.	

Content/ organization		Create an outline of the content you plan to include in your writing. After your draft is complete, compare it to your outline to ensure you covered everything you intended to. Edit accordingly. Show your work to someone outside your field.	
Wordiness		When writing and/or proofreading, consider whether each word is absolutely necessary in each sentence. Consider whether there are areas of your work that could be written more concisely. Stick to your main points and only include necessary comments and opinions if you are instructed to do so.	
Academic/ professional voice/Critical evaluation of literature		Read other professional writing pieces. Be cognizant of personal biases and how they may influence your writing style and tone. Maintain a professional tone throughout your work (e.g., utilize advanced vocabulary, avoid contractions, avoid personal pronouns unless advised to include them). Ensure you write from an active rather than passive voice. Critically evaluate what you have read in your writing; synthesize information and include your informed perspective about it rather than simply summarizing study results.	
Other			

Chapter 3
Attitudes toward Research

Introduction

At the beginning of your graduate program, you should aim to develop the *attitudes* necessary to critically evaluate research, conduct research in applied settings, and practice ethical and professional competence by learning the following:

- Attitudes toward science and practice in applied fields
- How do attitudes toward research in your program impact you?
- Appreciating your role when you conduct research in an applied setting
- Your attitude about your research resources, research ethics, and the institutional review board
- How ready are you to do the work? Stages and processes of change
- Your attitude toward self-evaluation and feedback

If you read the prior two chapters, you now know the knowledge and skills you need to acquire before conducting your final project. For example, you are now familiar with what it means to be scientifically minded, going beyond your personal opinions and embedding your interests within the context of existing research. You have read about various types of research designs and strategies for narrowing down potential project areas, as well as factors to consider regarding your options for faculty advisors and mentors. You have also learned how to get involved in faculty research and be a successful mentee, navigate applied research projects, conduct literature searches, begin to write, and incorporate feedback. You also know how to self-evaluate and begin to remediate any skills areas in need of improvement. Sounds like you may be all set—what could get in the way?

One common issue applied graduate students face is their attitude toward research. As we mentioned in the beginning, you may have entered an applied program because you were interested in focusing on practice rather than conducting research. Having to conduct a final project may be frustrating. You may think of it as a required means to an end: graduating. Although this is true, in Chapter 1 we reviewed additional benefits, such as becoming an educated consumer of research, increasing your marketability, evaluating your applied services to increase your credibility, and possibly deciding to conduct research in the future. Alternatively, some students enter applied programs with an initial interest in conducting research. Even so, the process of conducting your own project can be intimidating. Regardless of how you feel now,

Navigating Research in an Applied Graduate Program. Hilary B. Vidair, Pam L. Gustafson, and Eva L. Feindler,
Oxford University Press. © Oxford University Press (2024). DOI: 10.1093/oso/9780199352272.003.0003

we hope you will find ways to enjoy the process of your final project. Who knows? You may find it so rewarding that you decide you want to conduct research as part of your career. Either way, developing a positive attitude toward the conduct of research will help you navigate your way through your final project.

Attitudes toward Science and Practice in Applied Fields

Different graduate training models have traditionally fostered divergent attitudes about the role of research. For example, as we explained in Chapter 1, the scientist-practitioner, or Boulder, model of psychology training places an equal emphasis on research and practice. The practitioner-scholar, or Vail, model emphasizes the preparation for clinical practice while acknowledging the importance of training in science. Graduate students are taught to be local clinical scientists by applying research methods to address local (individual) and clinically significant issues (Peterson et al., 2006). According to Stricker and Trierweiler (2006), the "local clinical scientist brings the attitudes and knowledge base of a scientist to bear on the problems that must be addressed by the clinician in the consulting room" (p. 37). Clinical work is perceived as analogous to a research laboratory and represents an opportunity to integrate psychological science and "real-world" practice.

Despite the intent to integrate science and practice, students often do not follow suit. For example, a ten-year longitudinal study of over 200 psychology doctoral students who completed the Scientist-Practitioner Inventory (Leong & Zachar, 1991), a questionnaire including items that reflect both research and clinical activities, indicated that the Boulder model does not succeed in producing "scientists first and practitioners second" (Zachar & Leong, 2000, p. 579). The study revealed that only a small percentage of doctoral recipients continued to conduct research. Furthermore, doctoral recipients who become academic psychologists were shown to be significantly less interested in clinical practice than other clinical and counseling psychologists. A more recent survey of 653 clinical psychology graduate students focused on their experience in a scientist-practitioner training program indicated that the majority report confidence in their abilities to integrate science and practice and satisfaction with their training in the scientist-practitioner model (VanderVeen et al., 2012). However, more than one-third of the sample indicated they do not typically use science-based decisions when working with clients.

In response to the notion that the Boulder model may no longer be relevant, Overholser (2009) proposed a set of standards for determining who qualifies as a scientist-practitioner (S-P). These include the following:

- The S-P contributes to the field through scholarly work.
- The S-P remains active in scholarship.
- The S-P contributes scholarly work at a national level.
- Scholarship extends beyond teaching.

- The S-P remains active in clinical practice.
- The S-P provides clinical services on a regular basis.
- The S-P provides clinical services that are similar to standard clinical practice.
- Clinical practice extends beyond supervision.
- The S-P integrates the science and practice of psychology
- The S-P adheres to recommendations for evidenced-based practice.
- The S-P focuses on issues that are central to clinical psychology.
- The S-P in clinical psychology works with medical or psychiatric patients.
- The S-P in clinical psychology relies on psychological measures that have adequate psychometric properties and can easily be collected in most mental health settings.

Although these guidelines were designed to help Boulder model programs implement the ideals espoused in the model, professionals trained in a practitioner-scholar model can also actively contribute to research, even if they contribute in ways that are more aligned with local clinical scientists.

Stricker and Trierweiler (2006) emphasized several ways that scientific methodology contributes to the actual practice of the clinician. First is the recognition that research often exists about efficacious treatments for particular clinical problems. Many treatments have been empirically validated through clinical trials research. A second value of research to the clinician relates to the use of the scientific method in the clinical setting. Certainly, theory will guide the clinical observations and assessments of an individual client, but the scientific method will guide the intervention and outcome. For example, case conceptualization and treatment planning rely on hypotheses regarding triggers and maintaining factors for the presenting problem, along with historical and cultural influences. Clinicians can also systematically collect treatment outcome data on their individual clients and present and/or publish the results to inform their field.

In many applied fields, the gold standard is to ensure that practice is informed by research. Within the field of clinical psychology, three models emerged to help articulate the overall concept of research-informed treatment. In 1993, Division 12 (Society of Clinical Psychology) of the American Psychological Association (APA) established a task force charged with reviewing the available literature and identifying psychological interventions that were grounded in solid scientific research (Task Force on Promotion and Dissemination of Psychological Procedures, 1995). Later termed empirically supported treatments (EST), they were defined as psychological interventions that had been evaluated and met rigorous scientific criteria (e.g., found to be efficacious in randomized controlled trials). There was evidence available for the EST of a wide range of emotional and behavioral difficulties. However, the EST movement was criticized for ignoring key aspects of the therapeutic relationship, having homogeneous samples, and failing to consider the constraints of manualized treatments on treatment in real-world practice (e.g., Norcross, 2001).

As a result of criticism of the narrow range of treatments that met the EST research criteria, APA's Division 29 (Psychotherapy) originally created the Task Force on Promotion and Dissemination of Psychological Procedures in 1999 to examine factors other than the particular intervention techniques that contribute to the efficacy of psychotherapy (Norcross, 2001). In their search for "common factors" embedded in all therapies, common elements of the therapeutic relationship were identified as critical. They included therapeutic alliance, empathy, positive regard, therapist genuineness, client resistance, and collaboration. This second model emphasized more quasi-experimental and naturalistic research to identify both client and relationship variables that would contribute to effective change. Based on a series of meta-analyses, this task force had a number of specific research and practice recommendations and urged mental health groups such as the APA to advocate for the scientifically informed benefits of the therapeutic relationship (Norcross & Wampold, 2011). The evidenced-based relationships model, although it was another significant research-based model for psychological interventions, was perceived as being in contrast to the use of scientifically informed treatments (e.g., Norcross & Lambert, 2011).

The third model rests on an integrated principle that psychotherapy outcomes result from more than any individual factor (e.g., treatment factors: EST; client, therapist and relationship factors: evidenced-based relationships) alone. In 2005, an APA presidential task force was charged with determining the basis on which a clinician is to decide when a treatment is effective (APA Presidential Task Force on Evidence-Based Practice, 2006). The task force defined evidenced-based practice in psychology model as "the integration of the best available research with clinical expertise in the context of patient characteristics, culture and preferences" (APA Presidential Task Force on Evidence-Based Practice, 2006, p. 273). Specifically, they concluded that evidenced-based practice should be based on clinician judgment that incorporates not only the findings of the scientific literature, but also client characteristics and preferences and therapist factors such as experience and expertise. Without being tied to a particular orientation, a later, related task force compiled a list of sixty-one empirically supported principles that were either "common" (true for the treatment of most conditions studied) or "unique" (true for specific problem areas) (Castonguay & Beutler, 2006). The evidenced-based practice model of research-based practice integrates the previous two models and addresses how well a treatment approach, client, and therapist fit together to produce a good therapeutic alliance and positive outcomes.

Although faculty and program administrators often promote evidence-based practice models, in actual practice, surveys have indicated that therapists prioritize knowledge from their clinical experiences over research studies when making clinical decisions (Gyani et al., 2014). Practitioners more aligned with a cognitive-behavioral orientation seem more in tune with clinical research; however, a significant number of those in practice espouse other theoretical orientations. Regardless of your orientation or the kind of work you end up doing, we implore you to approach your practice in a scientifically minded matter. Lebow and Jenkins (2018) called for finding a common ground between research and clinical practice by asking the question: "Does it make any sense to engage in practice without reference to relevant research or to engage in research that fails to be informed by the work of clinicians and bears no relation to practice?" (p. 12). They cited numerous examples in which basic research has helped identify what would become core components of effective therapeutic treatments. For example, John Gottman (1998) studied couples' communication styles and deciphered the types of interactions that are most destructive to the relationship. Effective marital therapy techniques that targeted poor communication dynamics and the balancing of the ratio of positive interactions to negative interactions grew from these research results. Clearly, there are too many variables to consider in practice, such as therapist characteristics, theoretical orientations, setting differences, and/or varying symptom presentations, to have research results completely dictate treatment. However, our practices are most successful when they are informed by what current research indicates is most effective for helping the people we serve.

How Do Attitudes toward Research in Your Program Impact You?

As we suggested earlier, Gelso (2006) acknowledges that most applied graduate students enter training with the wish to be a practitioner rather than a researcher, and only a small proportion of graduates continue to produce research, even those who learn from a scientist-practitioner model. However, instead of faulting the clinical training model, Gelso suggests that there are serious deficiencies in the research training environment of most clinical programs that impede a student's involvement in research. He posits, "It is during graduate school that students' attitudes toward and investments in research are shaped" (Gelso, 2006, p. 4). An effective research training environment would stimulate students' interest in doing research and build students' sense of efficacy as clinical researchers. According to Gelso, positive attitudes toward conducting clinical research will hopefully develop across graduate training and are affected by the extent that the following occur:

- Faculty members model scientific behaviors and attitudes
- Research is positively reinforced by the environment, both formally and informally
- Students are involved in research early and easily in their training
- Varied approaches to research are taught and valued
- Students become aware that all research studies are limited in some way
- The bridge between science and practice is clear and valued

Once you begin your graduate training, you will become aware of the attitudes toward research within your program. You will also be able to assess two things early on: (1) the current climate or attitudes toward research and (2) the fit between the faculty members and the model. First, your program's overall attitude toward research is important to understand, because it will likely govern how you proceed with developing project ideas. As we mentioned in Chapter 1, there is substantially more overlap across training models than you might expect. For example, within psychology, some PsyD programs emphasize the importance of evidence-based practice and encourage students to conduct empirical research for their final projects. However, they might not have the time or resources to mentor independent student research projects outside the dissertation. In another case, you may be in a PhD program that is very clinically oriented. The faculty may not typically apply for grants or have the resources to teach students to apply for federal funding.

Your attitude toward the specifics of your training program will largely affect your ability to move forward in a way that balances your career goals with what can feasibly be done. We recommend being proactive by sharing your goals with faculty and asking them if they have suggestions for how you can move forward with your research goals within the context of your program.

Student Example: Attitude toward Program Research Climate

CLK began our PsyD program eager to conduct her own research. Our program encourages empirical dissertation research, research labs, faculty–student publications, and student-led presentations at professional conferences. However, students typically do not pursue their own lines of research outside the dissertation requirements. Aiming to find way to balance her research goals and her fit within the program, CLK decided to remain positive and take a proactive stance. She consulted with several faculty about how she could pursue some of her ideas in addition to the dissertation process. She was able to appeal to faculty by finding areas where her interests overlapped with theirs. She engaged in a variety of research projects with different faculty, including conducting a literature search for a comprehensive review article in a faculty member's area of interest, working on a research article based on data she collected as an undergraduate, and developing a research project evaluating a psychoeducational program she developed for a school setting.

Second, you will want to determine faculty member's attitudes toward conducting research, both on their own and with students. For example, you might have an advisor who has a long and productive research lab, but who does not engage in clinical practice. Or you might work with a faculty member who produces some scholarly work (e.g., presentations within local organizations), but who has generally not conducted any research since the completion of their own dissertation. Make an early assessment of the attitudes and interests in research and match them up with your own. If you are excited to conduct research, find a faculty mentor and/or advisor who shares this attitude, because this will increase the potential success of your own research process.

As we mentioned in Chapter 1, because of your research assistant assignments, you might be working with a faculty member on a research project for which you just are not interested in the topic or methods. Rather than responding negatively, think about what you can learn from the experience. Can you gain experience putting together a poster for an annual convention? Will you have the chance to practice systematically coding data or working in a team of student coders? This experience could help you learn how to train other students in a coding method for your own eventual project. Regardless of your specific initial research experiences, you can learn a great deal about research techniques and areas of your applied field that might help you later in your career. This is also an opportunity to learn about yourself as a potential researcher.

Student Example: How Keeping an Open Mind about Initial Research Experiences Translated into a Research Project

---

KU entered our doctoral program with a good number of years in residential care and she had risen to several administrative positions along the way. Her passion was working with adolescents suffering from emotional dysregulation. She began to think about a research project that would function as a program evaluation of an equine-assisted program she had been involved in for years. Although she had witnessed firsthand how valuable this type of adjunctive program was for the development of abused and neglected children, she had trouble finding both the empirical and the theoretical foundations on which the program was built. While she continued to gather published articles and critique them according to methodological rigor, she volunteered to be on a coding team for an upper-level student's project. The project called for interviews of ethnic minority students in doctoral training about their experience of being a student of color in training. As KU learned and coded these rich narratives, she understood that, rather than finding the evidence for a particular research question, the participants were teaching the researcher about what questions to ask and what was most important in their experiences. KU began to consider how qualitative research might be a better first step for her, too. Why not ask the participants about their experience with equine-assisted programs?

If research really is not your thing, find ways to express your interests and goals without sounding too negative about it. Try to avoid saying things to faculty who you potentially want to work with like, "I want to find a project that is as easy as possible" or "Tell me which research design will likely be the least amount of work." Think about it: Why would a faculty member feel motivated to work with a student who is not motivated themselves? Think of better ways to communicate your thoughts and feelings about the type of project you want to conduct, such as, "I find myself most interested in ideas that are very applied in focus. My goal is to conduct a final project that addresses [a specific clinical or educational issue]. Do you think we could discuss potentially feasible ways to pursue this area since I likely will not have access to a relevant sample?"

Overall, having a positive attitude will help you get through the research-oriented parts of your graduate program. Doing so will make each step in the process feel more manageable. Your positivity will also likely be clear externally, which will make faculty and other students eager to work with you.

Appreciating Your Role When You Conduct Research in an Applied Setting

In Chapter 2, we discussed how to navigate conducting research in applied settings, such as finding out the steps you have to complete to get started, learning about various opportunities to get involved, and creating a quid pro quo relationship. Successfully conducting research in applied settings also often requires you to adjust your attitude to fit in with the site and the professionals working there. Unfortunately, practitioners and organizations have sometimes had negative experiences with researchers coming in and trying to dictate what they will study and the changes that will take place in order to conduct their research. This top-down approach to conducting research is typically not well received.

A better approach to conducting research in an applied setting is to collaborate with professional staff and potentially even community members (e.g., clients) to determine what the needs are of the people involved with the site. At minimum, you will need to gain the support of key stakeholders at the site (e.g., principal, director) as well as the people who would need to help you implement a project (e.g., clinicians, teachers, hospital staff). The community-based participatory research involves fully partnering with people from the setting from the beginning. Via this approach, research is developed and conducted collaboratively, with the goal of finding outcomes that will benefit the community. Regardless of the level of collaboration between you and people at the site, take these points into consideration:

- Be humble! You are going into someone else's environment.
- Realize some staff have likely been working there for years and know a great deal about what is feasible, as well as what staff and community members will likely be interested in and willing to do.
- Inform staff and community members at the site about the potential benefits of participating in your project. In other words, what could be in it for them?
- Working with staff and community members can lead to the development of services they want.

- Staff can help you obtain access to the community and empower community members.
- Working with staff and community members can help you understand the community's perspectives.
- Working with staff and community members can help you earn trust in the community and assist with buy-in and support for your project.
- Working closely with staff at the site can help sustain an intervention or program you develop after your final project is completed.
- Successfully collaborating with a site increases the possibility that other students in your program will be able to conduct their projects there in the future.

Student Example: Collaborating with a School in Program Implementation

---

GS evaluated the effects of an anger management program for middle school students in a charter school. She first met with the school's personnel to discuss the potential benefits of the program. She also asked for their input regarding the time and location that would be most feasible for students and that would not be too disruptive to academic activities. By involving staff from the beginning of the project, GS was able to target issues that were most relevant to the student population. They were able to help her find a successful recruitment strategy and assist with buy-in from parents, who had to sign consent for their children's participation. The school provided her with positive feedback about the program and expressed interest in future collaborations.

Your Attitude about Your Research Resources, Ethics, and the IRB

The above-mentioned approach to collaborating with people in an applied setting also applies to working with people who can provide you access to research resources. Resources come from a myriad of places. Getting a degree in an applied field means that you will often interact with people across fields who have very different knowledge bases, skill sets, and attitudes toward your work, as well as their own work. These people may include academic librarians, writing center and technology staff, mentors, faculty, facility staff in applied settings, other students, and your peers, all of whom will be busy with other activities. Be sure to be professional, ethical, and kind when interacting with them.

It is easy to become frustrated with the people or the policies of offices you will have to go through to complete your project. Whether it is your institution's IRB, a site's administrative staff, or a group of parents, we recommend you be flexible in your expectations and methods for conducting your work. Being flexible not only builds rapport, but also indicates your level of professionalism.

There are some important attitudes to consider when thinking about the ethics of conducting applied research. Most applied graduate programs include course-work on research design, including ethical data collection and management, prior to the start of an applied research project. Most also require an ethics course that covers the detailed ethics codes of the profession. Each applied field typically has specific guidelines for the protection of the rights and welfare of the research par-ticipants, data management, and publication practices. The ethical challenges you face as you move toward your final project will differ based on your specific field, research design, and target population. For example, there are ethical considera-tions for developing and implementing informed assent procedures for children in an applied setting. If you conduct research with human subjects, you will have to address issues related to participant recruitment, risk assessment, and confiden-tiality in your IRB application. Thoughtfully addressing these issues will help your project move forward and protect the well-being of all involved. Conducting research ethically also demonstrates your ability to uphold the ethical standards in your field.

Your graduate training program is responsible for training you to understand the ethical standards in your field, which are important for developing and conduct-ing your final project. Research conducted by Fisher and colleagues (Fisher et al., 2009a, 2009b) has helped articulate aspects of the climate of an academic program's responsible conduct of research. These authors have developed four measures that assess the process of student socialization in the conduct of human subjects research (Fisher et al., 2009b):

- Mentoring the Responsible Conduct of Research Scale
- The Responsible Conduct of Research–Department Climate Scale
- The Responsible Conduct of Research–Preparedness Scale
- The Responsible Conduct of Research–Field Integrity Scale

These measures allow students to rate their department policies and practices relative to ethical research conduct, as well as their experiences with the direct instruc-tion and/or modeling received from research mentors about responsible and ethical research conduct. The results from a web-based survey of almost one thousand students indicated that the majority of research conducted in applied programs was characterized as having minimal risk, but almost all had some IRB challenges along the way (Fisher et al., 2009a). Most had positive ratings of their departments' respect for and adherence to research ethics principles and practices. The authors conclude that research ethics values are not simply transmitted through an ethics course, but also influenced by direct modeling from research supervisors as well as clear department policies and procedures relative to ethical issues. Upholding ethical standards is ultimately your responsibility, however.

You will likely receive some early exposure to the ethics of conducting research as a research assistant or a volunteer for someone's dissertation. Observe the ethics of how faculty and students conduct their research projects. Take note of each step of the IRB procedure and ask questions about anything you do not completely understand. When you get to the design of your own study, be prepared for questions related to ethical issues. Your research advisor should work carefully with you to prepare your IRB proposal, because they must sign off on it. It is almost inevitable that the IRB review of your research proposal will result in questions and a need for further articulation. Stay open-minded and nondefensive; the IRB committee members are just carrying out that which they are charged to do: protect the rights and welfare of human subjects. Have members of your research team or your cohort read a draft of your IRB proposal and make suggestions for clarification. Be open to feedback about your writing, your research objectives, your participant recruitment, informed consent, procedure, and data management. The more receptive you are, the smoother your research process will be.

How Ready Are You to Do the Work? Stages and Processes of Change

Even when you have many resources, making progress toward your final project will largely depend on how ready you are to put in the time and effort to do the work. You will have to be ready to make some behavioral changes, such as incorporating time to work on your project and avoiding temptations to engage in other activities. To make these changes, you will have to believe that the pros of getting the work done will outweigh the cons. You also will have to develop confidence that you can make progress and eventually complete the project. Your readiness to work on your project can be viewed as a process of attitudinal and behavioral change that can progress over time.

Prochaska and DiClemente (e.g., 1982; 1992) developed a theoretical model that includes six stages of behavior change: precontemplation (not ready for action), contemplation (thinking about being ready for action), preparation (ready for action), action, maintenance, and termination. The model was traditionally used to reduce problem behaviors such as smoking, but has been applied to making progress in changing many behaviors, such as exercise and stress management. We think it applies well to students' readiness to develop an idea and make progress on a project over time. Figuring out what stage you are in can help you determine how to move forward into the next stage of readiness.

Prochaska and DiClemente (e.g., 1982; 1992) also identified ten empirically supported processes of change over time, including five cognitive processes and five behavioral processes. The cognitive processes affect how you think and can facilitate movement through the first few stages of change and into action (e.g., from not being ready to work to getting work done). The behavioral processes mean beginning to make behavior changes and then maintaining these changes over time.

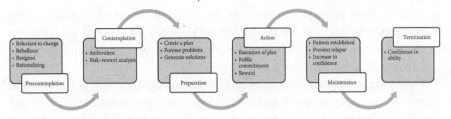

Figure 3.1 Stages of change

Figure 3.1 shows the characteristics of each stage of change. We review the characteristics of each stage, as well as strategies based on the ten processes of change to help you progress from one stage to another as you work toward completing your final project. Read the following information and then complete Worksheet 3.1 to determine your stage of change and strategies you can use to help you move into the next stage.

Stage 1: Precontemplation (a.k.a. Not Ready)

At this stage, you may not even be thinking of ideas for your final project. Think of a couch potato who has no intention of enrolling in a 5K. The costs of doing work at this stage (e.g., giving up fun activities, adding extra work to your schedule) may seem like they outweigh any pros. DiClemente and Velasquez (2002) identified four types of precontemplators, calling them the "Four R's." For our purposes, they include: (1) those who are reluctant to change (e.g., spend time doing literature searches, discussing ideas with faculty), (2) those who are rebelling against the idea of having to get to work, (3) those who are resigned to the idea that there is no hope of finding a good idea or a way to handle the workload, and (4) those who rationalize that their lack of work toward a project idea is not a problem. The good news is that if you are taking the time to read this section, chances are you realize you must be wary of these attitudes!

Processes That Can Help

Several cognitive processes can help you move out of the precontemplation stage. First, elevate your awareness about why you need to start working. Obtain information about the steps you can take to move forward, such as factors to consider when narrowing your interests into a potential project idea (which we covered in Chapter 1). Think about the consequences of not working on your project, such as the repercussions of missing major program deadlines (e.g., adding an extra year to your timeline). Talk to your mentor and upper-level peers, so they can provide you with constructive feedback and/or a reality check about how much you should be doing based on your point in the program and current skill level.

Second, focus on sitting with your emotions about starting the work. For example, feeling anxious about the need to get moving can increase your motivation. Ideally, you will feel hopeful when you hear how your upper-level peers are able to make progress on their projects. You may even feel inspired as you start to think about working on your idea! You can also conjure up emotions for how you will feel if you do not get started. You will likely feel intense anxiety, disappointment, and even some self-dislike, which might motivate you to get moving.

Third, be mindful about how delaying your work could affect others. For example, your loved ones may be counting on you to finish your final project within a certain time frame. Or your faculty mentor may be waiting to learn whether you will ask them to be your project chair. Making progress in your work can also positively impact your peers, which can improve your environment (e.g., communal work in a lab that benefits multiple projects).

Finally, consider the professional opportunities you will have once you move forward with your work. For example, showing diligence and dedication to your research can facilitate a positive relationship with mentors. Beginning to collaborate with professionals in an applied setting opens the door to developing collegial relationships and networking, which may lead to future job prospects. Moving forward with your project will also help you achieve certain program milestones, such as being able to apply for internships, not to mention getting your degree!

Stage 2: Contemplation (a.k.a. Thinking about Being Ready)

In this stage, you are ambivalent about whether working on project ideas right now is worthwhile. This is analogous to a person who thinks about exercising and getting into shape, but enjoys watching television and eating chips. If you are in this stage, you are likely interested in learning about your program's process for the final project and agree that you would benefit from working on it, but you are not doing so. You are likely conducting a risk–reward analysis of continuing to avoid the work versus getting moving. You may have a hard time believing that the reward of doing the work will be greater than the risk of procrastinating. This kind of thinking will prevent you from taking action.

Processes That Can Help

Re-evaluate how you feel about your current work habits. Are you okay with them or do you wish they would improve? Also take inventory of your values. How do you envision yourself? We expect that education and achievement are likely high priorities for you. (If your priorities have greatly shifted and you are not inspired by your program or your field, then perhaps now is the time to re-evaluate your decision to be in graduate school. This is not an easy decision, but completing a final research project requires a lot of time, dedication, and interest. It is better to decide it is not for you early on than to prolong leaving or following through on years of work that are miserable for you). If your long-term career goals remain focused on entering your applied field, you first need to take small steps toward your final research project. Imagine yourself behaving in successful ways (e.g., researching articles, talking through an idea with a prospective chair). This can help you build your motivation and confidence.

Stage 3: Preparation (a.k.a. Ready!)

In this stage, you will be ready to commit to taking action. You come to realize that the pros of working on your project goals outweigh the cons of doing it or the pros of avoiding it. Here, you can do research on what you will really need to know and do to move forward. It is like researching when the gym is open and planning how you will change your schedule to get there. Preparation allows you to develop a realistic plan of action before attempting to do the work. This is an important step that should not be skipped, because making your way toward your final project takes a lot of forethought and cannot be developed or executed overnight. Preparation for action can help you foresee potential problems and generate solutions before the problems occur. You can let your faculty mentors and peers know that you are serious about getting to work and that you are planning to take action in the near future.

Processes That Can Help

Three behavioral processes can help you get out of the preparation stage. The first involves believing you can get the work done and making commitments to doing it. Tell yourself you have the knowledge and skills to do the work, as well as the ability to acquire any new skills you will need. Try setting deadlines for the next parts of the process. Your commitments can be in the form of small steps (e.g., searching for articles on a topic of interest, making an outline of points you would want to make in a literature review). You will likely have to recommit to making progress on your work over and over. You may feel more motivated if you give yourself some choices. For example, this weekend, perhaps you can decide whether you will read and summarize articles, write up a potential method for an idea, or compile a typed list of the references you have found so far. Publicly committing to your action plan (e.g., telling your faculty mentor, family, and/or peers) can help hold you accountable.

The next two behavioral processes can be used to move beyond the preparation stage and out of any of the subsequent stages. The first refers to finding people who will be supportive of you and the steps you will need to take as you work. Ideally, you will be able to trust your mentor and/or chair to fulfill the roles found in Spillet and Moisiewicz's (2004) four C's: *cheerleader* as you move forward (e.g., be open-minded, available, encouraging); *coach* through each step of the process, helping you develop your research skills and keep your larger goals in mind; *counselor* through roadblocks you encounter (e.g., writer's block, time management); and *critic*, constructively evaluating your work and helping you take ownership of your project. Realistically, you will likely benefit from having more than one mentor to fill these different roles. Perhaps you can also find a student who is willing to work alongside you in the library or on the weekend. Outside school, figure out which friends and family you can trust to encourage your progress and listen to your struggles.

The second process involves learning how to replace problematic behaviors (e.g., procrastination) with more productive and healthy behaviors. For example, it means sitting down and writing even when you do not feel like it or doing deep breathing and practicing being assertive to counter anxiety you feel about meeting with a prospective chair. We review more strategies for managing procrastination in Chapter 6.

Practicing more healthy behaviors also means balancing work with self-care, which can help refresh you and prepare you to get back to work. Self-care practice is defined as participating in behaviors that help maintain your emotional and physical well-being, particularly when you are enduring the stressors involved in attending graduate school (Myers et al., 2012). Self-care practices can include physically healthy behaviors (e.g., diet, sleep, and exercise), emotional care (e.g., pleasant and/or relaxing activities, therapy), professional behaviors (e.g., taking breaks, stepping away from work to eat lunch), relational activities (e.g., spending time with a significant other, social support), and spiritual and/or religious activities (e.g., spending time in nature, attending religious services; Carter & Barnett, 2014). The goal of incorporating self-care practices into your life is to find time between professional responsibilities to maintain your physical and mental health. Unfortunately, given the academic and professional expectations involved in graduate training, it can be difficult to find time to engage in self-care, and financial limitations often exist as well (El Ghoroury et al., 2012). If this is the case for you, we recommend adding even small amounts of time into your schedule for free self-care activities. Preparing a self-care plan early on in graduate school will help you get into the habit of balancing your professional responsibilities with your physical and emotional well-being. We recommend getting a copy of the book *Self-Care for Clinicians in Training: A Guide to Psychological Wellness for Graduate Students in Psychology*, by Leigh Carter and Jeffrey Barnett (2014). The authors help students identify sources of distress, develop a self-care action plan, and help promote a self-care culture within their graduate program.

Stage 4: Action

This stage is just what it sounds like—it is when you put your plan into action! It is like getting up and going to the gym. Executing your plan will take a good deal of effort, because your goal is to develop new work habits, and forming new habits is hard work! Think of someone trying to climb a steep hill—it can be done, but there will probably be a lot of sweating and some pain. It will certainly not feel like a leisurely walk in the park! One thing that can help is to make your commitment to act known to people who can hold you accountable and be encouraging, such as your faculty mentors and peers. The good news is that starting to take action will likely reap rewards (e.g., feeling good about yourself, receiving praise from your mentor, seeing your progress), making it more likely that you will continue to follow through on your plan.

Processes That Can Help

Two behavioral processes can propel you forward from the beginning of the action stage. The first is rewarding yourself for your work! At the very least, be sure to be your own cheerleader and congratulate yourself on your accomplishments. Even completing small steps toward your larger project goals can feel intrinsically wonderful if you allow yourself to feel that way. Be sure to build in some external reward as well! Did you accomplish something on your list? Watch a movie or go for ice cream. It is important to build in reinforcement for your achievements, or they will likely feel anticlimactic. Contingencies, such as "If I complete X, I will reward myself with Y," can help motivate you to keep working. You can also reward yourself for putting effort into your self-care plan (e.g., "After I complete my workout, I can watch an episode on Netflix."). The trick is to only allow yourself the reward if you accomplish the work allotted for it. Try to involve your friends or family in this process. For example, as you move forward with your project, you might plan to go out to dinner once you submit a proposal draft to your chair or plan a vacation as a reward for getting through your proposal meeting. Having others involved in your reward system can increase the chances that you will have to do the work to obtain the reward.

The second process at the action stage refers to stimulus control, or creating an environment where you will feel cued to work. This should be a place that is free of distractions (e.g., from television, your friends) where you have adequate space to work. Getting used to working in a specific place can condition you to get started once you are sitting there. You might also try placing signs in your workspace, reminding you of your reasons to keep working. When you are planning to work, avoid places (e.g., your bed) and people (even well-meaning ones!) who are likely to distract you from your efforts. Similarly, try to create a separate space for engaging in self-care. For example, can you create a cozy spot reserved for reading fiction or meditating? Remember to maintain supportive relationships and productive behaviors that prevent procrastination.

Stage 5: Maintenance

You enter this stage when making progress toward your final project has become a real habit, like a person who sticks to their weekly gym routine. You will have finally established a pattern of working on your project that works for you (e.g., two hours per day, or one item on your list instead of a specific amount of time). In this stage, you will be able to see how far you have come and experience how making progress feels better over the long term than giving in to procrastination in the short term . You will remain aware of the importance of completing your project. Keep in mind that people who are supportive of your goals can help you stay on track. In this stage, it is important to be aware of triggers that could cause you to relapse into not working (e.g., challenging feedback from your mentor, summer). One strategy for preventing a relapse is viewing any slip-up as a temporary return to a prior stage that you have already surpassed and knowing that you can pass through it again, quickly. Over time, maintaining your work habits will increase your confidence in your abilities. Continue to ensure you are taking time to engage in self-care activities.

Stage 6: Termination

In this final stage, you will likely feel frustrated when something gets in the way of your desire to work on your project! You likely know someone who feels this way about working out. You will feel confident in your ability to complete the project and will not be concerned about relapsing into a state of paralysis. In this stage, you will see the light at the end of the tunnel and keep walking, even running, toward the finish line!

Your Attitude toward Self-Evaluation and Feedback

In Chapter 2, we reviewed several skills for evaluating and improving your research competence. Effectively developing your research competence is facilitated by a positive attitude toward self-evaluation and feedback on your work, which can lead to planning ways to improve. Having a positive attitude may involve something tangible, like being open to working with a writing mentor to remediate your writing skills. It can also mean being willing to ask your faculty advisor how well they think you speak to, engage with, and work with others. Ask yourself the following questions and answer honestly:

- *Your interactions with professionals (e.g., your faculty advisor, applied setting staff, librarians):* Are you open to their ideas? How about their feedback? Are you willing to ask their opinion about how you function in their setting? Do you feel comfortable asking for help in areas where you think you need improvement? Can you think about disagreements as opportunities to understand another's perspective? Are you able to diplomatically ask questions when something is unclear to you?
- *Your writing:* Are you open to feedback about your written ideas? Are you open to feedback about your writing skills (grammar usage? sentence structure? organization? clarity of thought? citation and referencing?)? If needed, are you willing to seek more assistance to get your writing to a professional level?
- *Presenting:* Are you open to standing and speaking in front of a room of professionals/peers/laypeople? Are you open to practicing discussing your project ideas with others? Are you open to welcoming others' feedback about your presentation?
- *Time to conduct your research:* Are you truly comfortable balancing your professional responsibilities with personal self-care? Are you willing to prioritize work on your project (e.g., reading, writing) in your schedule?

Use Worksheet 3.2 to record your answers to these questions. Answering them honestly will help you determine whether you could benefit from adjusting your attitude toward self-evaluation and feedback. It is common for students to have automatic negative thoughts in response to evaluation of their performance, whether it is through self-analysis or receiving input from others. If you find you have difficulty with your openness in any of these areas, the beginning of your program is a fantastic time to work on it. As a first step, you can use Worksheet 3.2 to help restructure your thoughts about situations you are likely to encounter while in school. Some examples of negative thoughts are listed in Table 3.1, along with examples of alternative, more positive attitudes. You may want to discuss any continued attitudinal concerns with a trusted peer and/or faculty advisor who can help you cultivate a plan for improving your attitudes toward self-evaluation and/or feedback.

If you find yourself struggling to change your attitude about self-evaluation and feedback, consider seeking a therapist who can work with you. Cultivating a positive attitude about such experiences can enhance your ability to embark on your final project and will likely facilitate growth in the quality of your work and professional relationships throughout your career.

Table 3.1 Examples of Restructuring Thoughts about Self-Evaluation and Feedback

Event	Negative thought	More positive attitude
The advisor you want to work with does not see the importance of your idea	Now I won't be able to ask her to be my chair.	I could ask her what did not seem important, try to clarify what I was thinking, and ask for guidance about moving forward in a way she would be interested in.
You receive feedback from a professor that your writing needs organizational improvement	This is ridiculous! He does not know what he is talking about! My writing is fine.	I am frustrated with this feedback; at the same time, there may be some truth in it. I will put it down for a couple of days and review it again when I have calmed down. I might also ask them for clarification and/or ask another trusted professor or peer what they think.
Class presentation is coming up and you do not have confidence in your presentation skills	I am so nervous. I know I will probably bomb this.	I know presenting is an important skill to develop. I can practice to prepare and be open to feedback about how I perform.
You are supposed to do work, but it is beautiful outside and you have a book you want to read	It is not fair. I shouldn't have to be working right now.	I would prefer to be outside and reading what I want, but I know I will feel better about myself for getting some work done. I can reward myself for getting a certain amount done by going out for a walk and reading later tonight.

Worksheet 3.1 Evaluating Your Stage of Change and Finding Strategies to Make Progress

Read the section in Chapter 3 called, "How Ready Are You to Do the Work? Stages and Processes of Change." Determine which stage of change you are in and find that stage on this worksheet. Answer the questions to help you find ways to progress through the stage. Use the information you read in the above-mentioned section of Chapter 3 to help you complete this worksheet.

If you have not been working on researching potential project ideas (precontemplation stage):

Question	Answer
Am I reluctant to change (e.g., spend time engaging in tasks such as doing literature searches, discussing ideas with faculty)?	
Am I rebelling against the idea of having to get to work?	
Am I resigned that there is no hope of finding a good idea or a way to handle the workload?	
Am I telling myself that my lack of work (e.g., toward a project idea) is not a problem?	
What information can I gather about steps I can take to move forward (e.g., factors to consider when narrowing interests, important program deadlines)?	
What are some potential consequences of continuing not to get work done (e.g., extending my timeline)?	
Who can I talk to for information, constructive feedback, and a reality check (e.g., mentor, upper-level peers)?	
What will it feel like to start to get the work done?	
What experiences of upper-level peers have I heard about that generate feelings of hope?	

Question	Answer
What inspires me when I think about working on my idea?	
What emotions will I likely feel if I do not get to work?	
How will delaying the work affect those around me (e.g., faculty, peers, significant other, family)?	
How could doing the work positively affect those around me (e.g., faculty, peers, significant other, family)?	
What professional opportunities will I likely have when I move forward with my work (e.g., positive relationships, useful collaborations, meeting program milestones)?	

If you are ambivalent about whether working on project ideas right now is worthwhile (contemplation stage):

Question	Answer
What are some reasons I am ambivalent about getting to work right now?	
What are some risks and rewards of getting to work?	
How do I feel about my current work habits?	
What are my values? My long-term career goals? How do I envision myself?	
Close your eyes and picture yourself behaving in ways that involve getting work done (e.g., researching articles, talking through an idea with a prospective chair). Ask yourself how this image makes you feel.	

If you are ready to commit to action (preparation stage):

Question	Answer
What is my plan of action? What are the next steps I can take?	
What potential problems with my plan may arise?	
What are solutions to address these problems?	
Who can I inform that I am about to put my plan into action (e.g., faculty, peers)?	
What can I tell myself to believe in my ability to get the work done? What knowledge and skills do I already have to do so?	
What skills do I have the ability to acquire to get the work done?	
Set deadlines for each initial step. List them here.	
What choices do I have regarding things I could work on next?	
With whom can I share my commitment to act on my plan (e.g., telling your faculty mentor, family, and/or peers)? Who can help hold me accountable?	
Who can I count on to be supportive of me and the steps I will need to take as I work (e.g., faculty, peers, significant other, family)? In what ways (e.g., as cheerleader, coach, counselor, critic, buddy system)?	

Question	Answer
What can I do to replace problem behaviors (e.g., procrastination) with more productive behaviors?	
How can I ensure self-care is part of my schedule? What kinds of self-care activities seem most important to add or maintain in my schedule?	

If you are ready to put your plan into action (action stage):

Question	Answer
What is the exact plan that I am starting?	
What self-care activities am I doing, and how will I balance them with my professional responsibilities?	
With whom can I share my commitment to act on my plan (e.g., telling your faculty mentor, family, and/or peers)? Who can help hold me accountable?	
What are some rewards that I am likely to receive that will motivate me to keep working (e.g., feeling good about myself, praise from my mentor, seeing my progress)? How about rewards for engaging in self-care?	
What rewards and/or reinforcement can I build in for myself (e.g., self-praise, movie, ice cream, dinner out, vacation)?	
What are some contingencies that could motivate me to keep working (If I complete X, I will reward myself with Y)? How about to continue to engage in self-care? What friends or family could I involve in this plan to make it fun and hold me accountable? How?	
Where are some places that are free of distractions and give me adequate space to get work done? How about where I can engage in self-care?	

Question	Answer
What can I put in my workspace (e.g., signs) to motivate me to get work done?	
When I aim to get work done, what places and people who are likely to distract me should I avoid?	
Who can I count on to be supportive of me and the steps I will need to take as I work (e.g., faculty, peers, significant other, family)? In what ways (e.g., as cheerleader, coach, counselor, critic, buddy system)?	
What can I do to replace problem behaviors (e.g., procrastination) with more productive behaviors?	

If making progress in your work has already become a habit (maintenance stage):

Question	Answer
What is a pattern of working that works for me (e.g., two hours per day, one item on my list at a time)?	
What are some ways I have progressed?	
What are some reasons it is worth continuing to progress rather than procrastinate?	
How can people supportive of my goals help keep me on track?	
What could trigger me to relapse into not working (e.g., challenging feedback from my mentor, summer)? If this happens, what steps I can take to quickly move past a slip-up?	

Question	Answer
What are some work habits I have developed that can help me feel confident about my ability to keep working?	
How can I continue to ensure self-care is part of my schedule?	

If you are almost done (termination stage):

Question	Answer
What makes me feel confident about my ability to complete my project?	
What are some benefits of finishing?	

Worksheet 3.2 Evaluating Your Attitude toward Self-Evaluation and Feedback

Read the section in Chapter 3 called, "Your Attitude toward Self-Evaluation and Feedback."

Part 1: Answer the following questions honestly, circling "Y" for yes and "N" for no. Answering these questions honestly will help you determine whether you might benefit from adjusting your attitude toward self-evaluation and feedback.

Your interactions with professionals (e.g., your faculty advisor, applied setting staff, librarians):	
Are you open to their ideas?	Y / N
Are you open to their feedback?	Y / N
Are you willing to ask their opinion about how you function in their setting?	Y / N
Do you feel comfortable asking for help in areas where you think you need improvement?	Y / N
Can you think about disagreements as opportunities to understand another's perspective?	Y / N
Are you able to diplomatically ask questions when something is unclear to you?	Y / N
Your writing:	
Are you open to feedback about your written ideas?	Y / N
Are you open to feedback about your grammar usage?	Y / N
Are you open to feedback about your sentence structure?	Y / N
Are you open to feedback about your organization?	Y / N
Are you open to feedback about your clarity of thought?	Y / N
Are you open to feedback about your citation and referencing?	Y / N
If needed, are you willing to seek more assistance to get your writing to a professional level?	Y / N
Presenting:	
Are you open to presenting in front of a room of professionals?	Y / N
Are you open to presenting in front of peers?	Y / N
Are you open to presenting in front of laypeople?	Y / N
Are you open to practicing discussing your project ideas with others?	Y / N
Are you open to welcoming others' feedback about your presentation skills?	Y / N
Time to conduct your research:	
Are you truly comfortable with balancing your professional responsibilities with personal self-care?	Y / N
Are you willing to prioritize work on your project (e.g., reading, writing) in your schedule?	Y / N

Part 2: Look at the areas where you answered "No." It is common for students to have automatic negative thoughts in response to evaluation of their performance, whether through self-analysis or in receiving input from others. If you find yourself having difficulty with any of the areas in Part 1, use the following chart to identify specific events in which you find yourself having negative thoughts. Then write down an alternative, positive thought. Use the examples in Table 3.1 to help you generate these thoughts.

Event	Negative thought	More positive attitude

DEVELOPING YOUR PROPOSAL
AND MANAGING YOUR FINAL PROJECT

Chapter 4
Knowledge Needed for Selecting Your Final Project Topic and Developing Your Proposal

Introduction

As you prepare to write your proposal and conduct your final project, you should develop your *knowledge* about the critical evaluation of research, the conduct of research in applied settings, and ethical and professional competence by reviewing the following areas of this chapter:

- Factors to consider when selecting your final project topic (and your project chair)
- Your final project proposal
- Research concepts to help you with your proposal: ethics, measure selection, and data analytic plan
- The proposal defense or meeting

Students in applied graduate programs are typically expected to be trained in empirically supported approaches to research and practice (e.g., American Psychological Association, Commission on Accreditation, 2018). It should follow that students completing a dissertation or thesis have evidence-based recommendations for navigating their final projects. However, as part of our research for this book, we conducted a systematic review of the research on the dissertation process in health services psychology. We found a limited number of studies, making it challenging to provide evidence-based recommendations for a successful dissertation process (Vidair et al., 2019). Nevertheless, in this chapter, we draw on existing literature as well as our experience mentoring students to provide you with requisite knowledge for successfully developing your final project topic and proposal.

Navigating Research in an Applied Graduate Program. Hilary B. Vidair, Pam L. Gustafson, and Eva L. Feindler, Oxford University Press. © Oxford University Press (2024). DOI: 10.1093/oso/9780199352272.003.0004

Factors to Consider When Selecting Your Final Project Topic (and Your Project Chair)

Selecting a topic for your final project is one of the most important decisions you will make in graduate school. If you are a doctoral student, your dissertation will likely be the first independent project for which you will be known. In fact, your dissertation might define your identity in your early career, because colleagues will want to know about your project and may come to consider you an expert in the area. If you are working on a master's thesis, your project could be a step toward applying to doctoral programs, developing a dissertation idea, or launching you on your career path. In addition to your project topic being a key professional decision, it may be one of the most difficult decisions you will face. It can feel like a daunting task; many suffer great angst as they select a topic to study and research questions to answer.

In Chapter 1, we indicated that the path from identifying your areas of interest to selecting a topic for your final project is a developmental process. Refer to Figure 1.6, "Factors to Consider When Narrowing Interests into a Potential Project Area." At this point, you have likely acquired a great deal of knowledge about various project possibilities and learned several ways in which you can select a topic that faculty would consider appropriate for your final project. For example, your topic could reflect an area of practice in which you want to establish yourself as an expert, or it might be rooted in something that will advance your practice with a certain population, problem or disorder, or intervention strategy. Your project is meant to contribute new information to your applied field that can have direct theoretical, methodological, and/or practical implications.

Ideally, you want to choose a topic that you are passionate about, that aligns with at least one faculty member's interests, and that is clearly achievable. On the one hand, a good project topic is delimited, since topics that are overly broad, excessively ambitious, and/or too vague are fraught with challenges and will delay achievement of your goal. On the other hand, your research or scholarly question should not have a simple "yes" or "no" answer, and there should be more justification for your idea than just the fact that no one has done the research yet. A research gap in your area of interest or an extension of previous research makes sense to build on. You can investigate a topic from a different angle, use different methodology, or look at extensions to other populations or settings. Some graduate programs include a dedicated research course or small group tutorial to help you develop your topic into a research question. In other programs, you might do this solely with a faculty member who functions as your research mentor or project chair. We review factors to consider when selecting your final project topic in Figure 4.1. After reading this section, we suggest you complete Worksheet 4.1 to help you move forward.

Figure 4.1 Factors to consider when selecting your final project topic

Am I Passionate Enough about This Topic to Immerse Myself in It?

In Chapter 1, we asked you to think about which parts of your field you could see yourself wanting to focus on for a year or more. This is still something to strongly consider! Given that you will devote a great deal of time to this one topic from the beginning to the end of your project, we recommend focusing on an area that is of great interest to you. The topic should be able to sustain your attention and motivation during the process of developing, executing, and completing your project, which at times can be challenging.

Who Should I Select as My Chair and Committee Members for This Project?

Selecting a chair to work with can be just as important as how interested you are in your topic. Your chair will be responsible for guiding you through the entire project process, including writing drafts, managing the execution of your project, and navigating professional relationships, including those you might have with your project committee, the institutional review board (IRB), research assistants, and/or any staff in applied settings you involve. Some programs will refer to this person as your project sponsor or advisor. Unfortunately, there is no course in how to be an effective dissertation or thesis chairperson. Most individuals learn this process by first being a dissertation student themselves and then being involved over time with helping students earn their degrees. There are many factors to consider when picking a chair. Next, we will explore what a chair does, who can typically be a chair, and factors to consider when reviewing your options.

What Does a Chair Do?

The chair of your dissertation or thesis usually has broad power and influence throughout the process of completing your final project. The specifics of their role may vary from program to program, so you will need to determine the roles, guidelines, and selection timeline adhered to in your program. Most likely, your chair will do the following:

- Be the first person who needs to approve your initial project topic, research question(s), research design, and methodology
- Help you pick or suggest additional committee members for your project (something we will discuss later in this chapter)
- Help you organize ideas for your research proposal (e.g., via an outline) and read through drafts of your written proposal, making edits and suggestions where needed
- Over time, help you navigate your relationships with committee members, the IRB, research assistants, and, if applicable, staff at applied settings who are assisting you with your research
- Approve of your proposal and signal your readiness to send the proposal to your other committee members
- Guide you through your proposal meeting (also discussed later in this chapter)
- Oversee revisions to your original proposal
- Guide your IRB application, sign off when it is deemed ready, and assist you in responding to the IRB's feedback
- Help you manage any challenges you encounter as you conduct your project
- Eventually give you the green light to send your complete written project to your committee members

- Guide you through your dissertation or thesis defense, which is typically the gateway to completing your degree
- Oversee revisions to your final project write-up and sign off on completion of your project

Who Can Be a Chair?

Typically, chairs are expected to be part of a program's core faculty, though some programs allow students to choose a chair from outside the department, such as an adjunct in the department, a faculty member from another department in the university, or someone with a doctoral degree who works outside the university. Choosing a chair from the latter situations may require your program's approval.

What Factors Should I Consider When Reviewing Potential Candidates for the Position?

Before making any decisions, take time to gather some "data," which will aid you in the selection process. Consider the factors we discussed in Figure 1.6 regarding which of your interests are compatible with faculty members' interests. Sometimes, deciding who you would like to have as your chair goes hand in hand with selecting a topic in a particular research area. As we mentioned, if you have already spent time working in a lab or on a research team, you might be aligned with a faculty member with whom you would like to continue to conduct your research. There might also be an "expert" in your program with whom you would like to do research. However, be careful not to equate being an expert with being a good research advisor! A faculty member's real interest in your topic and enthusiasm for working with you might suit you better. It may not be necessary for your chair to have expertise in your exact topic area; instead, they may have experience with the type of methodology or analyses you plan to use, and you can round out your team by choosing committee members who are familiar with your topic's content. Be sure to also think about whose feedback has been helpful to you, who appears interested in working with you, who you have heard is a good chair, and whose supervisory style would likely work for you.

If your program has a final project database, consider reviewing it to address some of the following questions: What types of projects has each of the faculty members chaired? What types of methodology have their students used? If a faculty member has chaired many projects using qualitative methodology, you might conclude that is their preferred research approach. If a faculty member has chaired and eventually published a number of meta-analyses, this might be a clue to their interests. If this information is not readily available in your program, you could consult alumni or see whether there is a listing of past projects in your university library's database.

It is also important to determine when you need to secure a chair and give yourself ample time to find and evaluate your options. Every program has its own timeline, which may be delineated in your program's handbook. Some programs include chair selection as part of a course, while others simply give a deadline. Prior to securing a chair, it makes sense to spend some time interviewing faculty members with whom you are interested in working. Prepare yourself to sell your proposal idea, particularly if you are approaching someone with whom you have not already done research. You might even have a short version of your proposal ready should they want to read it beforehand. Here is an example of what you might write to a potential chair over email:

Dear _____,

   I hope all is well. I have been thinking a lot about beginning the dissertation/thesis/final project process and have an idea/some ideas that I would like to discuss with you. Given your current enthusiasm/research/work for/in _____, I believe it would be helpful to hear your thoughts about my next steps. Would it be possible for us to meet to discuss this/these idea(s)? If so, what are some possible days and times when we could meet? Attached please find a written statement/outline/proposal of my idea(s). Please let me know if I should send you any additional information. I appreciate your time and consideration.

Best,
Student name

If the faculty member arranges to meet with you, prepare some questions to ask in advance. Some of these questions will be specific to your potential project topic(s). Others should be about what it would be like to work with them as your chair. Below are some questions to consider regarding how a faculty member might chair a project:

- Are you able to take on new students?
- What strategies do you use to help students hone their ideas and refine their hypotheses/research questions/scholarly projects?
- What types of projects or research designs are you willing to chair or do you feel comfortable chairing?
- How much do you generally expect students' topic areas to overlap with your areas of expertise? Are there any conditions under which you would chair a student's research idea if it was outside your area of expertise?
- What is your accessibility and availability during the time it will take for me to complete my project? (Ask about sabbatical or retirement plans.)
- What are your preferred ways and style of supervising research projects? (Determine frequency of contact and how to manage multiple drafts.)
- How collaborative would you like to be? Do you recommend that I work with other specific individuals as well?
- Are there other faculty members or outside experts with whom you suggest I consult?
- What are the average times to completion for your former or current students?

- Would we potentially be able to present our research/scholarly work together at conferences and/or submit our results for possible publication? How would credit for this work be assigned?

Be up front about what you are aiming to achieve at this point. In the sample email, notice that the student only indicated interest in the faculty member's feedback. There was no request for the professor to be their chair. We recommend just "window shopping" at this stage so you can weigh your options. This is usually acceptable, as long as you are clear about your intentions. Alternatively, if you *do* want to ask someone to be your chair, you can be more direct, either in your email or in person. Keep in mind, however, that once a faculty member agrees to be your chair, it will be difficult to change your mind. Students may also find themselves in a situation where they did not ask a faculty member to be their chair, but the person assumed they would hold the position. We will review skills for managing situations like this in the troubleshooting skills section of Chapter 5.

Working with Junior versus Senior Faculty
The faculty members in your graduate department likely vary in status: some may be new to the department, whereas others can be considered senior faculty. There are advantages and disadvantages to choosing a chair from either end of the continuum. Table 4.1 lists some pros and cons of working with a junior versus a senior faculty member.

Working Style and Personality Characteristics
Given that you will be working very closely with your final project chair for an extended period, we suggest that you consider their working style and personality characteristics. Some questions to consider include the following:

- How much time will they be able to give you and when? What is their turnaround time for drafts, IRB proposals, and general feedback? Are you fairly independent and want a more laissez-faire style? Or are you looking for regular feedback with agreed-on mini-deadlines?
- How well do you write and how important is that to your potential chair?
- How is feedback delivered? How detailed is the feedback?
- How empathically attuned might your potential chair be, and how much empathy do you need and/or expect?

Next, we will discuss some styles and characteristics to be wary of when chair shopping. Keep in mind that every student–chair relationship is interactional, and chairs likely vary at least somewhat in their behavior with different students. Although we include some extreme examples of the characteristics discussed here, we think it is important to consider whether your potential chair falls into one or more of these categories in general. Do keep in mind, however, that there is no such thing as a

Table 4.1 Pros and Cons for Working with a Junior versus a Senior Faculty Member

Pros for choosing junior faculty	Cons for choosing junior faculty
They are perhaps younger, more energetic, and more enthusiastic about working with graduate students because they remember the process well.	Junior faculty members might be inexperienced as far as mentoring graduate student research or scholarly projects, perhaps only having their own recent experience to draw from.
They are probably quite motivated to make connections with students and engage in collaborative research, and they may have some very cutting-edge interests.	Their status in the department might be tenuous or temporary depending on the faculty line and their process with tenure.
They likely have small labs and need and/or want to work with students as they embark on their professional journey.	They may not have established working relationships with other individuals needed for your committee.
They might be more likely to provide lots of hands-on mentoring and research supervision because they, too, are looking for positive evaluations as they approach promotion and tenure decisions.	Typically, junior faculty members are under enormous pressure to produce and might need you to conduct research for them rather than follow your own line of thinking.
	They may not have a track record in a defined research area and could have limited resources.

Pros for choosing senior faculty	Cons for choosing senior faculty
These faculty members are likely very knowledgeable in particular areas, might have significant research projects and/or publications, and perhaps enjoy a national reputation. Your affiliation with them could lead to a number of career opportunities.	The generation gap and/or age difference between you and your advisor could lead to misunderstandings.
They have trained far more students and might have significant research resources, including relationships with applied settings and already gathered data sets.	More senior faculty may be experiencing burnout after a long career, may not have much time or attention for you, could be in an outdated research area, and may have many outside responsibilities.
They have much more advisement experience and perhaps will foster your independence in research pursuits.	They may delegate the bulk of your final project supervision to someone in their lab who is less senior or even a postdoctoral fellow.
Senior faculty may have significant connections with other committee members who could be on your committee.	There is a chance they could go on sabbatical or retirement during your research process, which would likely impact your work together.

perfect chair, and you might not have many choices. Ideally, you will find a healthy balance of characteristics that works for you!

Overachiever

This type of chair might be caught up in their own research and scholarly goals, as well as their interest in publications and/or grant funding. In this case, their research productivity may be more important than supervising a student project, especially if it is unrelated to their own pursuits. You will likely have to be involved in their projects and have less room to explore your own research ideas.

Underachiever

This type of chair might eschew research and perhaps has not done much since their own dissertation. They likely did some publishing to achieve tenure status, but may not have what it takes to guide you in completing the type of final project you desire.

Micromanager

This type of chair wants too much control over your project. They may try to persuade you to shift the focus of your topic more than you think is necessary, dictate your exact method even though multiple options are presented in the literature, or expect to meet with you to review every detail of every step before you proceed.

Empty Cheerleader

This type of chair repeatedly tells you that you are doing well, but does not provide you with constructive feedback. Although they say you are doing a great job, they may not alert you to significant problems with your project or prepare you for questions your committee might ask. This kind of feedback alone will not help you improve the quality of your project.

Naysayer

This type of chair is hypercritical of your ideas and responds with negativity or cynicism to practically every idea you suggest. It is useful to receive honest feedback when an idea does not sound worthwhile; however, it is not helpful to have your thoughts repeatedly criticized or shut down, particularly if no constructive recommendations are made.

Contradictory

This occurs when you and a chair each have an idea that appears to directly contradict the other's, but either they expect you to find a way to do both or they explain the negatives of both pathways but do not suggest alternative options or solutions to the obstacles. This can also refer to a chair who does not help you problem-solve when your committee members have contradictory expectations for your project.

All about Me

This type of chair wants their own name to be in the spotlight. You can expect that they will tell everyone about your project, but connecting your name with it will likely be an afterthought, if it is mentioned at all. Be prepared for your ideas to somehow become the chair's ideas; they may even tell you how much they appreciate you deciding to carry the idea out for them. Also be prepared to repeatedly tell them how great they are—not only for the time and effort they put into your project, but also in general.

Perfectionist

This type of chair expects your work to be close to perfect before you can move forward. For example, small mistakes that most chairs would expect to be corrected after a proposal meeting might need to be fixed before scheduling the proposal meeting in the first place. The chair may know every formatting rule in the American Psychological Association's (APA's) style manual and expect you to adhere to it to the letter. It may be hard for this type of chair to allow you to move forward before revisiting the same written section, decision, and/or statistical analysis several times.

Unreachable

This refers to an unresponsive chair. They do not respond to emails you send and/or rarely agree to meet with you. You submit drafts and hear nothing, leaving you wondering how to proceed. They may make promises to send you things but keep you waiting.

Callous

This type of chair lacks sensitivity toward you and your circumstances. They may not be interested in small talk, wanting to keep every meeting very focused on your project. If you are feeling stressed and communicate that, they are not likely to convey much empathy. At worst, if you become emotional, they may firmly tell you to get yourself together or simply continue to discuss your project. This type of chair would not fulfill your need for psychosocial (i.e., life) mentoring!

Too Personal

This type of chair discloses more personal information than you are comfortable being privy to and/or asks you questions or makes comments about your personal life to the point where you feel uncomfortable. For example, they may go into excessive detail about personal relationship history or family conflicts or ask you to share information about your family dynamics and not respect your boundaries. In some cases, there may be sexual undertones or even more direct sexual comments.

What Engenders Positive Versus Negative Experiences with Chairs?

Students report both positive and negative experiences and interactions with their final project chairs (Burkard et al., 2014; Knox et al., 2011). In one mixed methods study using qualitative interviews, psychology doctoral students with positive dissertation experiences reported having supportive advisee and committee member relationships, which bolstered their confidence about conducting research and their professional advancement (Burkard et al., 2014). In contrast, those who reported negative experiences felt that they had challenging advisory relationships, including chairs and committee members who provided little guidance or took advantage of their power. They described how these relational difficulties negatively affected their emotions and professional development, even after graduation. These students' projects often focused on their own interests, and they had not worked with their chair prior to their dissertation (e.g., in a lab). A quantitative portion of the study found that students who reported positive experiences indicated having a significantly better working alliance with their chairs than those who reported negative experiences. A second qualitative study explored the experiences of chairs and found they expected students to maintain good relationships with them and their committee members, conduct independent work, and hold responsibility for their project (Knox et al., 2011). The chairs described positive experiences when they had collaborated with the student in the past, felt they had a positive working relationship, and found the student to be motivated and competent. Difficult relationships with students translated into negative advising experiences. Overall, it appears important to prioritize the cultivation of healthy, strong working relationships when considering chairs and committee members.

Choosing Your Committee Members

Applied graduate programs commonly include a requirement for students to gather a committee that will be responsible for evaluating their final project, even at the proposal stage. Once you and your chair have agreed on your proposed project, your attention can turn to selecting the other committee members (or outside readers, as some programs refer to them). Check your program's guidelines about who can serve as a committee member. Potential options typically include other faculty members in your program or university, someone with a doctoral degree who works outside your university who has expertise in your topic area, or a clinical supervisor from one of your practicum sites.

The overall responsibilities of committee members are to provide, in collaboration with the chair, timely and thorough guidance to a graduate student on their project, from the proposal draft to the project defense. At minimum, a committee member will read your proposal once it is approved by your chair, prior to your proposal meeting, and read your full research project draft once your chair approves it, prior to your defense. A committee member might also help you develop your specific research design or extract and analyze data.

The role of the project committee is to provide a system of checks and balances and act as an additional set of eyes to examine you as a candidate to be awarded a graduate degree, potentially of the highest distinction. No single professor can make this determination; rather, the decision of whether you pass your defense will be made by a group of professionals who have supervised you throughout the process. Having multiple committee members also helps to ensure that you have sufficient room for your own creativity and independent inquiry, because unfortunately, at times, overly powerful chairs or even committee members push their own agenda. Think of your committee members as watching out for you in this unique way.

Each committee takes its own form, and students must take responsibility for knowing what each committee member expects; students must also know what they expect of their committee members. Nevertheless, you can make the following generalizations.

Read the Guidelines in Your Department Handbook

Beyond consulting with your chair, check to see whether your program handbook contains any information about selecting committee members. For example, the number and qualifications of potential committee members may vary from program to program. Usually there are at least two other committee members, but there may be as many as four. Some programs require that at least one committee member be from within the department, while other programs encourage or require an outside reader. In addition, programs may have certain expectations regarding qualifications (e.g., an alumnus from your program might need to be four years postdegree).

Check the deadline and any paperwork necessary for obtaining committee members. For example, some programs will ask you to register for a course related to your final project and will need the names of your committee members to align with the course registration. You may also need committee members to sign an agreement.

Choose Committee Members Whom You Work Well With and Who Work Well Together

Hopefully, you have already established a good working relationship with possible committee members. You may want to contact former students who have worked with faculty members in your department and ask about their experiences. In addition, ask your chair about their relationships with the faculty members you are considering and see if you can learn any history that could indicate how the group might get along. You do not want to compromise your process because of faculty members who have a history of not working well together.

Consider Committee Members as Additional Sources of Expertise

Considering your topic, your methodology, and your working style, develop a list of possible committee members and review it with your chair. Your chair may have additional insights and suggestions. It might be helpful for your members to have expertise that your chair does not. For example, if you and your chair are enthusiastic about a project topic with a particular participant sample, but have minimal knowledge about assessment tools to use as dependent measures or how to plan for sophisticated statistical analyses, this might lead you to consider someone with those competencies for your committee.

If you are conducting your project in an applied setting, it can be useful to invite a key professional from the site to be part of your committee. This will enhance your rapport with them and strengthen their involvement in your project. They can also help inform your chair about the culture of the site and what is feasible to do there. Professionals in applied settings often work primarily in practice or administration and welcome the opportunity to be involved in an academic endeavor. Many also enjoy the training component of being part of a final project committee.

Be Clear about the Role a Particular Person Can Play on Your Committee

Try to meet or speak with potential committee members to determine whether they have the interest or time to commit to working on your project. Be sure they can provide the expertise or assistance you are looking for. You want to be sure you clarify what role they will play from the start. For example, a faculty member may have expertise in statistics but have guidelines about the kind of statistical support they can offer you as a committee member rather than as your chair. You do not want to be in a situation where you assume they will teach you how to conduct a certain analysis only to find out that they expect you to learn to conduct it independently or hire a consultant. Ideally, you want committee members who understand you and your research project, who are supportive of you, and who will provide you with timely and constructive feedback on your work.

Know What to Say to Potential Committee Members

Inviting other faculty members to be committee members on your research project takes a bit of planning. Prepare a short summary of your proposed research interests as well as an idea of your design and methodology, which you can first email to faculty members you think would be good to have on your committee. You can then ask if they would like to follow up with an in-person meeting. In your meeting, try to assess whether the person has enthusiasm for your ideas, initial thoughts about your project, and the time to contribute. You do not need a committee member who thinks your project is the ultimate investigation, but you will benefit from someone who is interested in exploring the area along with you.

In the face-to-face meeting, you can ask individual faculty members about being on your committee. Have a working draft of your proposal available, as well as an initial timeline of how you expect to meet all of the steps in the process. Make sure to complete all necessary paperwork. If they give you a firm commitment, your department might require you to sign and submit an official form. You can now indicate to your committee members when you expect to have your written proposal completed. Ask up front how each committee member wants to handle questions and/or revisions to your proposal. For example, some faculty will send you a written proposal with tracked changes and other edits before your proposal meeting, while others prefer to give their feedback at the meeting itself.

Working with Your Committee Members

Prior to your proposal meeting, you should touch base periodically with your committee members to keep them abreast of your progress. Some committee members are willing to read sections prior to reading a full final proposal draft. Most will just want a brief update on your progress. We advise you to have at least some communication so that your committee members do not receive the written proposal without having had opportunities to discuss your research and/or scholarly questions and methodology with you alone. Your chair may have preferences about how often you should communicate with your committee members or ask you to consult a committee member about a particular issue. Keep your chair apprised of any meetings you do have with committee members: a simple email will often suffice. We will address skills for managing difficulties with committee members in Chapter 5.

What Will Be the Purpose of My Project?

It can be hard to narrow down a specific purpose for your final project. As you read and critically evaluate literature in your topic area, take note of what has and has not been done. What are some key findings or products that seem to be missing? What do researchers in your area indicate as limitations and/or next steps for future research or scholarly work? Beyond what others say, what do you think are the limitations and potential future directions? Find a way your project could address gaps and serve as the next step in the existing literature.

Once you have a sense of what your project's purpose could be, experiment with writing it out in a clear, succinct sentence that includes key variables or concepts and foreshadows the type of research design you might consider. We will discuss more about how to word the purpose of your study in Chapter 5. For now, it can be helpful to create a brief working explanation of your project's purpose, because you will likely need to start sharing it with people who ask about it, including faculty, peers, and people interviewing you for practica, internships, and jobs.

Why Is My Project Important? How Can the Outcomes Make a Valuable Contribution to the Field?

It is important to have a convincing rationale for why people should care about what you plan to study or produce. As we mentioned in Chapter 1, the results of your final project should build on existing knowledge, generate or revise theory, and/or propose solutions to an existing issue. Ideally, the outcomes of an applied project have practical (e.g., clinical or educational) implications. Typically, your findings will also have theoretical and/or methodological implications that can guide directions for future research. We encourage you to share your ideas about your area of interest with your peers and faculty to determine if they think your idea could advance your field in some way.

Study Participants and Procedures: Who, What, Where, When, How?

You will have to determine whether you are going to recruit a new sample, have access to an existing data set, or conduct a project that does not analyze data. For some, this process is sequential (i.e., select a topic, find a chair, decide on a sample); for others, multiple parts of the process can occur at the same time. For example, you might have your research question and access to a data set and be looking for a project chair.

In Chapter 1, we discussed ideas for modifying your project by being creative about the sample you use and determining whether you have access to a data set. At this point, you will need to become clear on the specific methodology for your project. For example, if you plan to recruit participants, you will need to determine who you will include in the study and the sampling strategy you will employ. For student projects, it is typical to recruit a sample of convenience (i.e., eligible people who are willing to volunteer and to whom you have access). In qualitative research projects, sampling is often purposive; that is, participants are nonrepresentative of a population and are selected when they have information relevant to the study's purpose. This can be followed by snowball sampling, a method in which existing participants refer the researcher to other people who could potentially participate in or contribute to the study. This method is often used to find and recruit "hidden populations," that is, groups that are not easily accessible to researchers through other sampling strategies.

In addition, you will have to address the following procedural issues: where you will recruit from, whose permission you will need (e.g., the IRB, a leader in an organization), where and how you will advertise the study, who will recruit and/or administer your study's procedure, when and where you will be able to conduct the study, and what your procedure will be for collecting and/or analyzing data to answer your research questions (e.g., surveys, interviews, focus groups, observations). Will you be able to provide participants with some type of compensation, and if so, what will it be? Might you use a raffle, where only some participants would be awarded compensation?

Considering potential participant compensation, measures that may cost money to use, and/or survey or statistical programs that may be needed, project costs can start to add up. Now is the time to calculate total estimated costs and determine whether there are grants or other funding opportunities you can apply for to receive assistance in covering them (see Chapter 1 for comments on potential internal and external funding opportunities). Alternatively, think about any personal funds you may be able to obtain and set aside for these purposes (or family you might ask for assistance) and ensure you consider them in your overall budget.

You will also need to determine whether there are standard measures available to assess your variables or if you will be developing questions. If you plan to use the Internet to collect survey data, you will want to become familiar with survey programs you might use. Some current survey programs include SurveyMonkey, Google Forms, and REDCap.

The Importance of Consultation in an Applied Setting
If your project will involve conducting research in an applied setting, be sure to determine which key administrators and staff you can consult as you work on your

proposal. As we noted in previous chapters, it is valuable to consult and collaborate with people who work in the setting because they are likely to understand what is feasible and acceptable to staff and consumers attending their site, be knowledgeable about on-site resources you have access to, and help you navigate site limitations. Refer to Chapter 1 for ideas on what to discuss when developing your project. Remember to obtain permission to recruit and/or conduct the project and an understanding of who will be responsible for each part of the procedure. The IRB will typically request a letter of support from the director or key personnel at the site indicating that they have agreed to the procedure you outlined in your IRB application. Most students propose before developing their IRB application, so in order to work on your written proposal, you will want to have these discussions right away. We recommend discussing each person's role in the project as well as future authorship agreements up front to avoid later confusion or tension.

Student Examples: The Value of Consultation about Your Proposal in an Applied Setting

ML was interested in conducting an experiment focused on the Stanford marshmallow experiment, a study on delayed gratification, among children diagnosed with attention deficit/hyperactivity disorder in a community mental health setting. He consulted with the director there, who eagerly supported the project. Together, they worked out who would be eligible to participate, when the experiment could be conducted, and which staff could be asked to administer the study's procedure. ML invited the director to be on his project committee. She accepted and reviewed drafts of ML's proposal. She also helped ML coordinate a training session for the staff.

A student wanted to use an existing data set for their final project. They consulted with the principal investigator of the data and discussed potential project ideas based on the information available. The student asked about eventual authorship. They were told that even though it would be their dissertation, they would not be able to publish the project as first author. The student thanked the investigator for their time and consideration, but ultimately chose to pursue another dissertation idea.

Theoretical or Scholarly Projects

If you plan to conduct a theoretical or scholarly project, you will need to determine whether you have access to enough background literature, people, and/or other resources to conduct your project. Even if you are not collecting or analyzing data, your chair and committee members will likely expect a written proposal regarding how you plan to proceed with your project. Reviewing a written plan with your committee will allow you to assess what is feasible and what parts of your proposal need to be modified.

What Are the Strengths and Limitations of Different Research and Scholarly Designs?

In Chapter 1, we discussed the need to weigh the importance of internal versus external validity, because the strength of one is usually a limitation of the other. For example, you could conduct a study of program efficacy in a lab setting with very specific eligibility criteria and a methodologically rigorous procedure. Your findings would likely have strong internal validity, but would not generalize to a study conducted in a real-world setting where people present with multiple problems, such as comorbid diagnoses, a lack of resources, or time constraints. Conducting feasible research in settings such as schools or clinics necessitates more flexible study procedures to accommodate these realities. This would lead to stronger external validity, but weaker internal validity.

Also in Chapter 1, we provided a brief overview of several research designs and types of projects students may choose to conduct. Students sometimes ask which design will be easier for them to conduct, and we tell them that there is no such thing as an easy final project! They will all have challenging pieces. However, there is some truth to the fact that different types of designs have different kinds of challenges. By the time you are selecting your topic idea, you should have a good understanding of the strengths and limitations of different types of projects, as well as the practical issues that are important to consider. We provide a brief overview of the strengths and limitations of various quantitative designs in Table 4.2, followed by a description of the strengths and limitations of qualitative designs (see Table 4.3) and a similar description for theoretical and scholarly projects (see Table 4.4).

Strengths and Limitations of Qualitative Designs

As we discussed in Chapter 1, there are several types of qualitative designs, including narrative, phenomenological, grounded theory approaches, participatory action research, ethnography, and case studies. Although the specific goals and methods of these designs differ, they all generally include a focus on participants' experiences and the use of words in data analysis. Next, we describe the strengths, limitations, and practical issues involved in various types of qualitative research.

Table 4.2 Strengths and Limitations of Various Quantitative Research Designs

Study type	Strengths	Limitations	Practical issues
Quantitative	Allows for assessment of statistically significant differences between groups or significant associations between variables	Does not provide an in-depth look at participants' experiences	Will I obtain a large enough sample size for the analyses I plan to conduct? Am I generally comfortable with statistics (or the idea of learning to use them)? For a treatment study, how long will it take me to collect the data? What if my participants drop out prematurely?
True experimental	Methodologically rigorous, can assess cause and effect	Strong internal validity often means limited generalizability to the real world	Is it ethical and practical to randomize participants in this study?
Quasi-experimental	Allows you to get close to a true experiment when randomization to groups is not ethical or practical	Lack of randomization can mean that findings could be the result of extraneous variables (e.g., differences between groups at baseline)	How likely is it that my groups will be equal with the exception of how the independent variable is manipulated?
Single-case design	Can use individuals as their own control to systematically assess for behavioral changes in one or multiple individual participants	Lack of generalizability because of small sample size; ABAB designs may include an intervention that changes behavior even when it is removed, so you cannot expect a return to baseline levels of behavior	Can I expect participants to stay in my study across multiple assessment points?
Correlational or predictive	Can assess for associations between variables without intervening; good for assessing relationships along dimensions rather than between groups	Cannot assess causality; findings could be the result of extraneous variables	Do I have strong enough theory to support the need to assess my hypothesized relationships between variables?

Study type	Strengths	Limitations	Practical issues
Observational: comparative or case–control	Can compare existing groups without intervening when manipulation of the independent variable is not ethical or practical	Cannot assess cause and effect; existing groups can mean that findings could be the result of extraneous variables; retrospective designs rely on participants' memories, which can be faulty	How likely is it that these groups are the same with the exception of the naturally occurring independent variable? Can I expect to find a sample that includes participants both with and without the variable of interest?
Descriptive	Can explore characteristics of a sample without intervening (e.g., frequencies and percentages)	Cannot assess causality; some committees may criticize this type of study for its lack of traditional hypotheses	How can I develop a strong rationale for focusing my study on a description of characteristics within a particular sample?
Meta-analysis	Can assess outcomes from an aggregate of existing studies	Studies included have already been conducted, so procedures and variables are fixed	Can I find a project chair who is capable and willing to supervise my project? Do I have the unique statistical skills necessary to conduct this project?
Scale development	Can contribute an innovative and important assessment tool to the field	May take a long time to gather necessary data; may be challenging to find scales with which to compare for assessment of validity	Is there a strong rationale for an innovative scale in this area? Do I have access to a large enough sample and the time to collect these data? Are there existing measures that I can compare my scale to?
Program evaluation	Can assess the effectiveness of a program and how resources should be allocated	Not necessarily able to assume causation because of a lack of control group or randomization	Am I developing a program as well as evaluating it? If it is not my program, do I have an agreement up front about data ownership and agreement to report the results regardless of the findings?

Table 4.3 Strengths and Limitations of Qualitative Designs

Study type	Strengths	Limitations and practical issues
Qualitative	• Useful for describing complex phenomena • Flexibility and adaptability in research design, can work from participants' reactions • Ability to explore and capture subjective perspective • Can complement quantitative data by providing greater depth and detailed information than statistics	• Time-consuming for participants and researchers • Issues related to generalizability • Lacks objectivity • Patterns can be hard to detect • Not easily replicated when compared to quantitative research • Issues of anonymity and confidentiality present problems when selecting findings • More difficult to find scholarly resources that actively publish qualitative manuscripts • Interpretation is more individualized than with quantitative research • Potential researcher bias • If using coders, includes time to train them
Narrative	• Describes participants' oral stories in detail, emphasizing contextual factors in great depth • Active participation from researchers with a goal to accomplish very particular aims • Extra attention to participants' descriptions of sequences of action, analyzing intention and language	• Relies heavily on participants being able to recall information and experiences accurately • Findings are not easily categorized or comparable among participants • There is conflict and disagreement among those holding different perspectives • The working definition of narrative and related analyses varies across disciplines • The oral stories can go in many directions depending on the interviewer and/or researcher
Phenomenological	• Useful for describing how people perceive an event or phenomenon • Examines the uniqueness of each participant's experience	• Findings described from participants' subjective perspective, challenging the reliability and validity of findings • Open-ended interviews often leave room for interpretation and bias
Grounded theory	• Helpful in understanding phenomena that have not been explained with existing theories	• Questions in interviews are often very general and leave room for interpretation and bias

Study type	Strengths	Limitations and practical issues
	• Consists of a systematic, but flexible method meant for generating theory • Focuses on coding strategies that are inherently comparative and interactive throughout the research process	• There are no standard rules to follow for the identification of categories • There is often a lack of preexisting data to support findings
Participatory action research (PAR)	• Collaboration between researchers and participants at every stage, utilizing discussion, pooling skills, and working together • When compared to other quantitative methods, individuals or groups have maximum control over all aspects of the research	• Very time-consuming since problems are explored over time • Attrition • There is a possibility that participants' situations can change when studied over time • The PAR approach is often used loosely, rather than adhering to a particular method • Results are not always accessible, comprehensible, and immediately responsive to the needs of groups that use them • Lack of knowledge about PAR may make it less acceptable for use in a final project
Ethnography	• Useful to describe a culture's characteristics • Holistic outlook in research to gain a complete picture of a social group • Captures an understanding and description of a social and cultural scene from the insider's perspective	• Very time-consuming since problems are explored over time • Must be conducted on-site; all data collection occurs via fieldwork (less convenient than collecting data in a lab) • Ethnographers must be conscious of within-group diversity • It might be difficult to maintain a nonjudgmental stance about a given cultural practice
Case study	• Useful in describing the in-depth experience of one person, family, group, community or institution • Case studies can be a major source of theoretical innovation	• Uncontrolled and rely heavily on subjective interpretation • Tend to not focus on specific research goals • Less equipped for inferring external validity

Note: The information in this table is largely based on the *Sage Encyclopedia of Qualitative Research Methods* (Given, 2008).

Strengths and Limitations of Theoretical and Scholarly Projects

As discussed in Chapter 1, theoretical and scholarly projects aim to rely on existing theory and research to develop either an innovative way of understanding a phenomenon or case or an innovative program or treatment. These projects often do not include data collection. Table 4.4 describes some strengths and limitations of these types of projects.

Table 4.4 Strengths and Limitations of Theoretical and Scholarly Projects

Project type	Strengths	Limitations	Practical issues
Theoretical project or critical analysis of the literature	Demonstrates strong critical thinking skills; can contribute a novel and important theory or synthesis of existing literature with suggestions for next steps	Need excellent critical thinking and writing skills; some programs and/or committees are wary of approving theoretical or conceptual ideas that do not include any empirical study; even with a systematic review, some committees will expect statistical analyses	Do I think I can develop an innovative theory or critical review in this area based on a comprehensive review of existing literature? Do I have strong critical thinking and writing skills?
Extended case study	Very relevant to receiving an applied degree; an opportunity to study a case in depth	Some programs may have a clinical competency evaluation that expects you to conduct this type of project in addition to your final project; cannot generalize information to other cases	Have I worked comprehensively with a case that I can describe and study in rich detail?
Systematic development of an innovative program manual, curriculum, book, or guide	Contributes an innovative program manual or curriculum, book, or guide to your field or an adaptation of an existing one for a novel population, problem, or setting	Some programs and/or committee members will be wary of program manuals, curricula, books, or guides that are not empirically studied as part of the project; a study may not include a control group, meaning that findings could be the result of extraneous variables rather than the manual's protocol	Does there seem to be a strong rationale for the development of an innovative program, curriculum, book, or guide in this area?

How Will This Project Fit into My Graduate School Timeline?

Your final project will involve an extensive set of steps, such as a review of relevant literature, time to write and rewrite several times, meetings to approve next steps, potential collaboration with an outside organization, IRB approval, data collection, forming and training of coding teams, data analysis, time to ponder your results and develop thoughtful conclusions, and multiple consultations with your project chair and/or committee. Personally, you may be aiming to get married, move, and/or have a baby. Although life events cannot always be preplanned, it is important to at least have a general outline of your project timeline so you can plan as much as possible. A premeditated timeline can help you determine what is feasible to do and help you efficiently stay on task.

Make sure to review your program's suggested timeline and align it with a time-line for your final project. For example, in many psychology doctoral programs, students go on internship in their fifth or sixth year. Students in these programs often must successfully propose their final project before they can apply for intern-ship. Krieshok et al. (2000) found that psychology doctoral students who proposed prior to starting an internship made significantly more progress on their dissertations while on internship than students who did not. Once on internship, the best predic-tor of progress was the number of hours spent working on their projects. Programs often require students to remain enrolled in dissertation courses and pay additional matriculation fees until the project is complete.

Even if you familiarized yourself with your program's policies and procedures as a beginning student, you should not assume that they have stayed the same. Fac-tors such as staff changes, faculty restrictions, updated research competencies and policies, and institutional changes can engender changes to your requirements. It is your responsibility to research this information and develop a project that fits the requirements. Students sometimes assume that somewhere in the middle of the pro-gram someone will tell them the next step, be it in a class, a lecture, a meeting, or a formal correspondence. This may or may not be the case, so be sure you are up to date with your program's policies and procedures.

We recommend collaborating with your chair to determine a tentative timeline for completion of each of the steps of the final project process, as well as the responsi-bilities of both parties. For example, do they recommend you submit a fully written first draft by a certain date, or do they want to see an outline first and then discuss a subsequent deadline for something more fleshed out? A template for drafting a ten-tative timeline is provided in Chapter 5 (see Table 5.3). Over time, you should revisit your timeline (ideally with your chair's input), assessing the progress you have made, areas you have fallen behind on, and deadlines that make sense to readjust. In addi-tion, determine when and how you and your chair will generally correspond (e.g., via email, by phone, with regular or as-needed in-person meetings). What turnaround time is reasonable for you both? What are the appropriate prompts when you do not hear back or when something comes up that will cause a delay? Addressing these questions up front can help you stay on track.

Does This Project Topic Reflect My Initial Career Goals?

Your final project does not have to be your area of expertise for your entire career. There will likely be opportunities for you to lead or collaborate on projects in other areas throughout the time you spend in your profession. However, it can be strategic to choose an interest you would like to pursue once you complete your graduate program and move into the next stage of your career. Reviewing the literature in this area will help you develop a knowledge base for cutting-edge practices and current questions and concerns in this part of your field. It can also help you appear knowledgeable about a specific population or intervention area in future interviews.

Early in your career, your colleagues will likely view your project as part of your professional identity. They are also likely to turn to you for input in this area, since you will often be the resident expert in that area of your field. If you select a project topic that is not a direct step toward the work you want to do after graduate school, consult with a trusted advisor about how you can best describe the way your project fits into your overall career trajectory in applications and on interviews.

Student Example: How Your Project Topic Can Help Facilitate Your Career Goals

JR was interested in pursuing a career focused on adolescents and young adults. She had a particular interest in treating clients with eating disorders. She conducted her final project on adolescents diagnosed with eating disorders in a local hospital where she had been an extern. She spoke about her project on postdoctoral fellow interviews and was offered positions in both an eating disorders center and a hospital unit for college-age patients. Later, she interviewed in a private practice where the practitioners mentioned that they were excited to read about her dissertation work in her application because they were looking to hire someone with knowledge about that specific population.

Your Final Project Proposal

Once you have selected a project topic and a chair, you will typically have to develop a formal, written project proposal. This generally includes background literature supporting your idea, the purpose of your study and the rationale for conducting it, hypotheses and/or research question(s), and a step-by-step explanation of the method you will use to conduct your project. If you are beginning to write your proposal, chances are you have already reviewed a good deal of background literature and outlined pieces of your idea, as we suggested in Chapter 2.

Your written proposal will serve several purposes. First, it will help you clarify exactly what you want to study, why it makes sense to study it, and how you will do so. Second, the proposal will serve to communicate these ideas to your project committee so they can provide you with feedback and ultimately approve what you propose. Third, when you begin to conduct the project, you will often review your proposal to remember what you said you would do and help you plan the next steps. The document can also help you remember what you said you would do if you need to re-evaluate and change your method! It is common to stray from your original research plan. Referring back to that plan can help you prepare to explain any proposed changes to your committee; they will likely expect you to adhere to your original proposal, obtain their approval on any changes, and provide justification for why you made the changes you did. Fourth, the proposal will become the first section of your final written dissertation or thesis. A bonus reason for developing your written proposal is that you can consider converting the literature portion into a published paper.

Student Examples: Converting Parts of a Project Proposal into a Publication

GC successfully published a first-authored, peer-reviewed article comparing the construct of happiness in Western and Buddhist cultures after his committee came across a request for a special journal issue focused on philosophical foundations of therapy including happiness. The review was based on his dissertation proposal, and he invited his committee members to be coauthors.

BG published parts of the literature review from his proposal, which was focused on offering parent training in houses of worship, in a professional organization's newsletter. His dissertation chair was the second author.

We understand that writing a project proposal can be challenging. Each graduate program will provide a different amount of assistance, potentially in the form of research or professional development courses, faculty mentoring, peer mentoring, a writing center, and/or library, statistical, and technological support. Some of these types of assistance will be required, some will be optional, and some may be lacking (and some may even seem too basic). Here, we review the key components of a typical written proposal, key research concepts to help you with your proposal, and the structure of a proposal meeting.

Knowing the Key Components of a Written Proposal

When you begin writing your project proposal, you will want to understand and be familiar with the general format required by your program (see "Project Format" below for more information). For example, you will likely be expected to double-space your proposal and use one-inch margins and a clear, easy-to-read font (e.g., twelve-point Times New Roman). Most programs require you to follow specific writing guidelines (e.g., from the APA style manual).

The length of a final project varies, both across programs and across projects. Dissertation projects may comprise two hundred to three hundred pages, whereas theses tend to be shorter. We encourage you to limit the number of pages when possible because a typical manuscript submission to a journal is thirty-five pages, including the title page, abstract, tables, figures, and references. Some faculty expect students to keep their final project as close to this length as possible. Asking your chair to share examples of similar projects they have mentored can give you a general sense of the length they expect for each section of your project. Projects differ, however, and what worked for one topic may not work for another. Reviewing a project outline with your chair before you spend time writing will help ensure you go into enough detail without providing too much for your project's scope. Next, we review each of the typical components of a project proposal, noting when we think there may be differences across programs.

Title Page

Check your program's requirements regarding the format of your title page. For example, you may need to include the name of your specific department, the names of the professionals on your committee, and the date. Refer to the latest edition of the style guide in your field (e.g., the APA style manual) to determine whether there is an expected title page format.

Your title should summarize what you are proposing to study in a concise way that is limited to about twelve words and two lines. Ideally, you should include the key variables or methods and the population, intervention, and/or setting you are studying. It is common to have a working title that changes over time. You may not finalize your title until after you have written your proposal, and it might continue to change as you work on your project. Table 4.5 presents sample titles from students' final projects.

Table of Contents

Some programs require a table of contents, whereas others do not. A table of contents can help you outline what you will include in your proposal and provide a quick way for you and your committee to locate specific information, particularly during your proposal meeting. The table of contents should include each component of your proposal (e.g., "Abstract," "Introduction," "Method"). It is common to

Table 4.5 Sample Titles from Students' Final Projects

Acceptance and Change Skills as an Adjunct to Traditional Parent Training (Samantha Boutis)

The Effects of Sibling Incidental Teaching on Verbal Initiations of Children with Autism (Suzanne Buchanan)

Family Communication, Cohesion, and Adaptability in Families with Adolescent Drug Users (Giuliana Capone)

Improving Group Attendance of Acute Care Psychiatric Patients through Goal Setting and Feedback: A Field Study (Michael DeFalco)

Identifying Resiliency Factors in Commercially Sexually Exploited and Trafficked Youth: A Qualitative Study (Pamela Guthrie)

Comparison of Batterer Subtypes Using Structured Clinical Interviews (Olubukonla Kolawole)

number the components using roman numerals. You can also choose to include any subheadings you use in the body of your proposal (e.g., under "Introduction," you might include "Purpose of the Current Study"). For each component listed, include the corresponding page number. Be sure to update your table of contents over time as you make edits, or wait to add page numbers until the proposal is complete. Microsoft Word and other word-processing programs can generate a table of contents from your written headings and update page numbers as you write.

Abstract

In terms of structure, your abstract should appear on its own page. It should comprise one paragraph and include no more than 250 words. It should be written in the future tense because you have not yet conducted your study. The only exception to this is data that have already been collected. In general, the abstract should state whether actions have already occurred or will occur in the future.

In terms of content, your proposal abstract should provide an overview of what you plan to study. The abstract should begin with general background information about your topic area and then narrow down to a clear statement of what is lacking in the literature and the purpose of your project. You will also want to mention your hypotheses and/or research question(s), who your participants (or data, etc.) are or will be, the type of research design you will use, and a brief overview of the proposed procedure. Finally, you should include the potential contributions the project can make to your field (e.g., if your hypotheses are supported, what we might learn from your study).

Project Format

There are a few ways to organize your project proposal, and which you choose will likely depend on your program's guidelines for your final written dissertation or thesis, your chair, and your project's methodology. We are aware of three major formats for dissertations or theses, and you will need to select one to understand how to structure your project.

The first project format is based on a five-chapter dissertation or thesis model (with final written sections including Chapter 1: Introduction, Chapter 2: Literature Review, Chapter 3: Method, Chapter 4: Results, and Chapter 5: Discussion). If you select this format, the first three chapters would comprise your proposal, and the introduction to your proposal would include Chapters 1 and 2. In Chapter 1, you would provide a brief overview of the purpose of your study, summarizing relevant literature that supports your idea and its rationale and introducing your related hypotheses and/or research questions. In Chapter 2, you would provide a more comprehensive literature review.

The second format for a final project has been referred to as the three-article dissertation. In this format, you compile three different articles with a common theme that either are publication ready and/or have already been submitted for publication (Willis et al., 2010). These three articles can build on each other and may include a variety of methodology. For example, a student's first article could consist of qualitative interviews focused on experiencing a practical issue within a particular population. Their second article could build off the qualitative project by presenting data from a quantitative survey, and their third article could review the development of a program manual designed to target these issues as part of an intervention. The articles are linked together by an introduction that examines the main problem, provides a broad overview of the literature, and describes the three projects and their rationale. Once you have conducted your projects and written all three articles, this format typically includes a concluding section to discuss major findings, connections between the articles, and future research directions.

The third format of a dissertation or thesis project is similar to an article in structure (introduction, method, results, and discussion). At the proposal stage, you would present your introduction and method sections. If you are able to choose how to format your final project, we recommend the third model. It is likely the most feasible for a student in an applied program and is similar to a final manuscript format with regard to publication. Moving forward, we will focus on this third format.

Introduction

The introduction section typically begins with a broad overview of the literature and then narrows down to a critical evaluation of the studies most closely related to your proposed study. This is followed by a description of what is lacking in the literature; the purpose of the current study, along with the rationale for conducting it; and your hypotheses and/or research questions. We will walk you through how to write each part of the introduction in Chapter 5. Please note that some programs require very specific subheadings in each section of the write-up, while others allow more flexibility across projects.

Method

In your method section, you will describe each step of your project in detail. The method should be written so that theoretically another researcher could exactly replicate what you did. In an empirical project, the method section of a proposal includes a description of who the participants are expected to be and how they will be recruited (in past tense if data were already collected), the type of research design that will be used (e.g., true experiment, correlational design, grounded theory), the procedures that will be followed, descriptions of any interventions or conditions that will be administered, any measures that will be used, and the proposed data analyses (or the proposed method of assessing the data collected). For a nonempirical project, you would typically write about your method for developing a theory or product that will stem from your work. We will walk you through how to write each part of the method in Chapter 5.

References

In the references section, you will list all the articles, books, and/or websites you cited in the text of your proposal. Be sure to follow APA style or the format your program requires when you list the citations. The software programs mentioned in Chapter 2 can help you format your citations according to the desired style. Before you send your proposal, check that you have included all of the works cited in your references section, because committee members might want to look at the title and authors of a reference you mention.

Appendices

Appendices in a project proposal typically include materials that participants will be exposed to or expected to complete. For example, you might include fliers, advertisements, or emails designed to recruit participants; consent and/or assent forms; examples of measures you plan to administer, particularly any that you have adapted or developed; and any written or visual materials you plan to use as part of your procedure (e.g., case vignettes, worksheets). The expectations of your program and even your committee may vary with regard to the appendices included in your written proposal. For example, a chair may think you can wait until after your proposal has been approved to create your consent and/or assent forms, but a committee member may expect to see the forms before approving your project. Aim to clarify these questions ahead of time.

Research Concepts to Help You with Your Proposal: Ethics, Measure Selection, and Data Analytic Plan

In Chapter 1, we reviewed foundational concepts in statistics, psychometrics, and ethical conduct of research. At this stage, you will need to think about how these concepts apply to your proposed research. Next, we discuss issues related to the ethical conduct of research, measure selection, and proposal of a data analytic plan. The order of these concepts reflects the order in which they will likely be considered in your proposal.

Knowledge of Ethical Principles in Research

As you write, you must be cognizant that you are proposing a project that conforms to the ethical research principles in your field. As noted in Chapters 1 and 2, you should take your IRB's required ethics course or some equivalent to ensure familiarity with these principles. You have also probably taken an ethics course in your field by now. Table 4.6 provides a brief overview of ethical principles to consider and adhere to when you propose your project and conduct research with humans, based on the APA's (2017) "Research and Publication" section (standard 8) of the *Ethical Principles of Psychologists and Code of Conduct*. We then point out ways to avoid plagiarism. Additional ethical principles from standard 8 regarding presentation of results and publication will be described when we talk about completing your final project in Chapter 7.

A Note about Plagiarism

Students often think of plagiarism as directly copying someone else's sentences and passing them off as their own. While this is the most blatant form of plagiarism, more subtle kinds also exist. For example, it is not sufficient to simply switch words around in a sentence or use synonyms; you must still cite the original authors for their work. Even when you do provide a citation, it is important to reword the information; you can maintain the authors' meaning, but you should use your own words as much as possible. This can be more difficult for a research finding than for a conceptual idea. It is also important to cite an author when you present their general ideas about a topic; in other words, any idea that is not your original thought and is not common knowledge requires a citation. Be sure it is clear where any discussion of their ideas ends and your innovative perspective begins. It can sometimes be difficult to ascertain whether something is common knowledge or a concept that needs to be cited. If you are unsure, we recommend consulting with your chair and/or individuals such as faculty advisors or a librarian.

Understanding Measure Selection

In a quantitative study, you will be expected to propose measures you will use to assess your hypotheses and/or research questions. Quantitative measures typically include questionnaires, diagnostic assessments, standardized psychoeducational tests, and systematic observations. Generally, it is best to use measures that are well

Table 4.6 Ethical Principles You Need to Know for Your Proposal and Data Collection

Ethical principle	What you need to know
Institutional approval	Figure out if and/or when your research needs to be approved by the institutional review board. Get approval before you do the research. Do the research you were approved for.
Informed consent to research	Your participants should know: • The general purpose of your research (including how long it will take and what's involved). • Their right to participate in or withdraw from the study. • Any consequences, risks, and/or benefits of participating in or withdrawing from the study. • Confidentiality limitations. • People to contact with questions about the study and their rights. • Participants should have the chance to ask questions and obtain answers about the research.
Informed consent to research involving experimental treatments	Your participants should know: Your treatment is an experiment. How control and treatment groups are chosen. What treatments the control group will receive, if applicable. Treatment options if they decline participation or withdraw once the study has begun. Whether and/or how they are being compensated.
Informed consent for recording voices and images in research	You need consent for recording unless: The observation occurs in public places (i.e., naturalistic observation) and it will not cause personal harm or identification OR The study involves deception.
Client and/or patient, student, and subordinate research participants	If it is a client and/or patient, student, or subordinate, minimize negative consequences for declining or withdrawing from the study. If it is a course requirement or extra credit, provide equivalent options for credit.
Dispensing with informed consent for research	Forego informed consent only if your research will not cause distress or harm to any participants and you are: Examining typical educational and/or classroom content or practices in an educational environment; Solely using de-identified questionnaires, observations conducted in natural settings, or archival research that maintains confidentiality and does not place participants at risk of financial, criminal, civic, or reputable harm; Assessing factors related to occupational or organizational effectiveness conducted in work settings while maintaining confidentiality and ensuring participants' jobs are not at risk; Conducting research acceptable by institutional, federal, or legal guidelines.

continued

Table 4.6 *continued*

Ethical principle	What you need to know
Offering inducements for research participation	Provide reasonable incentives for participation. If the incentive is a service, clearly say what the service entails, including commitments, limitations, and risks.
Deception in research	If you use deception in your research, make sure it is justifiable and no other method would work. Do not use deception in your research if it could cause the participants to experience significant physical or emotional distress. Explain any features of deception to participants as soon as possible (i.e., at the end of their participation), but before your final data collection, and allow them to withdraw their data.
Debriefing	Provide information about the nature, findings, and conclusions of your research, and correct any misconceptions. Take steps to reduce harm.
Plagiarism	Do not use other's work as your own. Cite appropriately when using someone else's work.

Note: Based on the American Psychological Association's (2017) ethics code.

known in the field, are widely used in the literature on your topic, and have already demonstrated good reliability and validity. This strengthens the likelihood that your participants' responses will be consistent and capture the constructs you are interested in studying. You can review articles about research that is similar to your topic to see what measures have been used, but keep in mind that part of the rationale for a study may be to improve on the methodology.

Often, you can find measures to assess your constructs of interest, but remember that your idea of what a construct is may differ from what the measure is assessing. For example, you may want to assess changes in aggression over time, but do you intend to look at relational aggression or physical aggression? Review several reliable and valid measurements to determine which ones most closely reflect what you are aiming to assess.

You might need to assess constructs for which there are no existing measures that are an exact fit. In this case, it is best to look for a psychometrically sound measure that is most similar to what you want to assess and adapt it to your needs. A benefit is that your adapted measure will be based on a reliable and valid assessment. A significant limitation, however, is that the psychometrics may not be consistent with the way you change the original measure. In this situation, it is useful to assess content validity. For example, you can adapt the measure and then ask three experts in the field to compare your version with the original to determine whether the items remain as similar to the original questions as possible. In addition, you could conduct your own assessment of reliability and validity on the data you collect. Finally, you can contact the authors of the original measure to ask their permission to adapt it; you can also ask for their input. Ensure your chair is comfortable with you developing your own measures; some faculty may discourage this practice and work with you to find an alternative route.

Student Example: Adapting a Psychometrically Sound Measure

CG was interested in assessing adolescents' expectations for treatment at intake. She found a psychometrically sound measure focused on parental pretreatment expectations, but not one specifically for adolescents. In reviewing the parent measure, she realized she could change some of the item's basic wording (e.g., "I believe this treatment will be valuable in treating my child's problems" instead of "I believe this treatment will be valuable in treating my problems"). She adapted the measure in collaboration with her chair. She then asked three experts in the treatment of adolescents to compare the original items with her adapted items. Specifically, she asked them to indicate whether the adapted item (1) was worded well, (2) should be reverted to the original item, or (3) should be modified in another way (in which case she asked them to provide suggestions). She made revisions when two of the three experts suggested changing an item.

Occasionally, you will be interested in assessing a construct for which there is no measure. This is especially common for practice-focused projects in which the question of interest is on treatment preferences, likes, or dislikes, as well as projects focused on assessing the level of adherence to or competence in a particular protocol. Although there is no prior reliability or validity data for such a measure, creating one for the purpose of your project can lead to a novel and important contribution to your field. To strengthen the validity of the measure, you can assess content validity as described above. You can also search for measures used in similar situations (e.g., adherence to another protocol).

You might want to develop a system to code observable behaviors or verbalizations. To start, you can create categories informed by theory and prior research. You can ask two coders to categorize pilot data using the initial data and calculate their interrater reliability (e.g., the percentage of interrater agreement). You can then make any needed modifications to the coding system and retest.

Student Example: Developing a Novel Observational Coding System

CC wanted to code negative maternal cognitive content collected from mothers who watched a video of themselves engaging in a reportedly stressful interaction with their child immediately after it occurred. She reviewed literature based on the cognitive specificity hypothesis, which theorizes that cognitions match specific emotional states (e.g., one can have anxious cognitive content). CC developed initial thought categories that included anxious, depressive, and angry or hostile cognitive content. She created definitions for each category based on definitions she found in the literature. She then trained two coders, who practiced categorizing thoughts from pilot transcripts. She worked with the coders to revise the system until they reached an adequate level of interrater reliability.

In a qualitative study, your "measure" will often be your interview questions. Generally, your goal is to develop open-ended, nonbiased questions that will get your participants talking. Some qualitative methods suggest asking initial questions up front. It can also be helpful to prepare follow-up questions to keep your interview going should the conversation start to taper off.

Student Example: Qualitative Initial Question and Follow-Up Questions

SD conducted a qualitative study with low-income, depressed mothers for which one of her initial questions was: "What are some reasons that you don't currently talk to a mental health professional?" Her follow-up questions included:

- If a participant provides one barrier: "Any other reasons?"
- If a participant does not think they have a problem, probe for what having a problem worthy of therapy would be: "Can you imagine a scenario in which you'd need to go to therapy?"
- If a participant states that it will not help: "Why do you think it won't help?"
- What do you do instead to cope?
- If a participant mentions cultural barriers: "What is the common way people (in your culture) deal with emotional distress?"

At the same time, given the emerging nature of qualitative designs, some committees will expect your interview questions to evolve as you conduct your interviews and glean the type of responses you are receiving, as well as what you wish to ask more about. Consult with your chair about the degree to which your interview questions should be premeditated. In addition, ask your IRB if they are comfortable with a more flexible set of interview questions; some IRBs will be more familiar with and accepting of this type of procedure than others.

Knowledge You Need to Propose Your Data Analytic Plan

If you are working on a quantitative proposal, you might think you need to first get through your writing and worry about the statistics later. Although you will not be conducting the analyses now, you will need to propose your data analytic plan. If you are working on a qualitative proposal, your "data" will likely be words; however, you will still need to describe a plan for analyzing them. With a theoretical or scholarly proposal, you will usually need to demonstrate the type of product(s) your project committee can expect you to generate by the end of the project. Next, we discuss various types of proposed data analytic plans.

Data Analytic Plan for a Quantitative Proposal

The following steps can help you determine how to choose statistical tests to include in your data analyses.

What Are Your Hypotheses, Research Question(s), and Research Design?

These parts of your project will inform you of the type of statistics you need to conduct. Table 4.7 provides some examples. There will be caveats to the specific statistical tests you use, such as when you decide to control for extraneous variables and when your data violate statistical assumptions. Generally, however, just as the wording of

Table 4.7 Example Connections between Your Study and the Statistical Tests Used

Hypothesis/research question	Research design	Statistical test
Adults with mood and/or anxiety disorders who complete the sixteen-week transdiagnostic treatment will demonstrate significantly less depression and anxiety than those who complete the supportive therapy group.	Between-group design (e.g., true experiment, quasi-experimental)	t-test or analysis of variance
Graduate school training in evidence-based treatment will be significantly associated with later use of evidence-based treatment in private practice.	Correlational	Correlation, linear regression
What problems do parents endorse in their children's social–emotional functioning? How severely do they rate these problems? What do they prefer from a menu of options for related educational programming?	Descriptive	Frequency and percentages, means and standard deviations
It is hypothesized that children with hyperactive and impulsive behaviors will demonstrate improved ability to stay in their seat, raise their hand, and keep their hands to themselves after receiving a four-week behavioral classroom intervention.	Multiple baseline design	Visual analysis, z transformation, effect sizes

your hypotheses and/or research question(s) helped you decide what research design to use, the type of research design you employ should help you determine which statistical tests are necessary.

Note that, in the first example, the word "differences" indicated a between-groups design and statistic, while in the second example, the word "associated" indicated a correlational type of design that usually involves running correlations or linear regression analyses.

Review Your Statistics Class Notes, Statistics Books, and Websites

At this point, you have likely taken at least one graduate statistics course. It can be helpful to look back at your notes to jog your memory about statistical concepts and tests. Students often forget how much they learned in class, and it is possible that you are working on your proposal months or years after taking a related course. However, we recognize that you may not have learned about the specific statistics you need for your project, or you may not have enough information to run the tests independently.

The key to understanding when and how to run appropriate statistical tests is to find statistical resources that you find palatable. Some of our students have shared that googling statistical tests and reading about them from multiple perspectives has been most helpful. You can often find tutorials online for running through each step of a statistical analysis in programs like SPSS and SAS. We also recommend reading up on how to handle missing data, violations of statistical assumptions, and extraneous variables.

Review Studies Most Similar to Your Proposal Idea

What types of statistics were used? Did the authors discuss limitations to these analyses? Be sure to conduct your own critical evaluation. Do you want to replicate these analyses? Do you see ways you want to improve on what was done statistically?

What Does Your Chair Think?

Make sure to discuss options for data analyses when you and your chair are discussing your proposal idea. Your chair may have thoughts about which analyses to use based on their familiarity with the literature, statistical expertise, and analyses other students have successfully used. Your chair can also advise you when it is time to speak with someone who is a bit more knowledgeable about a particular statistical area.

Consider Hiring a Consultant

This step can be tricky, and attitudes about it vary. Find out whether your program offers statistical assistance and/or whether you are allowed to hire a statistical consultant. Some programs want their students to learn how to conduct the analyses themselves. Other programs encourage consultation as long as you are able to propose your own initial data analytic plan, write up your results section yourself, and clearly communicate how the analyses were conducted at your defense. Ideally, your consultant would discuss the purpose of your project with you to help you understand the rationale behind selecting specific statistical tests and offer potential interpretations of the results that go beyond the numbers. Also understand that hiring a consultant can be costly.

Regardless of the specific data analyses you use, it will be important to provide a rationale for why you are proposing specific analyses, particularly if you are asked about them in your proposal meeting. Your committee will expect your answer to be more thorough than saying that your chair or consultant suggested it! Some faculty will want a specific justification for your analyses in your data analysis section. In most programs, however, the proposal meeting is a time for you to make an informed suggestion and still request your committee's input.

Data Analytic Plan Needed for a Qualitative Proposal

For a qualitative study, the method you use to analyze your data will also largely depend on the type of research design you plan to use. For example, some qualitative research designs are more likely to call for your subjective reflection than for a coding process. Other designs, such as grounded theory approaches, are connected to specific methods of coding (e.g., open coding, axial coding, selective coding). The data analytic procedure should address the overarching purpose of the study. For example, if the goal of your study is to describe a particular group's recent experiences, the design would likely include interviews, whereas data analysis would likely involve categorizing interview transcripts into themes that would help provide an understanding of the group's aggregate experience.

Similar to our suggestions for conducting qualitative analyses, it is helpful to review similar qualitative studies and student projects to see how they analyzed their data. Talk to your chair about qualitative methods they are familiar with and comfortable using. This includes their thoughts on using qualitative data analytic software, such as ATLAS.ti and NVivo. Qualitative researchers have varying opinions of these programs. Some appreciate their ability to systematically search and code data, while others feel they remove too much of the researcher's subjective interpretation of the data.

It can be helpful to stick with a method used by prior students in your program, because this means people will be familiar with what you are trying to accomplish. In fact, if you plan to code data, it is very useful to first serve as a coder on someone else's qualitative project to learn about the process before trying to lead your own! In addition, get a qualitative methods book and read about options for conducting the type of analysis you plan to use. In any case, write up the steps you plan to take to analyze your data. We will provide an example regarding proposing qualitative coding in Chapter 5.

Plan for Products Generated from a Theoretical or Scholarly Proposal

If your project will include some sort of data analysis, you will want to describe your plan for it. For example, if you will be categorizing various studies as part of a critical analysis of the literature, explain how you will systematically code the articles and identify category names. By definition, nonempirical projects will not have a plan for data analysis. However, you should propose some way of presenting the products you say you will generate in your proposal. For example, if you propose to develop a new theory, you can include a general overview of how you plan to develop that theory or even a hypothetical outline of what might be included. If you are proposing to develop a treatment or educational protocol, you could include a final section in your proposed method where you describe the products you plan to create as part of your project (e.g., a manual, participant handouts).

The Proposal Defense or Meeting

In many graduate programs, students present their proposal in a meeting with their chair and committee members. Some programs have formalized steps leading up to a proposal: a research class, a preproposal, a group presentation, or a readiness evaluation. Be sure to check any written policies about the proposal meeting process. If your program does not have a process but you feel you or peers might benefit from it, suggest it to your advisor or chair. If it is something your program cannot do, seek other solutions.

Purpose of the Proposal Meeting

The proposal meeting typically occurs before you submit your IRB application for approval and before you begin to collect data (in cases where you might be using an already collected data set, it occurs before you begin to analyze your data). The proposal meeting varies in terms of formality from program to program, but there is a general theme of cooperation designed to help the student conduct a manageable research study. Your chair is responsible for running the meeting. After you provide an overview of your proposal (which meeting participants are expected to have read), committee members will ask questions and make suggestions to improve the quality of your project.

Timing

Once your chair has approved your written proposal, you will need to provide copies to all committee members prior to scheduling your proposal meeting. Usually, committee members require at least two weeks to read the proposal before you can schedule a meeting (but check your program's guidelines). This timing may also be influenced by where you are in your graduate program and whether you need to have the proposal completed by a certain date (e.g., before applying for internship). Think ahead about these time frames. You are likely responsible for scheduling the date, place, and time of the proposal meeting, which can take several emails as you negotiate everyone's schedules. We find the best approach is to suggest several potential dates and times. Online programs like Doodle, where individuals can log in and indicate when they are available, can be very helpful. A proposal meeting typically lasts ninety minutes and should not go beyond two hours.

Format

Just as every committee and every project is different, each proposal meeting is different. If more formality is expected, the meeting may really be a proposal "defense," which functions as a process of examination of you, the student, and your competency to explain, conduct, and complete the project. After an overview of your project, which may include a PowerPoint presentation, you should then be ready to answer questions. You might be asked to defend your rationale for the project, your hypotheses, your research design, and your chosen methodology. Remember, your chair may be able to offer some help, but you must answer the questions. Questions might include: "Why are you only using forty subjects?" or "Why have you not considered a multiple regression analysis?" or "How will you recruit subjects? What will you do if you do not obtain as many participants as planned?"

Other proposal meetings are less formal and include a discussion format in which the committee tries to problem-solve with the student to iron out any incomplete parts of the proposal. Changes might be suggested to make your project tighter or simpler. Either you or your chair should take notes concerning any suggestions and changes. Suggestions should be received with flexibility rather than defensiveness. In fact, your research study might be more efficient and you might achieve greater outcomes with suggestions from individuals who conduct research on a consistent basis.

If one of your committee members is not physically available either because they are an outside member located at another university or because they are out of the area, you can likely arrange other means of participation (e.g., over Zoom, Skype, or teleconferencing). You will need to set this up ahead of time and make sure there are no technical difficulties.

At the end of your proposal presentation and after all questions have been addressed, you will usually be asked to leave the room to allow the committee to deliberate. After a decision concerning your status is made, you will be called back into the room. Your chair will likely provide a summary of the feedback (hopefully including words of congratulations!). Then your committee members can chime in with additional suggestions.

Outcomes

Some programs require formal evaluation forms to be completed after the proposal meeting. You might be rated on a variety of aspects of your research project, in addition to your oral presentation and the written proposal. Make sure you know what forms are required and the process to obtain the go-ahead to begin your research. You will need to edit your written document and may have minor or even major revisions to make. Before the end of the proposal meeting, you and your chair should clarify how the committee members want these revisions handled: Do you need to make them and resubmit your proposal before they will sign off? Hopefully, all major revisions and/or suggestions were communicated before the proposal meeting, but if not, you must hunker down and make any needed changes.

In our experience, it is almost impossible for a student to not make it through a proposal meeting successfully, because so much of the feedback can be given before the meeting. Your chair will probably not allow a proposal meeting if they do not think you are ready. Committee members can also call off a proposal meeting if they think the proposal needs more work. However, it is possible for a project proposal to be rejected at the end of a proposal meeting. If you are told your proposal needs more work, talk with your chair and your committee members about the steps needed to improve your proposal. You might consider obtaining writing help and/or mentoring from a familiar professional who is not on your committee who can provide a more objective perspective. See Worksheet 5.2 for a template focused on helping you develop a remediation plan.

Worksheet 4.1 Factors to Consider When Selecting Your Final Project Topic

Once you have narrowed your interests into a potential topic area, use the information in the "Factors to Consider" section of Chapter 4 to help you complete this worksheet. It may be helpful to complete the worksheet more than once to think through a few possible project ideas. The purpose of answering these questions is to help you move forward in selecting your final project topic.

Project topic I am considering for this worksheet:

_____

_____

_____

_____

Factors to consider about this project topic:

Am I passionate enough about this topic to immerse myself in it?

Consider	Comments
Can I see myself wanting to study this for a year or more?	
Do I think I can sustain my attention and motivation through the development, execution, and completion of this project? Why or why not?	
What are the pros and cons of focusing on this topic in terms of my overall interests?	

Who would I like to have as my chair and committee members for this project?

Consider	Comments
Who is able to serve as a chair in my program? Who has the time to commit to my project?	
Am I already conducting research or being mentored by a faculty member? Can I see them being my chair?	
Is there someone expert in this area who can serve as my chair? How about someone with enthusiasm for the topic?	
Whose feedback has been helpful to me in the program so far?	
Who appears interested in working with *me*?	
Who is rumored to be a good chair?	
What supervisory style is the best fit for me (e.g., laissez-faire, pastoral, directorial, contractual)? Under what circumstances?	
What types of projects have the faculty I am interested in working with chaired? What types of methodology have their students used? Is there a program project database, library, or alumni contact to help me research this information?	

Consider	Comments
Have I "interviewed" faculty I am potentially interested in working with about their thoughts on my idea? How about on the way they chair projects? How clear am I being about my intentions to "chair shop" right now versus committing to working with them?	
Are my potential chairs junior or senior faculty? Core or adjunct professors? What pros and cons from Chapter 4 appear relevant to their level of seniority or involvement in the program? If my potential chair is an adjunct professor or someone external to my program's faculty, have I received program approval?	
How do my working style and personality characteristics match those of my potential chair?	
Who would I like as my committee members? How well do we work together? How well do they work together? What additional sources of expertise do they offer?	
Have I clarified the way potential committee members are willing and able to be involved in student projects?	
Have I thought about what I will say to potential committee members when I initiate contact? Have I asked about how my committee members want to handle questions and/or revisions to my proposal?	

What do I think would be the purpose of my project?

Consider	Comments
Based on what I have read so far, what about this topic appears to be missing in the literature?	
What have authors mentioned as the existing limitations and future directions in my topic area?	
Beyond what others say, what do I think are the existing limitations and potential future directions?	
How would my project serve as the next step in this topic area?	
How can I state the purpose of my working project topic in one clear, succinct sentence, in a way that demonstrates key variables and suggests the type of research design I might use? What can I do to feel ready to share this with others who ask about my project?	

Why is this project important?

Consider	Comments
How can the findings from a project like this make a valuable contribution to the existing literature and the field?	
How could findings from this project build on existing knowledge, generate or revise theory, and/or propose solutions to an existing issue?	
What would be the theoretical, methodological, and/or practical implications of my findings?	

Study participants and procedures: who, what, where, when, how?

Consider	Comments
What are some potential directions for future research based on this project?	
How might I have access to my sample of interest? Is there an existing data set? Would I collect new data? Would I not analyze data?	
Who would I include in this study? What sampling strategy would I use (e.g., convenience sampling, snowball sampling)?	
Where would I recruit from? Whose permission would I need?	
Where and how could I advertise the study? Who could recruit and/or administer my study's procedure? When and where might I be able to recruit and conduct the study? What could my procedure be for collecting and/or analyzing data to answer my research questions (e.g., surveys, interviews, focus groups, observations)?	
Will I be able to provide participants with some type of compensation, and if so, what will it be? Might I use a raffle where only some participants would be awarded compensation?	
What constructs would I need to measure? Are there standard measures available to assess these constructs? Are there any measures I might adapt? Do I think I would need to create my own measure? What are some pros and cons of these options?	

To develop and/or conduct a project in an applied setting: Do I have a setting in mind? How open do I think staff and the organization will be to my conducting a project in their facility? Whose permission would I need to recruit and/or conduct the project? How much do I think they will assist me? Expect to have control over my project? Allow and/or expect me to work independently? Who might be responsible for each part of the procedure? Will the setting's directors and staff be interested in helping facilitate my data collection? Would they want to claim primary ownership of the project? Would they allow me to publish my findings?	
What project costs do I anticipate (e.g., for participant compensation, measures for purchase, and/or survey or statistical programs)? What are some potential grants or other funding opportunities I can apply for to receive assistance with covering these types of costs (e.g., internal and/or external funding opportunities)? What personal funds may I be able to obtain and/or use, and how can I manage them within my overall budget?	
To pursue a theoretical review: Do I have a clear understanding of what is involved? Is there enough relevant literature to support the development of my theory? Do I have access to enough background literature, people, and/or other resources needed to conduct this project?	

What are the strengths and limitations of different research designs for my project (e.g., quantitative versus qualitative, strengths and limitations of specific quantitative or qualitative designs, strengths and limitations of theoretical or scholarly projects)?

Consider	Comments
What research designs could I consider for this project?	
What are the strengths of each possible design?	
What are the limitations of each possible design?	
What are the practical issues involved with each possible design?	
Which research designs have worked well with similar projects in the past?	

How will this project fit into my graduate school timeline?

Consider	Comments
What are my program's deadlines for specific project-related activities (e.g., what date must I propose by?)?	
Approximately how long do I anticipate this project taking to complete (e.g., writing, time for data collection)?	
How many years am I allowed and/or willing to stay matriculated in school to complete my project?	
How much does it cost to stay matriculated for extra semesters?	
What are creative ways I might study a similar topic with a more feasible method?	
Do I foresee myself undergoing a major life change during this time, such as getting married, moving, and/or having a baby? How would this fit into my project timeline? Do I foresee my chair undergoing major life changes during this time?	
Once I have a chair, can we make sure we are both clear on how we will work together? For example, do I know when and how we will generally correspond (e.g., via email, by phone, with regular or as-needed in-person meetings)? What turnaround time is reasonable for both of us? What are the appropriate prompts when I do not hear back or when something comes up that will cause a delay?	

Does this project topic reflect my initial career goals?

Consider	Comments
Does it reflect an interest I would like to pursue once I complete my graduate program and enter the next stage of my career? Does it create opportunities for me to lead or collaborate on projects once I graduate?	
What kind of knowledge base will it help me develop (e.g., about a specific cutting-edge issue in my field, a specific population or intervention area) that might prove useful in future interviews? Does my project depict a relevant professional identity for myself in beginning my career?	
Would I like to be considered an expert in this project area?	
If this project topic would not be a direct step toward the work I want to do after graduate school, who is a trusted advisor I can consult with about how I could best describe the way this project fits into my overall career trajectory (e.g., in applications and interviews)?	

Chapter 5
Skills for Writing Your Proposal and Managing Your Final Project

Introduction

As you prepare to write your proposal and conduct your final project, you should develop your *skills* with regard to the critical evaluation of research, the conduct of research in applied settings, and ethical and professional competence by learning the following areas of this chapter:

- Skills for finalizing your chair selection
- How to write your final project proposal
- Skills for successfully working with your chair
- How to finalize your proposal draft
- Preparing for your proposal meeting
- Writing your institutional review board (IRB) application
- Managing your project
- Managing changes to your procedure over the course of your project
- Keeping your project timeline on track
- Remediation planning

In Chapter 4, we reviewed factors to consider when selecting your final project topic, including issues related to selecting and obtaining your chair. We also reviewed key components of your written proposal, factors to consider when selecting committee members, and things to know about the proposal meeting. If you are making progress on your project in line with the order of this book, at this point you are likely ready to commit to both your final project topic and a project chair. Here, we look at skills to help you navigate finalizing your chair selection. We then review skills for writing each section of your proposal, working with your chair, writing your IRB application, and managing your project.

Navigating Research in an Applied Graduate Program. Hilary B. Vidair, Pam L. Gustafson, and Eva L. Feindler, Oxford University Press. © Oxford University Press (2024). DOI: 10.1093/oso/9780199352272.003.0005

Skills for Finalizing Your Chair Selection

If someone has already agreed to be your chair, congratulations! This is a big step in the final project process. Your next step is to make sure your paperwork for this stage of the process is complete. For example, some programs will expect your chair to sign off, stating that they agree to take on the role. In many programs, your chair will need to be listed as the professor for a course you take for credit.

Managing Potential Challenges When Selecting a Chair

Even after considering the variables on chair selection presented in Chapter 4, students can experience challenges with this process. Here, we list a few of the more frequent issues and some possible solutions.

What If You Cannot Secure a Chair?

You may have decided on a topic that has great meaning for you, but is not of interest to any of your faculty. In this case, you may need to alter your focus and/or yield to a faculty member's input on a project they would be willing to supervise. You may also need to examine whether you have had difficult relationships with the faculty in your program and whether you have a record of poor performance in any of your program's components. If you have a negative reputation with the faculty (e.g., poor grades, professional development issues), do not be surprised that no one wants to sign on. You might need to consult your program director or academic advisor and ask the difficult question, Are there reasons why no one wants to chair my research? If so, determine what steps you might take to remediate the issues and how long that might take (see the remediation planning section at the end of this chapter).

How Can You Handle a Faculty Member Who Assumes They Will Serve as Your Chair?

Students sometimes consult with a faculty member about their ideas without indicating they are simply window shopping, and the faculty member assumes the student plans to work with them. It is important to be clear about your intentions from the start to avoid this type of confusion; however, if you find yourself in this situation, we recommend clarifying your position as soon as possible. Even if they feel disappointed, hopefully the faculty member will appreciate your candidness and respect where you are in the process.

What to Do If You Are Firmly against Working with a Particular Faculty Member but Are Very Interested in Their Area of Research

This sounds like a political hot potato. Any given faculty may include prominent experts who have published in specific areas and are the only ones in the department to do so. Examine what has helped you develop this clear interest and whether it is independent of the faculty member. It is possible there was some kind of fracture in your relationship with the expert faculty member. If the impasse cannot be repaired, it might be inappropriate to ask a different faculty member to supervise research that might have sprouted under another's supervision. You may need to change your topic and start over, but the expert faculty member may also be amenable to you working with someone else. Try to consult with another faculty member about ways to proceed.

How Can You Switch to a Different Faculty Chair Even though You Were Working in Their Lab or as Their Assistant?

This situation is best handled with an honest conversation with the faculty member with whom you would prefer not to work. For example, you might explain that your interests have shifted and you hope to work with someone who has more familiarity with a particular topic area or type of statistical expertise. Or you might describe the need for a specific type of mentoring style, such as frequent meetings with a clearly laid out structure. If you can assertively advocate for meeting your own needs with a different faculty member while expressing appreciation for the lab you have been participating in, it will likely be a smooth transition.

How to Write Your Final Project Proposal

As we discussed in Chapter 4, there are a few ways to structure a proposal. Refer to that chapter to review the general key proposal components and be sure to check with your graduate program to determine whether there are specific written proposal guidelines. They can often be found on your program's website or in a program handbook. Although programs may have unique instructions, some general guidelines for how to write proposed introduction and methods sections likely apply. Here, we review skills for how to write these sections of your project proposal. If you read this section and think you would benefit from more in-depth information, several books focus entirely on writing literature reviews or proposals (e.g., Efron & Ravid, 2018; Galvan & Galvan, 2017; Krathwohl & Smith, 2005; Locke et al., 2013; Terrell, 2023).

Beginning to write your proposal does not typically follow a specific step-by-step process. Students often think they have settled on a topic area only to do some more reading and come across literature that points them in a slightly different direction. This can feel overwhelming and make you wonder if you are on the right course. In fact, this is exactly what the process of research typically feels like. Rather than a linear process, we think of a back and forth between reading and writing, writing and reading, which can lead to more refined research questions over time. Here is an example of a student who revised her topic during the course of her literature search.

Student Example: Revising a Project Topic as Literature Is Reviewed

AL was interested in exploring the perceptions of teachers when they work with students who have experienced trauma. She read a qualitative study that had been published in this area and planned to do another qualitative study about what teachers feel they need to help them manage trauma, expanding on what the researchers in the original study found. However, she then expanded the search terms she was using, trying synonyms for perceptions. She also searched through literature about people in other professions, such as police officers. These literature searches led to additional articles that provided her with a theoretical basis for developing a quantitative, correlational study focused on predicting what variables impact teachers' ability to handle student traumas.

You may feel that a substantial amount of literature is relevant to write about, and students often wonder when their literature review is complete! It is important to curate the set of articles you include in your introduction. For example, you may be wondering if older articles are important, or you may find a number of pilot studies on your topic and question whether they should be included. Your committee will expect you to have read more articles than you write about; they will evaluate you based on your ability to include and evaluate the literature that best develops your points for the purpose of your project.

It is helpful to create some decision points for what you include in your review. First, decide which topics you need to include to support each point you will be making and/or each variable you plan to assess. They should match the subheadings present in your outline. Second, you will want to write about articles in your subfield that are considered classic or seminal. For example, research projects regarding interventions for child anxiety often cite Phil Kendall's (1994) study because it was the first randomized controlled trial for treating child anxiety ever conducted. Other than classic articles, the majority of your review should include recent literature. Third, review the number of articles that have been written on a particular topic. If there are several, you can consider the following: Which are most closely related to your project topic and will need to be described in detail, which are somewhat related and perhaps can be summarized in a sentence or two about a group of studies and/or articles, and which seem on the periphery that you may end up leaving out? Determine the inclusion criteria you will use for research or scholarly work by assessing what is available. For example, if a handful of published randomized controlled trials are very relevant to your topic, you can likely exclude pilot studies or perhaps simply mention that they exist, citing them but not writing about them further. Ask your chair how much they wish to be involved in these decisions.

Writing about your idea can also prompt you to read more about a topic. You may feel the urge to write a sentence such as, "Research has indicated that . . ." and realize you need to find articles to support the idea! This can happen to anyone writing a proposal, but it is a particularly common occurrence for students who have chosen an idea before becoming familiar with the available literature. For example, you may have access to a data set and think of something interesting to study. You then need to go into the literature and find research that supports your idea. This can be tough, because you may not find exactly what you hoped for, and with an archival data set, you will not be able to change the variables you can examine. However, you should not be discouraged, because you can use existing literature to help formulate a slightly different research question. The main point, regardless of the type of project you are proposing, is to expect to have to shift between reading and writing several times throughout the development of your proposal, and even throughout the entirety of your project.

In addition, the order in which you write does not have to be sequential. Sometimes it can be easier to start writing in what will become the middle of your introduction section. As we discuss in the next section, this is where you would expect to find information about specific studies, such as their overall purposes, their methodology (participants, research design, procedure, method for measuring variables), their findings, and your evaluation of those findings. This section may be easier to write than the beginning or end of your introduction, because you have likely accumulated information about specific studies as part of your initial literature review and organization. Writing information about specific studies can help you feel that you are making progress and can shape the body of your introduction.

Alternatively, you might start by writing a draft of the problem statement, the purpose of your project, and its rationale. As discussed in Chapter 4, this will become the end of your introduction in a project emulating an article format or the first chapter of a five-chapter dissertation. We find that delineating the purpose of and rationale for a project is the most challenging because the goal is to make a compelling argument for why your study is important enough to conduct. Therefore, it can make sense to begin with this section, because you will want a lot of time to work on it. Part 1 of Worksheet 5.1 invites you to write out these parts of the proposal, as well as ideas for your method. You can expect to modify this information over time as you review literature that shapes your project idea. Part 2 of this worksheet can be used as a self-evaluation of your written project idea to ensure you have addressed all necessary items. It should be completed once you have a near-final draft of your proposal.

How to Write Your Introduction Section

There are different formats for writing an introduction to your proposal. As mentioned in Chapter 4, one format starts with a chapter including a statement of the problem, as well as the purpose of and rationale for your project. There is a separate chapter for the literature review, which might include a comprehensive review of each area you plan to include as part of your project. This method helps you acquire and demonstrate extensive knowledge of each subtopic found within your project. Another format begins with a literature review and narrows into the problem statement, as well as the purpose of and rationale for your project. We review the latter format, which is closer to the format typically found in an article. In this format, you do not have to provide a review of studies that are only remotely related to your topic; the goal is to develop an argument for the need for your project, supporting your points throughout the document with relevant literature. If you choose to follow the three-article format, each article will likely need this type of introduction, and you may also need to include an overarching introduction about all three articles. Check your program's required proposal format when deciding on your own, because programs often have rules for how to structure these projects.

The general structure of an introduction following an article format is illustrated in Figure 5.1. The upside-down triangle is commonly viewed as a funnel, starting off more generally and becoming more specific as you get closer to the purpose of and rationale for your project (e.g., Bell et al., 2019). Begin with a broad overview of your subfield and relevant operational definitions. Next, generally review any relevant theories and research in the main areas related to your project topic. You should then narrow your focus, getting more specific about research studies found

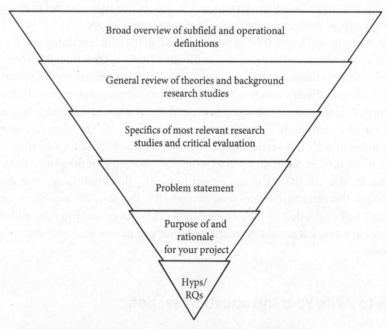

Figure 5.1 Order of an introduction section when structured like an article (hyps, hypotheses; RQs, research questions)

in the literature. Every point you make should help build an argument the reader can follow toward the purpose and rationale for your project. At the end of your literature review, you can summarize what has been found, as well as what is lacking in the literature, which becomes a statement of the problem. This should lead the reader to the purpose of your project and its rationale: how it will be innovative and important, how conducting it will fill gaps in the literature, and what your findings can potentially contribute to your field. Remember, you are not focusing on your specific topic just because it is interesting to you: you need to demonstrate how your project fits within the context of the prior literature. What evidence can you provide to support your argument? As you progress in your explanation, you want your reader to be nodding their head in agreement! Most empirical articles also include an introduction structured in this way, albeit shorter than what you will be expected to write.

There may be differences in your introduction's content depending on the type of project you are proposing. For example, qualitative studies often focus on emerging theory in areas with limited existing research, so their introductions do not always rely on building on particular studies as much as quantitative introductions usually do. The introductions of scholarly projects will also vary. For example, a critical review will likely follow the introduction format just discussed, while a case study might begin with demographic information and then review the literature supporting the intervention method. We find that most students can write their project proposals using the general structure discussed above. Next, we review each subsection of an introduction.

Broad Overview of the Subfield and Operational Definitions

The broad overview of the subfield refers to what you consider the general area of research relevant to your project. This is the introduction to your introduction, and it sets the stage for your reader to anticipate what literature you will focus on. Students often wonder where to begin their literature review. There is typically more than one possibility, because you likely need to review two or more bodies of literature to arrive at your project idea. Knowing what you want the main framework for your project to be as well as who your prospective audience is can help you decide the order in which you present your introduction.

Student Example: Determining the Order of the Introduction

CG proposed a project focused on adolescents' expectations and preferences from dialectical behavior therapy (DBT). She realized she could start her introduction in one of two ways: she could either begin her broad review of the subfield with a review of the literature on what DBT is and the evidence supporting it, or she could begin with reviewing the importance of addressing adolescents' expectations in therapy.

> She chose the first approach because she aimed to determine implications for how clinicians can best orient adolescents to DBT rather than use DBT for adolescents as an example of adolescents' expectations and preferences in treatment. She was also working with faculty who specialized in DBT and hoped to present and publish her findings for researchers and clinicians focused on DBT.

When you describe your general area of research, operationally define key terms and variables as they arise. This means you will clearly describe these terms and variables as they arise. This means you will clearly describe these terms and variables based on how you plan to define and measure them in your project. This is important, because there are often many ways to define one variable, and not all definitions hold the same meaning. Being clear about how you operationally define your variables will aid the reader in understanding how to interpret your findings, replicate them, and understand the limitations of your project (Kazdin, 2016). Variations across definitions can occur across articles you review. Be sure to alert the reader when an article includes a different definition of the same variable name.

Student Example: Indicating Various Operational Definitions for the Same Variable

KR proposed a study evaluating the effects of a peer support intervention for decreasing stress and increasing self-care in psychology doctoral students. A review of the existing literature on stress and self-care indicated that researchers had measured both in a variety of ways. KR and her chair spoke about the importance of writing about how each study she reviewed measured these constructs, to help compare findings across studies. She also provided a rationale for the measures she proposed to use.

Similarly, be sure to use consistent wording for key terms and variables. Do not worry about sounding too repetitive. Unlike creative writing, scientific and scholarly writing should not include synonyms, because they can confuse the reader. In fact, using the same words can help your reader follow along with your thought process.

For every citation you include, be sure to read the original source rather than obtain relevant information from a review article or other secondary source. The reason for this is that authors can interpret and/or report information inaccurately, and sometimes repetitively, as more authors use the same secondary sources over time. Be sure you understand the original authors' conceptualization and/or findings.

Paraphrase authors' key points and cite sources according to the style guide you are using (e.g., American Psychological Association, 2020). Be sure to allot credit to authors for their findings as well as their ideas. Use quotations sparingly (i.e., when an author provides a unique definition), because the goal is to write your own review rather than emulate what others have written. It can be difficult to rephrase points that sound great, but doing so can help you better understand the material and clarify important information.

General Review of Theories and Background Research Studies

After introducing your broad area of focus, you will need to provide a general review of theories and/or background research studies for each relevant area of the literature. Briefly summarize the theory and/or studies in each general area before transitioning to your next point. If you began with an outline, you can refer to it for ideas about the order of the review. You can also look at articles that are similar to your project for ideas about how to organize your literature review.

Student Example: Determining How Much Background to Provide in Your Introduction

In reference to CG's prior example, she first reviewed findings from original DBT studies and then mentioned several populations that have benefited from the treatment, including the citations. However, she did not go into detail about these articles, because they helped set up the background for her project but were not directly relevant to the purpose of her study. Similarly, later in her introduction, she reviewed reasons for assessing clients' treatment expectations and preferences. She wrote a few sentences about the known benefits of assessing the variables among clients of any kind, but held off on describing specific studies until she began her review of these variables among adolescent clients in particular.

If you are proposing a quantitative project, it can be useful to include theories that inform your research. Theories focus on how and why variables are related to each other (e.g., factors underlying a problem), what maintains a problem or pattern, and what can elicit change, such as a particular intervention (Kadin, 2017). Writing about theories helps build the foundation for testing your hypotheses. Note that theories do not necessarily need names; the goal is to explain your understanding of the predicted relations between variables. Some programs will ask you to include this information in a subsection of your introduction entitled "Theoretical Framework."

In a qualitative study, your introduction should typically take a neutral, open-ended stance, because you typically will not have guiding theory available, and you want to be careful not to bias your study with preconceived expectations. Instead, theoretical concepts may emerge from your data, which may be one of the major goals of your project, depending on the qualitative design you use. In any event, you can discuss theoretical concepts generated from a qualitative study as potential directions for future research.

As you write, use wording that clarifies when information found within a citation is conceptual rather than an empirical finding. It is fine to include both as long as the reader can decipher which points are ideas and which are the results of research studies.

Specifics of Most Relevant Studies and Critical Evaluation

Once you have covered generally relevant studies, review studies that are specifically relevant to your topic. The general rule of thumb is to cover in more detail studies that are more closely related to your specific topic area.

Student Example: Determining Which Specific Studies to Review toward the End of Your Literature Review

Returning to CG's example once again, she spent more time reviewing the details of research on DBT for adolescents and on studies regarding adolescent perceptions of treatment than she did on studies about DBT or client perceptions of treatment in general. The two studies that she reviewed in the most detail focused on adolescents' acceptability ratings of DBT.

Information you will want to provide for studies most relevant to your topic area include the purpose of the study, sample size, relevant methodology (e.g., research design, how they measured variables of interest), and relevant findings. If you model your methodology after these studies, be sure to include a description of how the study was conducted.

As we discussed in Chapter 2's section on critical evaluation of articles, keep in mind that your goal is not just to summarize the studies that are closest to your project idea. You should provide a critical evaluation of the literature along the way, explaining consistencies and discrepancies in findings across studies. How are the studies you are reviewing helping to build the case you are making for your project? What did they contribute to the literature? What is still unanswered, and how have findings been limited (e.g., methodologically?) Describe the strengths and limitations of the studies to help build the rationale for what your project will emulate, add to, or assess differently. This is where you can strengthen your proposal by using your own voice. Although authors of a study typically provide their own limitations and directions for future research sections, what do *you* think are the limitations and future directions you wish to build on? They may or may not be the same as what the authors indicated. Regardless, assert these limitations using your own analysis rather than writing a passive statement such as, "Author X said . . ." You can always reference the article at the end of your sentence. Your goal is to synthesize the information across articles in ways that provide a clear picture for your reader regarding what has and has not been done.

Problem Statement

The problem statement is where you summarize your evaluation of what is lacking in the literature. This is where you can restate key points of the argument you have built in your literature review. By this point, the reader should understand key research findings and procedures in this area, know the weaknesses and/or gaps in the literature, and be clear on exactly what you see as the next steps in research. If you have conducted a comprehensive search on a topic and do not find related articles, you can write something like, "To the author's knowledge, no studies have ..." This demonstrates that you did not find anything, but leaves room for the possibility that you may have missed something.

Student Example: Generating a Problem Statement

EC aimed to conduct a qualitative study examining parents' experiences with children with encopresis and implementing relevant therapies. Here is an excerpt of her problem statement:

"Empirically supported treatments for encopresis have been found to be effective in promoting more adaptive toileting behaviors and limiting the frequency of soiling episodes. The onus on successful implementation of these treatments lies with parents, yet little research has investigated parents' experiences conducting these prescribed treatments. It is crucial, then, to better understand how parents perceive their child's encopresis and related treatment. Only one quantitative study has looked at parents' perceptions of encopresis treatment (Bernard-Bonnin et al., 1993). As this study gathered most of its information from multiple-choice questions and forced-choice Likert scales and not with face-to-face interviews, there was no opportunity for parents to clarify or add to their answers. . . . No study, to this author's knowledge, has exclusively looked at the experience of parents who have provided encopresis treatment."

In terms of placement, some programs will ask that you include the problem statement as a separate subsection of your introduction, whereas others will not specify. In the latter case, you can transition into the problem statement at the conclusion of your literature review. Regardless, make sure you include one. Students sometimes skip the problem statement, which is a problem! Remember, the goal is to add a project to the existing literature base. You want to be clear about what research or scholarly work exists and where there are gaps, ultimately leading the reader to how you aim to address this gap by conducting your project.

Purpose of Your Project

You will also need to state a clear purpose for your project. You can place this statement either at the beginning of the section introducing your project or toward the end. Regardless, it is best to be clear with a sentence such as, "The purpose of the current study is to . . ." Be specific with your purpose; this sentence should be the only thing the reader needs to look at to understand the overall goal of your project. For a quantitative study, the purpose statement should provide the following: a clear overview of what you will study (e.g., what are the independent and dependent variables?), a foreshadowing of the kind of research design you will use (e.g., experimental, correlational), and who you will study. You might even be proposing a hybrid research design (e.g., partially experimental, partially correlational), which can be wonderful, but be clear in your language about both goals. For a qualitative study, the purpose is typically described in a more open-ended manner. The goal of this statement is to explain the phenomena being explored, as well as who will be included. If you will be conducting a theoretical or scholarly project, you will want to state your study's aims as clearly as possible. Table 5.1 provides examples of how students described the purpose of their projects in conjunction with their research designs.

Your Project's Rationale

It is also important to make the rationale of your project clear. In other words, explain why conducting it is important. Think of this as a response to the questions, "So what if this is lacking in the literature?" or "Why should we care?" Your goal is to have your reader thinking, "Yes, this is an important issue that needs to be addressed!" Describe how findings from your project could potentially add to theoretical knowledge, methodology, and/or empirical research in this part of your field. For an applied research project, be sure to address the potential practical implications of your findings. For example, how could results from your project inform clinical or educational practice? This is where you can indicate the potential contribution your project can make to your field, within the context of what is already known. Stick to what potential findings from your project may be able to indicate, and do not extrapolate further.

Stylistically, your rationale can lead up to the purpose of your current project, follow your statement of purpose, or be a mix of both. Consult with your chair if you are uncertain about the order. We also recommend not referring to "your project" until you have stated the project's purpose. This means that if you discuss the rationale first, speak about it in general terms, such as why research on "X" should be conducted.

Hypotheses and/or Research Questions

After describing the purpose of your project, you may include specific hypotheses and/or research questions, depending on the type of project you are conducting. They should directly relate to the purpose of your project. In quantitative research, hypotheses preemptively state the results you expect to find when you run your data

Table 5.1 Example Connections between the Purpose of Your Project and Your Research Design

Project purpose	Research design
The purpose of the present study is to examine parents' overall acceptability of exposure for pediatric anxiety as well as predictors of acceptability, namely, parent anxiety, engagement in accommodation, and knowledge of exposure (AR).	Quantitative, descriptive, and correlational
The present study will examine the effects of independent task engagement with minimal adult supervision or intervention on children's independence and resilience. The study will evaluate the effects of the Let Grow project (Skenazy, 2018), a school-based intervention aimed at promoting resilience and independence in children by assigning homework that engages them in tasks independently, in comparison to a control condition (ME).	Quantitative, true experimental
The purpose of this study will be to explore the experiences of clinical psychologists in providing cognitive-behavioral therapy to children and adolescents via telehealth. The research will use data from focus groups to generate a theoretical framework regarding how clinicians can successfully provide this treatment (CA).	Qualitative, grounded theory
This project will discuss the questions asked and models proposed by Western psychologists researching happiness and how they differ from the questions asked and models proposed by the Tibetan Buddhist tradition of psychology. It will also present an overview of scientific findings related to each of these models and suggest possible benefits of investigating the basis for underlying assumptions of theories of happiness and the effects of such assumptions on the outcomes derived from different models of psychology (GC).	Nonempirical, critical analysis of the literature

analyses. As mentioned in Chapter 1, they are part of the scientific method, because you predict what you anticipate to happen beforehand based on prior literature and then either confirm or disconfirm the hypotheses in the results section. Hypotheses are typically found in quantitative studies and can be either directional or nondirectional. Directional hypotheses predict what you expect to happen based on existing theories and/or empirical findings reviewed earlier in your introduction.

Student Example: Directional Hypotheses Based on Prior Research

AR, mentioned in Table 5.1, hypothesized that parents' knowledge about exposure would be positively associated with their acceptability of exposure. She did not find prior research on the relationship between parents' knowledge of exposure and acceptability to support her hypotheses; however, existing research demonstrated a negative association between therapists' beliefs about exposure and use of this therapy. Another study showed that clinicians who attended a workshop about exposure therapy had increased knowledge and a reduction in negative beliefs about exposure. She used these findings to support her hypothesis that parents' knowledge of exposure might be positive correlated with their ratings of acceptability.

Students are typically encouraged to make directional hypotheses and explain exactly what prior literature they are based on. However, it is not always possible to predict the direction of hypotheses. For example, suppose you were interested in predictors of children's engagement in a reading intervention. You might theorize that a child's level of inattentive symptoms will affect their engagement in the intervention, but you might not be clear about the direction of the findings. Perhaps children with inattention problems will not pay as much attention during the intervention as other children. Alternatively, perhaps the intervention will be very engaging for children who struggle with inattention, and those children will do better. Assuming you have no prior literature to help you determine the direction of your hypothesis ahead of time, you could leave it nondirectional by writing, "It is hypothesized that level of inattention symptoms will be significantly correlated with level of engagement in the reading intervention."

Write your hypotheses clearly, in a way that foreshadows the research design needed to assess the relationship between the variables. Specifically, each hypothesis should include the names of the variables being assessed; the type of relationship expected, including wording that foreshadows the research design that will be used (e.g., "significant difference between" for quasi-experimental, "positively associated" for correlation); and the relevant sample. Typically, you will not be expected to write out the specific names of measures and statistical tests in your hypotheses, because this can make them look clunky and the information will be covered in the measures and data analysis subsections of your method section, respectively.

Whereas hypotheses state an expected set of findings, a research question is open-ended and exploratory in nature. Qualitative studies typically include research questions as opposed to hypotheses, because the general goal of a qualitative study is to explore an experience or generate a theory about an experience. Often, one major research question is synonymous with the purpose of the study. The focus of this question is typically on understanding participants' perspectives about something they have experienced, including what the experience was like, how they experienced it, and what meaning it holds for them. Subsequently, you may ask smaller research questions under the overarching question. As with hypotheses, you should write research questions in a manner that foreshadows the type of research design needed to answer them. Some quantitative studies include hypotheses as well as research questions.

Researcher Bias: A Qualitative Study Section

In a qualitative study researchers acknowledge the role their potential biases may play during interviews, as well as in coding and interpreting data. If you are proposing a qualitative study, it can be helpful to include a brief description of what these biases might be, based on both personal and professional experiences and beliefs. Consider how much information you want to disclose. During this professional endeavor, we recommend sharing just enough to help readers understand where you are coming from while limiting the amount of detail you share (e.g., if you were proposing a project about poverty, you might say something general like, "Based on my family's experience, I anticipate . . ." rather than go into detail about the specific economic challenges your family faced when you were a child). Stylistically, you might place this section toward the end of your introduction or as part of your method section (almost like a second participant section). Speak with your chair about where a section about potential biases could best fit into your proposal draft. If you plan to use coders, think about whether you would want them to have experiences different from your own (e.g., if you were proposing a study about student mothers and you were one, would you want to try to include coders with or without children? Male or female?). This is something that is often discussed during the proposal meeting.

Additional Tips for Your Introduction
Use Subheadings to Help Organize Your Introduction
If you are proposing a quantitative study, consider including subsections for each variable you will assess. For example, if you plan to conduct a study assessing a moderating variable on an independent and a dependent variable, you could include subsections on the independent variable, the dependent variable, any correlations between them, and any correlations between the moderating variables and the other variables. Similarly, you might group your literature review based on different methodologies used. For example, if you are conducting a study on couples' cognitions during their interactions and a variety of studies have been conducted using self-report questionnaires, but a few assessed participants' responses to viewing videotapes of their interactions, you could review the former in one paragraph and the latter in another. If you are proposing a qualitative study, your subsections could highlight key areas of literature relevant to your topic.

Think about the Structure of Each Paragraph
Start with a topic sentence that orients the reader to the information that will be included. This is often an overarching sentence, such as "Research has indicated that . . ." Make sure all text in the paragraph falls within this topic sentence. At the end of

the paragraph, write a brief statement summarizing the information you addressed, and be sure to include words that help make a transition to the purpose of the next paragraph, even when subheadings are used.

Understand Where to Place Citations

The American Psychological Association's (2020) style manual, for example, indicates that you should cite any claims you make at the end of the first sentence. Write any subsequent sentences that stem from the same reference with wording that indicates it is part of the same citation. If it is not clear, you may cite the reference again.

Avoid Directly Cutting and Pasting Text from Sources into Your Working Draft

We recommend avoiding this completely; also refrain from adding sentences in another font color. This could lead to accidentally including other authors' exact sentences, which would be considered plagiarism. Refer to the note on plagiarism in Chapter 4 to ensure you avoid other forms of plagiarism.

How to Write Your Method Section

In Chapter 4, we listed each subsection you will likely include in your method section. We will now discuss what to write in each section. Remember to review your program's specific project proposal requirements to check for any differentiation from these guidelines.

Participants

If you plan to study human subjects, begin with the number of participants you plan to include. You should provide a rationale for this number. For a quantitative study, this typically involves conducting a power analysis, which is a test to determine how many participants you would need to include to have the power necessary to identify significant results. There are free programs available, such as G*Power 3 (Faul et al., 2007). If you are not familiar with power analyses or need to brush up on your skills, speak with your chair about seeking out helpful resources or appropriate consultation. Another good guideline is to review similar studies you mention in your proposal to see how many participants they used—this can help justify the number that you propose. For qualitative studies, it is helpful to cite literature that suggests a particular number of participants; however, you may decide to add participants or stop collecting data based on whether you achieve theoretical saturation, which occurs when you have collected enough repetitive evidence for conceptual categories and cannot generate any new conceptual insights.

Next, specify your eligibility criteria, including what kind of participants you plan to include and exclude. Who exactly do you aim to target? What kinds of participants need to be involved to answer your research question(s)? Does it make sense to aim for a broad or a specific sample when it comes to factors such as gender, race and/or ethnicity, ability, and geographical location? Examples of inclusion criteria include participants of a certain age, people belonging to a certain type of organization, or people who have a particular problem. You may choose to exclude participants with a particular diagnosis, those with a certain level of severity of symptoms, or those who have gone through a particular type of training. Be sure to include a specific method for identifying each criterion. For example, if you are assessing the effects of a reading program for school-aged children and you decide you want to exclude children with autism, how will you determine whether they have autism? Will you base the determination on parents' response to a yes or no question regarding whether their child ever received an autism diagnosis? A diagnostic screener for autism that the parent completes? Your own evaluation of some sort? In addition, be clear why you are choosing specific inclusion and exclusion criteria. In this case, why would you deem it necessary to exclude children with autism? Do you expect them to have difficulty completing your program in a way that typically developing children would not? Will your overall sample be too small to assess differences between children with and those without an autism diagnosis? Keeping your sample as homogeneous as possible can strengthen your internal validity, but at the expense of some of your study's potential external validity.

Think about the method via which you will obtain your sample. In a quantitative study, the ideal goal is to select a random sample from the population, so that your sample is as representative as possible of the entire population. This is not typically feasible, particularly without a good deal of time, resources, and money. This is why most student research projects tend to use convenience sampling, meaning you recruit in any feasible manner and accept all participants who meet your eligibility criteria. Snowball sampling is a common method for obtaining participants in a qualitative study. This means you begin with convenience sampling and ask your first eligible participant if they know others like themselves who meet your eligibility criteria. You contact these folks and ask them the same thing, building a larger sample over time.

You should also write about where and how you plan to obtain your participants. You can choose to have a specific recruitment section at the beginning of your procedures section. In the participants section, however, you can provide a brief overview of where they will come from. For example, do you plan to recruit teachers in local private schools by contacting each school's principal and informing them of your study? Will you advertise your study in an online chat forum regarding a particular issue or identity? Will you email family and friends a description of your study, explaining the types of participants you are looking for, and ask them to pass the word? Sometimes, if a student is uncertain at the proposal stage about the best means to obtain participants, they suggest a few potential sources and see what is effective as they go.

Nonhuman Samples

Some projects will involve nonhuman samples that can be described in place of a participants section. For example, if you conduct a comprehensive literature review or meta-analysis, you will likely want to write about the types of studies you plan to review in the method section, as well as inclusion and exclusion criteria, sources of information you plan to search, your search strategy, how sources will be selected, and how you plan to synthesize the information. It is useful to review what is referred to as the preferred reporting items for systematic reviews and meta-analyses (PRISMA) statement to help you identify a checklist of items to propose (Page et al., 2021). Similarly, if you conduct a qualitative analysis of photographs or text messages, you could write about these items, as well as perhaps the number of them you plan to assess and the number of people who generated them.

Design

Not every program requires a design subsection, but we think it helps you and your project committee to be clear on the type of research design you will use. This typically brief section states whether your study will be quantitative, qualitative, etc. It then specifies the type of research design within this larger category (e.g., true experiment, correlational design, grounded theory). It can also be helpful to state the independent variables and dependent variables, as well as specific conditions between groups, when applicable. Finally, include any inherent limitations to your design (e.g., potential threats to internal or external validity).

Procedure

In this subsection, you will walk your committee through what you plan to do, step by step. You want the procedure to be written clearly enough that someone could replicate it by following your instructions. You will likely begin with your recruitment procedure (unless it is simple enough to have been clear from your participants section). We recommend providing specific details here. For example, what exactly will your email advertisement to potential participants say? You can include the actual advertisement in your appendices. Some chairs will expect you to do this at the time of your proposal, but even if they do not, it is good to get it done because you will need it for the IRB.

If you are recruiting participants in an applied setting, you will want to think through who will approach them and when. For example, if you plan to recruit from a medical office's waiting room, who will approach people sitting and waiting for their appointment? What days and times of the week are possible? Talk with the directors and/or administrators there beforehand to determine what recruitment and procedural strategies are feasible for them. For example, one of our students was recruiting new clients in a private practice. She offered to recruit participants for her study herself, but the intake coordinator conducted the intakes at different times and it was easier for the externs in the practice to conduct the recruitment. Make sure they understand exactly what you are proposing to do. A site director may love your

Table 5.2 Sample of Factors to Consider in Applied Settings

Schools	Fingerprinting; security identification; district board time frames; recruitment restrictions; student schedules (alongside your schedule); parent groups; access to teachers, school personnel, and parents; students are considered a protected population by institutional review boards
Hospitals	Onboarding (e.g., obtaining identification, physical exams, proof of immunizations, drug testing, attending orientations), set hospital protocols, patient limitations, data access restrictions, separate hospital institutional review board, who can consent or will need a legal representative
Groups and private practices	Timing for study participation (before or after group, on break), multiple roles regarding who is able to recruit for the study (e.g., likely cannot be a client's therapist because of possible coercion)

project idea in theory, only to realize that the logistics will be challenging (e.g., difficulty obtaining permission from key stakeholders, offering a student intervention when students are typically in class). Table 5.2 includes factors to consider about various settings as you develop your project.

Student Example: Recruiting Participants in an Applied Setting

SI aimed to recruit participants for a study focused on assessing the feasibility, acceptability, and preliminary effects of teaching a specific skill to adolescents seeking dialectical behavior therapy, as well as their caregivers. Her chair was co-owner of a clinical group practice and regularly conducted intakes and treatment with adolescents who would be eligible. However, her chair knew from prior experiences with the IRB that she could not be the one to actively recruit participants whom she evaluated or treated. Therefore, SI met briefly with each potentially eligible family to inform them about the study opportunity and indicate that their treatment at the practice would not be impacted, regardless of whether they chose to participate. The IRB approved her procedure.

Beyond a site's expectations, the IRB will pay close attention to whether people feel coerced to participate in your study. They often suggest methods such as having a research assistant provide people with a flyer about your study and telling them to approach the assistant, email, or call a phone number if they are interested in participating. Typically, the IRB will also want recruitment to be conducted by someone other than a participant's clinician or educator, since they will not want them to feel that their participation is expected. It is worth thinking through who will do your recruiting now in preparation for the IRB process.

After you explain your recruitment process, write out the specific procedure for running your study. When working directly with participants, you will typically need to first state that you will review and ask them to sign informed consent or assent forms. Explain who will administer these forms and where (e.g., a private room). If the study will take place online, you could include a box to check off or click instead of requiring a signature. Check with your IRB for options. After writing about the consent process, explain any directions or instructions participants will receive, ideally providing a script of exactly what will be said (this is another item you could put in your appendix). For a study that only includes survey measures, you would then explain the order in which the questionnaires will be administered and how much time you expect it will take.

If you are assessing an intervention, educational curriculum, or other type of specific program, you can include it in a separate subsection of your procedures section. Describe the content in detail, including references to any already published materials you are administering or adapting. Then specify the following: How many sessions or lessons will be included? How long will each one be? How often will they occur? Be sure to describe who will administer the intervention or program. What are their credentials or training? Are they being supervised? By whom? Will you include any measure of their adherence to program material? Describe any control conditions you will use. In addition, explain whether you will have baseline assessments, continual assessments, and/or posttest assessments. Who will administer these assessments, and when and where will the assessments occur?

You should also indicate whether participants will be eligible for any compensation. For example, you might consider offering a gift card once a participant completes your study. In some studies, it might make sense to offer a book or free training. For a longitudinal study, you might try to incentivize participant retention by offering compensation at various times (e.g., after each set of assessments). Alternatively, students often tell participants they can choose to enter a raffle (e.g., three participants will be chosen at random to earn one hundred dollars).

If you are conducting an archival study, then your data have already been collected before you propose your project. Nevertheless, you need to describe your procedure for extracting relevant data. Here is an example.

Student Example: Writing the Procedure Section of a Proposed Archival Study

JR proposed to use self-report and diagnostic data from an eating disorders program in a major hospital. She wrote that she would only include cases that had a signed informed consent form from a parent as well as an assent form for those under the age of eighteen. She described the way the original research team recruited these adolescents, how the measures they completed were administered, who administered them, and the typical amount of time they took. She also wrote about the way she accessed data in an already de-identified manner, who had previously scored the measures, and how she would conduct data entry.

Measures

In Chapter 4, we determined options for selecting measures you might propose to use, including existing, adapted, and original measures. In a quantitative study, your measures section will consist of a description of each assessment tool you plan to use (e.g., demographics questionnaire, self-report, parent report, observational assessment). Each description should include the variable(s) measured, the number of items, the way the measure is scored, the range of scores, what the scores mean (e.g., higher scores indicate higher . . .), and any reliability and validity data that have been conducted, including the specific type assessed (e.g., internal consistency, convergent validity). It is a good idea to include a sample item or two. Clarify which of the variables in your study you will assess with this measure. If you do not plan to administer the entire measure, be clear about which portions you will use.

If you plan to adapt or create a measure for your study, include the procedure for modifying or developing it in the procedures section while describing what you expect the measure to look like in this section. If you have already developed it, is useful to include it in your appendices for your committee's review. Also, indicate whether you plan to analyze any psychometric data from your study.

You will need to either purchase or receive the authors' permission to use all or part of copyrighted measures. You will also need permission to add copyrighted measures to online surveys.

If you are conducting a qualitative study involving interviews, include the open-ended questions you plan to ask, as well as any potential follow-up questions, with an explanation of when you would ask them. It is common for committees to spend time discussing your interview questions and making suggestions for what you might change. This is normal, and the goal is to help ensure you have the best questions possible before proceeding with your study. Many qualitative methods include the understanding that your questions might evolve based on your initial interview experiences. Clarify with your committee the extent to which they feel comfortable with you modifying your questions over the course of the study.

Data Analyses

If you plan to collect and analyze data, you will likely need to include a proposed data analytic subsection in your method section. As we discussed in Chapter 4, your proposed analyses will need to align with the wording of the purpose of your project, as well as your research design. Various chairs and committee members will expect different levels of detail, so check with your chair about how much information to include. Your committee members may suggest additional analyses during your proposal meeting, at which time you will solidify an agreed upon plan.

We recommend writing about any descriptive statistics you plan to report (e.g., means and standard deviations, frequencies and percentages). This could include demographic information and scores on measures. For a quantitative study, you will also want to report your proposed inferential statistics. A good guideline is to propose analyses you would use to assess each of your hypotheses and/or research questions. In addition, consider any preliminary analyses you would need to conduct these analyses. For example, if you plan to run regression analyses, typically you would display correlations between all variables first. Some chairs may also want you to report any planned analyses of statistical assumptions (e.g., normal distributions, homogeneity of variance).

There are numerous ways to analyze qualitative data, ranging from a focus on your own subjective reflections and interpretation of the findings to working with coders to categorize your data. Although your method of choice likely depends on the purpose of your project and agreement with your committee, we find students are often most comfortable with the latter, because it provides a somewhat structured approach to analyzing your data. As much as possible, specify the procedure you will use for systematically organizing and evaluating your data. For example, if you plan to systemically code your data, indicate the procedure for doing so, including how you would train coders and address discrepancies in coding (e.g., consensus meetings).

Student Example: Proposing a Qualitative Data Analytic Plan

AS conducted a qualitative study exploring the experience of artists as parents. In his proposed data analysis, he indicated he would follow Auerbach and Silverstein's (2003) qualitative grounded theory methodology for analyzing focus group data. He and two graduate students would code the data. He planned to have each student read each group interview separately, with his overarching research question in mind. He then described how each coder would identify relevant text from each transcript and detailed how each new file would be labeled in a de-identified manner, including the interview number, coder's name, and level of data analysis. He indicated that after each stage of coding, coders would meet to discuss their results and describe how they would aim to reach consensus. He then detailed how each coder would independently review the master relevant text file and identify repeating ideas. They would meet for consensus as in the prior step and then move on to the theme level. Afterward, AS and his project chair would take both his data and existing theories into account to develop theoretical constructs and a theoretical narrative. Finally, he described how he would create his theoretical narrative, as suggested by Auerbach and Silverstein, to represent participants' collective experience.

It is helpful to mention any steps you would take to judge your qualitative research (e.g., on credibility, transferability). As an example, we will discuss strategies for conducting a member check to assess credibility in Chapter 8.

Abstract

It may seem strange to include information about your abstract after the key written section of your proposal; after all, as we discussed in Chapter 4, it appears before your introduction and method sections. At the same time, your abstract is a summary of your proposal and can serve as a check to ensure you understand exactly what you are proposing. Specifically, your abstract should include two to three sentences about the background research in your area of the subfield, a statement about what is lacking in the literature, and the purpose of your project. Next, include your hypotheses and/or research question(s) followed by details about your method section, including who your participants (or data, etc.) are or will be, the type of research design you will use, and a brief overview of the proposed procedure. Finally, include the potential contributions your project might make to your field, including theoretical, methodological, and/or practical implications.

Skills for Successfully Working with Your Chair

As you work on your proposal, you will be collaborating with your chair on everything, including the structure of your written proposal, hypotheses and/or research questions, project procedures, potential measures or questions to use, and methods for analyzing your data. As we discussed in Chapter 4, chairs vary in terms of how much involvement they want to have in your project. However, we think there are key skills for navigating this relationship. Next, we discuss skills for facilitating a positive student–chair interaction, as well as communication regarding when and how to submit proposal drafts and receive feedback. We also provide suggestions for troubleshooting issues you might encounter when working with your chair.

How Can You Facilitate Getting the Best from Your Chair?

The clearest suggestion is to be proactive! You are the author of your final project, which makes you responsible for all phases of the research endeavor until the final version is complete. You must take the initiative needed to move the project forward and to open a dialogue about any concerns or issues that arise. We recommend addressing responsibilities and expectations from the beginning to ensure they are clear. Some chairs might even like to develop a written agreement. If your chair has a positive experience with you throughout, the process will feel far more collaborative.

You can foster a positive student–chair experience through your level of enthusiasm and responsibility in completing this arduous journey. You will need to convey your excitement for the tasks ahead and let your chair know that you value their time. Be prepared for all meetings with an agenda, any tasks that require follow-up, and your best nondefensive self. Be sure to show up on time; cancel or change a meeting ahead of time, if needed; send follow-up emails about each meeting and each step of the process; and ask whether they would like you to bring hard copies of any written materials you will be discussing in person. Take notes when you meet and make sure that whatever you do submit is your best work thus far. Take the initiative with most everything, while asking for and expecting guidance. Last, we suggest that you maintain frequent contact with your chair and a professional attitude in your interactions, even when expressing concern about your project or personal roadblocks.

When and How to Submit Proposal Drafts and Receive Feedback

In Chapter 4, we reviewed various considerations for selecting your chair. One of those considerations is when and how they provide feedback. Check with your prospective chair about how often they want to see your drafts. Some chairs will expect prospective students to show them a written paragraph or two regarding their initial ideas for the purpose of the study and its rationale. Others will want to see a more detailed outline or even a first draft before committing to chair your project.

Though you may select a general topic area before choosing a chair, we recommend you develop your proposed project with their assistance. If your project is in an area of their expertise, they will likely have references to share that can help you develop your understanding of the relevant literature. They will also likely have ideas for the breadth of literature it makes sense for you to review, as well as suggestions for methods that would be useful for your project. If you are building on or taking a piece of your chair's own research project, it is best to negotiate your ideas about your role in the project up front.

Though there are many ways chairs and students can work together on written drafts, they typically share written documents at the following points: when you have a written purpose of your study with a supporting rationale, when you have a complete draft in outline form, and when you have an initial draft of the introduction and/or method section.

It is useful to develop a tentative timeline with your chair so they can know when to expect drafts from you. It is particularly important to ask about your chair's general schedule when timing these submissions. For example, your chair may take longer to review your written drafts around exam times, at the ends of semesters, and over holidays and in the summer or if they have a specific professional role that takes up time at a certain point in the year (e.g., an administrative role such as director of clinical training or the president of a professional organization). Ask them what you can expect regarding turnaround on your drafts at these times, as well as in general, so you can plan accordingly. Table 5.3 shows a sample timeline you might complete with your chair, from selecting committee members and drafting your proposal through conducting and completing your procedure. Keep in mind that timelines are typically tentative, and you will need to re-evaluate them as your project progresses. In addition, be aware of any required deadlines, such as when you need to propose by to meet program requirements (see Table 5.8 for related considerations). As you work through your proposal writing and the IRB process and begin your research, review

Table 5.3 Tentative Timeline

Task	Target date
Committee member(s) selection, if applicable	
Initial research problem, project purpose, and rationale	
Initial outline of literature review	
More detailed outline of literature review and proposed study	
Full introduction draft	
Initial method draft	
Full method draft	
Full draft of proposal	
Final proposal draft to chair	
Final proposal draft to committee	
Projected proposal date	
Actual proposal date	
Postproposal meeting revisions added	
Institutional review board (IRB) certification completion	
IRB application draft to chair	
IRB application draft for internal review	
IRB formal application submitted	
Recruit participants	
Begin to conduct project procedure	
Complete project procedure	
Conduct data entry	

your timeline to determine whether it is working and to establish solid deadlines for project pieces going forward.

In addition to deciding *when* to submit drafts to your chair, it is good to determine *how* you should submit drafts, as well as how you can expect to receive feedback. Does your chair want drafts in hard copy or electronically? Providing a hard copy means that you either need to snail mail copies (find out the preferred address) or be physically nearby to drop off copies. If you can submit them electronically, will the feedback generally be electronic as well? Do they use tracked changes in Microsoft Word? Would they welcome comments from you in tracked changes? Using tracked changes is a fantastic option for being able to track the edits each person has made. You can also add electronic comments to each other at the side of the document, including the date they were made. Alternatively, can you expect handwritten feedback in the margins? A mixture of both? How detailed do they expect the feedback to be? Some chairs will edit specific sentences, while others will tend to stick to broader suggestions. If your writing needs assistance, that is a different story. In that case, chairs may edit a few pages as examples of grammatical or structural concerns and suggest you get some writing help.

At any level of writing ability, it is common to make several sets of revisions before your chair gives you the go-ahead to set up a proposal meeting. This process typically begins with larger-level revisions, such as the order of your literature review or the specific methodology you will use. Over time, you will likely focus your revisions more on tasks such as making sure each paragraph includes a topic sentence, each section has a summary that transitions into the next paragraph, and each sentence clearly makes your point and is well written. We find that students spend the most time summarizing the statement of the problem and the rationale for their project, which makes sense considering that your goal in these sections is to convince your committee that your project is innovative, important, and has the potential to make a valuable contribution to the field.

As you work on revised drafts, it is a good idea to save and date each one separately so you can keep track of what has changed. You can also always go back to retrieve old text you did not think you would need. A bonus idea is to include notes at the start or end of each draft indicating what the major innovations were, as well as planned next steps.

Troubleshooting Issues Working with Your Chair and Committee Members

In every relationship, there are disagreements or misunderstandings. Working through them will most likely strengthen your working relationship; however, choose your "battles" wisely. If you have chosen the right person to direct your research process, any disagreements will be minor and short-lived.

Student Example: Effectively Managing Disagreement with a Chair

A student wanted to conduct a complex longitudinal study with multiple hypotheses. As impressed as their chair was, the chair wanted to simplify the method to make it more feasible and timely. The chair also wanted to use a different measure for one of the main variables. The student, however, was very committed to conducting the project as it was drafted. The student consulted about the issue with another trusted faculty member and went back to the chair with a clear description of their decision-making, as well as potential places to negotiate. The chair appreciated the student's thoughtfulness, as well as their willingness to be flexible. They were able to discuss the pros and cons of each choice and come up with a viable solution that addressed the goals and concerns of both parties.

Sometimes, conflict with a chair can intensify. In this case, you may need a third-party mediator, such as another committee or faculty member, or even someone outside your department for a more objective perspective. Ultimately, keep your end goal in sight: you want to finish. This may mean deferring to your chair's opinion, even when it is frustrating, for the sake of this larger goal. Remember, you can always pursue your ideas in other ways after you graduate. If you feel your chair is treating you in an unprofessional or unethical matter, be sure to consult with others. Review your program's handbook for steps you can take should you want to explore how to make a more formal complaint. Here, we list a couple of the more frequent issues that may arise when working with your chair, as well as some possible solutions.

How Do You Handle Requests from Your Chair That Seem Inappropriate or More along the Lines of Personal Favors?

Although this situation may seem awkward, you should handle it right away by indicating in a friendly but assertive manner that you are not comfortable with the request. Reference your current professional roles and acknowledge the possibility of future collegiality. If you want to do a "favor" for your chair, which might initially seem inconsequential, remember that you could be setting the precedent for additional requests over time. If you are not comfortable, get some feedback from peers or others who have mentored you during your graduate career.

What If Your Chair Just Does Not Respond to Your Emails or Phone Calls and Deadlines Are Fast Approaching?

Try an in-person meeting, which may mean that you try to catch the person during their office hours or after a class. Check in with them about your timeline (which you should have already created) and ask your chair about their availability and interest in your project. Maybe the lack of response indicates a switch in their support for your project. Ask directly, because you are better off switching early in the process rather than once you have begun. If your chair indicates they do still wish to work with you, acknowledge that they are likely busy, clarify the expected amount of time it will take to receive feedback, and ask if there is anything you can do to facilitate the editing process. For example, would they like you to send a reminder email at some point? Do they want to meet to walk through the draft instead of providing written edits?

What Should You Do If Your Chair Does Not Think You Are Ready to Propose?

Typically, chairs only allow students to send their final proposal draft to committee members once they think there is a high chance of passing. If your chair does not think you are ready, there is likely some truth to this. We understand that it is hard to accept this feedback, particularly if you are aiming to propose by a certain date and/or for a certain milestone (e.g., applying to an internship on time). At the same time, we recommend really thinking through what your chair is saying. What parts of your proposal do they think need work? Is it about the content, the organization, or the sentence structure? What do they suggest you do to improve? Once you are clear on the issues, determine what you will need to do to address them, and see if you feel confident doing so. In addition, consider whether you need some sort of assistance (e.g., with writing). If you do not agree with your chair's perspective, consider showing their feedback to one of your committee members and asking for their input. This will allow you to see if they share the same concerns. They may also be willing to help you figure out how to respond to your chair.

Troubleshooting Issues with Committee Members

You may also have difficulty with a committee member who is asking for favors, unresponsive, or dissatisfied with your proposal. Discuss the issues you are encountering with your chair and see how they recommend you handle it. Some of the suggestions for troubleshooting issues with your chair apply here as well. For example, if they expect several edits to your proposal before agreeing to a proposal meeting, it is likely worth making those edits. As frustrating as it may be, it will likely make your proposal stronger. If the committee member will not move forward with your proposal meeting because they do not approve of your research design, try to determine if there are adjustments you can make to satisfy their concern. It can be helpful to arrange a meeting with you, your chair, and the committee member to see if you can arrive at an agreement regarding what is expected. If you make these attempts and the issue seems beyond repair, consult with your chair and/or leaders in your program about policies for asking a committee member to step down from your committee. Handle this as diplomatically as possible. Encountering them afterward can be awkward, regardless, but this is sometimes a necessary step to take to ensure you can move forward with your project. It may even be a mutually desired parting!

How to Finalize Your Proposal Draft

Once you and your chair agree that your proposal is complete, you will need to finalize your proposal draft. A typical proposal draft includes the following: title page, abstract, introduction, method, references, and appendices, such as potential recruitment advertisements, informed consent and/or assent forms, questionnaires, vignettes, and treatment, curriculum, or coding manuals you are proposing to use. You do not necessarily need to include all these appendices, and it may depend on whether you consider developing some of them as part of your project (e.g., a treatment manual). However, the IRB will likely want to see many of these items, such as any questions from unpublished measures that you plan to ask participants, as well as consent and/or assent forms, so you might as well have them ready for your committee's feedback during your proposal meeting! Check with your chair about what makes the most sense to include in your full proposal draft.

Be sure to format your proposal draft according to the style guide you are using (e.g., American Psychological Association style). You will also need to make sure you are adhering to any required program and/or university formatting guidelines. Use the same font, font size, and headings throughout the draft. In addition, make sure your in-text citations and reference list are accurate and consistent.

It can be helpful to review a copy of the form your committee will use to evaluate you. Consider the form a self-evaluation. What would you rate yourself on each item? Is there anything you think you might improve on?

Be sure to proofread your final proposal draft. It can be useful to step away from your draft for a little while; taking a break may increase the likelihood that you will catch any issues when you return, such as spelling and grammatical errors, inconsistent headings, and problems with citations. It is normal to find mistakes, even when you have gone through your draft several times. Some chairs will want to see the complete final version of your draft before you send it to your committee members, whereas others will trust you to finalize the formatting. Either way, it can be worthwhile to ask someone (e.g., a mentor, friend, or family member) to review your final draft before sending it to your committee.

Preparing for Your Proposal Meeting

As we discussed in Chapter 4, once you and your chair have agreed that your proposal is ready to share with your committee members, they will typically have approximately two weeks to read it before agreeing to schedule a proposal meeting. Check with your chair and your program's guidelines to determine the exact steps you need to take. The five steps reviewed in the following sections include some relatively universal skills for successfully managing the proposal meeting process: tasks to complete before your proposal meeting, creating slides (if they are required), how to prepare for your oral presentation, how to respond to questions and feedback from your committee, and items to address after you propose. Table 5.4 provides a checklist of skills for each step. If you would like additional suggestions for preparing for the proposal meeting, please refer to Bell et al. (2019).

Before Your Proposal Meeting

Once your chair approves your written proposal, the typical next steps include sending it to your committee members and scheduling a meeting. Clarify the preferred way to send your draft. Most will be fine with an emailed draft, though some may prefer a hard copy. Make sure you also understand the acceptable procedure for scheduling a proposal meeting. In some programs, students can send their proposal draft at the same time they suggest dates and times for a meeting. In other programs, students must first give their committee members two weeks to read their proposal before they start to coordinate schedules. Sometimes it depends on the committee. Double check with your chair to ensure you are following the appropriate process and make sure you know how much time you should allot for the meeting.

You also need to prepare for the day of your proposal meeting. If you will be meeting in person, find out how to schedule a room and any equipment you will need (e.g., laptop, projector, adapter). If you will propose in person, try to spend some time in the room you will use to become familiar with the equipment and/or determine whether you need to arrange for someone at your school to have it there that day. We suggest having more than one copy of your slides with you in case of any technological difficulty. If one or more of your committee members will be online, be sure they have a video conferencing program they can use to join your meeting (e.g., Zoom, Skype), and offer to test a call with them prior to the meeting. Leave ample time to set up and check your Internet connection on the day of your proposal meeting. Finally, determine whether your committee members need to complete evaluation forms, and if so, be sure to get them the forms and instructions.

Talk with your chair about what you should prepare to present during your proposal meeting. For example, some chairs will ask you to put together slides, but others will not. If you have a choice, we recommend this because following a planned presentation can help you stick to key points and your audience can visually follow along. Find out how much time you should plan for your presentation and whether you or your chair will take notes on committee member feedback during the meeting.

Creating Slides

If your chair asks you to create slides for your proposal meeting, ask how much information to include. Some will want you to provide a comprehensive review of the literature, while others will want you to assume the committee is already familiar with your write-up and focus on your proposed project. Ask your chair and/or upper-level students for prior sets of proposal slides. They will help you get a sense of the format and the amount of information you might include. Ask your chair whether they would be willing to review your slides prior to your proposal meeting; if so, send

Table 5.4 Checklist of Skills for the Proposal Meeting Process

Before your proposal meeting	✓
I have checked with my chair and my program's guidelines to determine the exact steps I will need to take.	
I have sent my written proposal to committee members and scheduled a meeting.	
I have found out how to schedule a room and reserve any equipment I may need.	
I have spent time in the room I will be presenting in to familiarize myself with the environment.	
I have downloaded my slides onto my computer.	
I have more than one copy of my slides in case of any technological difficulties.	
If any committee members will be joining virtually, I have provided necessary instructions to join.	
If it is my responsibility to provide committee members with evaluation forms, I have provided them along with instructions.	
I have discussed with my chair how I will present my proposal in the meeting (e.g., show a PowerPoint presentation).	
I have decided who will be taking notes during my presentation.	
Creating slides	
I have discussed with my chair about the amount of information to include.	
I have determined whether my chair is willing and/or wants to look at a draft of my slides, and if so, by what date.	
I have determined whether I would like to distribute any supplemental handouts (e.g., tables, figures, copy of measures, copy of slides).	
My slides are visually simple, with bullet points and without excessive animations, multiple fonts, or colors.	
My slides begin with a title slide, including the title of my project draft, my name, and the names of my committee members.	
I included brief, key summary points of the background literature before discussing my project.	
I have provided information about studies similar to mine that discuss a gap in the literature that my proposal addresses.	
I have prepared a slide addressing the purpose of and rationale for my project.	
I have included my hypotheses and/or research questions and information about participants, research design, procedures and measures, and data analyses I will conduct.	
I have reviewed my slide set as a whole to determine whether I should cut any information.	
I have an introductory statement.	
I orient my audience to what I will be reviewing, briefly reorienting throughout my talk.	
Oral presentation	
I have envisioned speaking in front of my chair and any additional audience and/or committee members.	
I have practiced in front of a friend, family member, or classmate to receive feedback about the clarity of my slides, my presentation style, and my body language and eye contact.	
I have practiced presenting my slides within the time limit recommended by my chair.	

continued

Table 5.4 *continued*

Responding to questions and feedback	
In preparing to answer audience members' questions, I am clear on my reasoning for presenting the material I did, as well as the method I plan to use.	
I have envisioned the kinds of questions my committee might ask and have practiced potential responses.	
I am prepared to thank committee members for their questions and indicate that they asked a good question before responding.	
I am prepared to respond slowly and succinctly, keeping my response concise.	
I am prepared to acknowledge uncertainty to a question for which I may not have an answer.	
I am thinking of this meeting like a consultation and am committed to taking my committee members' suggestions seriously.	
I am prepared to take notes during the meeting, if this is what my chair and I decided, or ensure my chair is taking notes.	
I anticipate some potentially contrasting opinions, demonstrate appreciation for each committee member's input, and defer to my chair if it is unclear what I should decide.	
I am prepared to respond nondefensively to feedback about my writing and presentation.	
Postproposal meeting	
I understand the necessary final revisions to my proposal.	
My committee has signed any required forms or has a plan to return them to me.	
I have checked with my chair about the optimal order for completing next steps (e.g., institutional review board proposal draft, final draft approval).	

them your slides well in advance, so they can provide you with edits to integrate beforehand.

As you work on your slides, think about whether supplemental handouts would be helpful for your committee. For example, if you created a measure you plan to use, it could be useful for your committee to have a copy. If you will meet in person, print hard copies for your proposal meeting. If you and/or someone on your committee will be attending virtually, see whether you can send your slides and handouts prior to the meeting so they have time to review and print them and be able to follow along more easily.

Choose a layout for your slides that is relatively simple and easy to read. Do not use animations—there is no need to have text cartwheeling across your slide! Stick to one font type and try to use a consistent size for your titles and text. Text size can be decreased slightly if needed, but if you need a much smaller font, you probably have too much on that slide. In general, stick to key points. If you are worried you will forget something, you can add notes to the notes section of the slides; learn how to view them while presenting and/or print a copy for yourself.

The following are some general recommendations for slide preparation. Begin your slide set with a title slide, including the title of your project draft, your name, and the names of your committee members. Next, include a couple of slides with key points about the areas of background literature you reviewed in your introduction. Provide a bit more detail about the studies that are most similar to yours or that served as a springboard for your project. You can assume your committee has read your paper, so you just need to provide an overview, rather than all the specific details found in your draft. Next, acknowledge the problem you are attempting to address with your project. It often helps to have a separate slide or two regarding the purpose of your project and the related rationale. If relevant, include an additional slide with any hypotheses and/or research questions. Next, include slides about your participants, research design, procedures followed, measures used, and data analyses conducted. You will likely need a few slides for the method information.

Once you have written out your slides, review them as a set to see if you need to add or trim any key information. Usually it is the latter: you will likely want to decrease the amount of information you have included. As you go through your slides, reduce wordiness and determine whether there are places to add relevant visuals (e.g., a picture of the school where you will complete your project, a fun graphic related to your topic).

Once you have a full draft of your slide set, review them again, thinking through what you would say about each one. For example, think about your introductory statement. Typically, you would start with thanking your committee and presenting the title of your project. Sometimes students speak briefly about what motivated them to conduct their project. As you review each slide, think about the words you wish to say aloud. Make sure you can review each piece of information clearly and succinctly. This process often leads to revisions of the slide text, which is expected and useful for moving toward a final slide set.

Share a brief overview of the structure of what you plan to review, so your committee knows what to expect. Your chair might mention what they asked you to present at the beginning of your meeting. As you go through the slides, think about how you can orient your audience to each section. It can be helpful to let them know you are about to present key background information, as well as when you will be moving on to describe your method.

Oral Presentation

Once you have developed your full slide set, practice your presentation to get a sense of where you might still need to clarify information, both for yourself and in your slides. Imagine speaking in front of your chair and two committee members. Think about the layout of the room you will present in and whether you will sit or stand.

When you are ready, it can help to have a classmate, friend, or family member observe your presentation and provide feedback about the clarity of your slides. Can they repeat back what you are saying is lacking in the literature? What about the purpose of your project and why it is important? Can they explain how you will study it? If so, this is great news! If not, ask them to share what is unclear. Perhaps they would be willing to help you reword what you are trying to say. Also ask them to comment on your body language, such as your eye contact, volume, speed, and tone. Practice referring to your slides and even some notes while making eye contact with your imaginary committee. If you are anxious about presenting, more rehearsal will likely be helpful. Finally, time yourself to see if you fall within the time frame your chair recommended.

Responding to Questions and Feedback

The timing of your committee members' questions may depend on the level of formality of your proposal meeting. In a more formal meeting, you might present before your committee asks questions. In a meeting with a more collaborative style, your chair may invite committee members to ask relevant questions as you present. For example, someone might ask you a question about prior literature you are discussing before you move on to describe the purpose of your study.

The content of your committee members' questions can extend beyond what you are presenting to anything in your proposal or anything they deem relevant to determining your project rationale and method. The best way to prepare is to know the information in your proposal well and be clear on your reasoning for presenting the material you did, as well as the method you plan to use.

Try to anticipate potential questions and how you will respond. There is a good chance your committee members will have questions similar to ones you and your chair addressed while writing your proposal. For example, if prior literature in your area points to a few different measures, it is possible your committee will ask about your rationale for using the measure you proposed. In this case, it would be useful to walk them through your decision-making process, including the pros and cons of each measure and how you and your chair selected the measure you proposed. First, thank them for their question and acknowledge its merit. Second, practice speaking slowly so committee members can follow along, while providing concise answers that get to the point. It is nearly impossible to predict every question, however! It is okay to take a moment or two before responding. You can even say something like, "Thank you, that is a good question. I have to think about this for a moment." You can ask them to repeat the question or request further clarification. If you are unsure how to respond, it is okay to say you do not know. It is better to be open when you are uncertain than try to stumble through an answer. Remember, one of the goals of your proposal meeting is to help you develop the best possible project. You can ask the committee to consult with you about the issue, indicating you are eager to revise the project using their input.

Committee members will provide feedback about things they think you can present and/or do differently. This can be difficult to take in after you spent so much time thinking through your proposal, and you might feel the urge to become defensive. Just remember that the goal of this meeting is to create the strongest proposal possible so that your work has a good chance to meaningfully contribute to your field. Try to think of the meeting like a consultation, where you have the opportunity to elicit feedback from knowledgeable faculty and/or experts in your topic area. Take their ideas seriously and consider that they might have good points about improving your written work and/or project proposal. Take notes on any changes they suggest and/or ask your chair to do so prior to the meeting.

Sometimes committee members have contrasting opinions about how you should proceed with your method. If this happens, listen to each perspective. Strategically, it is beneficial to note the value of each committee member's idea. After making points about each side, you can respectfully suggest what you think makes sense. At the same time, indicate you are open to alternatives, and try to defer to your chair if the committee is having difficulty reaching consensus.

Your committee may also provide you with constructive feedback about your written and/or oral presentation. Critique is seldom easy to hear, but remember that it is the committee's job to provide you with this type of feedback. Try to consider it an opportunity to prepare for your future student work and career.

Postproposal Meeting

As we mentioned in Chapter 4, after you present your proposal, it is common for the committee to ask you to leave the room so they can evaluate your written and oral performance and discuss next steps. Your chair will let you know when to return, and hopefully the committee will congratulate you on passing your proposal meeting! If so, this is a milestone to celebrate—it means you can move ahead with your project and advance in your program.

Before you leave the meeting, make sure you understand any necessary revisions and who needs to see them before you move forward. In most cases, it is sufficient for your chair to approve the changes, but the rest of the committee may want to see your revisions as well. This could be the case if they expect major changes to your literature review, your hypotheses or research questions, and/or your method section. Finally, make sure your committee signs any required forms or has a plan to return them to you.

After your proposal meeting is complete, try to find some time to relax and do something fun to celebrate. You put a lot of time and energy into writing your proposal and preparing for this meeting, and you have a good deal of work ahead. Take time to do some tasks that are unrelated to your project, such as cleaning. Engaging in a combination of pleasurable and mastery activities will likely rejuvenate you for the steps ahead.

Once you have recuperated a bit, embark on the next steps, such as making proposal revisions, having your final draft approved, and writing a draft of your IRB proposal (if applicable). Check with your chair about the optimal order for completing these steps. In cases where IRB approval is needed (i.e., to collect data or use archival data with human subjects), it makes sense to complete your IRB application before working on your proposal revisions. In other cases, you may need to show your revisions to your chair and/or committee members before you move ahead with the IRB, particularly if you need to make major changes to your method section, which would affect your application.

If you need to submit an IRB application, do so as soon as possible, because it can take time for the IRB to review it. Check with your IRB to determine the expected timeline and any deadlines for submitting applications, particularly if your application will require full board review. In the next section, we will review the steps for successfully completing an IRB application.

Writing Your IRB Application

As we discussed in Chapter 2, it is important to become familiar with the specific IRB procedures, timelines, and application categories followed at your university well before you conduct your final project. If you will be working with human subjects, you will typically need to apply to receive IRB approval. Once you are ready to write your application, check your university's guidelines to determine which category your project falls under (i.e., exempt, expedited, or full board review) and the expected format and upcoming IRB meeting deadlines. Different IRBs will request slightly different information, but we review common components here.

IRB Application Components

Project Description
The project description includes a summary of your proposed research project, including the purpose of your study, your scientific rationale, and your study goals. Write in layperson language as much as possible, because the IRB members will come from a variety of scientific and nonscientific fields and may not be familiar with the jargon used in your specific subfield. The IRB will typically be less interested in knowing the literature in your area and more focused on the reasons you have for conducting your project.

Description of Participants or Subjects
Here, you will indicate the number of participants you aim to include, the anticipated gender breakdown, and the type of population. For example, if you plan to include any vulnerable populations, such as minors, prisoners, pregnant women, or individuals who are disabled, you will be asked to provide a specific rationale for doing so (or for specifically excluding those populations). You will be asked to include the inclusion and exclusion criteria for your study, as well as how you will determine these criteria (e.g., via responses to survey questions).

Recruitment and Enrollment
This is where you will describe your plans for making initial contact with prospective participants and procedures for enrolling them into your study. You will need

to explain when and how they will be informed about the study, as well as who will inform them, if applicable (e.g., a receptionist in a medical office will provide each client who signs in with a flier about your study). Include copies of any recruitment materials (e.g., fliers, scripts), as well as a letter of support from any applied settings involved in your study (e.g., if you are recruiting and/or working with participants off campus). If you will be obtaining participants from an existing data set, you will likely need to enclose a letter of permission from the data set's owner.

If you plan to collect data from participants directly, indicate who will officially enroll those who are eligible into your study and how (e.g., via phone, in person) it will be done. Include what you will tell participants about why they are eligible or ineligible. If you are recruiting for a study related to a treatment or a service and they are not eligible, consider providing them with referrals to a similar treatment or service.

Study Procedure

You will need to describe each step of what you will do once you have enrolled your participants. Write this section as if you were giving someone directions to conduct your study for you and you need them to get each detail exactly right. Begin with your procedure for obtaining informed consent and/or assent (see more information about these forms in the "Informed Consent and Assent" section) . Include information about who will conduct the procedure, as well as when and where it will take place. Then describe tasks such as how and when participants will be divided into groups, measures or activities they will be asked to complete (e.g., self-report questionnaires, responses to vignettes, participation in interviews), and any intervention or program content. If you are proposing the use of a procedure that is atypical or may be unfamiliar to your IRB, it is helpful to provide detailed information about what will be done, using citations to support your rationale. Talk with your chair about whether it would help to attach articles that discuss procedures similar to those presented in your application to educate the IRB about the kind of research method you are using. Regardless of the type of method you use, include copies of items such as consent and/or assent forms, measures, and/or interview questions as appendices.

Compensation

Indicate whether participants will receive any compensation or reward for participating in your study. If so, explain what the compensation will be (e.g., cash, reimbursement for travel, raffle), the amount, who will provide it, and when participants will receive it (e.g., after completion of the study forms).

Potential Risks and Benefits of Research Participation

Most IRB applications include questions about the possibility of a variety of risks, many of which relate to physiological procedures and medications. You will also be asked whether participants will be deceived in any way, and if so, how and when they will be debriefed. If any potentially vulnerable populations will be included, you will need to indicate what procedures will be in place to protect their rights and reduce the risk of coercion. Questions may address a possible invasion of privacy, based on the collection of personally identifying information (e.g., demographics, medical and mental health information). You will probably be asked to describe any questions participants will be asked related to sensitive information that might make them feel anxious, embarrassed, or violated, for example, questions about participants' mental health symptoms or drug history. You could also be asked whether participants might find any part of the study degrading, offensive, or threatening. The key is to describe how you will manage and reduce potential risks, such as by keeping data confidential and offering therapy referrals. If risks to participants' physical, psychological, or social well-being are potentially substantial, you will likely need to explain how the benefits of conducting the study outweigh the risks and are better than alternative methods.

Confidentiality of Data

This part of your application should include methods for keeping data anonymous or maintaining confidentiality of the data you collect. These methods can include the removal of identifying information from the data (de-identification), assigning each participant a code number known only to you and/or your research team, and storing your data in a place that only you and/or your research team can access (e.g., a locked file cabinet, secure electronic data set). Pay particular attention to the collection and storage of audio or video data (e.g., will faces be blacked out?). You should also indicate whether data will be disposed of after a specific period.

Informed Consent and Assent

The purpose of obtaining informed consent and assent is to ensure that participants understand what the study involves and that they have time to consider whether they want to participate, without any coercion. Consent forms are used for individuals ages eighteen and older, and assent forms are used to help children and adolescents under the age of eighteen make informed decisions about participating in your study. Individuals under the age of eighteen need written consent from a parent or guardian to participate; however, it is useful to inform them about the study via an assent form. In some instances, consent can be waived (e.g., when there is no possibility of more than minimal risk, participants' rights or benefits are not negatively impacted; the study cannot take place otherwise). In the case of an anonymous survey, the IRB will often allow you to include a letter at the front of your materials indicating that participating in the following survey verifies consent. Refer to your IRB's guidelines regarding how to determine when participants have the capacity to provide their own informed consent and how to handle those who cannot. There are also guidelines for how to obtain consent from non-English speakers.

Although you are asking participants who are capable of consent and assent to sign forms, you should walk them through the information and ask whether they have any questions. IRBs often recommend that you ask participants to summarize your study in their own words to be certain that they truly understand what is involved. The language you use in your consent and assent forms should be simple (i.e., at an eighth-grade reading level or lower).

The federal government outlines general requirements for informed consent (US Department of Health and Human Services, 2018). Typically, consent forms include the following pieces of information:

- Your name (as the primary investigator), your advisor's name, and your department
- Indication that this a research study
- One to three sentences about your study's purpose in layperson terms, at an eighth-grade reading level or lower (without sharing information that could potentially impact your results)
- The estimated duration of the study
- The expected number of participants
- An explanation that the study is voluntary and that they can withdraw at any time, without penalties (e.g., they can still receive their usual care on-site)
- A brief, specific description of the procedures they will be asked to complete
- Potential benefits of participating, including contributing to research in a certain area
- Potential risks of participating, including any emotional discomfort, and how they will be addressed should those risks arise
- Any compensation available
- How data will be kept confidential (e.g., de-identified, kept in a locked file cabinet) and any potential limits of confidentiality (e.g., in some qualitative interview studies, participants will be de-identified, but the researcher may report quotes from specific individuals).
- If audio and/or video will be obtained, who will be privy to the tapes, where they will be stored, and when they will be destroyed
- How long data will be retained and/or when data will be destroyed
- Ways to contact the primary investigator, your advisor, and/or your school's IRB with questions or concerns
- Alternative treatments (if it is a treatment study)
- An explanation that results of the study can be provided
- A place for the participant to sign their name and the date, indicating they understand the information on the consent form, have been given the opportunity to ask questions, and consent to participation
- A place for the researcher to sign their name and provide the date

Figure 5.2 illustrates a sample consent form from one of our former students, who was conducting a qualitative study with volunteer rape crisis counselors.

An assent form includes information similar to what would be found on a consent form, but in even simpler language, particularly if you design it for a young child. You should include a brief description of the study, the reasons you are conducting the study and asking them to participate, what participating will involve, and anything uncomfortable and/or beneficial. Make sure they know that their parent or legal guardian also signed permission for them to participate and that they can ask questions at any time. In addition, make sure they know they do not have to participate if they do not want to and that they can end their participation at any time.

Informed Consent Form for Human Research Subjects

You are being asked to volunteer in a research study investigating the experience of being a volunteer rape crisis counselor (RCC). This study is being conducted by CP, a clinical psychology doctorate candidate in the (PROGRAM NAME) under the supervision of HV, a faculty member in the program. Approximately 15 RCCs will be interviewed for this study. The purpose of the research is to better understand the experiences of volunteer RCC's as they work with survivors of domestic violence and sexual assault.

As a participant, you will be asked to meet with CP for approximately one hour at (LOCATION). She will ask you a number of open-ended questions about your experience as a RCC working with survivors.

There are no significant risks related to participating in this study. While there is no direct benefit for your participation in the study, it is reasonable to expect that the experience may be therapeutic, and the results may provide information of value for the field of psychology and volunteer organizations.

Your identity as a participant will remain confidential. For coding purposes, the interview will be audiotaped. The principal investigator, CP, will be the only one to hear the audiotape as she will promptly transcribe the content in a de-identified manner. Audiotapes will be used only for research purposes.Your name will not be included in any forms, questionnaires, etc. This consent form is the only document identifying you as a participant in this study; it will be stored securely in a locked file cabinet available only to the principal investigator. Data collected will be destroyed at the end of a legally prescribed period of time. Results will typically be reported in the aggregate, though some specific quotes from individual interviews will be reported in a de-identified manner. If you are interested in seeing these results, you may contact the principal investigator.

If you have any questions about the research, you may contact the principal investigator, CP, at (EMAIL), or the dissertation chair, HV, at (EMAIL). If you have questions concerning your rights as a subject, you may contact the Institutional Review Board at (NAME AND EMAIL).

Your participation in this research is voluntary. Refusal to participate will involve no penalty or loss of benefits to which you are otherwise entitled, and you may discontinue participation at any time without penalty. In particular, your decision to participate, refusal to participate, or withdrawal from this study will not affect any aspect of your volunteer position.

Your signature indicates you have fully read the above text and you have had the opportunity to ask questions about the purposes and procedures of this study. Your signature also acknowledges receipt of a copy of the consent form as well as your willingness to participate and to be audiotaped.

_____

Name of Participant

_____   _____
Signature of Participant   Date

_____

Name of Investigator

_____   _____
Signature of Investigator   Date

This consent form was based on a template provided by LIU Post's IRB.

Figure 5.2 Sample consent form

Finally, make sure they understand that signing means they have read the form and agree to participate. We provide a template of an assent form in Figure 5.3.

SAMPLE ASSENT FORM (UNDER 18)
UNIVERSITY/CAMPUS NAME
Assent Form for Human Research Subjects

Title:
Principal Investigator:
Supervising Investigator:

<u>Why are you here?</u>
The researchers (that's us) want to tell you about a study looking at how.... We want to.... We decided to invite you to be in the study because we want to learn more about....and because your parent or guardian thought you might like to be in the study too,

<u>Why is this study being done?</u>
We want to learn more about....

<u>What will happen to me?</u>
Only if you want, these things will happen:
    1) Answer questions about....
    2) Play with toys while we watch you....

<u>Will the study hurt?</u>
Nothing in this study will hurt.

<u>Will the study help me?</u>

<u>What if I have questions?</u>
You can ask us questions any time. You can ask questions now or later. You can talk to any of the people who are helping with the study.

<u>Do my parents know about this?</u>
This study was explained to your parents and they said that you could be in it. You can talk this over with them before you decide.

<u>Do I have to be in the study?</u>
You do not have to be in the study. No one will be upset if you don't want to do this. If you don't want to be in this study, you just have to tell us. If you want to be in the study, you just have to tell us. You can say yes now and change your mind later. It's up to you.

Writing your name on this page means that the page was read by you or to you and that you agree to be in the study. You know what will happen to you. If you decide to quit the study all you have to do is to tell the person in charge.

_____   _____
MY NAME   TODAY'S DATE

_____   _____
INVESTIGATOR'S SIGNATURE   DATE

Retrieved from: https://liu.edu/irb/forms

Figure 5.3 Assent form template

Additional Components of an IRB Application

Has IRB Approval Already Been Obtained from Another Institution?

There are times when you will need IRB approval from another institution in addition to your school. For example, if you plan to conduct your study in a school, hospital, or clinic or use their existing data, you will typically need to obtain IRB approval from that institution as well. If you are using existing data from an outside institution, the original researcher likely already has IRB approval. In this case, they can often add your name to the existing IRB protocol. Regardless, your school IRB will typically want you to submit the other institution's IRB approval. Sometimes this will facilitate your school IRB's review of your application, because your school may be inclined to defer to the outside institution's approval. At other times, you may have to go back to the outside institution's IRB and amend your application there to satisfy a request from your school's IRB.

Letters of Support from Applied Settings and/or Researchers

As mentioned earlier in this section, if you will be collaborating with any applied settings off campus, you will typically need to include a letter of support from someone of authority (e.g., the principal of a school, supervising therapist, lead administrator). This letter should indicate their agreement to be involved in your research. In addition, it should briefly outline the ways they will be involved. For example, if you will be recruiting there, how will this occur? If you will conduct your study on-site, what type of assistance, space, and/or time will they provide? If you will use some of their data, how will you access it? Similarly, you will typically need a letter from anyone whose archival data you will be analyzing, indicating their permission for you to do so.

Signatures

As the primary investigator of a research study, you will need to sign off on your IRB application. As a student, you will usually also need a faculty sponsor for the research project, who will sign off as well. The chair of your department will also typically need to sign off on your application. Make sure to know your program's procedure for obtaining the department chair's signature (e.g., in a large department, you may need to send your application to the chair by interoffice mail or submit it electronically through an IRB manager portal a certain amount of time before the application is due).

Checklist of Items to Submit

Once you have completed your IRB application, check to make sure you have included all necessary items. Each university will have its own requirements, but here is a typical list of the types of documents you will be asked to include:

- IRB application
- Consent and/or assent forms

- Description of how audio and/or video tapes will be managed (if a separate form is required)
- Recruitment materials (e.g., texts of emails, flyers)
- Unpublished questionnaires
- Interview questions
- Any unpublished manuals, vignettes, and/or protocols
- Any letters of support from applied settings or collaborating researchers
- Any required certificates of training (as discussed in Chapter 2)

Review Your IRB Application with Your Faculty Sponsor

At a basic level, your faculty sponsor (typically your chair) will serve as the gatekeeper for your submission to the IRB, since they will need to sign off on your application, but they can also help you navigate the IRB process. Faculty have experience with what your IRB wants and what they have approved in the past. As clear as you may think are in your writing, the IRB is looking for information that is much more specific than what is typically expected in a research proposal or article. Meet with your faculty sponsor while you are preparing the application to discuss and agree on the specific procedural steps you will follow. The good news is that nailing those steps down now will aid you in conducting your study. Your faculty sponsor can then review a draft of your application and point out any issues that need clarification or modification.

Sometimes faculty will talk about the IRB as a major obstacle to completing research. Understandably, the IRB's relationship with faculty as a check-and-balance system can lead to tension, since projects can be delayed or even disapproved by the IRB. As a student, if you are having difficulty getting a part of your research through the IRB, first meet with your faculty sponsor to receive their assistance in addressing the issue(s). In addition, find out if a member of your faculty serves on the IRB, because this person will have firsthand experience with what your school's IRB tends to expect.

Responding to the IRB's Feedback

Once the IRB has reviewed your application, they will either approve your project as is, ask you to make revisions, or decline your project. The latter is rare and would likely only occur if the risks to human subjects appear to greatly outweigh the benefits of the research. It is very common to receive requests for revisions, however. As we noted previously, take a few days to digest the feedback and ask to discuss it with your chair. After you think through the requests, your emotional response to the feedback will probably lessen.

Your IRB will likely want you to write a point-by-point response letter, addressing each of their queries. This does not mean you have to agree to change everything they asked about. You may just need to provide further clarification about what you intend to do and/or the rationale. Maintain a polite tone and thank them for their questions. Remember, your goal is to have them approve your project. In addition to a response letter, some IRBs will want you to revise your application based on their feedback. You may also have to revise your recruitment materials and/or consent and assent forms. The sooner you submit these changes, the sooner you are likely to receive approval to start conducting your research!

Making Amendments to an IRB Approved Study

After your study is IRB approved, you may want to revise something in your research study procedure. These changes need to go through the IRB, typically as an amendment to your application. For example, perhaps you found an additional site where you can recruit participants. Or maybe you are struggling to obtain participants and your committee agrees with a way to broaden your sample. You might have come across a measure you would like to add to your study. Check your IRB's process for submitting amendments, and make sure the IRB approves them before straying from your procedure.

IRB Renewal

IRB approval, once obtained, generally lasts about a year. At the end of this period, you and your advisor will typically receive a notice from the IRB asking about the status of your research and giving a deadline for renewing your application. If you have finished your project, you can indicate as such, but if not, you might need to ask for an extension. If you need additional time to complete your project, consider whether revising the procedure or consent and/or assent forms could be useful. Be sure to have the IRB stamp any recruitment materials and consent and/or assent forms for future participants with new expiration dates. The IRB committee is generally not interested in why you are taking so long to finish, but they remain vigilant in terms of monitoring interactions with participants, so be sure to keep your application active throughout the course of your project!

Managing Your Project

Once your proposal has been approved by your committee (and, in many cases, the IRB has provided you with written approval for your project), you are ready to go! The rest should be simple, right? You have a step-by-step plan to follow in your method section (and possibly your IRB protocol). However, these steps are often easier said than done. Next, we provide suggested steps to successfully manage your project.

Preparation and Assembly of Materials

First, go through all sections of your method and/or IRB protocol and make a to-do list of things you need to prepare and items you need to gather. If you are still awaiting IRB approval, you can work on your list while you wait. Table 5.5 includes a sample project preparation to-do list with columns indicating who you may need to contact and self-imposed deadlines.

Before beginning your final project, it can be useful to pilot test your procedure, either with a small number of participants or with mock participants (e.g., classmates, peers). As Bell et al. (2019) indicate, doing so can help you become aware of several factors, including the following: whether participants can complete your measures as planned, the ease with which online surveys may be used, the length of your procedure, places where you are less clear about the procedure than you thought, the quality of any necessary deception, and participants' reactions to your procedure. You can request feedback from your pilot study participants to help you improve your procedure and/or measures. Pilot testing can also be used to gather

Table 5.5 Sample Project Preparation To-Do List

To do	Who to contact	Deadline
If participants will complete hard-copy informed consent and/or assent forms, make copies of them, stamped by the institutional review board (IRB).		
Order standardized measures and/or other materials needed.		
If materials will be distributed in hard copy, make copies of all forms participants need to complete and create a place for participant identification numbers on each form (e.g., in the top right-hand corner).		
Create folders of all materials needed for each participant (hard copy or electronic).		
If materials will be electronic, seek permission to reproduce copyrighted measures online.		

continued

Table 5.5 *continued*

To do	Who to contact	Deadline
If materials will be electronic, upload or write in all questions and have them checked for errors.		
Write a step-by-step instruction manual for you and/or your research assistants to follow, including an itemized checklist of tasks and/or measures that need to be completed (e.g., as each participant or group is run).		
Prepare space and/or schedule to be in any space you will use to conduct your procedures. Pilot test any procedures and/or any measures you created. If electronic, pilot test usability of measures (e.g., can the participant move forward if they skip a question?).		
Secure a locked file cabinet in a locked room and/or password-protected computer files (adhering to how you said you would store data in your IRB application).		
Create a spreadsheet (separate from data entry for your project) to track any identifying information about each participant (e.g., the date[s] they participated, contact information, etc.)		
Obtain any compensation you will provide (e.g., gift cards).		
Prepare computer software (e.g., spreadsheet) for data entry (e.g., create column names for each variable you will enter, label values).		
Disseminate recruitment advertisements.		

observational or interview data to train coders and practice obtaining interrater reliability. Discuss any potential major changes with your chair before proceeding and determine whether any of them will require approval from your committee or IRB in the form of an amendment (Bell et al., 2019).

Student Example: Enrollment Checklist

JB developed this checklist to remind herself what she needed to do before and during her meeting with each study participant.

- Send reminder email to participants a day ahead of appointment with copy of consent attached
- Prep copies of all paperwork ahead of time: consent, demographic, knowledge test, attitudes scale, instructions for role play, instructions for writing sample
- Update participant spreadsheet with their contact information, book pickup, and preferred workshop time
- Complete consent
- Complete questionnaires
- Complete role play (filmed with camera and timed—five minutes for prep and ten minutes to complete)
- Complete writing sample (thirty minutes max)—record time length on sample and save file
- Check forms for completeness and write participant number and today's date on each one
- Remind about next steps (i.e., read book, attend workshop)

Obtaining and Managing Research Assistants (RAs)

Depending on your project, you may benefit from assistance with tasks such as recruitment, gathering materials, running your study's procedure, coding, and/or entering your data. There are a few solid reasons to obtain RAs for your project if possible. First, your method may call for assistance, such as when you need independent evaluators or more than one coder. Second, RAs can provide you with a fresh perspective on your project. By this point, you are likely so entrenched in the details of your study that someone with less knowledge about it might be better able to notice something that is not clear or have a good suggestion for handling any issues that arise. Third, managing research assistants will give you the opportunity to gain valuable interviewing, training, supervision, and even mentoring experiences that you can capitalize on as you move forward in your career.

Who to Obtain and What to Offer

The types of tasks you will want your RAs to complete will likely help you decide what level of education they would need and where you could recruit them. Consult with your chair first. In some applied programs, RAs are assigned to particular faculty members and may be able to focus their responsibilities on assisting with the research of upper-class students. In this case, your chair may already have RAs who can work on your project to fulfill their required research assistant hours. This is more likely to be true when your project is part of your chair's own research or student lab, but it never hurts to ask whether it is a possibility.

There are several possible options when it comes to finding RAs at different educational levels. Undergraduates (e.g., within your university's psychology department) or recent college graduates can be great research assistants, particularly when they are looking for experience to put on their curriculum vitae for graduate school. Some may be looking to volunteer for course or internship credit. They may also ask you to write them a letter of recommendation for graduate school or a job, possibly cosigned by your chair. You may have even served as this type of RA! Working with someone at this stage can provide you with a nice opportunity to pay it forward by mentoring someone through the graduate school application process.

Graduate students, particularly those from your own program, will likely be more qualified than undergraduates to manage tasks related to work in your field, such as administration of clinical assessments. You can tell lower-level graduate students that they will have the opportunity to learn the ins and outs of conducting a research or scholarly project, which could help demystify the process and even give them ideas for their own final projects. Upper-level students sometimes want to be RAs to acquire a particular skill set from your project, such as how to use a certain protocol or data analysis program. In our program, sometimes two students working on their final projects at the same time have agreed to be each other's RAs. The pro here is having someone who understands the importance of doing a quality and timely job on your work. The con is that it can feel like you are balancing a second project—think about whether it makes sense to make that time commitment.

Occasionally, high school students in advanced research programs can also serve as great RAs. Keep in mind that you will have to seek permission from their parents and/or legal guardians. You will need to be very specific about the dates and times you need them. Like undergraduates, they may also ask you for a letter of recommendation.

You may also find you have access to RAs who are members of your personal life, such as a parent, sibling, significant other, or friend. Sometimes this can work out, because these people usually are enthusiastic about your success and want to help you complete your project. Think about the kinds of tasks you are asking them to do and whether you can foresee your personal relationship interfering with the necessary work. If your proposal indicated your RAs would obtain interrater reliability and they can achieve this, then they may be good RAs. However, in some cases, the people in your personal life will not be qualified to conduct specialized activities, such as the administration of assessments or intervention sessions. We suggest talking to your chair about using personal contacts as RAs.

It is nice to offer your RAs some sort of compensation for their volunteer work, if possible, and it may add incentive to do a high-quality job on your project. We understand that most graduate students do not have extra money sitting around. However, if you are able to offer something, your RAs will surely appreciate it. You can provide compensation in several forms, including cash, a gift card, food during coding meetings, a small gift, or even assistance on a project. Think about what is feasible for you and makes sense for the people who agree to volunteer.

When to Obtain RAs

You may be tempted to secure RAs as soon as you receive IRB approval to recruit, or even earlier. The downside of this is that you may obtain their commitment prematurely. Suppose you are conducting a qualitative study and anticipate conducting interviews over three months. You obtain first-year graduate student RAs and train them in your qualitative method prior to obtaining participants, but it takes a month to obtain your first participant, and recruitment after that is slow. Six months later, your coders may have entered a new semester and stage of their own training. They may no longer be available or have forgotten their training. For this reason, we recommend obtaining RAs as close to the time they will conduct their work as possible. Of course, this is not always possible to predict. This means it is important to ask any RAs you do obtain to commit to the duration of your project from the start. It is reasonable for them to want an estimated timeline, but make sure they understand that the timeline is not exact, and see whether they will still be able and willing to work with you throughout the process.

Selecting RAs

Your chair may have lower-level RAs who can be allowed to serve on your project. In this case, you may not have a choice about who will work with you. If you do have the opportunity to select your potential RAs, you can ask to review their resumes for prerequisite experience. You can also ask to contact a few references to learn about their strengths and experience working with others.

If you have the opportunity to interview potential RAs, think about the kinds of questions you would like to ask ahead of time, for example, questions about prior research or job experience and the related tasks they were responsible for. Ask about their schedule up front, including the days or times that generally work for them to meet. Ask about any limitations they have, such as existing time commitments or upcoming scheduling issues. Also, ask them to tell you in advance about any meetings they will need to miss or attend late, as well as whether they anticipate a delay in submitting any work.

It is also a good idea to gain a sense of their interpersonal skills. If they will be interacting with participants, do they appear warm, friendly, and approachable? Are they polite? If they will be entering an applied setting, do you think they will be able to act professionally? In addition, how capable do you think they are of making decisions in complex situations? To assess this, you can ask them how they would handle specific scenarios that could arise. For example, if they see that a participant endorses suicidality, what ideas do they have about how they might handle it? Of course, you will train them in your specific protocol, but you might want to evaluate their sense of judgment from the beginning.

Finally, ask prospective RAs whether they have any questions for you about what they can expect to be doing. Demonstrating your approachability from the start can set the stage for them to feel they can come to you with any mistakes. You will want them to feel comfortable sharing concerns with you, because this will help you maintain the quality of your project.

Setting Expectations

When interviewing potential RAs, be sure to make your expectations clear. This includes what their training will entail, the length and frequency of training, what they can expect to be doing, when and where they can expect to work on these tasks, how often they will need to attend meetings, and the overall estimated time commitment for your project. It is helpful to present any opportunities they will have, such as experience learning a particular methodology and how it might benefit them. If they will be entering an applied setting, be sure to inform them about any site-specific requirements, such as background checks, fingerprinting, and/or the need for professional clothing. Consider writing up a contract where you both sign off on your roles and responsibilities, as well as how they will be evaluated. In addition, be clear about any compensation. Finally, ask whether they have questions about the opportunity to ensure you are on the same page about the work required.

Continue to review expectations at each stage of the process. It is helpful to check in with your RAs to see how they are feeling about their experience. The more you show interest in their professional development, the more likely they are to care about doing a good job on your project.

Training

Once your RAs have committed to your project, you will want to train them adequately. The first step is usually to inform them about your project, to the extent possible (sometimes you may want them to serve as independent evaluators and not be privy to all the details, such as the study's hypotheses or participants' assigned conditions). Walk them through your project's procedure and what you will expect them to do. Point out ways in which they will need to adhere to the IRB protocol, such as how to review consent and/or assent and maintain confidentiality. Role play what they are responsible for and various potential scenarios. For example, practice mock calls to prospective participants and handling emergencies.

It is also common to involve RAs in administrative tasks. Teach them how to complete these tasks, such as labeling documents and/or using tracked changes, various software programs, and databases. If they will be conducting data entry, walk them through a mock or first set of data and observe their performance. Review the importance of completing work in a timely manner, as well as how to check their work for accuracy. We will further discuss data entry and cleaning procedures in Chapter 8.

If your RAs will conduct coding, train them to use the coding system and practice using mock observations, video and/or audiotapes, and transcripts. If possible and appropriate for your project design, obtain interrater reliability on some initial data to ensure multiple coders are coding data in the same manner. Ideally, these data will not be part of your study data, unless they are chosen at random and attain adequate interrater reliability.

Throughout the course of your project, check in with your RAs to see how they are doing. If you have more than one RA, consider holding meetings to review project progress. Praise them for their efforts and mention times when they are clearly successful; this will make them more likely to care about the work they are doing for you.

Finally, talk to them about the importance of approaching you about any mistakes they might make. Tell them that you want to know what happened and determine how to address errors immediately, before any problems escalate. Reassure them that mistakes happen and that informing you will ensure the best project possible.

Table 5.6 Troubleshooting Issues with Research Assistants

Issue	Strategies
They do not show up on time and/or are hard to reach.	• Check in to see how they are doing. • Review expectations. • Brainstorm with them about ways to better accommodate their schedule and/or contact them. • Consult with your chair about how you are managing the issue and ask for feedback.
They delay submitting their work.	• Check in to see how they are doing. • Review expectations. • Assess barriers to completing work (e.g., is an assignment confusing or hard or are they overcommitted?). • Help them break the work down into smaller, manageable chunks and come up with a timeline for completion. • Re-evaluate after a specific period (e.g., four weeks) or after the next set of tasks. • Consult with your chair about how you are managing the issue and ask for feedback.

continued

Table 5.6 *continued*

They are not following procedures correctly.	• See whether they are aware of the problem and can think of any related barriers. • Review procedures and address barriers, if necessary. • Assess whether they have questions and clarify as needed. • Have them demonstrate their understanding by walking through an example, with either an actual or a hypothetical scenario, depending on what makes the most sense for your project. • Follow up and review their work with them after they complete the next real scenario. • Consult with your chair about how you are managing the issue and ask for feedback.
You train them thoroughly, but they do not grasp how to complete tasks.	• See whether they are aware of the problem and can think of any related barriers. • Consult with your chair about ways you might address barriers and try to do so. • If it is still not working out, determine whether there are other tasks they might find more manageable. • Consult with your chair about how you are managing the issue and ask for feedback.
They do not seem fully invested.	• Check in to see how they are doing. • Be honest about your observation that they do not appear fully invested. • Ask how they are feeling about their tasks, whether they had different expectations, and/or whether they feel differently about the project now compared to when they started. • Consult with your chair about possible options to re-engage them or modify their tasks to be a better fit. Ask whether they would like to try. If so, agree on the revised expectations and reassess after a specific period (e.g., four weeks). • If modification is not possible or they still do not seem invested after discussion and/or evaluation, consult with your chair about whether and how you should remove them from your project. • Ask you chair for feedback about how you handled the situation.
They quit your project prematurely.	• Ask whether they would be willing to discuss what happened. • Consider reminding them of the agreed-on time commitment. • Think about the pros and cons of trying to re-engage them in your project. It may not be possible, but it if is, there are surely potential benefits (e.g., they are already familiar with your procedure, they may complete tasks skillfully) and downfalls (e.g., they may not really want to be there, so they do a poor job; they might quit again). Consult with your chair about these pros and cons (of course, you may not have a choice!). • Ask your chair for feedback about how you handled the situation. • Consult with your chair about how to handle a case in which they might ask you to write them a letter of recommendation.

Troubleshooting Issues with RAs

As much as you try to vet and prepare your RAs, issues may still arise. Table 5.6 includes some common issues and strategies to help you address them. We recommend consulting with your chair about how to address each issue and asking for feedback about how you handled it afterward.

Keeping Track of Project Progress

As you make progress on your project, take notes on what you have done, what was successful, what was challenging, and what you wish you would have done differently. Recording the thoughts you have as you collect your data and/or conduct your project can help with writing up your discussion, such as the limitations of your project, practical implications, and directions for future research. In addition, take notes on any procedures that vary. It is easy to tell yourself now that you will remember what happens and when, but a few months from now, it may be surprisingly hard to recall!

Managing Changes to Your Procedure over the Course of Your Project

As you work on your project, you may realize you need to proceed differently. This is particularly true with research in applied settings, where you may be relying on the procedures of an outside site that you have little control over. Unfortunately, a site's explanation of what you can anticipate may not be the reality. For example, they may tell you they will have a free room available on two weekday evenings, so in your proposal you plan to administer an intervention at this site two times per week. What if that ends up not being possible? They likely had good intentions in offering you a room—it could be that they did not expect to add another class, client, etc. Ideally, you will have a good relationship with the site and they will work with you to figure out a solution. But what if their solution is to offer you a room one evening a week for double the time? This may be a good option (or your only option), but it would also mean conducting your intervention once per week instead of twice. How should you handle this?

The first thing to do when you need to make a change in your proposed procedure is determine whether it means making a major change to any part of your proposal, such as your hypotheses or your research design. In this example, you would need to determine whether you would expect your intervention to be as effective if you conducted it less frequently for twice as long each session. Could you justify offering this version of the intervention? Or would it make sense to add extra weeks to the intervention so that participants receive it in shorter sessions, even though it would be over a longer period?

Student Example: Switching from Collecting Data to Analyzing Archival Data

---

MM planned to conduct a quasi-experimental study comparing children who did and did not attend a mixed-age free-play club in New York City schools. She had successfully proposed doing so. Unfortunately, because of the COVID-19 pandemic, the groups were not running, which significantly affected her ability to move forward with her project. She was able to form a relationship with a school in another state that had run this type of play club in the past. They offered her the ability to analyze archival data both from the club and from a waitlist, including school attendance, lateness, grades, teacher-reported behaviors, standardized test scores, and demographic information. She sought approval from her chair, who then advised her to check in with her committee members, because this was a major change in her procedure. Fortunately, all agreed she could still produce a strong study!

You may have difficulty recruiting the number of participants you need. For example, the organization you planned to recruit through may have been too optimistic about how many of their members would be interested in participating. Or perhaps you hoped to recruit parents of children of a certain age with a specific disorder but you are not successfully recruiting from that population. The first thing might be to talk with your chair about ways to cast your net more widely. Can you add another organization or two to your recruiting pool? Widen your child age range a bit? Your chair may recommend sharing these types of changes with your full committee, particularly if you significantly deviate from your original proposal, to make sure everyone is on board.

As we mentioned earlier, in some qualitative methods involving interviews, it is normal to have interview questions evolve over time, based on responses from the initial participants. Although you may ask some new follow-up questions in the moment, we recommend running any revised premeditated questions by your chair before moving forward. You will be so close to the interviews that it is a good idea to have your chair serve as a check to what you are thinking, helping you see any potential biases and/or blind spots.

After you collect your data, you may realize some tasks are incomplete or were handled incorrectly (e.g., by RAs). This can happen even if you think you did everything you could to preserve the integrity of your project and prevent errors. You might be able to redo parts of your procedure. For example, if you had RAs code teacher behaviors in a classroom and they scored low in interrater reliability, you could retrain them, strengthening your operational definitions of each potential teacher behavior. However, some things cannot be redone, such as anonymous incomplete surveys or checking content validity of a measure after you have collected all of your data. These types of issues should be mentioned in your eventual discussion section (see Chapter 7 for limitations to include and Chapter 8 for how to write about them). We will also discuss skills for managing missing data in Chapter 8.

Keeping Your Project Timeline on Track

Over the course of your final project, how you manage your time will be important to ensure completion. Some students have prior success completing papers quickly, even pulling all-nighters at times and receiving a grade of A. This is not possible with your final project. As this book illustrates, there are several tasks you must complete, including gathering and reviewing literature, writing and editing, and collecting and analyzing data. As you work on the project, your responsibilities may change, including your coursework, training in applied settings, and personal responsibilities. It is helpful to talk about a timeline in collaboration with your chair, but you must effectively manage your own time. Here are some key factors for managing your time successfully:

- Schedule consistent times to work on your project (e.g., three times a week for two hours). Alternatively, schedule specific tasks to complete rather than durations of time. Leave yourself more time than you think you will need.
- Schedule time to work with the other people collaborating on your project. Ask for meetings ahead of time, prepare for the meetings, and send an agenda and materials beforehand.
- Continue working on any project tasks you can while waiting for feedback from others (e.g., your chair, the IRB, your coders).
- Make your "nonworking time" useful by keeping documents you need to work on easily accessible at all times (e.g., on the train, during slow practicum hours).
- Account for upcoming changes in your schedule (e.g., classes, practicum, life events).
- Maintain awareness of program policies and deadlines for your project and check with your chair and program administrator for confirmation.

Use Table 5.7 to assess whether you are managing your time effectively. Table 5.8 includes factors to consider regarding your program's requirements, deadlines, and resources. If you find you are having trouble making progress, see our strategies for addressing procrastination in Chapter 6.

Table 5.7 Are You Managing Your Time Effectively?

	1 You're never getting out of here	2	3	4 Excellent—see you at commencement soon!
Scheduling time to work on your project and adhering to it	Never	I try but something always gets in the way.	I schedule time but it is either not enough or I get interrupted.	I schedule time and am usually able to stick to it.
Scheduling time to work with the other people collaborating on your project	Never	I ask them to meet with little notice, or I ask them to meet but am unprepared.	I ask them ahead of time to meet and I prepare, but do not share my agenda ahead of time.	I ask them ahead of time to meet, prepare for meetings, and send them agenda and materials beforehand.
You work on any project tasks you can as you wait for feedback from others (e.g., your chair, the institutional review board, your coders)	Never	I think about tasks I should get around to.	Sometimes I do a little work here or there, but it is hard to get moving when I know I turned something in.	Yes, while I am waiting for feedback in one area, I focus on another part of my project.
Your "nonworking time"—be it travel time or otherwise—is useful	Never	I carry an article or two around but rarely get to them.	Sometimes, but other times I could be using the time and do not.	Always—I read and edit my documents wherever possible.
You have accounted for changes in your school schedule that could impact times you work on your project (e.g., data collection time)	Never	I probably should look at that again.	I think I know what needs to be changed; I just need to finalize the details.	Yes, I made sure my classes, practicum, and time to work on my project are all accounted for next semester.
The last time you checked on program policies and deadlines for your project was . . .	Never	I know I did at some point . . .	I read through it recently but need to double check the details.	Very recently, I made sure I understood them and checked with my chair and/or program administrator for confirmation.
Other				

Table 5.8 Questions about Your Program's Requirements, Deadlines, and Resources

Question	Answer
What classes do you need to take at this stage?	
What is your chair's schedule this academic year?	
When is the next time they will be on sabbatical?	
When must you propose by?	
What deadlines are there for the coming academic year?	
What formal forms, evaluations, and other procedures are in place in your program?	
Has anything changed since you started the program?	
Are there any new databases or other resources your library liaison has secured since last year?	
What are the associated costs related to the research component of your training?	
What are the consequences for not meeting deadlines?	
What are the financial consequences of not meeting deadlines?	
Which of the above topics am I assuming I know the answer to, but have not checked on recently?	
Other	
Other	

Remediation Planning

If you find you are struggling to complete your written proposal, do not succeed with your proposal meeting, or have trouble moving forward with the steps it takes to conduct your project, we recommend putting yourself on a remediation plan. Some programs will include a plan like this, with the goal of helping you take steps to improve your competence where needed. If you find you are having difficulty, speak with your chair about options for remediation. Worksheet 5.2 can help you develop a specific remediation plan. First, identify the areas of concern (e.g., academic knowledge, professional relationships, professional responsibilities, writing and/or oral skills). Second, write out the specific concerns in those areas. Third, list goals and specific steps you can take (i.e., objectives) to meet those goals. Specify criteria for knowing when you have attained your goals and indicate a deadline by which you should do so. You might discuss your plan with your chair or another mentor. They could even sign off and periodically check on your progress to help hold you accountable. When your deadlines arrive, evaluate how much progress you have made toward each goal, and revise your remediation plan if necessary.

Worksheet 5.1 My Project Overview: Planning and Self-Evaluation

Part 1: Planning

This form is intended to help you think through what you want to include in your written proposal about your project. Look at the section in this chapter entitled "How to Write Your Final Project Proposal" for guidance. You can use this worksheet to ensure you have thought through each component of your project. It can also serve as an overview to share with your chair and/or peers.

Part 2: Self-Evaluation

After you write your proposal, go back through each question and make sure you have addressed each item. Check it off (√) once it is complete.

Part 1	Part 2 √
Project title	
Statement of the problem: How can you summarize key points of the argument you will build in your literature review? How will conducting your project fill gaps in the literature?	
Purpose of your project: What is the specific purpose of your project? How can you state it clearly, in one to two sentences? If you will propose an empirical study, how can you write the purpose so it foreshadows the type of research design(s) you will be using? How can you make it clear who the participants will be?	
Rationale for your project: Why is conducting this research important? How can you explain this clearly? Why should the reader care about this topic? How can your project potentially add to theoretical knowledge, methodology, and/or empirical research to the literature? What are potential practical implications?	

Hypotheses/research questions: How can you directly relate your hypotheses and/or research questions to the purpose of your study? Will hypotheses be directional or nondirectional? If directional, how do existing theories and/or research influence your prediction? Does each hypothesis include the names of variables being assessed; the type of relationship expected, including wording that foreshadows the research design that will be used; and the relevant sample? How can you write any research questions so they are open and exploratory? Do they foreshadow your research design? Are there any smaller research questions under an overarching question?	
Researcher bias (for a qualitative study): What preconceived expectations might you have about the findings of your project, based on personal and/or professional experiences? How can you write about them openly but maintain your privacy? How will you aim to stay aware of biases and minimize their input on your project's results?	
Participants (nonhuman samples of data, photographs, etc., may alternatively be proposed): How many participants will you aim to include, and what is the rationale? What population(s) do you aim to include in your research (e.g., gender, race/ethnicity, ability, geographic location, age)? What sampling method will you use? How and where will you recruit them? What will be the inclusion and exclusion criteria for your study? What will be your method for determining whether participants meet each criterion?	
Research design: What research design will the study use (e.g., experimental, correlational)? If it is a quantitative study, what are the independent and dependent variables? If groups will be created, what are the various conditions? What are inherent limitations of your design (e.g., potential threats to internal or external validity)?	

Procedure: How will each component of the study be conducted? If you will be recruiting participants, what will advertisements say? Where will you recruit? If you will be recruiting in an applied setting, who will you approach and when? What directions or instructions will participants receive? What is the order of tasks to complete? If this is an intervention, educational curriculum, etc., what will specifically occur? If you will have different conditions, what will happen in each condition? What assessments will occur? Who will administer each part of your procedure, and when and where?	
Measures: What measures will you use for each variable and/or construct? Will your measures be existing, adapted, or original? How can you describe each assessment tool you plan to use (the number of items, the way the measure is scored, the range of scores, what scores mean, any reliability and validity data)? For each measure, will you use all or part of the measure? If you plan to adapt an existing measure, what will be modified? Will you analyze any psychometric data from your study? Do you need to purchase measures or obtain permission to use them? For a qualitative interview study, what open-ended questions do you plan to ask? Will there be any potential follow-up questions, and when you would ask them?	
Data analyses: What analyses will you use to interpret your data? Do these analyses align with the wording of the purpose of your project and research design? What descriptive statistics do you think you need to include? For a quantitative study, what inferential statistics do you think you need? Which preliminary analyses seem necessary? For a qualitative study, what data analytic approach seems to make sense for your project? If you plan to code your data, what steps would you take? How would you train coders and address discrepancies in coding? What steps could you take to judge your qualitative research?	

Worksheet 5.2 Remediation Plan

Date	Name
I. Areas of concern	
Please circle the appropriate area and provide behavioral descriptors and explanations.	
A. Research competency 1. Knowledge base 2. Skill level 3. Attitude toward research	B. Professional relationships 1. Student–chair 2. Student–committee member 3. Student–applied site member 4. Other
C. Professional responsibilities and/or ethics 1. Meeting obligations 2. Ethical responsibilities 3. Timely responses 4. Responsibility to an applied site 5. Motivation 6. Work ethic 7. Other	D. Language skills 1. Technical writing skills 2. Oral presentation skills 3. Organization 4. Critical thinking 5. Other
Concerns: Explanation and/or description	

II. Remediation plan			
Goals	Objectives to meet goals	Criteria for goal attainment	Date when objectives are to be met

III. Progress chart Complete after remediation is finished		
Goal	**Estimate of progress** (circle one and explain)	**Date**
	Full Some None Full Some None Full Some None	
Next steps:		

Chapter 6
Attitudes toward Your Research and Your Collaborators

Introduction

As you write your proposal and conduct your final project, you should develop your *attitudes* about the critical evaluation of research, the conduct of research in applied settings, and ethical and professional competence by reviewing the following areas of this chapter:

- Staying current, skeptical, open-minded, and aware of biases
- Attitudes toward research-informed practice by practitioners: Endorsing the local clinical scientist model
- Your attitude about working on a research team
- Balancing multiple roles
- Commitment to midcourse corrections on your project
- Reviewing the stages and processes of change: Where are you now?
- Reviewing your attitudes toward feedback

Chapters 4 and 5 focused on the knowledge and skills you needed to successfully narrow down your specific project idea and write a proposal, select and work with a chair, and manage necessary project procedures. If you are following along chronologically, you have likely written your proposal and started conducting your final project. As you continue with this process, we would like to provide some suggestions for maintaining a positive attitude toward your research and your collaborators. They include how you are thinking about what you are learning, including staying current in the field, maintaining healthy skepticism about your findings, and remaining open to multiple ways of knowing. You will also want to reflect on personal biases that may affect how you perceive what you are finding. Consider how you can benefit from appreciating your program's practitioner-scholar, local clinical scientist, or other encompassing model of training. If you are working with a research team, it is important to consider your attitudes toward others with whom you are working, as well as how to best balance multiple roles. As a developing professional, you will be expected to present your research ideas for the scrutiny of others, invest in providing constructive feedback, and commit to appropriate midcourse corrections to your project. We will also check in to see how you are doing with the stages and

Navigating Research in an Applied Graduate Program. Hilary B. Vidair, Pam L. Gustafson, and Eva L. Feindler, Oxford University Press. © Oxford University Press (2024). DOI: 10.1093/oso/9780199352272.003.0006

process of change from Chapter 3, as well as your attitudes toward self-evaluation and feedback.

Staying Current, Skeptical, Open-Minded, and Aware of Biases

As you work on your final project, it can become difficult to "see the forest for the trees." You will likely be so ingrained in the minutiae of day-to-day details that it will be hard to have a broader, objective perspective on your work. While this is understandable, as time passes, you will be more likely to miss key alternative viewpoints on your topic area, procedure, and results. There are several ways to combat this, including being aware of what can be found in the current literature, keeping a somewhat skeptical attitude about your findings, remaining open to multiple ways of knowing, and being aware of your and your collaborators' potential biases. Keep in mind that your project is one of many that will be viewed in context with existing and future literature. These attitudes will help you as you being to think through what you found and potential interpretations, limitations, and directions for future research, which we will address in Chapters 7 and 8. Practically, these attitudes will also help you as you prepare for your defense; committee members may bring up different ideas than you or your chair were able to think through, since the two of you may grow very close to the same way of thinking over time. This is normal and demonstrates why it is a good idea to have other professionals reviewing your work.

Recognize the Value of Staying Current in the Literature

As you conduct your project, periodically conduct a literature search for any new relevant research on your topic area. Familiarizing yourself with any new data can help you begin to formulate your ideas about how your project's findings will fit into the existing body of literature. Finding the latest articles as you work will also help when you later revise your introduction and write your discussion section.

Beyond your current project, however, the majority of practitioners in applied fields view scientific inquiry as important and view research as relevant across a number of applied areas. Most training models include in their competencies an objective for professionals to stay "active and informed consumers of research" even though the majority do not continue to conduct research beyond what is required for their graduate degree (Holmes & Beins, 2009, p. 6). Typically, graduate students receive training to actively and critically apply empirical research findings in their professional activities. Recognizing the importance of keeping up to date with current literature now will help you maintain this attitude as you move forward in your career.

Maintain an Attitude of Healthy Skepticism

According to the dictionary, skepticism is an attitude of doubt or the doctrine that true knowledge or knowledge in a particular area is somewhat uncertain. Unfortunately, too often mental health and educational practices and related public policies are driven by the media, conventional wisdom, and prejudice and/or bias rather than by scientific evidence. For example, the public view of psychology is often skeptical regarding the assertion that psychology is scientific. According to Lilienfeld (2012), this public skepticism might make potential mental health consumers hesitant to pursue therapeutic services and could create barriers to potential funding sources for psychological research. However, such uncertainty toward psychology's scientific status neglects the fact that applied research often incorporates robust scientific methods that indicate that effective interventions do ameliorate problems in daily living. Lilienfeld (2012) views public skepticism as an ally, in that it keeps applied scientists on their toes and calls for better communication about scientific methods and the applicability of research findings. In particular, mental health professionals have a valuable role to play in educating consumers about the substantial research base that exists for a variety of psychological interventions. Just how mental health providers might use research outcomes to inform better practice should be clearly articulated such that the provider sees the direct connection between research and practice.

Just as the public's skepticism keeps the applied researchers on their toes, so too should each individual researcher's skepticism focus them on evaluating the methodological adequacy of research studies before drawing conclusions. This means that each research article you read for your literature review, as well as each study you include to build a rationale for your own project and your own data collection, should be met with initial skepticism about the scientific value of the findings. Once you are assured that the methods of data collection are both reliable and valid, you can better accept the results obtained, even if they are not in the direction you had hoped. It will also be important to be skeptical about your own project findings! Remember, this is part of scientific inquiry and contributing to your field. Healthy skepticism rests on the knowledge and skills needed to critically evaluate the literature and to design, carry out, and evaluate new research.

Be Open to Multiple Ways of Knowing

How is it that people "know what they know?" McMillan (2021) reviews multiple ways of knowing, including personal experience and intuition, tradition, expert's authority, and logic and reason. Although all have some merit, they are all subjective. In contrast, research involves systematically collecting, interpreting, and disseminating information in as objective a manner as possible. As discussed in Chapter 1, quantitative research generally follows the scientific method, which involves the development of testable hypotheses to address research problems informed by prior theory and literature. Known research designs and procedures are used to test hypotheses, and results are interpreted with caution until further studies confirm the results.

Although quantitative methods still dominate the landscape of applied research, many researchers have recognized the potential of qualitative methods to explore the experiences of research participants and the deepened understanding gained from this approach (Roberts & Povee, 2014). Some maintain that qualitative research is particularly well suited to studying clinical practice (Silverstein et al., 2006), because the methodology allows for narratives about complex psychological experiences that may be missed when using only a quantitative method. In their development of the Attitudes toward Qualitative Research in Psychology measure, Roberts and Povee (2014) ascertained four factors that underlie attitudes about qualitative research, including a perceived lack of validity, perceptions of time and resource intensity, lack of experience and/or confidence in qualitative research, and the ability to capture lived experiences. The first three factors would combine to create a more negative attitude toward qualitative research.

You may have been exposed to the biases of academics and undergraduate experiences typically dominated by the traditional scientific method. Be aware that researchers in the applied field and/or program you are in may have been so focused on quantitative methods that there has been little to no exploration of qualitative methods. Alternatively, some faculty have a strong bias against quantitative research. An open, curious attitude around methodology will serve you better, because each method has its own strengths and limitations (as shown in Chapter 4). Interestingly, there has been a recent push toward mixed methods in applied research (discussed in Chapter 1), which can nicely integrate the advantages from both quantitative and qualitative methodologies. Regardless of the method(s) you are using for your final project, remember that all methods have their limitations, and your findings are from one sample or set of products developed under specific conditions during a certain time.

Reflect on Biases: Personal Biases and Key Stakeholder Bias

The topic chosen for your research endeavor likely has had an evolution from a fledgling idea to, hopefully, a dedicated direction and perhaps future career path. However, the topic also has a related backstory from your personal and academic experiences. It is important to consider the assumptions, expectations, and beliefs you already hold about the population or setting you will be focused on, as well as the research question and/or intervention you might be proposing.

Student Example: Reflecting on Personal Biases

Recently, SS proposed a qualitative study designed to explore the experiences that behavioral training experts had with challenging parents. During her proposal meeting, she was asked whether she had experiences with parent training, either in training or as part of her own family's therapy, and whether she had some preconceived notions about what would be effective for parents with emotional dysregulation in a parent training program. The committee thought it was important for her to examine her biases before engaging in her research, because they could impact the way she asked follow-up questions or coded her data. Since she was not a parent yet and had not implemented parent training programs, the committee discussed the potential use of coders who have had those experiences to balance perspectives and catch potential biases as they arise.

Beyond your own potential biases, consider potential biases emanating from key stakeholders involved with your final project. Stakeholders may include your chair, others on your research team, agency personnel from your participant recruitment site, parents and/or teachers of child participants, and anyone involved in funding your research efforts. All these folks may have a stake in the process and outcomes of your research project, and most often they have their own assumptions, attributions, and expectations of the results you will achieve. It can be helpful to think ahead about how you will publicly speak about any findings or products from your project that might conflict with stakeholder expectations. Be clear up front that potential publication of your project will be independent of what you find.

Attitudes toward Research-Informed Practice by Practitioners: Endorsing the Local Clinical Scientist Model

The local clinical scientist model, described in Chapter 1, views the clinician as functioning as a scientist and the applied setting as their laboratory. Stricker and Trierweiler (2006) suggested that scientific training includes the practitioner adopting specific attitudes about empirical support for interventions, an awareness of one's own personal biases, a consideration of the ethical implications of treatment, and the continued need for collegial interaction and feedback. The local clinical scientist model is built on an assumption that scientific training provides an attitude toward the presenting clinical problem such that a research-based perspective will directly inform the decision-making of the therapist in the service of the client.

Research has suggested that clinicians have varied attitudes about research and its implications for practice. It is possible that clinicians do not prioritize research evidence because they believe that efficacy outcome data from randomized trials do not generalize to clinical practice and that patients in practice are more troubled, complex, and difficult to treat than subjects in clinical research. Stewart et al. (2012) conducted a qualitative study of twenty-five practicing clinicians focused on their resistance to evidence-based practice. Their objections were concentrated on the idea that research was too controlled to be able to be generalized to actual clients who have more complicated clinical presentations. Further, clinicians suggested that the very nature of research diminishes the importance of the interpersonal dimensions of therapeutic relationships. However, clinicians reported they might be more likely to use empirically supported treatments if research was presented in a readable, user-friendly format and if research addressed how to apply treatments to diverse populations and settings. Interestingly, the most frequently cited facilitators to implementation of research-based treatments concerned policy changes (e.g., professional organizations and third-party payment) that support evidence-based practice (EBP) and increased availability of training through graduate programs, continuing education workshops, and postgraduate institutes. Practitioner-oriented books, blog posts, and online publications, as well as peer supervision groups, were cited as ways to make research outcomes more applicable to clinicians.

A study by Gaudiano et al. (2011) examined the attitudes of 176 licensed mental health providers about EBP (using the fifteen-item Evidence-Based Practice Scale) and attitudes about the use of intuition and alternative therapies. The majority of online respondents had been licensed and practicing for some time, with 34 percent being from a cognitive-behavioral therapy orientation. The respondents came from both the master's and the doctoral levels and were frequently in private-practice settings. Results indicated that therapists who possessed a more negative attitude toward the role of research in clinical practice were more likely to rely on intuition. Further, those with a greater reliance on intuition were less willing to comply with conditions used to provide evidence-based treatments. This calls for additional aspects of EBP programming to include perceived therapist attitudes that might present as barriers to providing EBP treatments. Interestingly, for some clinicians, the accumulation of data does not seem to override their reliance on "clinical intuition."

Practice-oriented research is focused on partnerships between clinical researchers and practitioners in the community, with the hope of a stronger connection between the science and practice of psychotherapy. Youn and colleagues (2019) surveyed 627 members of a large practice network of university counseling centers to assess areas, ideas, and/or topics that they would like researchers to explore. The hope was that if clinicians had the opportunity to give input for the development of research that was more applicable to their work settings, then they would have more positive attitudes about research and more readily incorporate results into their practices. Overall, the survey results indicated that practitioners viewed research on the processes of psychotherapy as most valuable. Related to the therapeutic process, providers reported interest in research focused on the generalization of therapeutic gains, insight, and corrective experiences. Of further value was research focused on the therapeutic alliance and related issues of relationship ruptures, countertransference, and the difficulty in establishing client engagement (resistance). These practice-oriented researchers then went on to design a multisite research project to test the feasibility of implementing two psychotherapy process measures focused on the therapeutic relationship, both from the clients' (i.e., the therapeutic alliance) and from the therapists' (i.e., countertransference or emotional, cognitive, and behavioral reactions to the client) perspectives. The inclusion of these measures in outcomes research across numerous applied settings was seen as the integration of researcher practitioner interests. The challenges encountered in this ambitious project included issues related to the institutional review board, as well as implementation difficulties in terms of subject recruitment and data collection. Most of the research components were not part of each practitioner's typical practice. According to Castonguay (2011), practice-oriented researchers are aimed at reducing empirical imperialism, where full-time researchers predominantly decide what should be studied and how, by having clinicians serve as active participants in all aspects of research, including the selection, development, implementation, and dissemination of research protocols. Although this seems ideal, it is difficult to organize and implement.

Another approach to improving practitioners' attitudes about research is the push for routine outcomes monitoring (ROM) in clinical practice. According to Boswell (2020), measurement-based care is now often incorporated into health care service delivery systems. This practice of basing clinical care on data that are systematically collected at the onset of treatment, throughout care, and on termination emerges as a direct link between practice and evidence, albeit on an individualized basis. Further, as the need for agencies to document the effectiveness of psychotherapy services and programs increases, clinical researchers are being called on to develop data collection methods that are reliable and valid across settings and that will track patient outcomes. Routine outcomes monitoring strategies for measuring the quality of psychotherapy focus primarily on three broad domains: structure (e.g., competency of clinicians to offer evidence-based psychotherapy), process (whether psychotherapy is delivered with fidelity to an evidence-based model), and outcome (improvements in initial presenting problems among individuals who receive psychotherapy; Boswell, 2020). Graduate training in clinical psychology and other types of applied programs will doubtless begin to incorporate ROM into their curricula and practicum experiences for developing practitioners, and likely your attitudes about ROM and measurement-based care will evolve throughout your career.

Your Attitude about Working on a Research Team

As we discussed in Chapter 5, you will be working with others on your final project. This may extend beyond your chair and committee members to include collaborators in an applied setting and/or research assistants. Sometimes they will be new collaborations, and at other times you may continue to work with people you have already worked with in some capacity (e.g., a faculty lab, clinical practice, school). In essence, you will be part of a research team!

Your attitudes and perceptions about research teams may influence your intentions and outcomes. For example, Wei et al. (2015) surveyed graduate students ($n = 281$) to explore their attitudes about working on research teams during their academic training. Their results indicated that students' attitudes regarding team research were positively associated with their attitudes about individual research. In addition, three factors—attitude about team research, subjective norm, and perceived behavioral control (i.e., level of difficulty)—alongside their field of study and degree level (doctoral vs. master's students), accounted for over half of the variance in their intention to engage in team research. They found that the subjective norm was the most prominent factor, followed by attitudes. Further results indicated that two-thirds of students did not submit any coauthored manuscripts during graduate school, with a median of zero students. Given the time it takes to publish an article, this indicates that most students will not have a coauthored publication by the time they graduate. However, greater intentions to conduct team research did significantly predict having coauthored publications.

As a student in an applied program, there are benefits to collaborating with others on a research team. For example, according to Aarons et al. (2020), there is about a seventeen-year lag between the development of scientific evidence and its broad use in practice. Research teams in implementation science can facilitate engagement between researchers and other stakeholders (patients, mental health providers, community members, and administrators) as well as the use of effective evidence-based treatments. Aarons et al. conducted a study in which they asked researchers focused on dissemination and implementation about strategies they have used to encourage team research. They found strategies that fostered research teams related to clear expectations and responsibilities, well-defined roles for team members, good communication between members, and having shared goals.

As part of a team, it is important for you to become invested in receiving and offering constructive feedback. For example, part of engaging in scientific work is presenting your research ideas for the scrutiny of others while being willing to provide feedback to others. It is also important to be open to providing and receiving feedback on collegial interactions. In Chapter 3, we spoke about being open to feedback provided by faculty (e.g., on your writing or professional development skills). Then, in Chapter 5, we spoke about times where you might have to give your chair feedback on issues you encounter in your working relationship with them. Also in Chapter 5, we spoke about opportunities to mentor research assistants and times where you may need to troubleshoot barriers to their progress. If you are lucky enough to have a research assistant, it is important that you take seriously your job as a teacher, role model, mentor, and supervisor. Your abilities to "grow" a relationship with your student assistant will go far in ensuring a successful partnership. Even though you may not select the person who will help you, you will be the primary person responsible for monitoring and maintaining the relationship. If you are working in an applied setting, you may also find yourself receiving and wanting to provide various types of feedback. Being open to this process as a student will help you reflect on your skill set, provide opportunities for professional growth, and practice skills that will benefit your performance in future jobs.

Another benefit related to collaborating on research ties in with the advancing world of technology. In a typical graduate school setting, new students tend to be more technology advanced than the existing faculty, and the existing faculty and graduate student population is usually more diverse in terms of needs, expectations, backgrounds, and levels of commitment and interests. The acquisition of knowledge and skills is therefore an important function of collaboration, and graduate students may benefit from participating in team research. We strongly endorse an attitude of collaboration and cooperation, especially around the formation of research teams.

Balancing Multiple Roles

As a graduate student, you may be required to play many roles while you are both completing your education and preparing to start your professional career. Because most students must complete their final project to receive their degree, you may also be working (even full-time) and/or have various family commitments. These personal roles and responsibilities may conflict with your own or your chair's expectations for research completion. The school–work–life balancing act is further complicated by the transition from being a graduate student to becoming an early career professional. From a contextual perspective, graduate work alone includes far more than coursework and project completion. You may also be juggling roles as a teaching assistant, grant writer, research assistant, mentor and/or mentee, or clinical supervisee. It seems inevitable that there will be tensions between some of these roles, and you will need to determine how to prioritize tasks and responsibilities in a timely fashion.

Faculty members also may play multiple roles as your research advisor, academic advisor, professor, and/or clinical supervisor. The following vignette is an example of one situation with considerations about multiple roles. Sometimes faculty members play a role in selecting and/or hiring students for assistantships, awards, and professional opportunities. The smaller your graduate program, the more likely this will be. Maintaining a positive attitude about these potential role conflicts and good communication with all of those in your school–work–life domain will be necessary even after your project is finished and you launch your career.

Student Example: Balancing Multiple Roles with Committee Members

At times, students' paths cross with faculty who have clinical commitments outside their graduate training program. We recently had an issue arise for a student related to these multiple roles. This student was completing a year-long externship at a placement where a faculty member from the student's academic program was a director and clinical supervisor. The graduate student had planned to conduct qualitative interviews with psychologists who were implementing a particular evidence-based treatment across a number of applied settings. The multiple roles of this psychologist (externship director, clinical supervisor, faculty member, and dissertation committee member) added extra pressure on the student about the best ways to code the narrative data. The psychologist who held all of these roles felt strongly that since this was an applied project about staff members' adherence to a treatment protocol, the student should yield to their suggestions about assembling a coding team familiar with the treatment for data analyses. However, the student's dissertation chair had strong feelings about qualitative research methodology that would have meant assembling a different and more objective coding team. The student felt caught in the middle and was particularly stressed about whom they should yield to. Ultimately, the three individuals sat down to discuss the issue and created a solution that all endorsed. Luckily, the student had good relationships with both psychologists.

Commitment to Midcourse Corrections on Your Final Project

Once your data start to roll in, you will become aware of the nature and direction of your research findings and whether the information needed to address your initial hypotheses, research questions, and/or goals is adequately being accumulated. Sometimes you might have to make changes based on your initial data collection. For example, in a quantitative project, you may do a small pilot study; based on the initial data obtained, you may want to change your research questions or your assessment measures to better align with your research objectives. For a qualitative study, may need to add or modify interviewing questions if the initial interviews do not seem to yield rich narratives.

Additionally, there is always the possibility that your applied research plan could fall through completely. For example, what if you base your study on the feasibility of recruiting a parent population after you were given access and then the agency or organization changes its mind? Participant recruitment can sometimes be difficult, and creative solutions are warranted.

Maintaining commitment to midcourse project corrections can be challenging, but they are key to successfully moving forward. The following vignette describes an unpredicted and necessary pivot for a student when their initial research plan fell through. She could have easily allowed the dilemma to derail her progress; however, she made sure to consult her committee, restructure her proposal, and generate a feasible idea that was similar to her initial topic.

Student Example: Commitment to a Midcourse Correction

Recently, EK, whose project had already been approved by her committee and had received IRB approval, had to make a major midcourse correction. The proposed study was an evaluation of a new group protocol for emotion dysregulation training for aggressive kindergartners, which she had proposed to conduct at several local elementary schools. However, as a result of the COVID-19 pandemic and subsequent shutdown of all in-person schools, the research as designed would not be able to be conducted for the foreseeable future. So as not to lose time or jeopardize her career trajectory, she consulted with her committee members and designed a treatment acceptability study for that very protocol. She recruited an online sample of school mental health practitioners to read case vignettes of aggressive children, as well as the group treatment manual. Then, they completed self-report assessments of treatment acceptability based on the manual. Participants also responded to questions about the format, settings, pacing, and applicability to particular types of children. Although it was not the outcomes evaluation desired by the student, the project was still in line with her research interests, and she successfully defended in a timely fashion.

Reviewing the Stages and Processes of Change: Where Are You Now?

In Chapter 3, we fully described the stages and processes of change (refer to Figure 3.1). At this point, you have likely moved through the first three stages and are somewhere in stage 4: action. In this stage, you are likely working through your research project and hopefully have developed some contingencies to reward your small steps forward (e.g., knocking items off your to-do list, recruiting a certain number of participants). Further, you may have created some stimulus control over your work behaviors such that you have figured out the best environments to cue working and to remove distractions and deterrents. Worksheet 3.1 contains questions you might ask yourself to help you keep moving through this stage of change.

In the fifth stage, maintenance, you will need to understand patterns of working that are effective for you, ways you have progressed, and the ways in which making progress has felt worthwhile. Stay connected to people who support your goals and continue to assess how they can help you stay on track throughout your project. In addition, note what triggers a relapse into not working. These triggers can be both external and internal, and you may temporarily need to return to the prior action stage to get back on track. The next set of questions in Worksheet 3.1 focuses on whether making progress has now become a habit and how you are balancing work and self-care. You might also focus on celebrating your positive work habits.

If you find yourself procrastinating, there is likely some negative thinking blocking your progress. Unfortunately, procrastination often results in negative outcomes when trying to complete a research or scholarly project. Patterns of task avoidance have been linked with anxiety and aspects of self-regulation and self-efficacy. Interventions for the reduction of procrastination often focus on finding ways to approach the work so you can achieve task completion. Table 6.1 details typical procrastination-related thoughts one might have when working on a research or scholarly project and potential solutions.

In an interesting article by O'Connor (2017), the barriers, blocks, and impasses encountered while writing a dissertation were examined through a psychoanalytic angle. Barriers, both internal and external, are connected to nonnegotiable realities that limit a student's ability to complete the work. One of the ironies O'Connor noted is the difficult position of the student to engage in quality research and writing on subjects they are not yet fully confident about, since they are still students in the field. A *block* is more likely a self-created defense reaction of an anxious student who responds to completion of their research and writing by shutting down. Since this reaction is often outside conscious awareness, many find it challenging to understand and work through. Finally, O'Connor theorizes there might be a particular type of block called an impasse, which reflects a dynamic process between the student and an advisor and/or mentor that essentially brings the work to a halt. He wrote, "There is a sense here that both parties contribute to this kind of stalemate, that there is a kind of stand-off, which halts development or drives things backward" (O'Connor, 2017, p. 518). This impasse may require an interpersonal intervention, perhaps mediated by another person familiar with your project. Overall, it will be helpful for you to consider these issues if you find that you are procrastinating or just cannot move forward.

Finally, you will achieve the sixth stage of change, termination, when you are almost done with your project and can see the light at the end of the long tunnel. In this stage, you might feel increased energy as you approach the finish line and frustration with things that get in the way. The most important attitude to take here is a "can-do" one; you are almost there, and you will achieve this!

Table 6.1 Procrastination Roadblocks

Procrastination-related thought	Potential solution
I do not know where to start.	Outline—start with small pieces (shape your behavior), and selectively attend to only that piece rather than the whole project. Accomplishing small steps will likely be reinforcing and help build your motivation.
I want my writing to sound better.	First write without editing. Then go back and read through your work, making minor edits. Then, give yourself some time away and approach your written piece with fresh eyes the next day.
I am not sure what to write for the first paragraph and/or section.	Start wherever you want and organize later. Do something that feels more exciting or easier in the moment.
My brain feels foggy or tired when I attempt to work.	Figure out what time you are most sharp and take advantage of that time!
Time keeps passing and I am not making progress.	Set specific, concrete, attainable, and measurable goals. Commit to working until a specific task is complete (e.g., a description of your procedure) rather than committing to a certain amount of time. Set deadlines for accomplishing small steps and share them with others who can hold you accountable. Things take longer than you think, but for now, focus on aiming to meet initial deadlines. You can re-evaluate later.
I get distracted from my work.	Stimulus control: create a specific work environment that increases your work output and minimizes distractions. Be mindful to observe when you are on or off task and return to a task as needed. Block technology and other distracters: turn off all devices, including your smart watch!
When I get work done, I feel blah afterward or I just think about how there is so much more to do.	Build in positive reinforcement: shape successive approximations toward completing sections and moving forward. Premack principle: start a work period with a less desirable section and follow it with a section that is far easier to complete.
I cannot imagine how anyone has done this!	Zone of proximal development/coping model—spend time with peers, both professional and personal, who have been successful in accomplishing a major applied research project. They will likely validate your concerns and roadblocks and tell you their stories of coping and eventually completing their projects.
I feel too anxious/frustrated/ uncomfortable to get work done.	Accept your emotions and work anyway: negative emotions and productivity are not mutually exclusive.

Procrastination-related thought	Potential solution
I cannot do it, I am an imposter, it is too much, I will not do a good job, or I worry what others will think.	Restructure your thoughts: cognitive restructuring helps to transform these negative statements into more moderate ones. It is more helpful to say, "I am capable of doing this, despite the struggles I am having."
I do not have enough time.	Prioritize your project. Put it in your schedule. Commit to fifteen minutes almost daily. This may motivate you. Assert yourself and say no to other activities.
I start worrying when I work.	Refocus your mind on the task at hand while pushing worry thoughts away—set aside a worry time and only worry during that time.
I cannot imagine getting to work.	Visually rehearse the sequences of sitting down and working.
I have trouble getting work done without an upcoming deadline.	Set deadlines and commit to them with your chair and peers.
I am waiting for feedback from my advisor and/or chair.	Keep working while waiting for feedback.
People in my life do not understand.	Surround yourself with positive supports. Communicate workload and needs to family and partners ahead of time.
I work better with others.	Find a project buddy to hold you accountable and provide support. Join a peer support group or higher a writing and/or executive functioning coach.
I did some work, but I am not sure it is enough or do not know what to do next.	Make to-do lists, regularly evaluate your progress, and set new goals or remediate as necessary.
I am sick of working on this!	Take short breaks and build in regular positive activities.

Reviewing Your Attitudes toward Feedback

You have likely continued to receive feedback from those around you during your writing and project management process, and you may have even been criticized for not sticking with certain ideas or not finishing your work fast enough. You also likely have an internal negative dialogue about your process thus far. These negative thoughts will certainly influence your distress level, motivation, and persistence at this stage and may even be a factor in project completion. In a qualitative investigation of experiences that led to completion or attrition of PhD students, Devos et al. (2017) interviewed twenty-one former doctoral students, including eight completers and thirteen noncompleters, about their research journey. The results indicated that what best distinguished these two groups during their research process was how much they felt they were moving forward, without too much emotional distress, on a project going in a direction they perceived made sense for them to pursue. Persistence for the completers seemed related to supervisor support, but this was not always the case, and some noncompleters had this support as well. Specifically, the following key ingredients differentiated the two groups:

1. Experiencing a feeling of progress in the development of the material that would constitute the final project (e.g., getting significant results, solving a mathematical problem, making a program work versus stagnating, going in circles, being stuck or blocked in this progression).
2. Experiencing little to no emotional distress (as opposed to experiencing high emotional distress about the work).
3. Being able to work on a project that made sense to them, in terms of it being their own, feeling passionate about it, and foreseeing that it could make a meaningful contribution (versus not having their own project or feeling they had to work in a direction that did not seem sensible).

At this point, if you are unhappy with the project you are working on, it will likely help to turn your mind toward accepting this reality. It will feel bad, and at the same time, it will help you achieve your goal of completing your degree. You can always pursue a different line of research or scholarly endeavor once you have that diploma! However, there are things within your control, such as taking stock of how you feel about how your project is going and working on how you think about it and persevere.

Table 3.1 included examples of how to restructure your negative thoughts about self-evaluation and feedback into more helpful ways of thinking. Table 6.2 includes similar examples for how to manage your thoughts about receiving feedback at this stage of your work. Look at these tables and then return to Worksheet 3.2 to restructure any of your own current negative thoughts about receiving feedback as you conduct your project.

Table 6.2 Examples of Restructuring Thoughts about Feedback

Event	Negative thought	More positive attitude
Your project committee requested several changes to your proposal.	It took me so long to write this, and now I have to go back and make so many edits. I will never be able to get this done.	It is tough to accept all of these changes, especially after I worked so hard on my proposal. I will give myself a small break and then ask my chair whether we can review what needs to be done. I can make a list including each item and work through the changes systematically.

Event	Negative thought	More positive attitude
A professional in your applied setting tells you they do not understand the purpose of your project or agree with its importance.	Maybe my project is stupid and pointless.	It is hurtful to hear this. At the same time, perhaps I can better clarify. It is also possible this person is not familiar with or up to date on the need for a project like this. I will consult with my chair to see what they think about this feedback.
A research assistant indicates they do not feel well-trained after you put a lot of effort into training them.	That is absurd! They are the one with the problem.	It is frustrating to hear this after all the time and effort I have put into training this research assistant. I will assess where they are getting stuck and see if I can clarify further. I can also review strategies from Chapter 5 for troubleshooting difficulties.
You were invited to present your project progress in your lab or in an applied setting.	I do not feel ready to present what I have so far. Others will see that my project has holes.	I know it is important to present work and hear others' feedback. I can view this experience as practice in front of a group where it is okay to make mistakes and receive feedback before presenting to a larger professional community (e.g., at a regional or national conference). I can share that my project is a work in progress and I can be open to receiving feedback that will give me ideas about next steps and help improve the project moving forward.
Your project timeline is delayed, and things are taking you longer than you expected.	What is wrong with me that this is taking so long? I should be further along by now.	I would have liked to be further along by now. But I have heard it is common for research and scholarly projects to take much more time than anticipated. I can assess whether I am consistent with moving forward and whether there is anything I can do to be more efficient or move forward more quickly. I can also re-evaluate my timeline so it is more realistic, based on the experience I have now attained.

SECTION 3

FINISHING YOUR FINAL PROJECT AND BEYOND

Chapter 7
Knowledge Needed for Finalizing Your Final Project

Introduction

As you get ready to finalize your final project, you should develop your *knowledge* about the critical evaluation of research, the conduct of research in applied settings, and ethical and professional competence by reviewing the following areas of this chapter:

- Factor to consider when completing your final project
- Knowing the key components of your results and discussion sections
- Ethical principles for completing your project
- The defense meeting

By the time you reach this chapter, you have likely completed your project's procedure (e.g., data collection) and are ready to analyze, report, and interpret your findings. Congratulations on reaching this point! We hope you have found a way to celebrate this milestone before turning to the next phase of your work. We will walk you through factors to consider as you move toward completion of your final project. We will then turn our attention to the key components of your results and discussion sections, ethical principles related to completing your project, and what to expect if your program requires you to defend your project in a defense meeting.

Factors to Consider When Completing Your Final Project

Similar to beginning your proposal, there are a number of factors to consider when completing your project. A good first step is to return to your proposal and update it to reflect the work you did. You will also want to consider ways to interact with your chair and committee members at this stage in the process to facilitate smooth completion. In addition, you will want to reflect on your findings in the context of the larger literature and think about their implications and contributions to the field, as well as your project's suggested limitations and directions for future research. You will also want to revisit your graduate timeline to ensure you are aware of important program and university deadlines. Finally, it can be helpful to clarify how your final

Navigating Research in an Applied Graduate Program. Hilary B. Vidair, Pam L. Gustafson, and Eva L. Feindler, Oxford University Press. © Oxford University Press (2024). DOI: 10.1093/oso/9780199352272.003.0007

Figure 7.1 Factors to consider when completing your final project

project aligns with your initial career goals. We review these factors to consider when completing your final project in Figure 7.1. Once you have read this section, we recommend you complete Worksheet 7.1 to help you think through the final stages of your project.

What Did I Do Differently Than I Stated in My Proposal?

You may have started working on your committee's expectations for revisions to your written proposal right after your proposal meeting. Or perhaps you made edits as you became clearer about your methodology, which often happens along with writing an institutional review board (IRB) application or conducting an actual project. However, if you have not done so yet, you are in good company! Now is a great time to get started. Even if you already began making revisions, it is worth going back and reviewing your latest proposal draft for any necessary updates. Here are some items to consider:

- Are your abstract, introduction, and method written in the past tense?
- Has any new literature been published (e.g., updated conceptualizations, recent studies) that makes sense to add to your introduction?
- If you conducted a qualitative study, did any unforeseen biases arise? Have you acknowledged potential biases of any coders you included?
- Within the method section, have you updated who your participants were and how many you had?
- Have you updated any changes to your research design?
- Have you updated any changes regarding how you conducted your procedure? What about the measures you used?
- Do you need to add or subtract any references?
- Do you have a table of contents to revise or wish to add one?
- Do you need to add or modify any appendices?

Revising Your Data Analytic Plan

It can be an exhilarating feeling to have all your data collected and ready for analysis. If you have spent time collecting data, take some time to review your data analytic plan to determine whether anything needs to be revised. For example, did you collect the exact data you proposed collecting? Do you have any new ideas about what you might want to analyze based on your experiences gathering your data? In a quantitative study, it is common to decide to conduct post hoc analyses, which refers to additional analyses you decide to conduct after completing your study. Post hoc analyses are typically based on new ideas about what would be worth evaluating after seeing your initial results. As we discussed in Chapter 4, if you use a statistical consultant, it is important to understand what you found and how to explain your findings to others. In a qualitative study, your original data analytic plan may have focused on how would code your data; however, when you are planning how to present your findings, you might decide to add descriptive statistics of your participants' demographic information in a table. If you have completed a theoretical or scholarly project, your experience over the course of your work might lead you to reconsider how you will present your findings or final product. For example, if you conducted a critical review of the literature, you may have planned to organize your findings around two contrasting perspectives only to determine that there is a third.

We recommend showing your chair a revised copy of your data analytic plan and/or an outline of your results section to be sure they agree with what you plan to analyze and present. If there are any major changes to your initial data analytic plan, it is useful to inform your committee about what you plan to revise and why, because it is better to hear any concerns they have before spending time conducting your analyses!

Theses and dissertations tend to include more results than a manuscript submitted for publication. For example, for a quantitative study, your chair may want you to include any of the following: missing data analyses, differences between participants who completed your study compared with those who did not, statistical assumptions, preliminary analyses (e.g., all correlations prior to regression analyses), nonsignificant results, and/or formulas to show that you understand what was calculated beyond what SPSS or another program ran. In a qualitative study, you may be expected to include sample quotes from individual participants to illustrate each theme or de-identified descriptions of each participant. Typically, this is not all necessary when you submit a manuscript, because there is not enough space to present this much information. Doing this now is analogous to showing your work in math class rather than using a calculator and providing only the final answer.

Student Example: Revising a Quantitative Data Analytic Plan

TW conducted a survey focused on assessing parents' acceptability and preferences for behavioral parenting training compared with a health maintenance model. When TW reviewed her proposed analytic plan after collecting her survey data, she opted to make a few changes. For example, some participants did not complete her survey, so she and her chair decided to compare completers and noncompleters on demographic and clinical variables to assess whether there were any significant differences between the two groups. She also had to address how to handle missing data. Before proceeding with her analyses, she consulted with the faculty member on her committee who teaches statistics. In addition, after speaking with her chair about the fact that this was a community sample, she decided to conduct post hoc analyses on a subsample of participants who reported elevated levels of behavior problems and distress.

Roles of Chairs and Committee Members at This Point

Now that your data are collected and/or you are ready to write up the results of your project, it is important to check in with your chair to ensure you are on the same page regarding how to proceed. For example, you may want to write an outline of your results and discussion sections to ensure your chair agrees with your plan before you spend valuable time writing.

It can also be helpful at this stage to talk with your chair about the length and style of your final project draft. Ideally, you will want to be able to transition your project into a manuscript for publication, which is often much shorter (e.g., about twenty-five to thirty-five pages total, including a title page, references, tables, and figures). Some faculty will encourage this style for your final project, while others will want to see a more comprehensive product before you take steps to turn your research into manuscript form. If you are given a choice, we recommend the former version; please note, however, that it is not necessarily easier to complete a shorter document, because it can be challenging to write concisely while still conveying all of the important information. The bonus to doing this work up front is that you are more likely to be able to publish your project.

In addition, your chair may recommend you follow the format of a prior student's dissertation, particularly if you are using similar analyses. Structuring your results and/or discussion section after a similar dissertation or article can save you a lot of time, because those before you already put effort into figuring out how to optimally present their findings.

Student Example: Planning to Write Up a Qualitative Results Section

LT was thrilled to have completed her qualitative interviews for her qualitative dissertation, focused on the retrospective experience of unaccompanied immigrant minors entering the United States. She reached out to her chair to propose an idea about how to organize and present her data. Her chair shared another student's (CP's) recently completed dissertation, because she had made use of the same grounded theory methodology for research focused on the experience of vicarious resilience in trauma workers. LT's chair encouraged her to organize her data in the same fashion, since a great deal of thought had already been put into how to communicate the findings, and CP had successfully defended her project. Although the content of the results was different, LT found it helpful to structure her results section in the same way. For example, she made a table including similar headers for each theme, with sample quotes to illustrate each repeating idea. Having a preexisting format to use as a template provided LT with an efficient way to organize her results and focus on the story of the participants she interviewed, as well as the practical implications.

It is also wise to keep in touch with your committee about your progress, particularly once you can estimate your defense date, so they have it on their radar for scheduling. This is also a good time to check with your chair and committee members about their schedules to determine whether they have any upcoming time away (e.g., conferences, vacations) that you will need to take into account when scheduling your defense. Regularly staying in touch reduces the possibility of anyone being surprised by your timeline when you attempt to find a meeting date and time.

Student Example: Keeping Committee Members Updated

Periodically, EC contacted her committee members to update them on her progress. About a month before she expected to defend, she let her committee know she was working on her final draft and asked them whether they had any upcoming vacations or dates they would not be able to meet for her defense. She expected to finish in December, a time when many faculty would be busy with final grading and the holiday season and right before her program's next conferral date. She acknowledged her program's policy, which indicated students should not set a defense date before the committee has time to review the final dissertation draft and approve moving forward. At the same time, she asked whether the committee would feel comfortable setting a tentative defense date, given the timing. The committee appreciated her regular contact and respectful request.

Some students may wish to ask for more input from their committee members at this point in the process. For example, if you have a statistician on your committee, you might want to show them the analyses you plan to use so you can obtain their feedback before proceeding. Some committee members may be willing to help you interpret your findings or organize your writing. However, committee members may expect your chair to address these steps with you. If you have not done so earlier, seek your chair's opinion now before going to your committee members to gauge what they think and obtain their approval. If you do seek a committee member's assistance, be sure to ask about the type and amount of assistance they feel comfortable providing.

What Did I Find or Develop? How Can I Understand My Findings and/or Project in the Context of the Larger Body of Literature?

In Chapter 1, we spoke about how your project would be embedded within the larger context of literature. Your project does not stand alone—it is only one part of a larger body of work. If you conducted an empirical study, you will need to demonstrate your ability to interpret your findings within the larger context of the research in your area, both in your discussion section and during your defense. As you think through your findings, compare and contrast them to the results of similar studies. Where do your results seem similar? Where do your findings differ? Think about why these similarities and differences might exist. If your results are consistent with prior studies, what do your specific findings add to this body of literature? Is it confirmation of prior findings or an extension in understanding? If your results contrast with prior research, could it be something about who was included in your sample? The way you asked specific questions? The time in history?

If you conducted a theoretical or scholarly project, your findings may be characterized as a product, such as a theory, a treatment or educational manual or book, or a description of a client or student's progress in an intervention; however, you will still likely need to describe how your project compares to similar prior work. For example, if you developed a treatment or educational manual, it will likely be important to compare and contrast your work to other manuals in your area, noting specific similarities and differences. If you engaged in a critical review of the literature in a particular area, note the key takeaway points and how your analysis can move our understanding of this area of the field forward.

What Are the Practical Implications of My Final Project? How Do They Make a Valuable Contribution to the Field?

You will want to have reasons why people should care about the results of your final project. How can you translate your findings into potential solutions to an existing practical problem? As we discussed in Chapter 4, this is your opportunity to suggest how your findings can build upon prior knowledge and make a practical contribution to the field. Additionally, can your results be used to revise or generate a theory or type of methodology? The implications do not have to be earth-shattering! Your findings can point to incremental, yet meaningful improvements in your area of study.

Student Example: Practical Implications Based on Students' Findings

RL conducted a qualitative study focused on student mothers' experiences within clinical psychology doctoral programs and supports they thought would be helpful. Based on her findings, she wrote up several practical implications for doctoral programs, externships, and internships, including ideas for policies (e.g., maternity leave), resources (e.g., pumping rooms), and supports (e.g., advisor check-ins).

What Are My Project's Limitations and Potential Future Directions?

Every project inevitably has limitations. This is normal and expected! As we noted in Chapter 1, studies with strong internal validity typically have less external validity and vice versa. There is no possible way your project can cover everything. As you think through your results, think about potential limitations. Here are some limitations of empirical projects:

- Sample: Are your participants possibly nonrepresentative of the population you aimed to study? Is generalizability limited based on demographic variables such as participants' gender, ethnicity, or age? In an applied study, could the setting or type of professionals involved impact your findings? Could people who chose to participate be different than people who did not?

- Sample size: In a quantitative study, did the size of your sample limit your ability to test for statistical significance? In a qualitative study, did you fail to reach theoretical saturation?

- Research design: In a quantitative quasi-experimental or correlational study, what constructs could serve as confounding variables? If vignettes were presented, could not actually going through certain experiences limit the generalizability of the findings? What were the limitations to your conditions or how your procedure was executed? In a qualitative study, how might your own bias or your coders' biases potentially have impacted your findings? See the limitations listed in Tables 4.2 and 4.3 for more potential design limitations.

- Measures: Could the type of measures or interview questions used have limited your ability to assess a particular construct or experience? In hindsight, was a key question not asked clearly enough? Could you have benefited from assessing the content validity of a new measure but did not do so?

- Procedure: Did what you expect to happen during your study occur as intended? How about in the time frame you proposed? Were there any procedural limitations related to your setting (e.g., amount of time you could spend with students out of class)?

- Analyses: In a quantitative study, were there any limitations to your analyses? Did you realize that some participants failed to respond to some questions? Were you unable to assess for differences between groups on certain key variables? Were any of your data skewed? Did your interrater reliability turn out to be low? In a qualitative study, did your coders have difficulty coming to a consensus? Was it difficult to develop theoretical constructs from your themes?

Even with a theoretical or scholarly project, you should think of limitations to your work. For example, if you developed a theory or a program manual, for whom might it not be applicable? If you engaged in a critical review of literature, what were the limits involved in the scope of literature included? If you wrote an extended clinical case study, what issues did your intervention not address?

Beyond limitations, you will need to consider potential directions for future research. These directions can be divided into theoretical, methodological, and practical directions. If you conducted a quantitative project, how might your results point to the next step(s) for advancing a theory? If your project was qualitative, you might generate a theory and related hypotheses that can be tested in future research. In terms of methodology, could researchers build on your work by assessing whether a diverse sample yields similar findings? What could knowing this add to the literature? What are the potential benefits of using another type of research design or additional ways you would suggest measuring the constructs you studied? Finally, what practice-oriented research questions can be generated from your findings?

How Do I Ensure That Completing This Project Aligns with My Graduate School Timeline?

When you are ready to analyze and write up your results, make sure you are aware of your program's suggested timeline and any related program and university deadlines, so you can plan accordingly. For example, make sure you know when you would have to defend by to be able to walk in graduation, avoid the next semester's matriculation fee, and complete your degree, typically referred to as degree conferral. Some universities allow you to walk during the graduation ceremony as long as you have already defended, even if you are still on an internship. Some universities require you to apply for graduation by a certain deadline.

After defending, you will typically have to make edits to your final project, and you might have to adhere to a deadline for official conferral of your degree. Keep post-defense deadlines like this in mind when scheduling your defense date, because you will likely have to submit a final version of your project to your department and/or university library a certain amount of time before the conferral date to have your degree conferred.

How Does My Final Project Fit with My Initial Career Goals?

As we discussed in Chapter 4, your final project does not have to dictate your career. At the same time, you can think about whether and how it does fit into your initial career goals. For example, when writing a cover letter or interviewing for a job, how will you want to describe the work you conducted for your project? Sometimes this is very clear, for example, if you conducted a project focused on students with learning disabilities and aim to continue your career in special education. If it is not so clear, think about ways you can tell your story. What did you learn from your project that motivated you to apply for your next position? How did the research complement your applied experiences?

Student Example: How Your Project Can Fit with Your Initial Career Goals

EY had an interest in working with families grieving the loss of a child. While in graduate school, he served as a research assistant for a professor conducting research in rural Uganda. He spoke with the professor about being able to assess grief in this population, especially considering that it has one of the highest child death rates in the world. The professor agreed, and EY traveled to Uganda with the professor's research team, adding survey measures about parental bereavement, depression, and trauma to the larger research study. Conducting this research allowed EY to become familiar with literature in his area of interest while finding a feasible project and chair. He was then able to speak about his research on job interviews and is now in private practice, with grief counseling as an area of focus.

Beyond the specific content of your final project, think about how leading a project to completion has enhanced your skill set. For example, did you have the opportunity to supervise research assistants? You can highlight this experience to demonstrate your ability to train and possibly even mentor others. Did you learn more about conducting research in a particular applied setting and/or identify ways to translate research-based knowledge for use in real-world practice? Many training and job opportunities will appreciate this type of knowledge. In addition, did you have the opportunity to network with any professionals who might be useful contacts moving forward?

Student Example: How Your Project Can Create Future Opportunities

CLK developed and pilot tested a mindfulness curriculum in an Orthodox Jewish school for females. She spent time training the school's teachers and offering support as they implemented the lesson plans. The school's administration appreciated her project so much that they asked her to continue mentoring teachers and administrators so they could sustain the curriculum for years afterward. Once she was a licensed psychologist, she also supervised a postdoctoral fellow who taught monthly class lessons and provided mentoring to the teachers.

Knowing the Key Components of Your Results and Discussion Sections

Now that we have addressed factors to consider when completing your project, we turn to the key components needed within your results and discussion sections. As with your proposal, be sure to check the American Psychological Association's (APA's) style guide or any other style manual you need to adhere to for details about formatting. Also check to see whether your program has specific guidelines for formatting these sections, such as subsections to include or the placement of tables and figures. We will discuss strategies for how to present your results and discussion sections in Chapter 8.

Results

In the results section, you will report what you found. It is important not to interpret the data in this section; rather, you will report your findings as if you are a newscaster, leaving the editorializing for the discussion section. For an empirical project, it is common to begin with descriptive data (e.g., means and standard deviations, frequencies, and percentages) on each of your measures. You might also compare these statistics to existing norms. It is helpful to present these data in a table, highlighting anything important or unusual in the text. For a quantitative study, you will then likely present your findings in order of your hypotheses and/or research questions. For a qualitative study, you would likely report your data in the most logical order of your themes and/or theoretical constructs. The order of your results section will likely match the order of your data analytic section.

Theoretical or scholarly projects will probably differ in how results are presented. Consult with your chair about format ideas. Some may be more straightforward than others. For example, development of an intervention program may involve presenting session-by-session content, along with participant handouts. Results from a critical analysis of the literature or development of a theory will likely involve writing a summary of your review, along with tables categorizing your findings and/or figures organizing your ideas.

It is helpful to write about your key findings in the text and present more detailed information in tables. You can also illustrate key points with figures. You will likely have more tables and figures for your final project than you would for a manuscript, where you are typically limited to approximately five items. We will present ideas for reporting your results in Chapter 8.

Discussion

In the discussion section, you will interpret the results of your project within the context of the larger body of literature. This section typically begins with a reminder of the purpose of your study, as well as the main findings (or products). Subsequent paragraphs describe each of the main findings, followed by any post hoc findings. As mentioned earlier, it is important to embed your findings in the context of the existing literature. In other words, you should explain how your results compare to prior research and comment on any similarities or differences. Once you have completed the interpretation of your findings, you should explain their practical implications. For example, how can your results inform clinical practice or teaching in the classroom? The next step is to report on your project's limitations. As mentioned earlier in this chapter, these could be methodological limitations, such as the limits of your sample, the type of design you used, how you conducted your procedure, or what you measured. Although limitations are expected, theses and dissertations often have numerous limitations described in substantial detail, which can make it sound as if the study was problematic. You will probably want to reduce the number of limitations reported if you turn your project into a manuscript for publication. Your discussion should conclude with directions for future research, including theoretical, methodological, and practical directions. Some students add a brief conclusion summarizing their project's purpose, findings, and overall implications. This section can be very short, even a paragraph, and is primarily a stylistic choice.

Ethical Principles for Completing Your Project

In Chapter 4, we presented ethical principles related to developing a proposal and conducting research with humans. They were based on the APA's (2017) "Research and Publication" section (standard 8) of the *Ethical Principles of Psychologists and Code of Conduct*. In Table 7.1, we present ethical principles from standard 8 that are relevant to presenting results and publishing your final project.

Table 7.1 Ethical Principles for Presenting Your Results and Publication

Ethical principle	What you need to know
Reporting research results	Do not falsify or alter your data. If you discover mistakes in published work, aim to correct them by submitting a correction or a retraction to the journal with the published work.
Plagiarism	Do not use other's work as your own. Cite appropriately when using someone else's work.
Publication credit	Authorship credit should only be granted for substantial effort and contributions to publication. Authorship should reflect those whose efforts were involved in the research; credit should not be granted to those who did not actively participate in the project. Ensure that minor contributions to the work are recognized in acknowledgment sections. You will be listed as the principal author on any publications that are based on your dissertation research, except under unique circumstances. Discuss publication credit with your chair and/or advisor early in the process of conducting research and consider whether you need to revisit the discussion of authorship as you proceed with publication.
Duplicate publication of data	Do not publish data that have already been published and cite them as original. If republishing existing data, indicate where and when data were published before.
Sharing research data for verification	After publication, you must provide data to other professionals in the field who wish to re-evaluate your work. If you do this, ensure that confidentiality of your participants is maintained.

Based on the American Psychological Association's (2017) ethics code.

Authorship

Issues related to authorship order and the manuscript writing process can be complex to navigate. If you are interested in presenting and/or publishing your final project, discuss authorship and related expectations as early as possible in the process, because this can decrease the potential for later problems. Once you know the results of your project, ask your chair whether they think the project will be possible to present and/or publish, and if so, what they would like that process to look like. If you have been collaborating on your project with professionals in an applied setting, recall that in Chapter 4 we mentioned the importance of discussing authorship with them up front. Now is a good time to meet with them to review your findings and revisit your authorship agreement. We will discuss strategies for presenting and publishing in Chapter 8, but it is important to discuss authorship as a first step.

The APA's (2017) ethics code indicates that students should be the principal authors of their dissertations, except under exceptional circumstances. Studies of faculty and students have typically supported this APA standard (e.g., Bartle et al., 2000; Tryon et al., 2007). Potential "exceptional circumstances" are not listed in the standard; however, some possible examples are as follows:

- You do not wish to do the work of converting your dissertation to a manuscript for publication, and your document will require significant revisions to be appropriate for a journal article.
- You and your chair agree up front that you would be able to maintain first authorship if you worked on the manuscript for a certain amount of time after graduation (e.g., one year).
- You were given permission to use archival data for your project that belongs to your chair or a professional in an applied setting, provided with a research idea the data could help address, given relevant articles to read, and guided through the data analysis.

Faculty have been found to be more hesitant about a student assuming first authorship at the master's level (Bartle et al., 2000). If you are in a field that adheres to an ethics code, see whether they have any guidelines about authorship.

When you are thinking about who to include for authorship, consider the amount and type of work each possible author put into the project. As indicated in the APA's (2017) ethics code, authorship is reserved for those who made meaningful contributions to your work. This might include having helped you conceptualize the research problem, structure your research design and procedure, and/or interpret your findings (APA, 2020b).

Typically, if you will be the first author, you will be expected to list your chair as the second author, although you will need to consider how much each potential author contributed to your topic development, research design, and manuscript writing (Bartle et al., 2000). An exception would be if a professional from an applied site was more involved in helping you develop the project and collect and/or analyze data, while your chair served as your advisor given your program's academic requirements. In that case, you might make your chair the third author. Alternatively, professionals from your applied site who contributed to your project but not as much as your chair may be invited to be authors after your chair.

Your committee members can be considered as authors, but they might not have contributed enough to the project to warrant authorship. For example, simply reviewing your draft and providing commentary does not mean they should be invited to be an author on a resulting paper. If a committee member helped run analyses or is willing to help convert your project into a manuscript, however, you and your chair could invite them to serve as a coauthor.

Research assistants who were involved with your project might also be invited to be authors on your study, but they would need to contribute more than simply conducting observations or entering data to be considered meaningful contributors. Sometimes it is sufficient to involve research assistants on poster presentations before or instead of involving them in a publication. Speak with your chair about whether it makes sense to include them and what tasks they might help you complete at this time that would warrant authorship of various kinds.

The APA has developed scorecards to help determine who has contributed enough to warrant authorship, as well as authorship order (see APA, 2015). They also include common reasons for changes in authorship, as well ideas about how to address authorship concerns.

IRB Renewal

As mentioned in Chapter 5, if you have an active IRB-approved study, keep on top of when your approval is set to expire and be sure to determine whether you need to renew it. Typically, a full board application will require annual review, while exempt and expedited studies might require a shorter renewal process. Even if you have completed data collection, some IRBs require you to keep your application active while you analyze data. They will likely also ask you to report any modifications you have made to your study, as well as any study findings to date.

The Defense Meeting

Similar to the proposal meeting we discussed in Chapter 4, many programs hold a defense meeting where a student presents their complete project, with their chair and committee present to discuss and evaluate it. Some programs add additional committee members at this point, sometimes referred to as outside readers. Next, we provide an overview of the defense meeting, including the purpose of the meeting, defense requirements, format, and possible outcomes. We will review skills for defending in

Chapter 8, including tasks to complete before your defense, how to prepare your slides, how to ensure you are ready for your oral presentation, how to respond to questions from your committee, and items to address immediately after your defense.

Purpose of the Defense Meeting

One of the main points of a defense meeting is to determine whether you have achieved an expected or higher level of research competence for someone completing your program. Your committee will likely evaluate you on some or all of the following:

- Did you ethically conduct your project?
- How well did you carry out your proposed research design and procedure?
- Can you intelligently communicate what you found, both in writing and orally?
- Did you adequately interpret results of any assessments and/or measures used?
- Can you adequately respond to questions about your design or findings?
- How well can you explain your findings in the context of the existing literature?
- Are you aware of your project's limitations and do you have directions for future research?
- Do you demonstrate understanding of how individual and cultural diversity played a role in your project's findings?
- Can you respond to feedback in a thoughtful and nondefensive manner?

Another goal of defending is to have the opportunity to share and discuss what you found with faculty and/or professionals who are about to become your colleagues. It is normal to be anxious about defending; at the same time, keep in mind that after all of the work you have accomplished, you are the main expert on your project—no one will know the ins and outs of it better than you! We hope you find it exciting to review your project with experts in your field.

Defense Requirements

Check with your program to see whether there is any written policy outlining the defense process or any time when the requirements and timeline will be reviewed. Some programs have specific requirements leading up to the defense, such as sharing your abstract with the entire department, creating a flier announcing your defense, and/or inviting other students. Some programs open defense meetings up to other members of the university community or professionals from your applied setting. You may also be allowed to invite family and friends to your defense meeting. Some programs hold closed defense meetings that include only the student and the committee.

As with your proposal meeting, once your chair approves your full project draft, you will typically then send it to your committee members. You will usually be expected to give them at least two weeks to read your final dissertation draft before you schedule your defense meeting. Some committee members may provide you with feedback on your written draft before the meeting. Ask your chair whether you should send any revised drafts to your committee before your defense or wait to address them in the meeting. As with the proposal meeting, a defense meeting typically runs about ninety minutes.

You might wonder what to wear to your defense. Most programs do not have a particular dress code; however, it is best to look professional. This is your moment to present your work to your committee, who are about to become your colleagues. It will likely be easier to get into the professional mindset you need if you are dressed for a professional setting. This can include anything from business casual (e.g., cardigan and dress pants) to a suit.

Many departments have an unwritten tradition of students providing food and drinks for the committee when defending. Check whether your department has policies around this practice. Bringing refreshments should not impact your committee's evaluation of your project. If you decide to do so, we recommend bringing a small amount of food and a few water bottles or coffee. Some students choose to check in with the committee about dietary restrictions beforehand.

Defense Format

The defense meeting includes your presentation, committee members' questions for you, some discussion about your project, what could have been different or what is important to study next, and the evaluation of your written project and oral presentation performance. The evaluation portion typically includes asking you to leave the meeting so your committee members can discuss your written and oral performance, complete written evaluations, and come to a consensus on whether you attained competency in the required areas (e.g., ethics, research).

Speak to your chair about what to include in your presentation. You can think of your presentation as an extension of what we reviewed in Chapters 4 and 5 about a proposal meeting; this time, however, you will be spending most of your time discussing your findings. Many programs ask students to present using an accompanying PowerPoint presentation. We will review how to prepare slides for a defense in Chapter 8. It can also be helpful to bring hard copies of your slides and/or the tables and figures you want your committee to be able to refer to during your presentation.

At the start of your meeting, your chair will likely set the tone for how formal or informal the structure of your presentation will be. Some may want the committee to hold their questions until you complete your presentation. In this case, they may ask you to prepare to talk for a certain amount of time (e.g., thirty minutes). Other chairs will encourage committee members to jump in and ask questions as you go through your talk, allowing things to evolve into more of a discussion about your work. In this case, follow your chair's lead to know when to proceed from discussion to your next point. Talk with upper-level students who worked with your chair about their experiences.

Your committee members typically will have read your draft ahead of time and come prepared with questions and comments. Questions can range from clarifying specific information (e.g., the number of participants who completed various parts of your study) to open-ended questions about your methodology, findings, comparisons of your findings to existing research or scholarship, practical implications, limitations of your findings, and directions for future research. They might also ask you to comment on how you could do something differently if you had the opportunity to conduct the project again, given what you have learned.

Questions and comments are not the only behaviors you can expect from committee members. Sometimes they will end up in discussions among themselves! This is a positive sign; some of the most successful defenses we have attended engendered deep discussion about topics such as the best strategy for measuring a particular variable or creative ideas for implementing practical implications of a student's study into an applied setting. If two committee members end up in strong disagreement, however, recognize that this is likely more about their own ideologies than about your work! We will discuss how to respond to questions and feedback in Chapter 8.

Possible Outcomes

Formal evaluation forms often must be completed near the end of your defense meeting, when you are asked to leave the room. Be sure you have these forms ready for your committee members at the start of the meeting, if they are meeting with you in person, and electronically if they are video conferencing. Typically, your committee will rate you on your written draft, your oral presentation performance, your understanding of your results and the implication of your findings, and your reaction to feedback. Some programs will give you a final overall rating on a Likert scale (e.g., from 1 to 5, where 3 indicates passing). Many committees will also rate you using one of four final outcomes: passing with no required revisions (which is very rare); passing with minor revisions, where only the chair needs to approve your edits (probably the most common); passing with major revisions, where all or part of your committee needs to approve your edits; and failing (also rare).

After you committee is finished deliberating, they will call you back into the room, usually to say, "Congratulations, you passed your defense!" Try to be appreciative of this moment, because it is the culmination of all of your hard work over a long time. Once the committee has congratulated you, your chair will likely review the committee's overall impressions about the strengths of your work, as well as any competency areas that need improvement and any parts of your project that you could have handled differently or that still need revisions. Each committee member may then add their individual comments. Your committee may require you to make some revisions and recommend others.

We understand the fear of failing, yet failing is actually hard to do! A chair will typically not allow a student to schedule a defense meeting unless they feel confident the student will pass. In our experience, students run into trouble when they push to defend before their chair thinks they are ready, for example, to start a job or graduate by a certain time. If your chair thinks you are ready to defend, you likely are. You have come a long way to get to this point in your program, and your chair will want you to succeed. If you want to be extra confident, find out what would happen if you failed. Typically, you would be able to remediate your work and schedule a second defense meeting when you and your chair feel you are ready.

Postdefense

Once you pass your defense, we hope you spend time celebrating before you do anything else! After doing all of this work, it can feel surreal and/or anticlimactic. It is important to build in some fun and relaxation. After all, you have really earned it! After commemorating your achievement, you will need to take the steps necessary to finalize your project, which may include completing revisions and showing them to your chair and/or committee as necessary, as well as filing any necessary paperwork with your program and university (e.g., submitting defense evaluation forms or your final project copy). Many students choose to include an acknowledgments section toward the front of their final project draft. In addition, you may be required or want to publish your final project in an open-access repository or a database, such as ProQuest Dissertations & Theses Global. We will discuss binding your final project, writing your acknowledgments section, and skills for presenting and publishing your work in Chapter 8.

Worksheet 7.1 Factors to Consider When Completing Your Final Project

Once you have completed your project's procedure (e.g., data collection) and are ready to analyze, report, and interpret your findings, use the information in the "Factors to Consider" section of Chapter 7 to help you complete this worksheet. The purpose of answering these questions is to help you move forward with completing your final project.

What did I do differently than I stated in my proposal?

Consider	Comments
Are my abstract, introduction, and method written in the past tense? Have I updated who my participants were and how many I had? Have I updated any changes to my research design?	
Have I updated any changes regarding how I conducted my procedure? What about the measures I used?	
What about any changes I made to my data analytic plan?	
Do I need to add or subtract any references?	
Do I have a table of contents to revise or wish to add one? Do I need to add or modify any appendices?	

How should I revise my data analytic plan?

Consider	Comments
Did I review my data analytic plan to determine whether it needs to be revised?	
Did I collect the exact data I proposed collecting? Do I have any new ideas about what I might want to analyze and/or present based on my experiences gathering my data and/or developing my final product?	
If I used a consultant, do I understand what I found and how to explain my findings to others?	
Did I show my revised data analytic plan to my chair to determine that they agree with my plan?	

Have I communicated with my chair and committee members?

Consider	Comments
Have I reviewed an outline of my results and discussion section with my chair to ensure that I am headed in the right direction?	
Have I spoken with my chair about the length of my final project?	
Am I using a prior student's dissertation format?	
Have I notified my chair and committee members of my expected defense date and determined whether they will be available?	

What did I find or develop? How can I understand my findings in the context of the larger body of literature?

Consider	Comments
Are my results and/or product similar to prior research or work? Are they different in some way?	
Why do these similarities and differences exist?	
If my results are consistent with prior studies, what do my specific findings add to this body of literature? Is it confirmation of prior findings or an extension in understanding?	
If my results contrast with prior research, could it be something about my sample? The way I asked specific questions? The time in history?	

What are the practical implications of my results and/or project? How do they make a valuable contribution to the field?

Consider	Comments
How could findings and/or products from my project build on existing knowledge, revise or generate a theory, and/or propose solutions to an existing practical issue?	
Can my findings and/or products be used to make recommendations that could practically advance my field?	

What are the limitations of my project and potential future directions?

Consider	Comments
Are my participants possibly nonrepresentative of the population I aimed to study? Is generalizability limited based on demographic variables such as participants' gender, ethnicity, or age? In an applied study, might the setting in which participants work or the type of professionals they are have impacted my findings? Could people who chose to participate be different than people who did not?	
In a quantitative study, did the size of my sample limit my ability to test for statistical significance? In a qualitative study, did I fail to reach theoretical saturation?	
In a quantitative quasi-experimental or correlational study, what constructs could serve as confounding variables? If vignettes were presented, could not going through certain experiences limit the generalizability of the findings? What were the limitations to my conditions or how my procedure was executed? In a qualitative study, how might my own bias or my coders' biases potentially have impacted my findings?	
Could the type of measures or interview questions I used have limited my ability to assess a particular construct or experience? In hindsight, was a key question not asked clearly?	
In a quantitative study, were there any limitations to my analyses? Was I unable to assess for differences between groups on certain key variables? Were any of my data skewed? Did my interrater reliability turn out to be low? In a qualitative study, did my coders have difficulty coming to a consensus? Was it difficult to develop theoretical constructs from my themes?	
If I conducted a quantitative project, how might my results suggest the next step(s) for advancing a theory? If my project was qualitative, could I generate theory and hypotheses that can be tested in future research? In terms of methodology, are there ways researchers could build on my work using a different sample? How about another research design or other measures? Finally, what practical research questions can be generated from my findings?	
If I conducted a theoretical or scholarly project, what are the limitations? For example, if I developed a theory or manual, for whom may it not be applicable? If I conducted a systematic literature review, what were the limits of the scope of literature included? If I wrote an extended case study, what were the limits of my intervention? What are some potential next steps based on my project?	

How do I ensure that completing this project aligns with my graduate school timeline?

Consider	Comments
Am I aware of my program and university's timeline for graduation and conferral of my degree (i.e., make sure you know the date by which you have to defend to be able to walk in graduation)?	

How does my final project fit with my initial career goals?

Consider	Comments
How will I describe the work I conducted for my project?	
What have I learned from my project?	
Does my final project reflect what I plan to pursue in the future? If not, consider how to tell the story of my trajectory.	
How did this research compliment my applied experiences?	
How does this research apply in real-world practice?	
What experiences did I have within the project that can help me in my career moving forward (e.g., supervised and/or mentored research assistants, learned to conduct research in an applied setting and/or implement findings, networked with professionals who might be useful contacts)?	

Chapter 8
Skills for Finalizing Your Final Project

Introduction

As you analyze, write up, and present the findings from your final project, you should develop your *skills* with regard to the critical evaluation of research, the conduct of research in applied settings, and ethical and professional competence by learning about the following:

- Continuing to write up your final project
- Analyzing your data
- Writing your results section
- Writing your discussion section
- Skills for successfully working with your chair
- How to share results with professionals in your applied setting
- Keeping your project timeline on track
- How to finalize your full draft
- Preparing for your defense
- Remediation planning
- Practical strategies for presenting and publishing

In Chapter 7, we reviewed factors to consider when finalizing your final project. We also reviewed key components of your written results and discussion sections and things to know about the defense meeting. At this point, you are likely ready to analyze your data and write your results and discussion sections, so we begin this chapter by discussing how to do so. We then review skills for working with your chair and committee members at this stage, putting your entire draft together, and keeping your timeline on track. Your program may require a defense meeting, so we present skills to help get you through it and ready to graduate! We wrap up with skills for presenting and publishing your findings, which we highly recommend.

Continuing to Write Up Your Final Project

It can be tough to get back into writing after you have conducted your project, especially because working on the end stage of your project is not usually part of a class, like the proposal phase might be. In fact, you may already be finished with

Navigating Research in an Applied Graduate Program. Hilary B. Vidair, Pam L. Gustafson, and Eva L. Feindler, Oxford University Press. © Oxford University Press (2024). DOI: 10.1093/oso/9780199352272.003.0008

coursework and not in regular contact with your cohort. Try to think of this piece as the light at the end of a tunnel. You have come a long way through selecting a topic, writing your proposal, and conducting your project.

As we discussed in Chapter 6, there are strategies you can use to reduce procrastination and keep your project writing moving. Take notes whenever you think of important points, even if this means jotting them down in the notes section of your phone. Break the sections you need to work on into smaller tasks. For example, the first author of this book set a goal to complete about a third of this chapter at a time. From there, she divided that third into even smaller pieces, taking notes on what she aimed to accomplish under each heading. Before ending a writing section, jot down some notes about the next steps you want to take so you have somewhere to start when you return.

As you revise drafts, consider using tracked changes in Word to temporarily keep yourself aware of what you add, delete, or move around. This will allow you to easily see what is new and revert to a previous version if you change your mind. Save new drafts as you go, so you can return to prior work should you have a question about something you deleted. It also helps to periodically email your work to yourself or set it up to save automatically on an electronic drive.

As you are working, remember that you should recharge periodically so you have the energy to keep going. This means scheduling in breaks, including time for socialization, family time, exercise, relaxation, sleep, television shows, or anything you find relaxing or rejuvenating.

We recommend completing Worksheet 8.1 to help you prepare to conduct your data analyses and write your results and discussions sections. Part 1 of this worksheet invites you to think through each of these pieces of your project. Part 2 can be used to track the completion of each related project task.

Analyzing Your Data

Data Planning

In Chapter 7, we spoke about revisiting your data analytic plan to be sure you and your chair are clear about the analyses you will be conducting. As we discussed in Chapter 5, the particular analyses you conduct will depend on the purpose of your project, your research design, and your committee's agreement during your proposal meeting; however, there are some universal strategies for planning your data analyses. For example, it can be helpful to write an outline of the specific steps you plan to take, even including basic steps.

In a quantitative study, you can include preliminary analyses, such as analyzing descriptive data, running statistical assumptions (e.g., normal distribution, homogeneity of variance), and conducting analyses that serve as prerequisites to statistical tests that will address your hypotheses (e.g., correlations prior to regression analyses).

Writing out these initial steps will give you a plan to follow and ensure you do not miss anything. You may decide to present some of these preliminary analyses in your method section. This could include descriptive information about your participants, interrater reliability of coding (e.g., coding child observations for specific behaviors), or any reliability and/or validity analyses you conducted on your measures (unless the focus of your study was on scale development, in which case it might be better to present this information in your results section). Speak with your chair regarding their thoughts about where to place these kinds of analyses.

Once you have determined your preliminary quantitative analyses, you will want to list the analyses you need to conduct in the order of your hypotheses and/or research questions. Next, think about any addendums, such as variables you may want to control for (based on theory, prior literature, or the results of your preliminary analyses) and any statistical corrections you might need to use to account for multiple comparisons. In addition, ask your chair whether you should analyze confidence intervals, which will illustrate the potential range of your findings and/or effect sizes, which go beyond statistical significance to determine the magnitude of your findings.

After you start analyzing your data, you may think of additional analyses you want to conduct or post hoc analyses. For example, you could conduct a survey in a community sample and realize you have a subgroup of participants who meet the criteria for clinically significant problems. You might want to add some post hoc analyses examining whether your results differ between participants with clinical and nonclinical presentations; however, this might not be part of your initial hypotheses. Speak with your chair about adding post hoc analyses. They can be worth examining, but at the same time, you do not want to stray too far from the initial purpose of your study. In addition, developing hypotheses after you conduct your study usually means they are not rooted in the theory or prior research you reviewed. Consider your post hoc analyses exploratory results that might point to future research rather than confirming your hypotheses. Here is an example of a step-by-step outline for a quantitative data analytic plan.

Student Example: Writing an Outline of Your Data Analytic Plan

MR conducted a quantitative survey study to determine whether there were significant differences in the type of cognitive-behavioral therapy (CBT) approaches that psychologists accept, prefer, and use to treat generalized anxiety disorder in practice. Participants read two case vignettes, one using imagine exposure (IE) and one using cognitive restructuring and relaxation training (CRRT), to treat a potential client with generalized anxiety disorder. She also examined clinicians' beliefs about conducting imaginal exposure and the amount of CBT training and exposure training they had received. In her proposal, her initial data analytic plan focused on analyses for her hypotheses and did not include some of the preliminary and post hoc analyses she and her chair thought were important. Together, they developed the following outline of steps to follow for her data analyses:

Step-by-Step Data Analytic Plan

- Preliminary analyses
  o Means and standard deviations, frequencies and percentages for demographic and clinical training variables
  o Means and standard deviations for acceptability, preference, and use (A/P/U) in the overall sample
  o Means and standard deviations of the Treatment Evaluation Inventory (TEI), Therapists' Beliefs about Exposure Scale (TBES), and Treatment Likes and Dislikes questionnaire
  o Statistical tests for assumptions for analyses below
  o Correlations between demographic variables and A/P/U
- Analyses for hypotheses
  o Comparison between vignettes
    ▪ t-test for difference in acceptability (TEI) between the two vignettes
    ▪ Chi-square tests for preference and use between the two vignettes
    ▪ Correlations between TBES and A/P/U
    ▪ Correlations between amount of CBT/exposure training and A/P/U
- Post hoc analyses
  o Correlations among A/P/U
  o Correlations between TBES and amount of CBT/exposure training
    ▪ Pearson when continuous, biserial when one is continuous, chi square when both are categorical.

As we discussed in Chapter 5, qualitative data analytic methods range from a process of subjective reflection to systemic coding. Regardless, it is helpful to make a list of the steps you will need to take to conduct your analyses. For example, if you are using grounded theory methodology, you will likely list the steps you need to take for coding (as shown in AS's example in Chapter 5). It can be useful to list steps prior to coding as well, such as how you will color code individual participants' commentary. You may also benefit from conducting descriptive analyses on the demographics of your sample. For instance, what was the mean age of your sample? How about their education level? What percentage of your participants were recruited from the same location? This information may be useful to present in a table in the method section of your final paper. Ideally, you will also be able to plan to judge your analyses using some of the concepts we discussed in Chapter 1 (i.e., credibility, transferability, dependability, confirmability) to assess your data's trustworthiness. For example, if you interviewed participants, we recommend planning to conduct a member check with some of them in a group meeting (see the data analysis section for more about this).

For a nonempirical study, your "data" will likely take a different form. However, it can still be useful to list the findings you plan to share. For example, if you developed a theory, how will you organize its presentation? If you designed a treatment manual, would it be useful to include checklists for each session?

Regardless of your project's design, it can also be useful to determine what data you plan to present, including what to present in tables and figures, as well as whether details of supplemental, detailed, and/or nonsignificant analyses might be best suited for your appendices. You can also look at examples from the final projects of other students your chair has mentored, because they will probably recommend similar analyses and formatting. Overall, agreeing with your chair about how to present your final project can save you ample time moving forward and give you a ready-made to-do list!

Data Entry and Cleaning

Now that you have your data analytic plan, it is important to ensure your data are entered, organized, and ready for analysis. This involves data entry and cleaning, which are necessary steps to take, at least with quantitative and qualitative research projects.

Prior to beginning data entry, refer to your institutional review board (IRB) application and ensure you adhere to any steps you said you would take to de-identify and store data. If you are dealing with hard copies, it is useful to de-identify data as they come in. For example, you may need to separate consent and/or assent forms with identifying information from survey measures. In this case, you would create an ID number and connect that number to both the consent and/or assent form and the surveys. Only you and the research team you included in your IRB application should have access to this information. You will also need to ensure the data are stored as you indicated they would be in your IRB application. Hard copies are typically stored in a locked file cabinet in a locked room. Hard copies of qualitative transcripts and audio and/or video recordings may be destroyed once they are transcribed, if this is what you indicated would occur. Any electronic data files should be backed up and stored in separate locations. In addition, it can be helpful to note the date by which data can be destroyed in a place where you will easily see it when you open your files years later.

Make sure you are familiar with any spreadsheet and/or statistical programs you can use to enter and analyze your data. Determine whether you have access to programs of interest through your school or if they are available for free or must be purchased. Students can often receive a discount on programs that require a purchase. If you need help figuring out how to lay out data in a particular program, there are probably many sources of information, including textbooks, online instructional videos, tutorials made by the program creators, and other students familiar with the program.

If you will be analyzing quantitative data and you have not already entered data into a spreadsheet, such as Microsoft Excel, SPSS, or another statistical package, now is the time to do so. Sometimes it is not clear how much data to enter. For example, standardized measures might include questions you do not plan to analyze. There are pros and cons to entering all the data you have. Pros include having the data on hand if you decide it could be useful to analyze, having the statistical program calculate summary scores from individual question items, and being able to check more detailed information (e.g., individual subscale scores) when there is a question about total scores. The biggest con is the amount of time you will have to spend on data entry and cleaning for data you might not need.

Once you know what data you plan to enter, create a mock spreadsheet and try to enter one participant's information. This should help you clarify what needs to go in each column. It can help to enter the data in the same order it was collected. Label your columns clearly so you remember what each one stands for (e.g., the abbreviated name of the measure, then Q1 for the response to question 1). Keep a codebook of any values you assign categorical responses to so you can recall them later. For example, if you numerically code categorical variables like gender, race/ethnicity, and income, be sure to record what you coded as answer choice 1, choice 2, etc. It may seem clear and a codebook may seem unnecessary now, but in a few weeks or months you may find yourself wondering what you did! Some statistical programs, like SPSS, include a place to track the names of values.

You may have used a survey program (e.g., SurveyMonkey or Google Forms) that will allow you to export your data into a spreadsheet rather than having to manually enter it. If this is the case, you will still want to review the labels of columns and determine whether they could benefit from any editing for clarity.

If you are working with qualitative data, you will want to review your transcripts of interviews, field notes, photographs, and/or documents several times, so you can really become familiar with the content before beginning any analyses. Then, decide how you will organize your data. For example, if you have transcripts from interviews, will you enter data from each interview into a Word document and then create documents for each coding step, color coding text from individual participants? Or will you enter data into a qualitative data program such as ATLAS.ti or NVivo, which can help organize and interpret qualitative transcripts, visual, or audio data? Although these programs can be incredibly helpful when it comes to systematic data analysis, they take time to learn and can be costly. Some qualitative researchers feel that using them removes too much of the possible subjective interpretation, even with a coding team. You can discuss the pros and cons of these options with your chair.

As with quantitative data, make sure to label each qualitative data file clearly (e.g., individual participant ID number, focus group number, document number). Keep a codebook to record what each label means. Be sure to have a system for naming files in a consistent manner to stay clear about what the file includes (e.g., Coder A, Participant 8, date). If you will be manually coding, consider using different colors and fonts to indicate codes selected by a specific coder or by more than one coder, as well as a code indicating the participant who shared the quote. And if you have a coding team, create and retain master files of each coding step, with a list explaining any decisions made (i.e., an audit trail).

Regardless of the kind of data entry you are doing, make sure you save your work often and back up your files! It can be very upsetting after all your hard work to realize your file has somehow not been saved or become corrupted. Make sure to label the data file name clearly, so you can be clear exactly what the file includes.

Once you have entered all your data, you will need to clean it, which can include checking for missing data, codes that appear outside the allowable numerical range of a measure (i.e., outliers), and any data entry errors. For a quantitative study, check for any missing data. Some options include deleting any participants with missing data, using the means of other items on a scale to estimate what missing responses would have been, or using statistical procedures called multiple imputation, which generate many potential responses and average them together. Talk with your chair about how to handle your specific situation.

Outliers may reflect data entry errors, or you may have obtained some participants who endorse or have extreme responses. It can be difficult to determine whether you should keep outliers in your study; on the one hand, they may reflect the true responses of someone who is representative of your population. On the other hand, they may represent participant error, and/or they will throw off the results of your study (e.g., the mean score in a group). Sometimes it is helpful to compare your data with and without any outliers to determine whether it significantly impacts your findings. Talk with your chair about whether it makes sense to leave outliers in your data set and, if so, how to address them.

To reduce human error, it is also helpful to have a second person verify that each number was entered accurately, particularly with a large data set. They can visually check the initial data entry and flag any errors. One strategy for doing this well is to have one person read the information from the raw data out loud while the other manually checks to ensure it matches what is in the data set. Some database programs (e.g., SAS) will let two people enter the data independently and then compare the entries, checking for inconsistencies. You can also enter each raters' responses into separate columns in Excel and create a formula to subtract the columns from each other. Any answer other than zero would demonstrate a discrepancy in response.

If you are using a spreadsheet of archival data, you will need to review the data you have to determine whether anything is unclear. If so, determine who is in the best position to help you figure out what you need to know (e.g., the principal investigator, someone who entered the data). For example, you may not understand how some of the data were coded or what a particular variable means. You may request access to the initial raw data if you notice potential errors (e.g., a number outside the allowable range for a variable). You may also inquire about any missing data (e.g., was it not entered, or is it actually missing? Are there any theories for why certain data are missing?).

If you are using coding in a qualitative study, check to be sure that you labeled data clearly and accurately before and during every step of the coding process. For example, if you conducted qualitative interviews, make sure to label participants' transcripts correctly and color code text from group interviews by participant. After you clean your data, you are ready to proceed with your analyses.

Data Analysis

Now is the time to analyze your data. Each project will entail different steps, and covering how to conduct the specific analyses needed for each type of hypothesis and/or research question would be well beyond the scope of this book! However, there are some general guidelines to follow. Start going through each step of your data analytic plan, checking off your progress along the way. It is useful to title each document, so you can keep track of what you have done and be clear about what is included in each section later. Make sure to save any findings you generate, in case you realize it could be useful to return to old drafts! This can save you significant time if you realize something you discarded earlier is worthwhile. If you follow each step of your data analytic plan, this should then become the roadmap for writing your results section.

With quantitative data, you might start analyzing and run into an unexpected issue. In fact, this is likely! For example, parametric statistical tests include statistical assumptions about the distribution of your data. If one or more of the statistical assumptions you need for any of these tests has been violated, this may change how you can interpret your findings. Talk with your chair and/or committee members who are familiar with statistics about how to handle this problem. There are a few ways to address it, and the best way to do so is somewhat of a subjective decision. For example, some statisticians would recommend using a nonparametric statistical test in this situation, because these tests can be used when statistical assumptions are not met. Others would tell you to proceed with a parametric statistic, while acknowledging the violation(s). Still others might suggest running the data both ways to assess whether there is any difference in the outcome, as in the following example.

Student Example: Using both Parametric and Nonparametric Tests When Statistical Assumptions Have Been Violated

MR ran her planned t-test to compare her CRRT and IE vignettes. Some assumptions were violated, so she and her chair decided to run a nonparametric test to determine whether the results differed. She presented her results as follows:

"A dependent means t-test was used to examine if participant ratings of the acceptability of CRRT and IE were significantly different from one another. The t-test showed that although the mean acceptability was higher for CCRT ($M = 29.14$; $SD = 8.70$) than IE ($M = 27.81$; $SD = 8.70$), this difference was not statistically significant ($t = 1.50(243)$, $p = .14$). As the t-test assumes normal distributions and equal variances, and in the present data, the acceptability ratings did not appear to fit a normal distribution, a nonparametric, Wilcoxon signed-rank test was also used to test the difference between the acceptability ratings of the two treatments. However, the Wilcoxon signed-rank test also suggested that the difference was not statistically significant ($Z = -1.51$, $p = .13$). Therefore, the first hypothesis was not supported."

You might have also planned to conduct analyses that depend on significant preliminary results. For example, if you proposed conducting a mediational study, you would expect your variables to significantly correlate with each other first. It is not your fault if this does not end up being the case! Nonsignificant results can also provide valuable information. When there is any type of diversion from your proposed data plan, the key is to make sure you can clearly explain what you did and the justification for doing it. Then, in your discussion section, you can try to interpret what may have happened. Ultimately, your committee will be evaluating your ability to think critically about your options, clearly explain the rationale for what you did, and share an informed potential explanation of the results based on your findings and the existing literature.

If you conducted a quantitative study and are working with a statistical consultant, take the time to discuss the outline of your data analytic plan with them to ensure they are clear on each step and what you aim to determine conceptually. Once they have conducted the analyses, be sure you understand what they mean, because you will need to understand your findings to write about them, as well as to present and answer questions about them during your defense.

There are several typical steps for analyzing qualitative data. Although there are many qualitative coding methods, the general goal is to approach the task with an open mind, acknowledging any biases while withholding preconceived notions about what you will find. If you are working with coders, orient them to your overall research question and go through coder training until you are confident they can review data on their own. Ask them to read through the data several times, as you should have already done and continue to do. Try to estimate the time it will take for them to independently review transcripts and/or documents at each stage of analysis (e.g., sorting through relevant text, then grouping text into repeating ideas and/or themes). Periodically check in with them while they are independently coding to see how things are going and to help hold them accountable. Devise a structure for how you want to proceed during consensus meetings and determine how you will manage discrepancies, which can differ depending on the methodology you are following (e.g., majority rules, need unanimous consensus, principal researcher has the final say). In addition, determine at what point in the process you will involve your chair in the decision-making (e.g., once you have a full draft of themes). Once your chair makes suggestions, return to your coders with any questions or ideas for potential revisions and obtain their input before making any edits. After all, you and your coders will know the data much better than your chair. Finally, finalize your themes and/or theory and determine how to present your findings (e.g., order of themes, presented in a table or figure).

Even with a great deal of preparation and training, sometimes you will encounter unexpected issues. Perhaps you are conducting qualitative interviews and your initial participants speak about a phenomenon you are not familiar with but about which you would like more information. In many qualitative methods, you could go back and alter your interview questions for your next set of interviews. Qualitative coders also lead to additional considerations. It may take longer than you predicted for them to code the initial stage of your data, or you might run into issues reaching consensus. More practically, a coder could quit your study prematurely. If you run into any issues with your coders during your data analytic phase, please refer to the information in Chapter 5 regarding troubleshooting issues with research assistants.

Next, you can turn your attention to the concepts we discussed in Chapter 1 (i.e., credibility, transferability, dependability, confirmability) to assess the reliability and validity of your qualitative data analysis. For example, earlier we recommended that if you interviewed participants, you should conduct a member check with some of them in a group meeting. During this meeting, you would present your data at the themes or theoretical construct level. The goals of a member check can be to assess for agreement with the data, any additional information participants contribute, or discrepancies they indicate. Finding places where there is agreement would help demonstrate the credibility of your findings. However, any discrepant findings from a member check do not necessarily call for changes to your existing results, because they only represent a subsample of your sample. Instead, you can add information from your member check into your results section, as in the following example.

Student Example: Including Results from a Member Check in a Qualitative Results Section

RK conducted a qualitative study focused on assessing clinicians' experiences collaborating with families in child inpatient settings. She used Auerbach and Silverstein's (2003) grounded theory methodology and then conducted a member check meeting. One of the themes that emerged from her data was that conflictual family interactions need repair before discharge. Within this theme, one repeating idea was the importance of separately preparing children and parents for family therapy sessions. During her member check, however, participants explained how this could be challenging in an inpatient setting. Here is how she included this information in her results section.

"Once the family is engaged, the clinician ideally works individually to prepare both the child and the parent before they meet together for family therapy (Repeating Idea 2). During the member check, participants explained that while this is best practice, the pressure of a short-term setting does not always allow for this type of work. Often, there is not enough time to work with the child and parent individually, and family engagement must begin regardless of the parent or child's readiness."

You may have difficulty obtaining a large number of participants, particularly if a lot of time has gone by since they were initially interviewed. However, even meeting with a couple or a few of them can help provide actual participants' perspectives on the way you interpreted your data. You can also present your data to a key informant or stakeholder in the community to obtain their perspective on your findings. In terms of confirmability, some researchers will have a second set of coders audit your data or even try to organize your data into the same themes and/or theoretical constructs and assess interrater reliability. The latter method is typically used with quantitative analyses, and using such analysis will usually depend on the preference of your chair and/or committee.

Writing Your Results Section

Once you have analyzed your data, you will be ready to write your results section. The goal of the results section is to report what you found in a clear and thorough manner. As we discussed in Chapter 7, you will only want to highlight the main findings in your text, while placing complete information in tables and/or figures. It is also important to remember not to interpret your findings in the results section—leave that for your discussion section.

Regardless of the type of results you write up, try to keep your wording consistent and clear. As discussed in Chapter 7, you will likely want to present your results in the order of your data analytic plan. You and your chair might decide it is helpful to have an introductory paragraph orienting readers to the organization of this section. Be consistent in your wording for each variable throughout the entirety of your draft. This may feel redundant, but will help readers follow along across project sections. There are several resources that can help you with writing up this section, including style manuals (e.g., the American Psychological Association [APA] style guide), statistical books and/or online resources, prior student projects in your program, articles based on studies that are similar to yours, and, of course, your chair and/or committee members. We will now provide some general tips for reporting quantitative and qualitative results.

In a quantitative study, you will typically have to report a variety of numbers. You may even present some descriptive statistical information in a qualitative study (e.g., demographic data, means and standard deviations on an eligibility measure, frequencies and percentages of participants who endorsed specific themes). And even if you conducted a nonempirical project, you may find yourself having to report some numbers in your results section (e.g., if you are summarizing data from prior studies). Check with the required style manual (e.g., APA style) to determine the appropriate information to include about each statistic presented and the related formatting (e.g., how many decimal points to include, when to italicize names of statistics), as well as your program's and/or university's guidelines.

With quantitative data, you will typically start with reporting the results of any preliminary analyses (e.g., descriptive data about your measures, analyses comparing participants who dropped out vs. those who remained in your study, missing data analyses), follow with your hypotheses and/or research questions, and end with any post hoc analyses. It can be useful to place information about statistical assumptions right before each analysis presented. Be sure to title each subsection of your results clearly, using the wording of your constructs so readers can understand the key variables being presented in that section. Remember the example of MR's outline of her data analytic plan? Here is the list of subsections in her results section.

Student Example: Subsections of a Results Section·

Remember MR, who had conducted a quantitative survey study focused on determining whether there were differences in two types of CBT approaches (imaginal exposure vs. cognitive restructuring and relaxation training; IE vs. CRRT) psychologists accept, prefer, and use to treat generalized anxiety disorder in practice? She also examined clinicians' beliefs about conducting imaginal exposure on the Therapists'

Beliefs about Exposure Scale (TBES) and explored their likes and dislikes about each CBT approach. Here are the subtitles of the results section in her final project:

- Descriptives of Key Study Variables
- Comparing Acceptance, Preference, and Use of IE and CRRT
- Associations between Acceptance, Preference, Use, and the TBES
- Associations between Demographics and Acceptance, Preference, Use, and the TBES
- Associations between Clinical Training and Acceptance, Preference, Use, and the TBES
- Descriptives from the Treatment Likes and Dislikes Questionnaire

When presenting results from your main hypotheses and/or research questions, remind your readers what you hypothesized. If you have several related results to place in a table and/or figure, refer the reader to it (e.g., "All correlations among variables can be found in Table 3."). Include any information about statistical assumptions before presenting your findings, as well as any related nonparametric tests you needed to use as a result of these analyses. Then write a sentence including the inferential statistical test used and the numeric values typically reported with it (e.g., t for t-test, df for degrees of freedom). Also remind the reader if you statistically controlled for any variables. It is often helpful to include another sentence that explains the finding conceptually. Sometimes it makes sense to report a few findings from the same types of analyses and then summarize what they mean conceptually. Here is one example from MR's dissertation.

Student Example: Reporting Statistical Findings Statistically and Conceptually

MR ran chi-square analyses to assess for differences in preference and use between her two vignettes. She first reminded readers of her hypotheses. She then described her findings and the results of her chi-square tests for each analysis before summarizing what the two results meant conceptually.

"Hypotheses regarding preference and use of CRRT vs. IE were examined. Comparing preference ratings showed that 61.0% ($N = 147$) of the sample endorsed a preference for the treatment portrayed in the CRRT vignette; 39.0% ($N = 94$) preferred the treatment in the IE vignette. A chi-square goodness of fit test was conducted to examine whether the observed frequencies differed significantly from the expected frequencies (i.e., a 50/50 split) with regard to treatment preference. As hypothesized, this test demonstrated that this higher preference for CRRT was significant ($\chi^2(1) =$ 11.66, $p < .01$). Similarly, as predicted, a higher number of participants reported higher use of CRRT in their practice (66.8%; $N = 161$), as compared to IE (33.3%; $N = 80$). Another chi-square goodness of fit test showed this higher frequency of CRRT use was significant ($\chi^2(1) = 27.22, p < .001$). Thus, overall, respondents reported significantly preferring and using the CRRT treatment over the IE treatment."

If you ran any statistical corrections to account for multiple comparisons, you would also want to report them as part of your description of a particular finding. Then present any exploratory and/or post hoc analyses, describing them as such.

There are many ways to present qualitative data. If you engaged in a coding process, you might first present an overview of your themes and/or theoretical constructs, in the order that makes the most sense conceptually. Then you could review each one individually, using the text to highlight examples of key findings and tables to provide more comprehensive details. As with quantitative data, clear subheadings can help orient the reader to the results being reviewed in a particular section. Our students often present repeating ideas within each theme in text and then examples of relevant quotes for each theme in tables, as illustrated in the following example.

Student Example: Reporting Qualitative Results in Text versus in a Table

RK conducted a qualitative study using Auerbach and Silverstein's (2003) grounded theory methodology focused on clinicians' experiences seeing families on inpatient units. Here is an example of how she described key findings for a particular theme in text while keeping specific quote examples of each repeating idea that comprised the theme in a table.

"**Theme 1: To implement evidence-based family therapy and/or family systems therapy, I need more family sessions than the length of stay can provide.** The first theme in this construct conveys the challenges clinicians face in implementing evidence-based family therapy within a short-term setting (see Table 2—first supporting theme). Furthermore, it discusses the benefits to the child, when clinicians are able to make those adaptations. This theme was discussed by 75% (9/12) of the participants and included four repeating ideas. Clinicians are only able to provide approximately two family meetings during the child's inpatient stay, which occur on a weekly basis (Repeating Idea 1). At a state facility, this frequency is standard practice for the first month, and family meetings occur monthly afterwards. To implement family systems therapy, clinicians need more sessions than the inpatient unit can provide (Repeating Idea 2). Likewise, clinicians do not believe they have enough time with the family to implement evidence-based protocols (Repeating Idea 3). Clinicians believe that if they could ensure the child will continue to receive evidence-based services after discharge, the child's treatment would be more effective. Despite this, clinicians have difficulty finding such referrals (Repeating Idea 4).

Sometimes it might be difficult to determine which information to include in the results versus the discussion section, since one could argue that all reflections and/or categorizations are interpretive. Speak to your chair and/or committee members who are familiar with qualitative methods for ideas about how to best present your results.

Tables and Figures

As you work on writing up your results, the need for specific tables and figures may become even clearer than when you wrote your data analytic plan. Make sure to refer readers to any corresponding tables or figures in text (e.g., see Table X for all descriptive data from the outcome measures). In addition, enumerate tables and figures by number, in chronological order, and place them right under the paragraph where they are discussed (although they are typically placed at the end of the document when a manuscript is submitted for publication). Some students may also choose to include a table of contents for figures and tables as part of their final project. Next, we discuss some specific skills regarding how to create tables and figures.

Tables

Tables can be used to organize descriptive data, means and standard deviations, and frequencies and percentages of demographic information, as well as measures used. In a quantitative study, it is also common to use tables to present inferential statistical analyses, including correlational, chi-square, *t*-test, analysis of variance, multivariate analysis of variance, and regression analyses. If you coded qualitative data into themes and/or theoretical constructs, you might present each one in a table, perhaps including the percentage of your sample that endorsed it. If you have conducted a theoretical or scholarly project, your use of tables will likely vary. For example, if you completed a critical literature review, you might include tables summarizing the relevant articles. If you wrote an educational curriculum, you might include a table of items in your week-by-week lesson plans.

When formatting your tables, it is important to check the style manual you are expected to follow (e.g., the APA manual; APA, 2020), as well as any program and/or university guidelines. Each table is numbered in consecutive order, starting with Table 1. If you included any tables in the method section, you would continue numbering from there. Consider whether a table would be worth including in your appendices instead of in your results section (e.g., tables demonstrating all nonsignificant quantitative findings, tables of all qualitative open coding used in each axial coding category).

Table titles should include the exact information presented, while being as concise as possible. For example, in a quantitative study, make sure the title indicates exactly which variables are included, as well as the statistics being presented. Solid titles sound like the following:

Differences in Baseline Anxiety and Depression between Completers and Non-completers
Frequencies and Percentages of Participants' Reported Teaching Strategies
Correlations among Demographic and Outcome Variables
Regression Coefficients for Predicting Parental Cognitions from Observed Behaviors

Figures

Figures are useful when you think it is best to demonstrate your findings visually. They enable you to present trends, patterns, or stark differences in your data in the form of bar graphs, line graphs, or pie charts. For example, a bar graph can be used to demonstrate significant between group findings or a line graph to indicate changes in participants' scores on a measure over time. Pie charts are useful for displaying percentages, such as the percentage of participants who endorsed specific items or the percentage of people who preferred one of several choices. In a qualitative study, you might also use a visual diagram to depict how various themes represent participants' experiences or even a theory generated from your data. Figures can also include arrows to demonstrate directionality of results. When it comes to formatting, it is important to consult any style manual you are using, as well as any relevant program and/or university guidelines for presentation.

Student Example: Figure Demonstrating a Theoretical Model from a Qualitative Study

Figure 8.1 is an example of a theoretical model generated from a qualitative dissertation by RK, who, as mentioned earlier, studied clinicians' experiences collaborating with family members of children attending psychiatric inpatient care. Note how she used a legend to indicate each of her four theoretical constructs on a theoretical pathway, based on her participants' interviews, toward successful discharge.

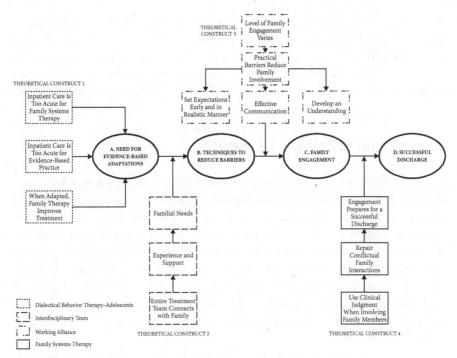

THEORETICAL CONSTRUCT 3 · Level of Family Engagement Varies

Practical Barriers Reduce Family Involvement

THEORETICAL CONSTRUCT 1

Inpatient Care Is Too Acute for Family Systems Therapy

Set Expectations Early and in Realistic Manner

Effective Communication

Develop an Understanding

Inpatient Care Is Too Acute for Evidence-Based Practice

A. NEED FOR EVIDENCE-BASED ADAPTATIONS

B. TECHNIQUES TO REDUCE BARRIERS

C. FAMILY ENGAGEMENT

D. SUCCESSFUL DISCHARGE

When Adapted, Family Therapy Improves Treatment

Familial Needs

Engagement Prepares for a Successful Discharge

Experience and Support

Repair Conflictual Family Interactions

Dialectical Behavior Therapy–Adolescents

Interdisciplinary Team

Working Alliance

Family Systems Therapy

Entire Treatment Team Connects with Family

THEORETICAL CONSTRUCT 2

Use Clinical Judgment When Involving Family Members

THEORETICAL CONSTRUCT 4

Figure 8.1 Theoretical model of facilitators to a successful discharge

Writing Your Discussion Section

In your discussion section, you have the opportunity to discuss the meaning of your findings and make suggestions about how they might influence the field. You will want to show more than you tell, meaning there is no need to explicitly state how awesome your findings are! Let your readers determine the significance of your project based on your findings and the related implications. As discussed in Chapter 7, your goals in this section are to briefly restate your key findings, interpret them in the context of existing literature, point out the implications of your project, acknowledge limitations, and make recommendations for future research directions. You and your chair may also decide to include a brief concluding paragraph. We review how to write each of these sections next.

Summary of Findings

Open your discussion section with a paragraph reminding readers about the purpose of your project and what made it innovative. Then summarize your main findings. In contrast to your results section, there is no need to include specifics here, such as hypotheses by number or actual statistics. It is okay to assume readers know your findings by now; a topic sentence to orient them is useful, but there is no need to rehash detailed findings at this point. The idea is to briefly remind readers what you found, knowing they have already read the specific details. Similarly, now is not the time to introduce new analyses. Any post hoc analyses should be kept in the results section.

Comparison to Existing Literature

You may recall from prior chapters that the opportunity to make a significant contribution to your field means embedding your findings in the context of the existing literature in your area. With an empirical project, this means comparing your results with prior studies. You likely want to organize this by discussing your main findings up front. In a quantitative study, it is common to write about your findings in the same order as your hypotheses, followed by a discussion of any exploratory analyses. However, if your hypotheses are unsupported, you might decide to write about some exploratory, more interesting findings first. In a qualitative study with coding, you can write about your findings in the same order as your organized themes and/or theoretical constructs.

Once you determine the order, you should compare your findings to prior studies and/or theory. Go back to any similar studies you reviewed in your introduction and search for additional studies that may help explain your findings. Finding results similar to those of prior studies helps to confirm previous findings, strengthening support for a particular theory and/or area of knowledge. If your results are different from those found in prior studies, however, it is important to theorize possible reasons that this may be the case. For example, perhaps your study sample included a different age range or you assessed a construct differently than in prior studies. If so, explain why you think these differences could have accounted for contrasting findings. In some cases, the reason for differing results may be unclear; in this case, you can acknowledge this.

As you write about your interpretation of your research findings in the context of existing work, think about any potential biases you may have, as well as any alternative explanations others might have. If you will have to defend your project, anticipating and writing about other potential perspectives up front can be particularly helpful.

With a theoretical or scholarly project, it likely will still be important to discuss the outcome or product of your project within the context of the existing literature. For example, if you developed an educational curriculum, compare it to existing curricula and describe any similarities and/or differences. If you conducted a clinical case study, explain how your intervention adds to our knowledge of existing methods for treating similar problems.

Implications of Your Findings

After you have compared your findings to those in the prior literature, include a section on the practical or clinical implications of your project. This is your opportunity to suggest how to practically implement your findings or project in real-world settings.

Many researchers also list potential theoretical and/or methodological implications of their findings. For example, in terms of theory, can we speculate how findings from a quantitative study add to our understanding of relationships between variables? Did your work contribute any methodological innovations? It is okay to suggest creative possibilities here, as long as you use speculative language about your ideas. At the same time, it is important to make recommendations solely from what you know based on your findings and those from prior research. In other words, do not extrapolate beyond the limits of research findings to date. For example, if you found evidence demonstrating acceptability of a treatment technique with people who have a particular problem, be sure to make related recommendations for treatment of that specific issue only. Save any theoretical reasons to study the technique with other populations for your section about directions for future research, which comes later in the discussion section.

Project Limitations

As we mentioned in Chapter 7, as great as your final project is, every project inevitably includes some limitations. In fact, researchers are expected to include their study's limitations in published manuscripts. Review the possible limitations we mentioned in Chapter 7 (e.g., about your sample, research design, procedures, measures, analyses).

Consider two types of project limitations: premediated project choices versus unexpected limitations that came up during the context of your study. Some programs may refer to the former as delimitations, or planned decisions about what a particular study would include and exclude. You do not have to apologize for failing to cover areas beyond the scope of your project. For example, many researchers write about their study being limited by the sample they included. However, if your study was designed to study parenting preschoolers and your sample was made up of parents of preschoolers, your results may not be generalizable to parenting adolescents. This is a reasonable limitation, not a design flaw. We expect there are good reasons you made the decisions you made up front! In this case, when you acknowledge this limitation, also include a brief justification. Here is an example of a student justifying a premediated type of design used in her final project.

> **Student Example: Acknowledging Limitations of a Measure while Supporting the Choice**
>
> KK presented parents with two vignettes of evidenced-based time-out interventions, room time-out and deferred time-out, partially to assess their acceptability. In her limitations section, she acknowledged that reading about a hypothetical intervention is not the same as engaging in it. However, she supported her choice for using an analog method by citing other acceptability studies that did so and indicating the advantages of this design (e.g., gathering data on more than one intervention simultaneously, obtaining a large sample).

In addition, consider including delimitations as potential directions for future research. If you encountered an unexpected limitation, however (e.g., you were not able to recruit a representative sample), acknowledge this limitation and consider whether it is worth proposing ideas for addressing it in future research.

Students sometimes come up with long lists of their project's limitations, beyond the scope of what is necessary. While you want to be forthcoming about project limits, consider consulting with your chair about which limitations are important to point out. As we mentioned in Chapter 7, students typically list more limitations in their project write-ups than they would include in a journal article.

Directions for Future Research

As indicated in Chapter 7, directions for future research can include theoretical, methodological, and practical directions. Think about what the potential next steps could be if someone were to continue in this line of study and be sure you can justify why they make sense. It does not have to be you (though it could be!). Write about a few key future directions rather than a long list of ideas. As with implications, make sure your recommendations follow your study's findings as much as possible. It may be hard to imagine, but someday, a student may review your project to see what you thought was an important next step in the research.

> **Student Example: Suggesting Directions for Future Research**
>
> Remember KK, from the earlier limitations section? In her section regarding directions for future research, she suggested theoretical, methodological, and practical directions for future research. Theoretically, she suggested further study of deferred time-out outcomes, because their effectiveness has yet to be established, and it is

not clear whether younger children understand the concept or whether older children can navigate their own environment to the point where this disciplinary strategy is ineffective. She also suggested going beyond treatment vignettes to determine whether there are differences in parents' acceptability and preference once they receive the interventions. Methodologically, she recommended examining whether there are cultural differences in parents' acceptability and preferences for different disciplinary strategies, given prior research that suggested cultural values might influence these variables. She also suggested using methods of data collection beyond self-report measures to reduce the impact of shared assessment methods. Practically, she suggested studying ways to examine whether the acceptability of room time-out could be improved, either by making minor modifications to the intervention or by increasing parents' understanding of it (e.g., adding information about the rationale, providing successful parent testimony, troubleshooting).

If you conducted a qualitative study or theoretical project, it is helpful to suggest hypotheses based on your data. Be sure your hypotheses are clear and specific and that they can be tested empirically. You can also refer to our description in Chapter 5 regarding how to write hypotheses.

Skills for Successfully Working with Your Chair

As we discussed when you started conducting your project in Chapter 5, it is important to remain proactive in your communications with your chair. Keep them posted on your tentative timeline and progress regarding each significant step, such as your data analyses, written results section, and written discussion section. Check in with them to be sure you understand how they want to work with you on this part of the process. For example, are they able to review tentative outlines with you to ensure you are headed in the right direction? Will they review pieces of your results or discussion sections to provide feedback before you move forward, or do they want to wait and see an entire first draft of these sections before commenting? It is possible they will want to maintain the same type of working style the two of you had when you worked on your written proposal; however, do not assume this is the case. Your chair may like to provide specific feedback about how to approach these sections. Now that the two of you have experience working together, your chair may want to find ways to improve your joint working style.

We know you are likely eager at this point to finish your project! Your chair knows this as well. Be aware of how you come across when communicating with your chair about a timeline for completion and/or defense. It can be helpful to communicate excitement about reaching the finish line while acknowledging that you know your chair is busy and you are hoping to determine a timeline that makes sense for both of you. Ask about any upcoming times when they are likely to be busier or unavailable. Then you can suggest a tentative timeline and ask your chair's opinion. Be sure to leave reasonable turnaround time for drafts, (e.g., two to three weeks), as well as time for additional revisions you did not anticipate (e.g., some students only need a couple of rounds of edits on a section, while others require several).

Troubleshooting

How Do You Ask Your Chair to Help You Meet a Quickly Approaching Deadline?

As you have read, we recommend having a timeline in mind for completing your project. There are times, however, when your timeline does not go as planned or needs to change. For example, we have had psychology doctoral students who accepted a postdoctoral position with a certain start date, contingent on having defended. When the student accepted the position, they were certain their project would be completed by their start date, but they hit some barriers along the way (e.g., with data collection) and needed to figure out how to finish quickly, in time for the start of their postdoctoral position. We understand this concern. If you are in a situation like this, the best thing you can do is explain your dilemma to your chair immediately. Propose a timeline and ask whether they think it is realistic, based on the status of your project. Acknowledge that the timeline is tight and that you know they must be busy. Propose ways you can keep the project moving while your chair is reviewing your draft. Ask whether it makes sense to send pieces of the draft to other committee members for additional assistance. At the same time, be honest with your pending job about the dilemma with your timeline and see if they are willing to either negotiate a later start date or start you while knowing you will have a later defense date.

How Do You Handle It If It Is Taking a Long Time to Obtain Feedback from Your Chair?

It can feel so good to get drafts to your chair, especially as your hard work gets closer to the finish line! So what do you do if you send the drafts and do not hear back or if it usually takes a while to obtain feedback? Initially, you can send a friendly follow-up email to ensure they received your draft and ask when they estimate they will be able to provide feedback. It can help to acknowledge that they are likely busy and note that your message is just a friendly reminder. Chances are they know you sent the draft, but could use a gentle push to get it higher up on their to-do list. If a long turnaround time becomes a pattern, we recommend asking your chair whether there is anything you can do to help facilitate feedback. For example, if you sent a long draft and they typically send a lot of writing edits, would they prefer to provide feedback on the first part and then have you try to integrate similar feedback throughout the rest of the draft before they read through the rest?

What Should You Do If Your Chair Does Not Think You Are Ready to Defend?

We know this is a rough position. You are likely looking forward to finishing your project, which is often tied to graduation as well as other professional and personal goals. As difficult as it can be to receive this feedback, we recommend taking it seriously. Students usually pass their defense when their chairs think they are ready. Pushing to defend when your chair is not supportive means there is a high risk of failing. As hard as it is to hold off, addressing existing issues prior to defending is usually the best route to take. First, try to understand the reasons they do not think you are ready. For example, are they saying you need to conduct additional data analyses? Are they concerned about your understanding of what you found or developed? Do they think your writing needs improvement? Once you think you understand the general reasons for their concern, try to figure out how you can address them. Take your chair's recommendations and try to implement them. If you struggle to do so, now may be the time to hire a statistical consultant or an editor or to go to your university's writing center. You might also ask your committee members to review your work and see what they recommend. They may be hesitant to let you move forward with a defense meeting as well and might be able to provide further suggestions for improvement.

How to Share Results with Professionals in Your Applied Setting

If you conducted your project within an applied setting, you may be eager and/or expected to share your findings. Once you feel clear about your findings, you can check with professionals who helped you with the project about when and how it makes sense to share.

Some sites will provide you with the opportunity to present, even before you defend. This is a great way to obtain feedback from professionals who are familiar with the population you studied, the data you analyzed, and/or the issue you set out to address. Think about creating slides for this talk, which will help you organize your findings, think about what they mean, and prepare for your eventual defense. In addition, determine whether it makes sense to provide any supplemental handouts (e.g., tables, figures). Hearing this group's feedback and responding to their questions can help you prepare for your defense.

Keeping Your Project Timeline on Track

As you get closer to completing a full draft of your final project, we recommend revisiting the key factors for managing your time successfully, which we discussed in Chapter 5. You can also revisit the questions posed in Table 5.7 to assess whether you are managing your time effectively. In addition, revisit your program's requirements and deadlines. Related questions can be found in Table 8.1.

Table 8.1 Questions about Your Program's Requirements and Deadlines

Question	Answer
What is your chair's schedule this academic year?	
When must you defend by?	
What formal forms, evaluations, and other procedures are in place in your program?	
What are upcoming deadlines for degree conferrals?	
What are the financial consequences of not meeting the next conferral deadline?	
How about any licensing, certification, job, and/or career-related consequences?	
Which of the above topics am I assuming I know the answer to, but have not checked on recently?	
Other:	
Other:	
Other:	

As we discussed in Chapter 5, working on a tentative timeline with your chair can keep your expectations for finishing your project aligned. It can also serve as a motivator as you get closer to the finish line. Table 8.2 presents a sample timeline you can use as a template at this point in your project trajectory. As with our last tentative timeline (see Table 5.3), it is important to remain flexible and be willing to re-evaluate your timeline as you proceed and determine what is realistic.

How to Finalize Your Full Draft

Once you have written drafts of the majority of the sections in your final project, it is useful to start placing various written sections together. Typical final project sections include the following: title page, acknowledgments (postdefense), abstract, table of

Table 8.2 Tentative Timeline

Task	Target date
Proposal draft revised (e.g., future tense converted to past tense, updates to method section)	
Data analytic plan outlined	
Data entry and cleaning complete	
Data analysis conducted	
Outline of results and discussion	
Full results draft	
Full discussion draft	
Tables and figures complete	
Full draft of final project to chair	
Final project draft to committee	
Projected defense date	
Actual defense date	
Postdefense meeting revisions and acknowledgment section added	
Final copies submitted and bound, if necessary	

contents, introduction, method, results, discussion, references, and appendices. The latter can include recruitment advertisements used, informed consent and/or assent, questionnaires, vignettes, treatment, curriculum, or coding manuals, as well as other materials developed for your project and additional tables and figures. It is worth working on any outstanding edits in older sections while you are awaiting feedback from your chair on new sections; just be sure to keep track of the latest drafts of each section as you go!

Be sure to revisit your abstract before wrapping up your project. Besides switching the project's purpose and updating the method information (if you have not already done so), you will need to add your main findings and a sentence or two about their overall implications. The APA (2020) style manual indicates an abstract can be approximately 250 words, but the acceptable length differs across peer-reviewed journals. For your final project, check to see whether your program and/or university guidelines include an allotted abstract word count.

As you finalize your full draft, double check that everything is in the format of the style manual you are using, as well as any program and/or university guidelines you are expected to follow. Be sure to use a consistent font, font size, and headings. Double check that your table of contents has accurate page numbers, make sure tables and figures are numbered consecutively, and ensure all references cited in the text are accurately listed in your references section and vice versa.

As we mentioned in Chapter 5, when you were preparing to propose, it can be useful to review a copy of the form your committee will use to evaluate you and complete it as if it were a self-evaluation. See how you think you would rate yourself on each item and if there is anything you want to improve based on your evaluation.

When you are almost done, try to leave yourself at least a few days to take time away from your full draft, so you can return to it with fresh eyes. Reduce the size of your overall document and scroll through to check headings, indents, tables, and figures. You will usually find a few mistakes. This is expected and may even occur after you have completed your absolute final draft! One of the keys to success is knowing when it is time to move on. In many cases, moving on in your program will mean you and your chair agree you are ready to defend!

Preparing for Your Defense

It can be tempting to want to relax after sending your full project draft to your committee and setting a defense date. This makes sense after all the hard work you put in getting to this point! However, the time when your committee is reviewing your draft is the best time to prepare for your defense. For example, most chairs will want you to put slides together, and you will want to spend time practicing what you plan to present. We have divided the skills needed for defending into five steps: tasks to complete predefense, how to prepare your slides, how to ensure you are ready for your oral presentation, how to respond to questions and feedback from your committee, and items to address immediately postdefense. Table 8.3 provides a checklist of skills for each of these steps. You can also look at Bell et al. (2019) for an additional perspective on how to prepare for your defense meeting.

Table 8.3 Checklist of Skills for the Defense Process

Predefense	✓
I have sent my committee my final project draft and any necessary evaluation forms and/or other required paperwork.	
I have scheduled a date, time, and place.	
I have sent my committee (or printed) any necessary forms (e.g., evaluation forms, blank title page they will need to sign).	
I have clarified with my chair approximately how long I should plan to present.	
I have determined who I can and want to invite to my defense.	
I know what equipment I need and how I will set it up.	
I have determined whether I would like to distribute any supplemental handouts (e.g., of tables, figures).	
I have decided who will take notes during the meeting.	
I have decided what to wear.	
I have decided whether I will provide refreshments.	
Slide preparation	
I have determined whether my chair is willing and/or wants to look at a draft of my slides, and if so, by what date.	
If applicable, I have supplemental handouts (e.g., of tables and/or figures) for committee members to be able to refer to while I present.	
My slides are visually simple, with bullet points and without excessive animations, multiple fonts, or colors.	

continued

Table 8.3 *continued*

I have a title slide, including the title of my project draft, my name, and the names of my committee members.	
I will begin with brief, key summary points of the background literature.	
I include the research problem, purpose of my project, and rationale.	
If relevant, I include my hypotheses and/or research questions.	
I review my method, including number of participants, any key participant demographic variables, research design, main procedures, and measures and analyses used.	
I present my results, one hypothesis or research question at a time.	
I have decided whether I will compare my results to existing literature one point at a time or after I have presented the results.	
I have determined which tables and/or figures are worth placing in slides, if any.	
I compare my findings to existing literature.	
I review potential theoretical, methodological, and/or practical implications.	
I present project limitations.	
I indicate directions for future research.	
I have reduced wordiness.	
I have an introductory statement.	
I orient my audience to what I will be reviewing, briefly reorienting throughout my talk.	

Oral presentation	
I have envisioned speaking in front of my committee.	
I have envisioned speaking in front of any additional audience members or guests.	
I have practiced making eye contact while flipping through my slides and/or notes.	
I have practiced my facial expressions (e.g., smiling, relaxing my jaw).	
I have practiced my pace, volume, and tone.	
I am able to sound engaging and keep my audience's attention.	
I am able to explain the information on each slide clearly and succinctly.	
My findings are clear to someone listening to me practice.	
I have specifically practiced parts where I feel less confident.	
I am able to stay within the time limit agreed on with my chair.	
Responding to questions and feedback	
I have asked my chair whether they will ask my committee to ask questions as they arise or wait until I have finished presenting. I am prepared for both!	
I have envisioned the kinds of questions my committee might ask and practiced potential responses.	
I am ready to truly listen to what committee members are asking and pause to think before answering.	
I am ready to thank committee members for their questions and indicate that they asked a good question before responding.	

continued

Table 8.3 *continued*

I am ready to diplomatically ask for clarification about confusing questions.	
I am ready to respond by speaking slowly and succinctly, keeping my response concise.	
I am ready to say I am not sure if I truly do not know.	
I anticipate some potentially contrasting opinions and plan to listen to each perspective, demonstrate appreciation for each committee member's input, respectfully share my thoughts, and defer to my chair if it is unclear what to decide.	
I anticipate feedback about what I could have done differently and am ready to thank the committee for their ideas.	
I am ready to clarify what needs to be integrated into my final project draft (and who needs to see these revisions) versus what is a suggestion for future publication.	
I am ready to respond nondefensively to feedback about my writing and presentation.	
Postdefense reminders	
I understand the necessary final revisions.	
I understand who needs to approve my final draft.	
I have either obtained any forms I need signed (e.g., evaluation forms, title page) or made a plan for when and how I will receive them.	
I have someone who will remember to take pictures.	
Celebrate!	
I understand the final steps to take to officially submit my final project to my program and/or university.	
I have sent any compensation to eligible project participants and/or research assistants.	

I have planned a reward for accomplishing each step toward final project completion!	
I have considered adding an acknowledgment section that includes thanking my chair and committee and acknowledging any professors, supervisors, and other mentors who played a role in my training, as well as any other professionals who helped make this project possible.	
I have also considered acknowledging family, friends, and key graduate school peers, significant other, children, and/or pets, as applicable.	
I have considered whether I want to dedicate my final project to someone.	
I understand how to submit final copies of my final project and how many copies I will need.	
I have checked that I have correctly formatted the document (including the title page, required committee signatures, table of contents, headings, tables and figures, references, and appendices).	
I have considered making a bound copy for my chair, my committee members, anyone else involved with my study, family/friends, and/or myself.	

Tasks to Complete Predefense

As we discussed in Chapter 7, once your chair approves your full project draft, you will likely need to show it to your committee members. Email is currently the most common way to send drafts, but some members may request a hard copy. If you have any large files accompanying your write-up (e.g., videos), you may need to get them to your committee another way (e.g., an online drive, a USB stick).

In any event, be sure you understand your program's timeline and the process before asking to schedule your defense date. For example, your committee may expect to have two weeks to review your draft before agreeing to schedule a meeting. If you will meet in person, learn how to obtain a date and time to use a designated room for the meeting. If you will defend online or have someone attend online, be sure you are familiar with the computer program you will use (e.g., Zoom, Skype). Also, be sure to send your committee any necessary forms (e.g., evaluation forms, blank title page they will need to sign). If you will meet in person, print copies for the day of the defense. If any committee members will be online, resend the forms the evening before or the morning of your defense, along with a link for the meeting.

Once you have a date, time, and place for your defense, consider who you can invite and who you want to invite. Some programs have a closed defense process, meaning only your committee can be present. In this case, family, significant others, and friends can usually be present after the formal presentation and evaluation is complete (hopefully to celebrate!). Others are more open, allowing you to invite people to your presentation, though they will have to step out to allow the committee to deliberate. Some programs like to encourage lower-level students to attend to help demystify the process. Still other programs have you present to a larger audience and may ask you to present more formally (e.g., stand in front of a podium).

Make sure you are familiar with any equipment and/or technology you will need on the day of your defense. For example, if you plan to use a PowerPoint presentation, find out whether the room includes a projector and the necessary adapters. Determine whether you will need your own laptop or if one is provided. We recommend having a couple of copies of your slides in different places, or even a paper copy, in case something goes wrong with the technology. If you will be defending in person, try to spend some time in the room you will use to become familiar with the room layout and equipment. Also, leave ample time to set up and check your Internet connection on the day of your defense.

As you prepare for the day of your defense, be in touch with your chair with any questions. Ask approximately how long you should plan to present for, which will help facilitate your slide preparation. In addition, ask whether you should plan to take notes about suggested revisions during the meeting or if they would be willing to, and confirm the plan at the start of the meeting. If you have questions about the dress code, now is the time to ask.

One other consideration if you will be meeting in person is whether you are going to bring food and/or drinks that day. Again, you are not expected to do this, and it should not affect your committee's evaluation. If you choose to provide refreshments, leave yourself ample time to pick them up and get to the place where your defense will be held early (to set up, envision presenting).

How to Prepare Your Slides

Most chairs will want you to prepare a slide set to use during your defense. This is a great way to visually help your audience follow along with your talk. Consult with your chair about the breadth and depth you should include in your slide set. You can also ask your chair and/or students in your program who have defended whether they have defense slides they are able and willing to share, so you can use them as a template. It is a good idea to ask your chair whether they would be willing to review them before your defense. Provide ample time for them to do so by drafting slides early, as tempting as it may be to take a break once you send your final draft to your committee.

Beyond your slides, consider whether any supplemental handouts (e.g., tables and/or figures) might be useful for committee members to refer to as you are presenting. Label them clearly so you can easily refer them to specific pages and places in the handout as you present. If you will meet in person, print copies. If you and/or someone on your committee will be online, think about whether you want to send slides and any handouts to committee members beforehand, so they can follow along more easily.

Sometimes you will have slides from your proposal meeting. If so, you can return to those and make updates to your introduction and method section, similar to the way you revised your written draft (e.g., put the purpose of your study in past tense, revise the method to match what you actually ended up doing). You can likely remove some of the background information you had previously included and stick to key points, because your committee will probably be more interested in discussing what you did, what you found, and the implications of your findings. In addition, you can refer to the section on creating slides in Chapter 5 for formatting considerations.

Beyond the information that was in your proposal slide set, you will now want to present what you found. For a quantitative study, results are often presented in order of the hypotheses and/or research questions. For a qualitative study, you might review a slide with all themes and/or theoretical constructs before reviewing one at a time. It can be helpful to review the results and discussion points of each theme or theoretical construct together, to avoid repetition of information. If you conducted a theoretical or scholarly project, you will likely present an overview of what you found or developed in a similar fashion to how you presented this information in your draft. As you create slides about your findings, determine whether it might be helpful to present some tables and/or figures in the slides. Supplementary handouts of these visuals can be useful for your committee's review as you present the information.

If you have not yet presented how your findings compare and contrast with the existing literature, now is the time to do so. Then you should review the same points you wrote about in your discussion section, including potential theoretical, methodological, and/or practical implications, present project limitations, and indicate directions for future research. Once you have written out your slides, you can refer to Chapter 5 for ideas about how to edit them and orient your audience to what you will discuss.

Preparing for Your Oral Presentation

We next recommend starting to practice your oral presentation. As you do so, envision speaking in front of your committee and anyone else you expect to be present. Picture where you will be standing or sitting while presenting, looking out at your audience. Often, we are not aware of how we come across while presenting. Have someone you trust watch you rehearse your presentation and provide feedback. It can be useful to present in front of student peers in a lab meeting, ideally with your chair present, if possible. Practice looking out at your mock audience. Making eye contact while following along with your slides is a skill that takes some practice. You might also want to refer to your notes. If you are not comfortable presenting, take more time to rehearse. Beyond eye contact, consider your facial expressions and body language. Make sure to smile occasionally and relax your face.

While you are speaking, practice your pace, volume, and tone. It is common to start speaking quickly when nervous, so practice focusing on each point you are making and even pausing a second to look at your audience before moving on. Make sure you are loud enough to be audible, based on where your committee will be sitting. Ask those who listen to you rehearse whether you are keeping their attention and what you might do to improve.

You will also want to ask your mock audience whether your findings are clear. This is useful if the person is not familiar with your research. Can they repeat back what you found? If so, you are doing a good job explaining yourself! If not, perhaps they can help you make your explanation more clear. Spend more time practicing the parts of your presentation where you feel less confident. For example, if you have some complex results to explain, review what you will say about them several times.

Finally, time your presentation and see if it falls within the amount of time your chair suggested. If your presentation has become too long, you might ask your chair what makes sense to cut out.

Responding to Questions and Feedback

It is useful to anticipate what the questioning portion of your defense meeting might be like. In some defense meetings, committee members will wait until you finish presenting before asking questions. Other times, they inquire along the way. For example, if you recruited participants, they may ask you questions about your recruitment strategy when you present that information. Be prepared both to give a continuous presentation and to have people cut in to ask you questions.

You can also plan ahead by thinking about questions your committee may ask you (see Chapter 7 for possible types of questions) and ways you would respond. First, truly listen to what they are asking. This can be hard to do, because you may feel anxious. Remember, you are the person who knows your project the best. It is okay to pause to think about your answer. It is also acceptable to ask them to repeat their question or diplomatically ask for clarification about a question you find confusing. It is good etiquette to thank the committee member for their question and/or say you think the question is a good one. Once you have thought about your answer, respond slowly and succinctly, keeping your response concise. If you are truly unsure about the answer to a question, it is okay to state that. It is usually better to say you do not know something than to make up an answer; your committee will likely be able to tell that you do not know how to address the question.

As we mentioned in Chapter 7, sometimes your committee may end up answering the question themselves, or even debating with each other! This is usually a good sign, because it means they are engaged in the discussion and likely are enjoying themselves. If a positive discussion occurs during your defense, listen carefully and look for a place you can jump in and contribute. Try to find a valid point on both sides of the debate and respectfully share your own thoughts. If the debate seems contentious, look to your chair for cues regarding when and how to move forward.

Your committee will likely also provide you with feedback about what could have been done differently. This is a normal part of the process. As we have discussed, every project inherently includes limitations, and research and scholarly work is meant to be critically evaluated and improved on. Thank the committee for their comments and make sure you understand which ideas need to be integrated into your final project draft. They may expect some revisions, whereas others may be simply suggestions for possibly moving forward with publication. Also make sure you understand who needs to see the revisions.

Your committee may provide you with constructive feedback about your oral presentation and/or writing skills. Be prepared to respond nondefensively to this feedback. There is usually room for improvement in these areas, even for a skilled researcher. Committee members are expected to provide feedback on your strengths, as well as areas where you could improve. Try to view this as an opportunity to learn and to improve for future endeavors.

Postdefense Reminders

As we discussed in Chapter 7, your committee will send you out of the room and ask you to return, hopefully to congratulate you on successfully defending. This is an amazing moment! In this moment, you are transitioning from being your committee's student to their colleague! Before you wrap up the formal meeting, be sure you are clear on what, if any, revisions need to be made to your final project copy and to whom they need to be shown for final approval. Also be sure to obtain any forms you need signed, including evaluation forms and the title page. If your committee still needs time to complete the forms, determine when and how you will receive them as well as any deadline for submission.

Then it is time to celebrate! Try to have someone take pictures of you, your chair, and/or your committee to commemorate this special day. Then take some time off to relax and enjoy your achievement. Plan something exciting to do later that night or weekend; otherwise, completing all that work may feel anticlimactic. You have achieved a major milestone—take the time to revel in it.

Once you have celebrated, be sure to complete any final steps, such as making final edits, getting your final draft approved, binding your final copy (discussed below in the section about binding), submitting it to your program and/or university, and submitting it to an open-access repository or database (discussed below in the section about publishing). If you offered any compensation to participants or research assistants, make sure they have received it. After putting in so much time, effort, and energy leading up to your defense, it can be hard to feel motivated to complete these steps. At the same time, you are so close to the finish line! You will need to complete those final steps to graduate, so this is the time to push yourself through in whatever way you can. Make a list of the steps you need to take and reward yourself for completing each one.

Acknowledgments Section

Once you defend and work on finalizing your draft, decide whether you want to add an acknowledgments section to your final project. It is customary to do this after your defense to ensure that you do not bias your committee beforehand. There is no set format for this section, but anecdotally, there is a common order to loosely follow. Students tend to begin by thanking their chair and committee. They then acknowledge the professors, supervisors, and other mentors who were key to their training, as well as any other professionals who helped make the project possible (e.g., leaders from a supporting applied setting). Then students typically thank their family, friends, and key graduate school peers, significant other, children, and/or pets, as applicable. The order of this section is up to you. The tone is also something to consider: do you want it to be sentimental, humorous, or a combination of both? Although there is no requirement to include this section, we believe it is a nice final touch. One of us may even be known to look up acknowledgment sections (e.g., in ProQuest Dissertations & Theses Global) and consider them projective tests! Just kidding (sort of!). Some students also choose to dedicate their final project to someone.

Binding and Electronic Final Copies

Check with your program about how to submit the final copies of your final project. Some programs require you to have the project bound. This is sometimes completed through your school library, but you may also be asked to handle the binding on your own, such as at a Staples store. Some schools will want you to obtain a spiral- or tape-bound copy with a clear cover and thick, black backing. Also find out how many copies you will need. For example, you might need one copy for your department and one for your university library. Many programs now request electronic final copies. Either way, be sure you have correctly formatted the document, including the title page, required committee signatures, table of contents, headings, tables and figures, references, and appendices. It is also a nice gesture to make a bound copy for your chair, your committee members, anyone else involved with your study (e.g., your applied setting, research assistants), and/or proud family or friends. On that note, we recommend binding a copy of two for yourself. This makes your project easily accessible to you for future reference. It is also nice to see a copy of your completed project on your own bookshelves, both at home and in your eventual workspace!

Remediation Planning

We have discussed many potential successes. But what if you find you face difficulties completing your final written draft or getting your chair to approve your final draft? What if your chair does not think you are ready to defend, or in the worst case, what if you defend and your committee does not pass you? We recommend first speaking with your chair, committee member(s), and/or another trusted mentor or advisor about the problems you are facing and asking for suggestions. We then recommend going back to Worksheet 5.2 to write out a remediation plan with specific goals, objectives, and criteria to determine whether you have met your goals by certain deadlines. Complete this plan on your own or, better yet, with your chair or other advisor or mentor. As deadlines arrive, evaluate your progress and determine whether the problems have been addressed or if further remediation is necessary.

Practical Strategies for Presenting and Publishing

At this point, your final project required for the completion of your degree is done, and you may need a break from it. However, whether or not you want to continue the research pathway you began with your dissertation and/or thesis, we hope you will consider presenting and publishing to disseminate your findings into your professional community. Presentation and/or publication of your work increases your exposure in the field and has the potential to increase the use of your research or scholarly work. Your project may influence another graduate student or researcher's work.

Publication considerations include open-access and closed databases, and some programs require students to submit their project to a database like ProQuest Dissertations & Theses Global to graduate. Open access allows you to quickly get your work out there. However, publishing with a database allows you to track your project's reach and possibly make royalties from downloads and purchases of your work. Another good steppingstone is to submit your work to a professional conference, because the criteria for acceptance are often more flexible than those for publication, and presenting at a conference enables you to potentially get some feedback from other like-minded professionals. In addition, some professional associations publish proceedings from their conferences, which may be your segue into publishing. There are many additional ways to pursue publishing your final project, including as a chapter, a book, or an article. Kamler (2008) suggests using "safe spaces" for your first writing attempts. These might include nonrefereed professional journals, professional society newsletters, online blogs, and even online journals.

Coauthorship with academic and clinical mentors and/or supervisors might be the best way to start out. As a coauthor, you will be an assistant in the writing process, but it is the best way to learn the ropes. In fact, Kamler (2008) suggests that coauthorship should become a more intentional pedagogic practice, like a scaffolding process, to help launch scholars and researchers into the field. If this opportunity is not offered to you, ask your mentors whether they would like your help to publish some of their work or your joint work.

Collaborating with others who have already published can be very informative. We recommend asking a colleague to review anything you want to submit, whether for a conference presentation or for publication. You might create or join a regular writing group or buddy system to help hold you accountable for continuing to write and meet self-imposed deadlines. Some professional organizations or societies have writing groups you might want to consider. These groups provide not only writing support and feedback, but also the camaraderie you might benefit from once you leave your academic home. Plus, regular meetings might hold you accountable for producing written material. Check with your various professional associations when you join.

To begin preparing for publication, start with an overall summary or the take-away points from your project and consider whether the results are methodologically rigorous and/or impactful to the field. Then consult with your chair, committee members, and other mentors to determine where your work might fit. Some students even secure more than one publication from their project. There may be too much in your final project to easily fit journal publication guidelines, so you could think about writing a set of articles emphasizing different aspects of your work. For example, if you made clinical recommendations that could easily map onto clinical sites providing services, then newsletters or conferences attended by your target professional audience may be the best forum for this part of your project.

As you tell others about your work, you may be offered opportunities, such as the chance to submit your project in the form of a chapter for someone's book. If you conducted a theoretical or scholarly project, such as a theoretical paper or practice-oriented manual, you might aim to turn your work into a book. It is common, however, to aim to turn a research study into a manuscript, with the hope of publishing it as an article in a peer-reviewed journal. Peer review refers to other researchers in your subfield critiquing your paper and providing feedback. These types of journals are the most prestigious, and publishing in one will add credibility to an already successfully defended project. Some peer-reviewed journals also publish critical analyses of the literature, which can be good to keep in mind if you conducted one for your final project or think you might be able to turn your project's introduction into an independent article. Next, we present practical strategies for publishing in an open-access repository or database, presenting, and publishing in a peer-reviewed journal.

Publishing in an Open-Access Repository or Database

Note that, for the most part, your work must be in publish-ready condition for open-access repositories and databases. This means there are no editor or peer-review services available when using these publication options. You can hire a professional for writing and editing assistance if you feel your writing needs further improvement. Your university may have a writing center that is able to help you with this as well. Note that if you consider publishing in a journal or with a book publisher, you will have an editing process to go through (likely including peer review and more extensive editing processes).

Here, we list some current options available for publishing to a database or open-access repository; however, to be sure you have the most up-to-date list of possibilities, check with your university's librarians. They will be able to tell you if there are additional resources you should consider.

- ProQuest Dissertations & Theses Global (PQDT Global): Over three thousand academic institutions around the world have access to this database (through an institutional subscription). Your work will also be indexed in their partner search tools (other databases). Publishing with PQDT Global is nonexclusive, meaning your work will have no restrictions, so you can publish your work elsewhere as well. You may receive royalties. Check their website for the most up-to-date information for authors. Be sure to use their formatting guide before submitting. The current URL for information about this ishttps://about.proquest.com/products-services/dissertations/Authors.html.
- ProQuest ETD Administrator: This may be used by your institution as the place to submit your work. In some cases it may be a program requirement and in others a suggested step. Using this management system will help manage the review, edit, and revise process with your chair. The system seamlessly allows you to submit to PQDT Global. The current URL ProQuest ETD Administrator is https://www.etdadmin.com/. The site also has information about copyright and other important things to be aware of as you make publication decisions.
- Digital Commons: This platform hosts universities' open-access collections of university faculty- and student-produced research and scholarship. Currently servicing over six hundred academic institutions, Digital Commons is able to give access to the research community and create a network of scholars within and outside the university. Your university may also make use of other products available from Digital Commons, like journal publishing, conference management, archives, and more. If your university utilizes Digital Commons, it will be accessible through the library. Ask a university librarian for assistance.
- ScholarWorks: Like Digital Commons, this platform is utilized by universities to manage the scholarly output of their faculty and students. If your university uses it, it will be accessible through your school's library website. Find a university librarian for assistance.
- Open-access repository: There are a plethora of open-access repositories to submit your work to. An extensive list is currently available from the University of California Library System at https://www.library.ucsb.edu/scholarly-communication/open-access-repositories. If you have questions regarding

whether submitting your work to these repositories is useful in your field, check with your university librarians as well as your program faculty.

- Professional networking sites: Some professionals choose to publish their work to a professional networking site, like LinkedIn or ResearchGate. Doing so allows you to get your work out there. However, work published to these sites is often seen as less credible because it does not go through the vetting process, as in repositories like PQDT Global or Digital Commons (which verify your credentials with your institution before publication).

It is important to reiterate that these resources might be great places to start when beginning your research or working to expand your network. You may be able to find researchers (faculty or students) at your institution to connect with by searching the university's internal repository. You can also utilize the search tools in PQDT Global to search by institution and find the names of those who have published from your institution in the past.

Presenting

In Chapter 1, we spoke about joining professional organizations and attending conferences. Now you can consider becoming one of the professionals presenting your final project! An initial first step might be to check whether your university has a research conference to which you can submit to present. This can be a great opportunity if you are new to presenting and wish to practice your presentation skills. However, presenting outside your university is considered more prestigious. Options include local, regional, national, and, on occasion, international conferences. Consult with your chair about forums they think would be most appropriate for presenting your work, and check the deadlines for submitting a proposal, which typically takes the form of an abstract.

Many students aim to present their research in the form of a poster presentation or as part of a research symposium, which includes an oral presentation of several different research projects with a unifying theme. If your project is a theoretical or scholarly project, it will likely make more sense to present your work as part of a panel discussion, which is typically a semistructured discussion among professionals focused on a particular topic. Professional organizations with regular conference meetings often advertise a theme for each of their conventions; assess whether and how you can frame your work within this context.

Once you select a conference to apply to present at, determine who you will ask to serve as coauthors (refer to Chapter 7 for information on authorship decisions). You will typically need to submit an abstract to a conference portal by a specific deadline. If possible, highlighting how your project fits in can increase your chance of acceptance. It typically takes a few months to hear whether your work has been accepted to present.

If your work is chosen, you are expected to attend the conference to present your work or at least arrange for a coauthor to do so. Keep in mind that conferences typically cost money to attend, including conference registration fees, transportation, hotel fees, and food, even if you are presenting. Sometimes your university, internship, and/or place of employment will provide travel reimbursement for presenting. Conferences are a great opportunity for you to practice describing your work, as well a chance to network with other researchers with similar interests. It is possible you will cross paths with these professionals again—it has happened to us!

Publishing in a Peer-Reviewed Journal

Publication in a peer-reviewed journal is certainly a goal for students aiming to disseminate their final research project results to a wider audience. However, according to Evans et al.'s (2018) review of peer-reviewed publication outcomes of psychology PhD research projects in the United States, only a quarter of them were eventually published, and the rates were lower for applied subfields like clinical and counseling psychology than for research-oriented fields. The peer-review process can be daunting, because it is often arduous and very competitive, with many journals accepting fewer than 20 percent of the manuscripts submitted. If you aim to submit your project to a peer-reviewed journal, we encourage you to have serious conversations with your chair, advisors, and/or mentors about the possibility of a publication from your research project. They are usually best positioned to suggest revisions that meet various publication guidelines and to suggest which journals might be the best match for your project (Kamler, 2008).

Once you decide to submit your work to a peer-reviewed journal, there are several steps to take. We recommend reviewing the information about authorship from Chapter 7. Determine whether your chair and other potential coauthors are willing to join you in revising your final project draft into a manuscript and determine author order up front, if you have not already. Consider using the APA scorecards (see APA, 2015) to guide your decision-making about the tasks to complete and who will work on each one. It also helps to make a tentative timeline to keep your project on track and hold everyone accountable for making progress. Think about asking your coauthors to sign an author agreement, confirming a plan.

As we mentioned in Chapter 4, a manuscript draft is often significantly shorter than a thesis or dissertation. To cut your written draft down, focus on the main purpose of your project and make sure everything in your manuscript relates. For example, make sure each paragraph in your literature review leads to the need for your project. See what references you can cut out; you likely only need a maximum of two to three citations for each point. Determine where your description of your procedure can be more succinct. Review your results section and see which analyses seem essential to report on versus what you might be able to cut. Challenge yourself to reduce the limitations and directions for future research subsections of your discussion down to about a paragraph each.

As you are revising your manuscript, consider which journals might make sense for your project. One way to determine this is to review your references section and see whether any journals are repeatedly mentioned. This might give you an idea of which forums would be interested in publishing a paper on your topic. We have also had success sending a letter of interest to a journal's editor to ascertain whether they thought a paper was a good fit for their publication.

Another important consideration is the prestige of the journal. Journals receive various ratings. For example, the impact factor, a number based on how often articles from the journal are cited elsewhere, provides a general idea of the journal's impact in its field. Although there are criticisms of these types of rating systems, they can give you an idea of where a particular journal stands relative to similar publications. A journal with a relatively high impact factor will typically be more competitive. It can be beneficial to aim high, because although these journals will sometimes reject your paper, they may provide you with a review that can help you improve your paper for submission to another journal. Sometimes the editor may simply tell you your paper is not a good fit—ideally this happens rather quickly, so you can submit to another journal.

It can also be helpful to review journal descriptions and tables of contents from recent issues of journals you are considering. Familiarize yourself with the range and scope of accepted articles. In addition, carefully review the author guidelines for each journal to help determine what they require (e.g., page length, subheadings). Come up with a list of about three journals to apply to and rate your first choice.

Once you know which journal you plan to submit to first, refer to a few recent articles with similar topics or methodology to get a sense of the writing style, scope, and format of articles the journal decided to publish. Check the authors' guidelines and any checklists for submission to ensure you have adhered to all requirements. The amount of time it can take to hear back varies, even for the same journal.

When you receive the editor's feedback, you will typically also be given the status of your paper. The least common is acceptance of a manuscript with no changes. Sometimes you will receive acceptance contingent on minor changes. More common is an invitation to revise and resubmit. This means your paper has not been accepted yet, but you are being given an opportunity to improve it and receive a second review. This does not mean your paper will ultimately be accepted, but you have a good shot! Still, it can be hard to read the feedback. Take a few days to acknowledge your emotions and digest what they have said. Consult with your chair and/or coauthors about a plan for responding. You will need to develop a point-by-point response to the reviewers' comments, similar to how you respond to an IRB (see Chapter 5 for those suggestions, because they apply here as well).

If your manuscript is accepted, congratulations! If your manuscript is rejected, we know that can be upsetting, particularly if you waited a long time for a response. But it does not mean your work is unimportant! Perhaps it just was not a good fit for that journal. Nearly everyone receives multiple rejections, so expect to remain persistent. Sometimes, the comments from the reviewers and/or editor will be helpful to you as you revise and resubmit your article. Consult with your chair and/or coauthors about next steps. If you received feedback from reviewers and/or an editor, see if you can make at least some of the suggested changes. Many academics we know are fond of saying that every project has a home. You may have to submit to several journals. If you still have difficulty after a few submissions, consider switching to another forum for disseminating your work (e.g., a newsletter published by a professional organization).

Worksheet 8.1 Planning Your Data Analysis, Results, and Discussion Sections

Part 1: This worksheet is designed to help you prepare to conduct your data analyses and write your results and discussions sections. We begin each item by indicating whether it is relevant for all projects or for quantitative, qualitative, or theoretical/scholarly projects specifically. Review the data analytic, results, and discussion sections in this chapter to help guide you through this worksheet. Remember to consult with your chair on these decisions before proceeding.

Part 2: After you have completed each task related your project, place a checkmark (√) next to the corresponding box to track your progress.

Part 1	Part 2 √
Data analytic plan	
What type of project will you be conducting: quantitative, qualitative, theoretical or scholarly?	
Quantitative: If applicable, which preliminary analyses will you be using (e.g., descriptive data, statistical assumptions, prerequisite analyses, analyses for your method section)?	
Quantitative: List the analyses you need in the order of your hypotheses and/or research questions.	
Quantitative: What addendums might you need to make (e.g., variables you may want to control for, statistical corrections to account for multiple comparisons, confidence intervals, effect sizes)?	

Quantitative: What post hoc analyses might you consider?	
Qualitative: Will you use subjective reflections to interpret your data or will you use a coding system? What steps will you need to take to analyze your data? If you will be coding, what steps will you need to take prior to doing so? How can you assess reliability and/or validity (i.e., credibility, transferability, dependability, confirmability)?	
Qualitative: Have you considered conducting descriptive analyses on the demographics of your sample? If so, would you present it in your method or results section?	
Theoretical or scholarly project: How do you plan to present your findings?	
All: What data do you plan to present in tables, figures, and appendices?	
All: According to your institutional review board, how will you de-identify and store data? Who is allowed to have access to this information? Where will you store hard copies? When can they be destroyed?	
All: What spreadsheet and/or statistical programs will you need to analyze your data? Do you have access to the necessary software? What training might you need to obtain, and how can you receive it?	

Quantitative: Have you entered your data into a spreadsheet or started a mock spreadsheet? Which data will you enter? Have you assigned values to variables (e.g., categorical) and created a codebook listing those values?	
Qualitative: How will you organize your data (e.g., color code text from individual participants, enter data into a program such as ATLAS.ti or NVivo)? What are the pros and cons of your various options?	
Qualitative: Have you labeled files clearly and created a codebook listing the values? Have you been consistent with your labeling? Have you considered creating an audit trail?	
All: How are you backing up your files? Do it now!	
All: What is your plan for cleaning your data (e.g., check for missing data, review outliers, check data entry for accuracy)?	
Quantitative: If you encounter any issues while analyzing your data (e.g., violation of statistical assumptions, nonsignificant prerequisite analyses), how will you address them?	

Quantitative: If you have a statistical consultant, have you discussed your data analytic plan with them? Do they understand what you aim to determine conceptually? After they have conducted the analyses, how well do you understand what the results mean?	
Qualitative: What biases or preconceived notions might you have when analyzing your data?	
Qualitative: What is your plan for checking in with coders and addressing any potential discrepancies in coding? At what point will you involve your chair in the decision-making?	
Qualitative: How might you handle unexpected issues (e.g., wanting to gather more information after initial interviews, problems with coders)?	
Qualitative: What steps do you need to take to assess the trustworthiness (i.e., credibility, transferability, dependability, confirmability) of your analyses?	
Results section	
All: How will you organize your results section (e.g., results in the order consistent with the data analytic plan; will you include an introductory paragraph to reorient the reader?)?	

All: What descriptive statistical information will you present (e.g., means and standard deviations, frequencies, and percentages)? Did you consult a relevant style manual (e.g., the APA style manual) to assess what information to include about each of the statistics presented?	
Quantitative: What are the statistical assumptions you will present? If necessary, what nonparametric tests do you need to use? How can you summarize the meaning of your findings conceptually, without interpretation?	
Quantitative: What are your findings from any preliminary analyses, main analyses (e.g., from your hypotheses), and post hoc analyses?	
Quantitative: What inferential statistics will you include (e.g., t test, correlation)? Did you consult the APA style manual to determine which numerical values are typically reported? How can you write your findings conceptually?	
Quantitative: Which, if any, variables should be statistically controlled for? Are there any statistical corrections you need to report?	
Qualitative: How will you present an overview of your themes and/or theoretical constructs (e.g., review each one individually with key findings highlighted)? What will you present in the results section versus the discussion section?	
All: What information would be worth placing in tables? Have you checked the style manual you are expected to follow for formatting guidelines and relevant information to present? How about any program and/or university guidelines?	

All: Which (if any) tables should be placed in your appendices rather than in the text (e.g., tables displaying all nonsignificant findings)?	
All: What information would be worth placing in figures? What types of figures will you use to display your data? How could you create them? How might you code different parts of your figure in a legend? Have you checked your style manual and program and/or university guidelines regarding formatting?	
Discussion section	
All: What will you report in the first discussion paragraph (e.g., restatement of your project's purpose, summary of main findings, what was innovative about your project)?	
All: How will you organize your findings (e.g., for a quantitative study, you could write about your findings in the same order of the hypotheses or lead with the most interesting ones; for a qualitative study, consider reporting findings in the same order as your organized themes and/or theoretical constructs)?	
All: How can you embed your findings or product into the context of the existing literature in your area? For an empirical study, how do your findings compare to existing studies and/or theories? How do your findings strengthen support for the larger body of existing literature? What do you theorize occurred in places where you found results that contrast with existing literature? What are some alternative explanations and/or perspectives? For a theoretical or scholarly project, how can you discuss the product of your project within the context of the existing literature?	

All: What are some practical or clinical implications of your project? How about any theoretical implications or methodological innovations?	
What are some limitations of your project? What were premediated project choices versus unexpected limitations? Could any of your limitations be considered directions for future research? Have you consulted with your chair about limitations to include versus those to leave out?	
All: What recommendations can you make for directions for future research (e.g., theoretical, methodological, practical)? For a qualitative study, are there any testable hypotheses you can suggest based on your data?	

Chapter 9
Attitudes about Research after Your Final Project and Beyond

Introduction

Now that you have successfully completed your final project, you should develop your *attitudes* about the critical evaluation of research, the conduct of research in applied settings, and ethical and professional competence by reviewing the following areas of this chapter:

- Letting go while staying in touch
- Transitioning into an early career professional
- Methods and attitudes for continued lifelong learning
- Decisions about commitment and focus for the future
- Final thoughts

Letting Go while Staying in Touch

At this point, you have likely completed your applied research project and your graduate degree. Hopefully you have been able to find employment in a setting that is exciting for you. There are so many transitions happening at the same time, and you will leave the academic program that you have been in for quite a while. As you prepare to make this first postgraduate transition, it is important to show an *attitude of gratitude*. Many people have helped you achieve your dream, so be sure to thank the advisors, mentors, supervisors, associated professionals, friends, and family who supported you in this journey. We hope you remain thankful and do not become entitled, because these same people may still play large roles in your early career, even in ways that may not yet be apparent.

There is a kind of anticlimax period once you have successfully defended a research project you have likely spent years working on. This letdown is also accompanied by the dissolution of your cohort members who have also completed their degrees. It is common to doubt the worth of your efforts once you leave your academic research environment. Recently, Kaplan-Berkley and colleagues (2019) examined this postdissertation period for three new doctorates who ended up far from each other geographically. These researchers were interested in the postdissertation

Navigating Research in an Applied Graduate Program. Hilary B. Vidair, Pam L. Gustafson, and Eva L. Feindler, Oxford University Press. © Oxford University Press (2024). DOI: 10.1093/oso/9780199352272.003.0009

process when graduates shift from the usual cohort model to individual work settings and wondered whether reflective practice and digital technologies would help maintain their connection and collaboration. They collected data that examined each participant's perspective about their postdoctoral experience and its impact on their identity, self-efficacy, and sense of professionalism. Their qualitative data analyses revealed that grieving was a natural experience postdissertation, and digital communication helped to maintain established connections from their graduate program. Using reflective practices helped to maintain a positive attitude about their research accomplishments and identify the next steps in their professional journeys. Leaving the role of a graduate student requires alterations to existing professional relationships, as well as the acquisition of new skills and competencies within a new work environment. All of this can be quite a challenge for a new graduate.

We encourage you to stay in touch with other researchers: likely you will have had collaborators in a research lab, as part of a coding team, and/or as part of a cohort or class in your graduate program. You may also have already networked with other researchers in your field of interest at conferences, within special interest groups, or during workshops you have attended. There are many options to maintain your affiliations with those who have already mentored you, as well as the new professionals who might guide this next phase of your professional development. Maintaining a relationship with your advisor or mentor is always a good idea, and the relationship might transition into that of colleagues. See the following student example.

Student Example: New Professional Opportunities through a Continued Relationship with a Chair Postdefense

Prior to beginning her fifth-year clinical internship, AMS, who had completed her dissertation on a new treatment protocol for preschoolers with emotional dysregulation, had her abstract accepted for a national conference. While on internship, she presented a poster about her study and talked with many professionals attending the conference about her treatment ideas for young children. This increased her confidence as an applied researcher and allowed her to embrace the clinical implications of her dissertation. She then used it as a springboard for her postdoctoral job interviews to discuss her passions for working with disruptive young children. This "specialization" was seen as a key factor in her success at landing an excellent postdoc position. During her postdoctoral year, AMS was asked by her chair to be a cofacilitator of a multisession in-service training program at a state-run inpatient facility for children. AMS had kept close contact with her chair, and they talked about collaborating on just such projects. AMS had spent a year on externship at the same facility, so she knew many of the staff who were set to receive the training. The postdoc agency then hired her as an early career professional and tasked her with developing clinical services for young children at their group practice. Her creative dissertation research helped her to establish the start of her clinical career. Further, an opportunity arose for her to cowrite a chapter with her dissertation advisor and to showcase her treatment protocol in an edited volume on treatment applications for young children. The edited book was to be about new interventions for young children, and AMS's novel program was to be the highlight of the chapter. This was AMS's first publication opportunity made possible by her close and collaborative association with her chair and her willingness to take on additional work.

For many, once the research project is completed, there is tremendous relief, and with a graduate degree in hand, research becomes part of the past. There are still several ways to cultivate and maintain a scientific attitude toward practice beyond your academic training (see Maddux & Riso, 2007). For example, you can continue to be an educator consumer of practice-oriented research in your field, formulate hypotheses about your clients' and/or students' problems, use relevant evidenced-based interventions to test your hypotheses, and evaluate and revise your plan as warranted (i.e., local clinical scientist model; Stricker & Trierweiler, 1995). You can also use assessment measures in your practice and systematically collect data on any individual and/or group interventions you have implemented. This might lead you to pursue publication in practice-oriented journals. In addition, you can encourage research and evaluation of clinical or educational practice in your job setting. You might even serve as a clinician on a research study or collaborate with researchers on implementing interventions at your job.

For others, completing their research project has awakened an interest and at times even an enthusiasm for doing research. Depending on where you land for your first professional job, there may be research opportunities you can easily join. The American Psychological Association (APA) recently published an online piece entitled *Moving into Your First Independent Research Job*, which contains strategies for success if research is in your career plans (APA, 2021). With a primarily practice-oriented degree, however, your most viable pathway is likely to become involved as a collaborator on research projects, as opposed to aiming to become a principal investigator of research grants. Larger settings like hospitals or federal settings (e.g., Veterans Affairs and prison facilities) often have an active research division that looks for new professionals to join. Some clinical and educational settings have never really considered conducting research but are amenable. In these environments, you could eventually assume a leadership role as someone who conducts program evaluations and/or develops a research program. Or you might maintain a collaborative relationship with your graduate program and participate as a committee member or research advisor to a graduate student beginning their research journey. See the following example.

Student Example: Providing Research Mentorship as an Alumnus

When TW was a doctoral student, she was very involved in her faculty advisor's lab and quickly became its research coordinator. She presented research at conferences and mentored more junior students just starting out with research. She also developed advanced statistical knowledge, eventually becoming a statistical consultant for students conducting theses and dissertation projects. For her dissertation, she collaborated with her chair on submitting a small faculty research grant, which they were awarded and which paid for her study measures and participant compensation. After graduation, she secured a postdoctoral position in a large, well-known evidence-based private group practice. Once she completed her postdoctoral fellowship, she became licensed and was invited to stay on as a psychologist as well as the research coordinator of the practice. Eager to give back to her doctoral program, TW continued to serve as a coauthor on poster presentations and write manuscripts with her chair and current students, based on research she was involved in as a student as well as her dissertation. She also served as an alumni mentor, meeting with a first-year student about various topics, including getting involved in research in graduate school. Recently, a current student was inspired by TW's dissertation research and proposed a similar final research project with the same research design and chair. The student invited TW to serve on her dissertation committee. TW was honored to hear someone was pursuing a similar project and thrilled to give back to her doctoral program in this capacity.

Last, if you have the "bug" to continue research efforts after your own project, consider becoming a part of a practice research network (PRN). PRNs originated in the medical field, with physicians working collaboratively to collect data from community settings. Over the past decade, psychotherapy researchers have begun to collaborate by asking practitioners to use a common outcome measure to evaluate treatment effectiveness across clinical practices. One of the first successful PRNs was a collaboration between a community practice association and an academic institution (see Castonguay et al., 2015, for a fuller description). Those involved wanted to create an active partnership between experienced community practitioners and clinical researchers to design, implement, analyze, and disseminate clinically meaningful and scientifically rigorous research. This approach not only helps to support practice-based research but also helps the practitioner to adhere to a scientist-practitioner model as they move forward in their professional career. Koerner and Castonguay (2015) emphasized the potential in this collaborative process across clinical practitioners, educators, trainers, and researchers who work together to develop, implement, and evaluate the most effective treatments for enhanced client outcomes. Participation in a PRN rests on positive attitudes about the value of research across one's clinical career, independent of the work setting.

Transitioning into an Early Career Professional

As exciting as it is to embark on a long-awaited career, early career professionals (ECP) must usually juggle multiple roles in their professional and personal lives. Given the high cost of graduate education, many have increased debt-related issues and must generate an income quickly. Others are focused on the varying licensure requirements in their states and are looking to obtain supervised postdoctoral hours to become license eligible. In addition to these complexities, you are also just beginning your career and likely want to think about establishing your professional identity and balancing that with your personal identity (Green & Hawley, 2009). Any professional development and/or mentoring you can obtain around these issues will likely be helpful.

Elman et al. (2005) summarized the outcomes of a professional development workgroup subcommittee from a competencies conference devoted to issues of credentialing professional psychologists. They proposed the following definition for professional development (PD): "PD is the developmental process of acquiring, expanding, refining and sustaining knowledge, proficiency, skill, and qualifications for competent professional functioning that results in professionalism" (Elman et al., 2005, p. 368). There are several components of this developmental process to consider as you turn toward your postgraduate applied career, including self-reflection, responsibility and accountability, critical thinking, and interpersonal skills (see Elman et al., 2005, for recommendations on how to develop these skills). Many strategies will help you to develop your professional identity, including attending professional development conferences and professional meetings, as well as participation in professional associations (Elman et al., 2005). There are also many mentoring opportunities for ECPs about career steps, professional networking, finances, and professional leadership (Andrews & Cook, 2020; Arora et al., 2017; Doran et al., 2018; Grapin et al., 2020; Green & Hawley, 2009; Sim et al., 2016). In addition, many professional local organizations and divisions of larger organizations provide mentoring programs for ECPs.

Boot camps can also provide opportunities for fostering mentoring relationships beyond graduate school. For example, Foran-Tuller and colleagues (2012) reported on a specialty early career training program for psychologists beginning their careers in academic health centers. Specifically, the Association of Psychologists in Academic Health Centers (APAHC) Early Career Boot Camp is an intensive, biannual, interactive workshop for postdoctoral fellows and ECPs held during the first day of the APAHC Annual Conference. Application to the boot camp is open to psychologists within ten years of receiving their doctoral degree; however, preference is reportedly given to individuals who are newer to their field. APAHC also offers a midcareer boot camp for those who are further out from their professional degree or those changing work settings. These boot camps generally focus on professional effectiveness, clinical supervision, strategic career planning, and academic research, all within the work context of an academic health center.

If you are excited about continuing your applied research, it also might be important to consider what you might bring to the next research environment. Did you learn a particular research methodology that might be useful to agencies competing for grant monies or wanting to conduct needs assessments and program evaluations? Those in applied settings may not have the research skills you have already acquired to write grants proposals for funding. You can also look for opportunities to increase your knowledge about obtaining funding. For example, the National Institutes of Health (NIH) Grant Writing Boot Camp is a two-day intensive boot camp that includes lectures, discussions, and other activities focused on the NIH application process. This training will teach you how to identify relevant NIH funding, tailor your application to what reviewers are looking for, and write clear and effective grant proposals. Even if you do not plan to be a principal investigator of a grant, attending a boot camp like this can help you acquire the knowledge and skills necessary to serve as a valued co-investigator or practice-oriented collaborator.

Methods and Attitudes for Continued Lifelong Learning

Although at this point you are finished with your graduate training and can begin your professional work life, your commitment to the importance of research and evaluation will hopefully involve a lifetime of learning. This can include continuing professional development (CPD), which Taylor and Neimeyer (2017) refer to as a wide assortment of activities designed to maintain your competence, including those that are informal (e.g., learning from peer-reviewed articles), incidental (e.g., learning as a byproduct of teaching), or formal (e.g., a course). There is typically more oversight and organization for formal activities, whereas informal learning can occur on your own as self-directed but unsupervised learning. Incidental learning can occur spontaneously as your career develops and you engage in supervision, case consultation, or various peer-related activities in new areas. Continuing education (CE), which refers to more formal structured learning activities, involves course credits and sometimes leads to certifications or specializations. Licensing and/or certification requirements vary somewhat across the United States, but most states have requirements for CE. Once you are established in your first more permanent job, check with your state's education department about exactly what is required each year in terms of CE credits. Some states have clear guidelines on the types of courses acceptable for CE credits and some require more explicit courses that must be taken periodically.

Several professional clinical psychology groups convened meetings of APA members to consider the standards for and quality of CE programs. Washburn et al. (2019) reported on their recommendations to better organize the CE process for psychologists. One recommendation involved transitioning from CE courses based on evidenced-based practice to science-based practice, to move from a sole focus on outcomes to include a scientifically plausible rationale for assessment and interventions. In addition, the group suggested a transition from attendance-based programs to competency-based learning experiences. CE programming can be accomplished in many formats (seminars, workshops, home-based study, webinars, online courses, and certifications), but the most effective learning method seems to be an interactive one that builds on didactic training (Washburn et al, 2019). Similarly, Rossen et al. (2019) reviewed CPD and CE requirements across various state agencies that credential school psychologists and agencies that conduct national credentialing. Consult their article to understand these continued learning activities and the state agencies with requirements for credentialing and renewal of certifications. There seems to be a good amount of variability in regard to time frames and types of CPD and/or CE that are acceptable. The authors suggest that states eventually move toward adoption of a consistent set of requirements for school psychologists.

Once you start to attend professional conferences, perhaps first to showcase your research project via a poster or a presentation, but then to grow your professional network, you will discover there are numerous pre- and postconference workshops and/or courses that you can complete and for which you can receive CE credits. For example, as a clinician, whenever a new version of the *Diagnostic and Statistical Manual of Mental Disorders* or an intelligence test arrives, you will likely need to attend some CE about their new developments to stay current in your field. You also may have landed a first job that includes work with a population you have little experience with or treatment approaches with which you are less familiar. These are good reasons to seek out additional training opportunities, and we suggest offerings that also provide the necessary CE credits.

As CE opportunities move toward science-based practice, so should your continued professional development such that, as a clinician or educator, you practice in a manner that is consistent with scientific standards. After you complete your degree, you have several choices of professional organizations to join on many levels: local, state, national, and international. We encourage you to carefully review these organizations prior to joining and consider their scope, their training opportunities, their networking potential, and their reputability. Membership often costs a great deal per year, so the fees should match the opportunities. Often, you may subscribe to professional journals through these organizations. We suggest that you review these options just as carefully, perhaps reading several articles of interest from several journals.

To keep your research knowledge and interests alive, we suggest you read and even subscribe to the journals that "bridge" the science and practice elements in your field (Maddux & Riso, 2007). The following is an initial list of journals we encourage you to read from:

- *Clinical Child and Family Psychology Review*
- *Clinical Psychology Review*
- *Clinical Psychology: Science and Practice*
- *Cognitive and Behavioral Practice*
- *Contemporary Educational Psychology*
- *Evidence-Based Practice in Child and Adolescent Mental Health*
- *Journal of Child and Family Studies*
- *Journal of Clinical Psychology*
- *Professional Psychology: Research and Practice*
- *Psychotherapy*
- *Contemporary School Psychology*
- *School Psychology Review*
- *Psychology in the Schools*

The APA also publishes a monthly newsletter called the *Clinician's Research Digest* (with different editions for adult and youth populations), which highlights summaries of one hundred clinical articles reviewed by editors each month. Reading a digest such as this one or newsletters from your professional groups will help you to stay current with practice-oriented research. Further, there is a newer peer-reviewed journal by the APA entitled *Practice Innovations*, which includes articles on the ever-changing practices, methods, and standards in professional mental health. Other mental health and education fields have their own organizations, newsletters, and journals that might be of interest as you seek to stay up to date.

Beyond lifelong learning about your profession, you will want to maintain an attitude that supports lifelong curiosity and learning about yourself. Consider any feedback that you may have gotten along the way from your advisors and/or supervisors as you developed your career, and consider which areas of practice or professional development could use some attention. Have you received some kind of consistent but negative feedback you would want to remediate? Perhaps you have had feedback about your timeliness or organization with paperwork or an interpersonal issue that you can now focus on. You can always go back to Worksheet 5.2 to develop your own remediation plan to address these issues, either alone or in consultation with a trusted consultant, advisor, or colleague. We consider professional development an ever-evolving process across your career. Openness to continued self-evaluation and feedback from others will likely foster significant professional as well as personal growth.

Finally, we encourage you to think about how you can continually integrate self-care into your lifestyle. Beyond the self-care activities we discussed in Chapter 3, you will likely best flourish over the course of your career if you cultivate positive and supportive relationships with colleagues, mindfully make meaning of your work, practice in ways consistent with your values, and actively engage in continued learning with other professionals (Wise & Reuman, 2019). Consider joining a peer consultation group or team and try to attend some CPD and/or CE activities in person to receive support and have opportunities to discuss topics such as legal, ethical, and professional issues (Wise & Reuman, 2019).

Decisions about Commitment and Focus for the Future

One of the benefits of having a master's or doctoral degree in an applied field is that it is versatile. There are many options you can pursue, and many practice-oriented professionals are involved in more than one work setting. It is easy to take on too much or be uncertain about which direction makes the most sense. Try to decide what you want to commit to based on which opportunities can help you move forward with your initial career goals. Here are some questions to help you clarify your thoughts about next steps in training, research, professional practice, and online:

1. *What kinds of clinical, educational, or research experiences do you want to obtain after graduating to continue to advance your career?* Should you pursue formal training, certifications, or specializations? If you have completed a master's degree, what are the considerations in terms of moving forward with doctoral education? Or do you think a master's degree is sufficient for your goals?
2. *What opportunities will allow you to integrate scientific attitudes and values into your practical work?* Are you interested in pursuing research and evaluation? What are some ways you can function like a local clinical and/or practicing scientist? Would you consider taking on a leadership role as a researcher and/or evaluator in an applied setting?
3. *How can you apply scientific findings to your practice?* If you are leaning in the direction of practice only, what are some considerations for establishing your professional practice and areas of expertise? Are there ways you can apply scientific findings to your practice, such as reading peer-reviewed journals, using a local clinical scientist model, or incorporating routine outcomes assessment?
4. *How might you incorporate technology into your professional practice?* In a survey of 164 professional psychologists, technologies such as mobile telephone, email, and videoconferencing that are used to deliver clinical services were deemed increasingly popular and include numerous practical and professional challenges to consider (Glueckauf at al., 2018). And that was prior to the COVID-19 pandemic! The APA (2020) found that 76 percent of clinicians they surveyed were providing solely remote services, compared to 5 percent before

the pandemic began. If your professional training program did not prepare you to use technology in practice, you should consider CE options for preparing yourself in this area.

5. *How do you want to present yourself online and in social media?* Developing a professional website and working to establish your areas of expertise seem to now be necessary parts of postgraduate professional life. Many in practice now develop their own professional website and use it to showcase their training, their areas of expertise, and their research interests. A professional website can be used to network with other like-minded professionals across many contexts and as a way to market your practice and/or publications. Many professionals also create blogs or respond to discussions on popular social media platforms like Twitter, Facebook, and LinkedIn to advertise their specialties and attract possible clients. Further, there are numerous professional listservs and discussion blogs to elicit interaction. More graduate training programs have developed technology and social media policies for their graduate students to get them thinking about possible conflicts in terms of private and professional online identities. Pham (2014) suggests a plan for navigating social networking and urges new graduates to consider ethical challenges, possible digital dual relationships, issues of confidentiality, and how to think through what you might post online. It will be important to design a social media policy for your postgraduate career. Creating your professional identity on social media should be an intentional plan with consideration about issues of privacy and off-duty interactions with clients (Kolmes, 2012).

Overall, there are many choices about how to take your research and practice interests forward and integrate them into your professional identity, including your online identity. See the following example.

Student Example: Transforming Student Research Interests into a Professional Identity, in Practice, in Print, and Online

As a graduate student, AC had a passion for working with eating disordered clients. After completing her dissertation research on substance abuse following bariatric surgery, AC published the research in a medical journal and began to write essays for popular magazines on diet culture. Once she finished with her degree, she completed postdoctoral training at a hospital integrated with bariatric surgery and obesity nutrition research, furthering her specialty after her formal degree training. She continued in her professional development by becoming certified in mindfulness-based eating awareness therapy. She opened a specialty private practice and contributed to an eating disorders blog sponsored by *Psychology Today*. Further, she developed her own website and blog, along with social media accounts on Facebook, Twitter, and Instagram.

Although she no longer maintains an institutional research affiliation, AC stays current with new research findings in the fields of bariatric surgery and eating disorders. She regularly attends and presents at research conferences and serves as a peer reviewer for bariatric surgery medical journals. She serves as the research liaison for the International Association of Eating Disorder Professionals, New York Chapter, and is a board member of the Center for Mindful Eating. Most recently, AC published her first book: *The Diet-Free Revolution: 10 Steps to Free Yourself from the Diet Cycle with Mindful Eating and Radical Self-Acceptance* (published in 2021 by North Atlantic Books and distributed by Penguin Random House).

Final Thoughts

Congratulations, you made it! We hope our book helped you navigate your way from beginning your research in graduate school to completing your final project. We also hope we have inspired you to continue a lifelong process of seeking scientifically based knowledge, continuing to use your research skills in some capacity, and maintaining an open-minded, scientific attitude about your practice and performance in applied settings. We recommend you continue to seek mentorship and/or consultation throughout the various stages of your career and hope that you feel motivated to give back by mentoring others in your applied field who aim to embark on research. Best of luck to you as you move on to the next stage of your professional journey!

Further Recommended Reading

Bell, D. J., Foster, S. L., & Cone, J. D. (2019). *Dissertations and theses from start to finish: Psychology and related fields* (3rd ed.). American Psychological Association.

Efron, S. E., & Ravid, R. (2018). *Writing the literature review: A practical guide.* Guilford Press.

Galvan, J. L., & Galvan, M. C. (2017). *Writing literature reviews: A guide for students of the social and behavioral sciences* (7th ed.). Routledge.

Given, L. M. (Ed.). (2008). *The Sage encyclopedia of qualitative research methods.* (Vols. 1 and 2). SAGE.

Kazdin, A. E. (2023). *Research design in clinical psychology* (6th ed.). Cambridge University Press.

Krathwohl, D. R., & Smith, N. L. (2005). *How to prepare a dissertation proposal: Suggestions for students in education and the social and behavioral sciences.* Syracuse University Press.

Locke, L. F., Spirduso, W. W., & Silverman, S. J. (2013). *Proposals that work: A guide for planning dissertations and grant proposals* (6th ed.). SAGE Publications.

McMillan, J. H. (2021). *Educational research: Fundamental principles and methods* (8th ed.). Pearson.

Rudestam, K. E., & Newton, R. R. (2014). *Surviving your dissertation: A comprehensive guide to content and process* (4th ed.). SAGE Publications.

Terrell, S. R. (2023). *Writing a proposal for your dissertation: Guidelines and examples* (2nd ed.). Guilford Press.

Willis, J. W., Inman, D., & Valenti, R. (2010). *Completing a professional practice dissertation: A guide for doctoral students and faculty.* Information Age Publishing.

References

Preface

National Council of Schools of Professional Psychology. (2007, August 15). *Competency developmental achievement levels (DALs) of the National Council of Schools and Programs in Professional Psychology (NCSPP).* https://thencspp.org/wp-content/uploads/2022/05/DALs-of-NCSPP-9-21-07.pdf

Chapter 1

Alvarez, A. N., Blume, A. W., Cervantes, J. M., & Thomas, L. R. (2009). Tapping the wisdom tradition: Essential elements to mentoring students of color. *Professional Psychology: Research and Practice, 40*(2), 181–188. https://doi.org/10.1037/a0012256

American Psychological Association. (2017). *Ethical principles of psychologists and code of conduct* (2002, amended effective June 1, 2010, and January 1, 2017). https://www.apa.org/ethics/code/

Auerbach, C. F., & Silverstein, L. B. (2003). *Qualitative studies in psychology. Qualitative data: An introduction to coding and analysis.* New York University Press.

Bieschke, K. J. (2006). Research self-efficacy beliefs and research outcome expectations: Implications for developing scientifically minded psychologists. *Journal of Career Assessment, 14,* 77–91. https://doi.org/10.1177/1069072705281366

Bieschke, K. J., Fouad, N. A., Collins, F. L., Jr., & Halonen, J. S. (2004). The scientifically-minded psychologist: Science as a core competency. *Journal of Clinical Psychology, 60,* 713–723. https://doi.org/10.1002/jclp.20012

Bloomberg, L. D., & Volpe, M. (2012). *Completing your qualitative dissertation: A road map from beginning to end* (2nd ed.). SAGE Publications.

Borders, L. D., Wester, K. L., Granello, D. H., Chang, C. Y., Hays, D. G., Pepperell, J., & Spurgeon, S. L. (2012). Association for counselor education and supervision guidelines for research mentorship: Development and implementation. *Counselor Education and Supervision, 51*(3), 162–175. https://doi.org/10.1002/j.1556-6978.2012.00012.x

Brown, R. T., Daly, B. P., & Leong, F. T. L. (2009). Mentoring in research: A developmental approach. *Professional Psychology: Research and Practice, 40*(3), 306–313. https://doi.org/10.1037/a0011996

Burkard, A. W., Knox, S., DeWalt, T., Fuller, S., Hill, C., & Schlosser, L. Z. (2014). Dissertation experiences of doctoral graduates from professional psychology programs. *Counseling Psychology Quarterly, 27,* 19–54.

Callahan, J. L., Smotherman, J. M., Dziurzynski, K. E., Love, P. K., Kilmer, E. D., Niemann, Y. F., & Ruggero, C. J. (2018). Diversity in the professional psychology training-to-workforce pipeline: Results from doctoral psychology student population data. *Training and Education in Professional Psychology, 12*(4), 273–285. https://doi.org/10.1037/tep0000203

Charmaz, K. (2006). *Constructing grounded theory: A practical guide through qualitative analysis.* SAGE Publications.

Chen, P., Weiss, F. L., & Nicolson, H. J. (2010). Girls Study Girls Inc.: Engaging girls in evaluation through participatory action research. *American Journal of Community Psychology, 46*(1–2), 228–237. https://doi.org/10.1007/s10464-010-9328-7

Clark, R. A., Harden, S. L., & Johnson, W. B. (2000). Mentor relationships in clinical psychology doctoral training: Results of a national survey. *Teaching of Psychology, 27*(4), 262–268. https://doi.org/10.1207/S15328023TOP2704_04

Creswell, J. W., & Plano Clark, V. L. (2011). *Designing and conducting mixed methods research* (2nd ed.). SAGE Publications.

Drotar, D. (2013). Lessons learned from a career in clinical research: Implications for mentoring and career development. *Professional Psychology: Research and Practice, 44*(6), 384–390. https://doi.org/10.1037/a0035228

Feindler, E., Klein, J. S., & Smith, T. (2019). Innovative PsyD training: The development of an alumni mentorship program. *Open Access Journal of Behavioural Science and Psychology, 2*(2), 180020.

Gatfield, T., & Alpert, F. (2002, July 10–12). The supervisory management styles model. In T. Herrington (Ed.), *Quality conversations* [symposium]. Proceedings of the 25th HERDSA Annual Conference, Perth, Western Australia.

Gelso, C. J. (2006). On the making of a scientist-practitioner: A theory of research training in professional psychology. *Training and Education in Professional Psychology, S*(1), 3–16. https://doi.org/10.1037/1931-3918.S.1.3

Hoch, E. L., Ross, A. O., & Winder, C. L. (1966). Conference on the professional preparation of clinical psychologists: A summary. *American Psychologist, 21*, 42–51. https://doi.org/10.1037/h0021107

Johnson, W. B. (2002). The intentional mentor: Strategies and guidelines for the practice of mentoring. *Professional Psychology: Research and Practice, 33*(1), 88–96. https://doi.org/10.1037/0735-7028.33.1.88

Johnson, W. B. (2003). A framework for conceptualizing competence to mentor. *Ethics & Behavior, 13*(2), 127–151.

Johnson, W. B., Koch, C., Fallow, G. O., & Huwe, J. M. (2000). Prevalence of mentoring in clinical versus experimental doctoral programs: Survey findings, implications, and recommendations. *Psychotherapy: Theory, Research, Practice, Training, 37*(4), 325–334. https://doi.org/10.1037/0033-3204.37.4.325

Jones, J. L., & Mehr, S. L. (2007). Foundations and assumptions of the scientist-practitioner model. *American Behavioral Scientist, 50*(6), 766–771. https://doi.org/10.1177/0002764206296454

Kazdin, A. E. (1982). Symptom substitution, generalization, and response covariation: Implications for psychotherapy outcome. *Psychological Bulletin, 91*(2), 349–365. https://doi.org/10.1037/0033-2909.91.2.349

Kazdin, A. E. (2016). *Research design in clinical psychology* (5th ed.). Pearson.

Kidd, S. A., & Kral, M. J. (2005). Practicing participatory action research. *Journal of Counseling Psychology, 52*(2), 187–195. https://doi.org/10.1037/0022-0167.52.2.187

Knox, S., Burkard, A. W., Janecek, J., Pruitt, N. T., Fuller, S. L., & Hill, C. E. (2011). Positive and problematic dissertation experiences: The faculty perspective. *Counselling Psychology Quarterly, 24*, 55–69.

Lincoln, Y., & Guba, E. G. (1985). *Naturalistic inquiry.* SAGE Publications.

Luyten, P., Blatt, S. J., & Corveleyn, J. (2006). Minding the gap between positivism and hermeneutics in psychoanalytic research. *Journal of the American Psychoanalytic Association, 54*(2), 571–610. https://doi.org/10.1177/00030651060540021301

Mapes, B. M., Foster, C. S., Kusnoor, S. V., Epelbaum, M. I., AuYoung, M., Jenkins, G., Lopez-Class, M., Richardson-Heron, D., Elmi, A., Surkan, K., Cronin, R. M., Wilkins, C. H., Pérez-Stable, E. J., Dishman, E., Denny, J. C., Rutter, J. L., & All of Us Research Program (2020). Diversity and inclusion for the All of Us research program: A scoping review. *PLOS ONE, 15*(7), Article e0234962. https://doi.org/10.1371/journal.pone.0234962

McMillan, J. H. (2021). *Educational research: Fundamental principles and methods* (8th ed.). Pearson.

Peluso, D. L., Carleton, R. N., Richter, A. A., & Asmundson, G. J. G. (2011). The graduate advising relationship in Canadian psychology programmes: Advisee perspectives. Canadian Psychology, 52(1), 29–40. https://doi.org/10.1037/a0022047

Ragins, B. R., & McFarlin, D. B. (1990). Perceptions of mentor roles in cross-gender mentoring relationships. *Journal of Vocational Behavior, 37*(3), 321–339. https://doi.org/10.1016/0001-8791(90)90048-7

Raimy, V. C. (Ed.). (1950). Training in clinical psychology. Prentice Hall.

Ready, R. E., & Santorelli, G. D. (2014). Values and goals in clinical psychology training programs: Are practice and science at odds? *Professional Psychology: Research and Practice, 45*(2), 99–103. https://doi.org/10.1037/a0036081

Rogers, D. T. (2009). The working alliance in teaching and learning: Theoretical clarity and research implications. *International Journal for the Scholarship of Teaching and Learning, 3*(2), Article 28. https://doi.org/10.20429/ijsotl.2009.030228

Schlosser, L. Z., & Gelso, C. J. (2001). Measuring the working alliance in advisor–advisee relationships in graduate school. *Journal of Counseling Psychology, 48*(2), 157–167. https://doi.org/10.1037/0022-0167.48.2.157

Schlosser, L. Z, Lyons, H. Z., Talleyrand, R., Kim, B. S. K., & Johnson, W. B. (2011). Advisor–advisee relationships in graduate training programs. *Journal of Career Development, 38*(1), 3–18. https://doi.org/10.1177/0894845309358887

Shannon-Baker, P. (2016). Making paradigms meaningful in mixed methods research. *Journal of Mixed Methods Research, 10*(4), 319–334. https://doi.org/10.1177/1558689815575861

Spring, B. (2007). Evidence-based practice in clinical psychology: What it is; why it matters; what you need to know. *Journal of Clinical Psychology, 63*(7), 611–631. https://doi.org/10.1002/jclp.20373

Stricker, G., & Trierweiler, S. J. (1995). The local clinical scientist: A bridge between science and practice. *American Psychologist, 50*(12), 995–1002. https://doi.org/10.1037/0003-066X.50.12.995

Sue, S. (1999). Science, ethnicity, and bias: Where have we gone wrong? *American Psychologist, 54*(12), 1070–1077. https://doi.org/10.1037/0003-066X.54.12.1070

Trierweiler, S. J., & Stricker, G. (1992). *Research and evaluation competency: Training the local clinical scientist.* In R. L. Peterson, J. D. McHolland, R. J. Bent, E. Davis-Russell, G. E. Edwall, K. Polite, D. L. Singer, & G. Stricker (Eds.), *The core curriculum in professional psychology* (pp. 103–113). American Psychological Association. https://doi.org/10.1037/10103-012

Trierweiler, S. J., Stricker, G., & Peterson, R. L. (2010). The research and evaluation competency: The local clinical scientist—Review, current status, future directions. In M. B. Kenkel & R. L. Peterson (Eds.), *Competency-based education for professional psychology* (pp. 125–141). American Psychological Association. https://doi.org/10.1037/12068-007

US Department of Health and Human Services. (2018, June 19). *2018 Requirements (2018 Common Rule): Subpart A. Basic HHS policy for protection of human research subjects.* Office for Human Research Protections. https://www.hhs.gov/ohrp/regulations-and-policy/regulations/45-cfr-46/revised-common-rule-regulatory-text/index.html

Willis, J., Inman, D., & Valenti, R. (2010). *Completing a professional practice dissertation: A guide for doctoral students and faculty.* Information Age Publishing.

Chapter 2

American Psychological Association. (2006). *Introduction to mentoring: A guide for mentors and mentees.* https://www.apa.org/education/grad/intromentoring.pdf

Bell, D. J., Foster, S. L., & Cone, J. D. (2019). *Dissertations and theses from start to finish: Psychology and related fields* (3rd ed.). American Psychological Association.

Bieschke, K. J. (2000). Factor structure of the Research Outcome Expectations Scale. *Journal of Career Assessment, 8*(3), 303–313. https://doi.org/10.1177/106907270000800307

Bieschke, K. J., Bishop, R. M., & Garcia, V. L. (1996). The utility of the Research Self-Efficacy Scale. *Journal of Career Assessment, 4*(1), 59–75. https://doi.org/10.1177/106907279600400104

Bishop, R. M., & Bieschke, K. J. (1994). *Interest in Research Questionnaire* [Unpublished scale]. Pennsylvania State University.l

Crane, D. R., Wampler, K. S., Sprenkle, D. H., Sandberg, J. G., & Hovestadt, A. J. (2002). The scientist-practitioner model in marriage and family therapy doctoral programs: Current status. *Journal of Marital and Family Therapy, 28*(1), 75–83. https://doi.org/10.1111/j.1752-0606.2002.tb01175.x

Deemer, E. D., Martens, M. P., & Buboltz, W. C. (2010). *Research Motivation Scale (RMS)* [Database record]. APA PsycTests. https://doi.org/10.1037/t03669-000

Efron, S. E., & Ravid, R. (2018). *Writing the literature review: A practical guide.* Guilford Press.

Galvan, J. L., & Galvan, M. C. (2017). *Writing literature reviews: A guide for students of the social and behavioral sciences* (7th ed.). Routledge.

Gelso, C. J. (2006). On the making of a scientist-practitioner: A theory of research training in professional psychology. *Training and Education in Professional Psychology, S*(1), 3–16. https://doi.org/10.1037/0735-7028.24.4.468

Gelso, C. J., Mallinckrodt, B., & Judge, A. B. (1996). Research training environment, attitudes toward research, and research self-efficacy: The revised Research Training Environment Scale. *The Counseling Psychologist, 24*, 304–322. https://doi.org/10.1177/0011000096242010

Kahn, J. H., & Miller, S. A. (2000). Measuring global perceptions of the research training environment using a short form of the RTES-R. *Measurement and Evaluation in Counseling and Development, 33*(2), 103–119. https://doi.org/10.1080/07481756.2000.12069001

Knox, S., Burkard, A. W., Janecek, J., Pruitt, N. T., Fuller, S. L., & Hill, C. E. (2011). Positive and problematic dissertation experiences: The faculty perspective. *Counselling Psychology Quarterly, 24*(1), 55–69. https://doi.org/10.1080/09515070.2011.559796

Leong, F. T. L., & Zachar, P. (1991). Development and validation of the Scientist-Practitioner Inventory for psychology. *Journal of Counseling Psychology, 38*(3), 331–341. https://doi.org/10.1037/0022-0167.38.3.331

Leong, F. T. L., & Zachar, P. (1993). Presenting two brief versions of the Scientist Practitioner Inventory. *Journal of Career Assessment, 1*(2), 162–170. https://doi.org/10.1177/106907279300100205

McMillan, J. H. (2021). *Educational research: Fundamental principles and methods* (8th ed.). Pearson.

Owenz, M., & Hall, S. R. (2011). Bridging the research–practice gap in psychotherapy training: Qualitative research analysis of master's students' experiences in a student-led research & practice team. *North American Journal of Psychology, 13*(1), 21–34.

Papanastasiou, E. (2014). Revised Attitudes toward Research scale (R-ATR): A first look at its psychometric properties. *Journal of Research in Education, 24*(2), 146–159. https://doi.org/10.1037/t35506-000

Schlosser, L. Z., & Kahn, J. H. (2007). Dyadic perspectives on advisor–advisee relationships in counseling psychology doctoral programs. *Journal of Counseling Psychology, 54*(2), 211–217. https://doi.org/10.1037/0022-0167.54.2.211

US Department of Health and Human Services. (1998, November 9). *Expedited review: Categories of research that may be reviewed through an expedited review procedure.* Office for Human Research Protections. https://www.hhs.gov/ohrp/regulations-and-policy/guidance/categories-of-research-expedited-review-procedure-1998/index.html

US Department of Health and Human Services. (2018, June 19). *Exemptions (2018 Requirements): Subpart A. Basic HHS policy for protection of human research subjects.* Office for Human Research Protections. https://www.hhs.gov/ohrp/regulations-and-policy/regulations/45-cfr-46/common-rule-subpart-a-46104/index.html

Chapter 3

APA Presidential Task Force on Evidence-Based Practice. (2006). Evidence-based practice in psychology. *The American Psychologist, 61*(4), 271–285. https://doi.org/10.1037/0003-066X.61.4.271

Carter, L. A., & Barnett, J. E. (2014). *Self-care for clinicians in training: A guide to psychological wellness for graduate students in psychology.* Oxford University Press.

Castonguay, L. G., & Beutler, L. E. (Eds.). (2006). *Principles of therapeutic change that work.* Oxford University Press.

DiClemente, C. C., & Velasquez, M. M. (2002). Motivational interviewing and the stages of change. In W. R. Miller & S. Rollnick (Eds.), *Motivational interviewing: Preparing people for change.* (pp. 201–216). Guilford Press.

El-Ghoroury, N. H., Galper, D. I., Sawaqdeh, A., & Bufka, L. F. (2012). Stress, coping, and barriers to wellness among psychology graduate students. *Training and Education in Professional Psychology, 6*(2), 122–134.

Fisher, C. B., Fried, A. L., & Feldman, L. G. (2009a). Graduate socialization in the responsible conduct of research: A national survey on the research ethics training experiences of psychology doctoral students. *Ethics & Behavior, 19*(6), 496–518. https://doi.org/10.1080/10508420903275283

Fisher, C. B., Fried, A. F., Goodman, S. J., & Germano, K. K. (2009b). Measures of mentoring, department climate, and graduate student preparedness in the responsible conduct of psychological research. *Ethics & Behavior, 19*(3), 227–252. https://doi.org/10.1080/10508420902886726

Gelso, C. J. (2006). On the making of a scientist-practitioner: A theory of research training in professional psychology. *Training and Education in Professional Psychology, S*(1), 3–16. https://doi.org/10.1037/1931-3918.S.1.3

Gottman, J. M. (1998). Psychology and the study of marital processes. *Annual Review of Psychology, 49*(1), 169–197. https://doi.org/10.1146/annurev.psych.49.1.169

Gyani, A., Shafran, R., Myles, P., & Rose, S. (2014). The gap between science and practice: How therapists make their clinical decisions. *Behavior Therapy, 45*(2), 199–211. https://doi.org/10.1016/j.beth.2013.10.004

Lebow, J. L., & Jenkins, P. H. (2018). *Research for the psychotherapist: From science to practice* (2nd ed.). Routledge.

Leong, F. T. L., & Zachar, P. (1991). Development and validation of the Scientist-Practitioner Inventory for psychology. *Journal of Counseling Psychology, 38*(3), 331–341. https://doi.org/10.1037/0022-0167.38.3.331

Myers, S. B., Sweeney, A. C., Popick, V., Wesley, K., Bordfeld, A., & Fingerhut, R. (2012). Self-care practices and perceived stress levels among psychology graduate students. *Training and Education in Professional Psychology, 6*(1), 55–66.

Norcross, J. C. (2001). Purposes, processes, and products of the task force on empirically supported therapy relationships. *Psychotherapy: Theory, Research, Practice, Training, 38*(4), 345–356. https://doi.org/10.1037/0033-3204.38.4.345

Norcross, J. C., & Lambert, M. J. (2011). Psychotherapy relationships that work II. *Psychotherapy, 48*(1), 4–8. https://doi.org/10.1037/a0022180

Norcross, J. C., & Wampold, B. E. (2011). Evidence-based therapy relationships: Research conclusions and clinical practices. *Psychotherapy, 48*(1), 98–102. https://doi.org/10.1037/a0022161

Overholser, J. (2009). Ten criteria to qualify as a scientist-practitioner in clinical psychology: An immodest proposal for objective standards. *Journal of Contemporary Psychotherapy, 40*, 51–59. https://doi.org/10.1007/s10879-009-9127-3.

Peterson, R. L., Peterson, D. R., Abrams, J. C., & Stricker, G. (2006). The National Council of Schools and Programs of Professional Psychology Educational Model. *Training and Education in Professional Psychology, S*(1), 17–36. https://doi.org/10.1037/1931-3918.S.1.17

Prochaska, J. O., & DiClemente, C. C. (1982). Transtheoretical therapy: Toward a more integrative model of change. *Psychotherapy: Theory, Research & Practice, 19*(3), 276–288. https://doi.org/10.1037/h0088437

Prochaska, J. O., & DiClemente, C. C. (1992). *The transtheoretical approach.* In J. C. Norcross & M. R. Goldfried (Eds.), *Handbook of psychotherapy integration* (pp. 300–334). Basic Books.

Spillet, M. A., & Moisiewicz, K. A. (2004). Cheerleader, coach, counselor, critic: Support and challenge roles of the dissertation advisor. *College Student Journal, 38*(2), 246–256.

Stricker, G., & Trierweiler, S. J. (2006). The local clinical scientist: A bridge between science and practice. *Training and Education in Professional Psychology, S*(1), 37–46. https://doi.org/10.1037/1931-3918.S.1.37

Task Force on Promotion and Dissemination of Psychological Procedures. (1995). Training in and dissemination of empirically-validated psychological treatments: Report and recommendations. *The Clinical Psychologist, 48*(1), 3–23. https://doi.org/10.1037/e554972011-003

VanderVeen, J. W., Reddy, L. F., Veilleux, J. C., January, A. M., & DiLillo, D. (2012). Clinical PhD graduate student views of their scientist-practitioner training. *Journal of Clinical Psychology, 68*(9), 1048–1057. https://doi.org/10.1002/jclp.21883

Zachar, P., & Leong, F. (2000). A 10-year longitudinal study of scientists and practitioner interests in psychology: Assessing the Boulder model. *Professional Psychology: Professional Psychology Research and Practice, 31*(5), 575–580. https://doi.org/10.1037/0735-7028.31.5.575

Chapter 4

American Psychological Association. (2017). *Ethical principles of psychologists and code of conduct* (2002, amended effective June 1, 2010, and January 1, 2017). https://www.apa.org/ethics/code/

American Psychological Association, Commission on Accreditation. (2018). *Standards of accreditation for health service psychology.* http://www.apa.org/ed/accreditation/about/policies/standards-of-accreditation.pdf

Burkard, A. W., Knox, S., DeWalt, T., Fuller, S., Hill, C., & Schlosser, L. Z. (2014). Dissertation experiences of doctoral graduates from professional psychology programs. *Counseling Psychology Quarterly, 27*, 19–54.

Given, L. M. (Ed.). (2008). *The Sage encyclopedia of qualitative research methods* (Vols. 1 and 2). SAGE.

Knox, S., Burkard, A. W., Janecek, J., Pruitt, N. T., Fuller, S. L., & Hill, C. E. (2011). Positive and problematic dissertation experiences: The faculty perspective. *Counselling Psychology Quarterly, 24*, 55–69.

Krieshok, T., Lopez, S. J., Somberg, D., & Cantrell, P. J. (2000). Dissertation while on internship: Obstacles and predictors of progress. *Professional Psychology: Research and Practice, 31*, 327–331.

Vidair, H. B., Kobernick, C. L., Rosenfield, N., Gustafson, P., & Feindler, E. L. (2019). A systematic review of research on dissertations in health service psychology programs. *Training and Education in Professional Psychology, 13*(4), 287–299. https://doi.org/10.1037/tep0000250

Willis, J., Inman, D., & Valenti, R. (2010). *Completing a professional practice dissertation: A guide for doctoral students and faculty*. Information Age Publishing.

Chapter 5

American Psychological Association. (2020). *Publication manual of the American Psychological Association 2020: The official guide to APA style* (7th ed.).

Auerbach, C. F., & Silverstein, L. B. (2003). *Qualitative studies in psychology. Qualitative data: An introduction to coding and analysis*. New York University Press.

Bell, D. J., Foster, S. L., & Cone, J. D. (2019). *Dissertations and theses from start to finish: Psychology and related fields* (3rd ed.). American Psychological Association.

Efron, S. E., & Ravid, R. (2018). *Writing the literature review: A practical guide*. Guilford Press.

Faul, F., Erdfelder, E., Lang, A.-G., & Buchner, A. (2007). G*Power 3: A flexible statistical power analysis program for the social, behavioral, and biomedical sciences. *Behavior Research Methods, 39*, 175–191. https://doi.org/10.3758/BF03193146

Galvan, J. L., & Galvan, M. C. (2017). *Writing literature reviews: A guide for students of the social and behavioral sciences* (7th ed.). Routledge.

Kazdin, A. E. (2016). *Research design in clinical psychology* (5th ed.). Pearson.

Kendall, P. C. (1994). Treating anxiety disorders in children: Results of a randomized clinical trial. *Journal of Consulting and Clinical Psychology, 62*(1), 100–110. https://doi.org/10.1037/0022-006X.62.1.100

Krathwohl, D. R., & Smith, N. L. (2005). *How to prepare a dissertation proposal: Suggestions for students in education and the social and behavioral sciences*. Syracuse University Press.

Locke, L. F., Spirduso, W. W., & Silverman, S. J. (2013). *Proposals that work: A guide for planning dissertations and grant proposals* (6th ed.). SAGE Publications.

Page, M. J., McKenzie, J. E., Bossuyt, P. M., Boutron, I., Hoffmann, T. C., Mulrow, C. D., Shamseer, L., Tetzlaff, J. M., Akl, E. A., Brennan, S. E., Chou, R., Glanville, J., Grimshaw, J. M., Hróbjartsson, A., Lalu, M. M., Li, T., Loder, E. W., Mayo-Wilson, E., McDonald, S., . . . Moher, D. (2021). The PRISMA 2020 statement: An updated guideline for reporting systematic reviews. *BMJ (Clinical Research ed.), 372*, n71. https://doi.org/10.1136/bmj.n71

Terrell, S. R. (2023). *Writing a proposal for your dissertation: Guidelines and examples* (2nd ed.). Guilford Press.

US Department of Health and Human Services. (2018, June 19). *2018 Requirements (2018 Common Rule): Subpart A. Basic HHS policy for protection of human research subjects.* Office for Human Research Protections. https://www.hhs.gov/ohrp/regulations-and-policy/regulations/45-cfr-46/revised-common-rule-regulatory-text/index.html

Chapter 6

Aarons, G., Reeder, K., Miller, C., & Stadnick, N. (2020). Identifying strategies to promote team science in dissemination and implementation research. *Journal of Clinical and Translational Science, 4*(3), 180–187. https://doi.org/10.1017/cts.2019.413

Boswell, J. F. (2020). Monitoring processes and outcomes in routine clinical practice: A promising approach to plugging the holes of the practice-based evidence colander. *Psychotherapy Research: Journal of the Society for Psychotherapy Research, 30*(7), 829–842. https://doi.org/10.1080/10503307.2019.1686192

Castonguay, L. G. (2011). Psychotherapy, psychopathology, research and practice: Pathways of connections and integration. *Psychotherapy Research: Journal of the Society for Psychotherapy Research, 21*(2), 125–140. https://doi.org/10.1080/10503307.2011.563250

Devos, C., Boudrenghien, G., Van der Linden, N., Azzi, A., Frenay, M., Galand, B., & Klein, O. (2017). Doctoral students' experiences leading to completion or attrition: A matter of sense, progress and distress. *European Journal of Psychology and Education, 32*, 61–77.

Gaudiano, B. A., Brown, L. A., & Miller, I. W. (2011). Let your intuition be your guide? Individual differences in the evidence-based practice attitudes of psychotherapists. *Journal of Evaluation in Clinical Practice, 17*(4), 628–634. https://doi.org/10.1111/j.1365-2753.2010.01508.x

Holmes, J. D., & Beins, B. C. (2009). Psychology is a science: At least some students think so. *Teaching of Psychology, 36*(1), 5–11. https://doi.org/10.1080/00986280802529350

Lilienfeld, S. O. (2012). Public skepticism of psychology: Why many people perceive the study of human behavior as unscientific. *American Psychologist, 67*(2), 111–129. https://doi.org/10.1037/a0023963

McMillan, J. H. (2021). *Educational research: Fundamental principles and methods* (8th ed.). Pearson.

O'Connor, J. (2017). Inhibition in the dissertation writing process: Barrier, block and impasse. *Psychoanalytic Psychology, 34*, 516–523.

Roberts, L. D., & Povee, K. (2014). A brief measure of attitudes towards qualitative research in psychology. *Australian Journal of Psychology, 66*, 249–256. https://doi.org/10.1111/ajpy.12059

Silverstein, L. B., Auerbach, C. F., & Levant, R. F. (2006). Using qualitative research to strengthen clinical practice. *Professional Psychology: Research and Practice, 37*(4), 351–358. https://doi.org/10.1037/0735-7028.37.4.351

Stewart, R. E., Stirman, S. W., & Chambless, D. L. (2012). A qualitative investigation of practicing psychologists' attitudes toward research-informed practice: Implications for dissemination strategies. *Professional Psychology, Research and Practice, 43*(2), 100–109. https://doi.org/10.1037/a0025694

Stricker, G., & Trierweiler, S. J. (2006). The local clinical scientist: A bridge between science and practice. *Training and Education in Professional Psychology, S*(1), 37–46. https://doi.org/10.1037/1931-3918.S.1.37

Wei, T., Sadikova, A. N., Barnard-Brak, L., Wang, E. W., & Sodikov, D. (2015). Exploring graduate students' attitudes towards team research and their scholarly productivity: A survey guided by the theory of planned behavior. *International Journal of Doctoral Studies, 10,* 1–17. http://ijds.org/Volume10/IJDSv10p001-017Wei0558.pdf

Youn, S. J., Xiao, H., McAleavey, A. A., Scofield, B. E., Pedersen, T. R., Castonguay, L. G., Hayes, J. A., & Locke, B. D. (2019). Assessing and investigating clinicians' research interests: Lessons on expanding practices and data collection in a large practice research network. *Psychotherapy, 56*(1), 67–82. https://doi.org/10.1037/pst0000192

Chapter 7

American Psychological Association. (2015). *Tips for determining authorship credit.* https://www.apa.org/science/leadership/students/authorship-paper

American Psychological Association. (2017). *Ethical principles of psychologists and code of conduct* (2002, amended effective June 1, 2010, and January 1, 2017).

American Psychological Association. (2020, September). *Other research transparency standards and disclosures for journal articles.* https://www.apa.org/pubs/journals/resources/standards-disclosures

Bartle, S. A., Fink, A. A., & Hayes, B. C. (2000). Psychology of the scientist: LXXX. Attitudes regarding authorship issues in psychological publications. *Psychological Reports, 86,* 771–788.

Tryon, G. S., Bishop, J. L., & Hatfield, T. A. (2007). Doctoral students' beliefs about authorship credit for dissertations. *Training and Education in Professional Psychology, 1*(3), 184–192.

Chapter 8

American Psychological Association. (2015). Tips for determining authorship credit. https://www.apa.org/science/leadership/students/authorship-paper

American Psychological Association. (2020). *Publication manual of the American Psychological Association 2020: The official guide to APA style* (7th ed.).

Bell, D. J., Foster, S. L., & Cone, J. D. (2019). *Dissertations and theses from start to finish: Psychology and related fields* (3rd ed.). American Psychological Association.

Evans, S. C., Amaro, C. M., Herbert, R., Blossom, J. B., & Roberts, M. C. (2018). "Are you gonna publish that?" Peer-reviewed publication outcomes of doctoral dissertations in psychology. *PLOS ONE, 13*(2): Article e0192219. https://doi.org/10.1371/journal.pone.0192219

Kamler, B. (2008). Rethinking doctoral publication practices: Writing from and beyond the thesis. *Studies in Higher Education, 33*(3), 283–294, https://doi.org/10.1080/03075070802049236

Chapter 9

Andrews, E. E., & Cook, A. J. (2020). Relational mentorship for doctoral psychology interns: A formal preceptor model. *Training and Education in Professional Psychology, 15*(4), 306–314. https://doi.org/10.1037/tep0000352

Arora, P. G., Brown, J., Harris, B., & Sullivan, A. (2017, March) Professional development needs and training interests: A survey of early career school psychologists. *Contemporary School Psychology, 21*(1), 49–57.

American Psychological Association. (2020, June 5). *Psychologists embrace telehealth to prevent the spread of COVID-19.* http://www.apaservices.org/practice/legal/technology/psychologists-embrace-telehealth

American Psychological Association. (2021, July 1). *Moving into your first independent research job.* https://www.apa.org/monitor/2021/07/career-first-research-job

Castonguay, L., Pincus, A., & McAleavey, A. (2015). Practice research network in a psychology training clinic: Building an infrastructure to foster early attachment to the scientific-practitioner model. *Psychotherapy Research, 25*(1), 52–66. https://doi.org/10.1080/10503307.2013.856045

Doran, J. M., Galloway, M. P., Ponce, A. N., & Kaslow, N. J. (2018). Leadership mentoring: A survey of early career psychologist leaders. *Mentoring and Tutoring: Partnership in Learning, 26*(2), 165–182. https://doi.org/10.1080/13611267.2018.1471339

Elman, N. S., Illfelder-Kaye, J., & Robiner, W. N. (2005). Professional development: Training for professionalism as a foundation for competent practice in psychology. *Professional Psychology: Research and Practice, 36*(4), 367–375. https://doi.org/10.1037/0735-7028.36.4.367

Foran-Tuller K., Robiner, W. N., Breland-Noble, A., Otey-Scott, S., Wryobeck, J., King, C., & Sanders, K. (2012). Early career boot camp: A novel mechanism for enhancing early career development for psychologists in academic healthcare. *Journal of Clinical Psychology in Medical Settings, 19*(1), 117–125. https://doi.org/10.1007/s10880-011-9289-5

Glueckauf, R. L., Maheu, M. M., Drude, K. P., Wells, B. A., Wang, Y., Gustafson, D. J., & Nelson, E.-L. (2018). Survey of psychologists' telebehavioral health practices: Technology use, ethical issues, and training needs. *Professional Psychology: Research and Practice, 49*(3), 205–219. https://doi.org/10.1037/pro0000188

Grapin, S. L., Gelbar, N. W., January, S.-A. A., Reinhardt, J. S., Ochs, S., Peterson, L. S., & Grossman, J. A. (2021). Professional needs of doctoral-level students and early career professionals in school psychology. *Contemporary School Psychology, 25,* 491–502. https://doi.org/10.1007/s40688-020-00291-z

Green, A., & Hawley, G. (2009) Early career psychologists: Understanding, engaging, and mentoring tomorrow's leaders. *Professional Psychology: Research and Practice, 40,* 206–212.

Kaplan-Berkley, S., Strickland, C., & Dimartino, L. (2019). Post-dissertation: Surviving and thriving amidst doctoral transition. *Reflective Practice, 20*(6), 705–719. https://doi.org/10.1080/14623943.2019.1689940

Koerner, K., & Castonguay, L. (2015). Practice-oriented research: What it takes to do collaborative research in private practice. *Psychotherapy Research, 25,* 67–83.

Kolmes, K. (2012). Social media in the future of professional psychology. *Professional Psychology: Research and Practice, 43*(6), 606–612. https://doi.org/10.1037/a0028678

Maddux, R. E., & Riso, L. P. (2007). Promoting the scientist-practitioner mindset in clinical training. *Journal of Contemporary Psychotherapy: On the Cutting Edge of Modern Developments in Psychotherapy, 37*(4), 213–220. https://doi.org/10.1007/s10879-007-9056-y

Pham, A. V. (2014). Navigating social networking and social media in school psychology: Ethical and professional considerations in training programs. *Psychology in the Schools, 51*(7), 767–778.

Rossen, E., Guiney, M., Peterson, C., & Silva, A. (2019). Alignment of CPD/CE requirements for credential renewal with best practices for professional learning in psychology and school psychology. *Professional Psychology: Research and Practice, 50*(2), 87–94. https://doi.org/10.1037/pro0000231

Sim, W., Zanardelli, G., Loughran, M. J., Mannarino, M. B., & Hill, C. (2016). Thriving, burnout, and coping strategies of early and later career counseling center psychologists in the United States. *Counselling Psychology Quarterly, 29*(4), 382–404. https://doi.org/10.1080/09515070.2015.1121135

Stricker, G., & Trierweiler, S. J. (1995). The local clinical scientist: A bridge between science and practice. *American Psychologist, 50*(12), 995–1002. https://doi.org/10.1037/0003-066X.50.12.995

Taylor, J. M., & Neimeyer, G. J. (2017). The ongoing evolution of continuing education: Past, present, and future. In T. Rousmaniere, R. Goodyear, S. Miller, & B. Wampold (Eds.), *The cycle of excellence: Training, supervision, and deliberate practice* (pp. 219–248). Wiley–Blackwell. https://doi.org/10.1002/9781119165590.ch11

Washburn, J. J., Lilienfeld, S. O., Rosen, G. M., Gaudiano, B. A., Davison, G. C., Hollon, S. D., Otto, M. W., Penberthy, J. K., Sher, K. J., Teachman, B. A., Peris, T., & Weinand, J. (2019). Reaffirming the scientific foundations of psychological practice: Recommendations of the Emory meeting on continuing education. *Professional Psychology: Research and Practice, 50*(2), 77–86. https://doi.org/10.1037/pro0000235

Wise, E. H., & Reuman, L. (2019). Promoting competent and flourishing life-long practice for psychologists: A communitarian perspective. *Professional Psychology: Research and Practice, 50*(2), 129–135. https://doi.org/10.1037/pro0000226

Index

Tables, figures, boxes, and worksheets are indicated by an italic t, f, b, and w following the page number.